AKU-AKU

by Thor Heyerdahl

THE KON-TIKI EXPEDITION
AMERICAN INDIANS IN THE PACIFIC

AKU-AKU

THE SECRET OF EASTER ISLAND

THOR HEYERDAHL

Ruskin House
GEORGE ALLEN & UNWIN LTD
MUSEUM STREET LONDON

THIS EDITION FIRST PUBLISHED IN APRIL 1958
SECOND IMPRESSION APRIL 1958

*

Original Norwegian Edition
published by Gyldendal Norsk Forlag, Oslo
Aku-Aku: Påskeöyas Hemmelighet
with simultaneous editions in Swedish, Danish and Finnish
©Thor Heyerdahl 1957

English translation
made under the personal supervision of the author
© George Allen & Unwin Ltd., 1958

PRINTED IN GREAT BRITAIN
in 11 pt. Baskerville type
BY C. TINLING & CO. LTD.
LIVERPOOL, LONDON AND PRESCOT

COLOUR PLATES BY EGMONT H. PETERSEN
COPENHAGEN

To
His Royal Highness
Crown Prince Olav
the Patron of the Expedition

CONTENTS

ILLUSTRATIONS

A*

CHAPTER I

DETECTIVES OFF TO THE END
OF THE WORLD

I HAD no *aku-aku*.
Nor did I know what an *aku-aku* was, so I should hardly have been able to use it if I had one.

Every sensible person on Easter Island has an *aku-aku*, and I too got one there. But at the moment I was organizing a voyage to that very place, so I did not possess one. Perhaps that was why the arranging of the journey was so difficult. It was much easier to get oneself home again.

Easter Island is the loneliest inhabited place in the world. The nearest solid land the inhabitants can see is in the firmament, the moon and the planets. They have to travel farther than any other people to see that there really is land still closer. Therefore they live nearest to the stars and know more names of stars than of towns and countries in our own world.

On this remote island, east of the sun and west of the moon, mankind once had one of its most curious ideas. No one knows who had it, and no one knows why. For it happened before Columbus led white men to America, and in doing so opened the gate for voyages of exploration out into the great unknown Pacific. While our own race still believed that the world ended at Gibraltar there were other great navigators who knew better. In advance of their time they ploughed unknown seas in the immense floating vacuum off the desolate west coast of South America. Far out in it they found land. The loneliest little island in the world. They landed there, whetted their stone adzes and set about one of the most remarkable engineering projects of ancient times. They did not build fortresses and castles, or dams and wharves. They made gigantic stone figures in man's likeness, as tall as houses and as heavy as railway trucks, they dragged them in great numbers across country and set them up erect on huge stone terraces all over the island.

How did they manage this, before the mechanical age? No one knows. But there stood the figures they had desired,

towering into the sky, while the people fell. They buried their
dead at the feet of the colossi they themselves had created.
They raised columns and buried themselves. Then one day the
blows of the adze on the rock face fell silent. They fell silent
suddenly, for the tools were left lying and many of the figures
were only half finished. The mysterious sculptors disappeared
into the dark mists of antiquity.

What happened? Yes, what had happened on Easter Island?

I bent over my writing-table for the thousandth time and let
my eyes sail over the large-scale chart of the Pacific, that
treacherous sheet of paper on which the islands bulk large in
capital letters and one travels with the ruler as easily up as
down the ocean currents. I was beginning to know this ocean
now. There in the wild valleys of the Marquesas group, just
south of the equator, I had lived for a year in native fashion
and learned to see Nature with Polynesian eyes. There too I
had heard for the first time old Tei Tetua's stories of the man-
god Tiki. And down in the Society Islands, among the palms
of Tahiti, the great chief Teriieroo had once been my teacher.
He had adopted me as his son and taught me to respect his
race as my own. And there, on the coral reef in the Tuamotu
group, we had landed with the *Kon-Tiki* raft, and learned that
even the salt sea has its inexorable treadmill, the route from
South America out to those distant islands. However lonely
the islands were, they all lay within the natural range of the
Inca Indians' old balsa rafts.

And from over there, from the dry cactus forests of the
Galapagos group, I had other strange memories. We had nearly
landed there with the *Kon-Tiki* raft, so I went later with a
new expedition to see what secrets this remote group of islands
concealed. In a fairy-tale world, among giant lizards and
the world's largest tortoises, I had taken part in collecting
a veritable Aladdin's lamp, which lay crushed to fragments,
buried in an old rubbish heap among the cactus trees. One had
only to rub the dirty old fragments to see broad sails on the
eastern horizon. It was the Inca Indians' mighty forerunners
that we saw, steering out with their rafts from the coast of
South America on the wild sea. They crossed the sea once,
twice, many times, and came ashore on the waterless cliffs of
the Galapagos group. There they encamped, and as time passed

they broke one after another of the curious jars they had on board, jars of a type the like of which no other civilized people in the whole world has made. It was fragments of these jars we dug up at the old settlements; and they played the part of Aladdin's lamp, reflecting their owners' maritime enterprises and casting their light right into the darkness of prehistoric times.

No archaeologist had investigated the Galapagos group, and therefore no one had found anything. We were the first who believed that the Indians had sailed so far out to sea, and so we went out and searched. The archaeologists Reed and Skjölsvold and I had dug up over two thousand of these ancient fragments, from 130 different jars. The experts in Washington analysed the fragments as detectives examine finger-prints, and were able to establish that a thousand years before Columbus opened the door into America the Incas' forerunners had thrown open the door of the Pacific and paid repeated visits to the remote Galapagos Islands.[1]

These were the oldest traces of humanity that had so far been found out on the real ocean islands of the Pacific. They revealed that before the islands of Polynesia were inhabited, and before the Vikings set out on their voyage to Iceland, the ancient people of South America had begun to explore the Pacific and gained a foothold on islands as far from their own coast as Iceland is from Norway. They had fished there, planted native cotton and left many traces at their settlements before they forsook the inhospitable and waterless islands for an unknown destination.

From the Galapagos the same fierce ocean current rolls on unchecked, swifter than the Amazon and a hundred times as wide, till, only a few weeks later, it rolls its water-masses in among the South Sea Islands.

An uncertain little dot, with a note of interrogation beside it, was marked on the chart out in the middle of the ocean current. Was it land? We had steered right over the spot with the *Kon-Tiki* raft and discovered that it was only eddies. But far to southward, where the southernmost branches of

[1] For further details see: Thor Heyerdahl and Arne Skjölsvold: *Archaeological Evidence of pre-Spanish visits to the Galapagos Islands*. Published in 1956 as Mem. No. 12 of the Society of American Archaeology.

the current turn off, lay another little dot, and this had a
name, Easter Island. I had not been there, and it was there I
wanted to go. I had always wondered how the prehistoric
men had got themselves to that desolate spot. Now, for a change,
I was wondering how I should get myself there. It was rather
irrational to try to solve the travel problems of Stone Age
people, when one could not solve one's own.

As the *Kon-Tiki* drifted past, far to the north, we had sat
on deck in the moonlight and talked about the mystery of
Easter Island. At that time I had a secret dream of coming
back some day and going ashore on that lonely island. Now I
was trying to make the dream a reality.

Easter Island belongs to Chile. A warship goes there just
once a year with provisions for the inhabitants: then she turns
round and goes back to Chile, which is as far away as Spain is
from Canada. Easter Island has no other communication with
the world outside.

The warship offered no solution of my travel problems. To
explore Easter Island in a week, while the warship lay waiting,
was of course futile. To be left on the island for a whole year
with busy scientists was an equally unattractive prospect, for
they might find after a month that there was nothing more to
do there. It was possible to drift there on a balsa raft from South
America with the current and wind, but I might not get any
archaeologists to go with me, and there was no sense in trying
to explore Easter Island without them.

So I must get a boat of my own, a kind of expedition ship.
But there was no harbour at Easter Island, no reliable
anchorage, and no access to a wharf, oil or water supply. The
ship, therefore, must be large enough to carry oil or water for
the voyage out and home again, and, moreover, for mobility
during the time of waiting. She began at once to be quite a big
ship. And suppose the archaeologists found in a couple of
weeks that there was nothing to dig for. In that case it would be
a bad business to have come all the way to Easter Island in our
own ship, unless we could use her to go on to other unexplored
South Sea islands. Well, there were enough of them in the
eastern part of Polynesia. A whole string of exciting islands lay
awaiting excavation just in that part of the Pacific where the
ocean current rolls in from the Galapagos and South America.

About voyages to remote seas I have always consulted Thomas and Wilhelm. One day, while my plans were still only a secret dream, we were sitting together in the cosy old shipping office of the Fred Olsen Line down by the wharves at Oslo. Thomas smelt a rat when I came in and he produced a fat globe, which he placed between us. I turned it round till it was nearly all blue. That can only happen when the immense southern Pacific is swung forward so that both America and Asia disappear, as well as Europe, on to the back half of the globe. I pointed to Easter Island.

"There," I said. "But how?"

Two days later we were sitting round the globe again, and Wilhelm produced a calculation.

"The best thing for you would be a diesel-propelled boat about 150 feet long with a speed of twelve knots and space for fifty tons of water and 130 tons of oil," he said.

I did not doubt for a moment that this would be the best thing for me. I had learnt to rely on Wilhelm's nautical calculations since he had helped me to estimate the *Kon-Tiki*'s drift so exactly that we should have been there to the day if only we had managed to throw a rope ashore as we drifted past Angatau.

Wilhelm rang me up a few days later. He had an offer from a canning factory at Stavanger. They had a suitable trawler on the Greenland fishing grounds: I could hire her for a year if I took her from September.

I looked at the calendar. It was towards the end of April, and September was not six months away. The offer was "bareboat" —i.e. I was to take over the vessel empty, without crew or equipment.

My own shipping experience had never got beyond the timber raft stage. Nor could the other fellows from the *Kon-Tiki* voyage man a real ship: licences and papers were required: it was all much simpler on an Inca raft.

"Our office can help you with all nautical problems," Thomas said.

So we suddenly found ourselves sitting at the big green conference table with the marine superintendent, the signing-on authority, the provisioning authority, the insurance authority and all the other experts higher and lower. And the result was a

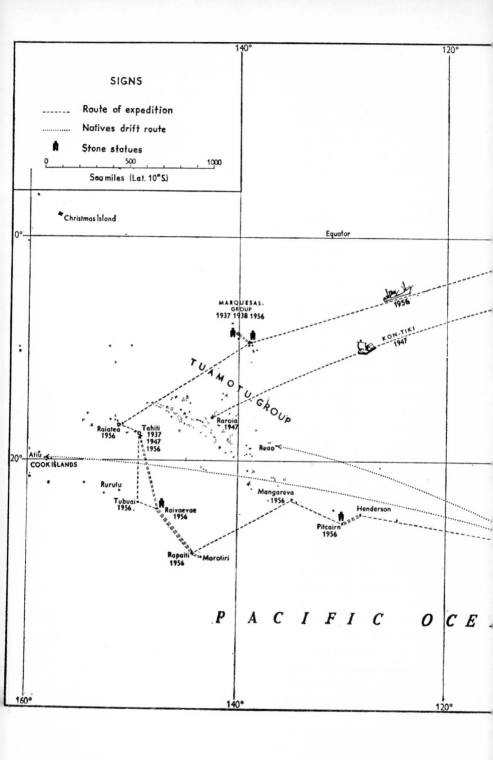

SIGNS

------- Route of expedition

·········· Natives drift route

🗿 Stone statues

0   500   1000

Sea miles (Lat. 10°S.)

Christmas Island

Equator

0°

MARQUESAS.
GROUP
1937 1938 1956

TUAMOTU GROUP

KON-TIKI
1947

1956

Raroia
1947

Raiatea
1956

Tahiti
1937
1947
1956

Reao

20°

Atiu

COOK ISLANDS

Rurutu

Tubuai
1956

Raivaevae
1956

Mangareva
·1956

Henderson

Pitcairn
1956

Rapaiti
1956

Morotiri

P A C I F I C   O C E

140°

120°

160°

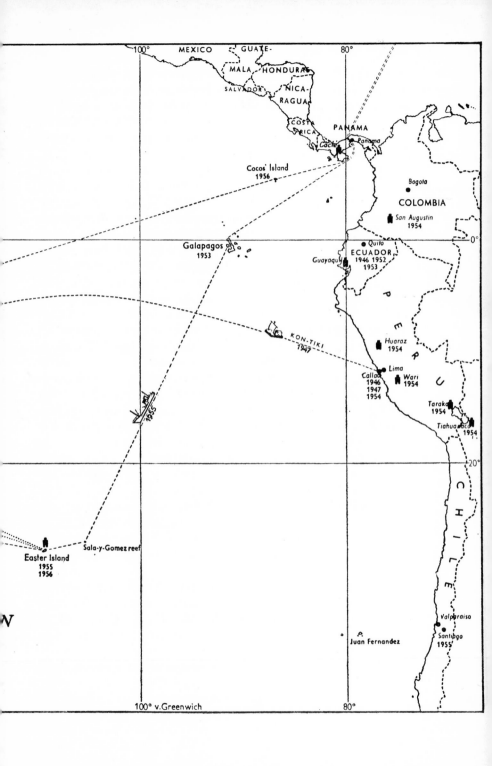

MEXICO GUATE-
MALA HONDURAS
SALVADOR NICA-
RAGUA
COSTA
RICA
PANAMA
Cacte
Panama

Cocos' Island
1956

Bogota

COLOMBIA

San Augustin
1954

Galapagos
1953

Quito
ECUADOR
Guayaquil 1946 1952
1953

KON-TIKI
1947

Huaraz
1954

P
E
R
U

Callao Lima
1946 Wari
1947 1954
1954

Taraka
1954

Tiahuanaco
1954

1955

Sala-y-Gomez reef

Easter Island
1955
1956

C
H
I
L
E

Valparaiso

Juan Fernandez

Santiago
1955

N

100° v.Greenwich   80°

real ship. Barely four months remained now, and I could almost hear hungry, impatient hootings from the big boat which lay at Stavanger waiting to start, without a spark of life in her funnel, her deck empty of men, and not a thing in the large holds where naked iron girders projected cheerlessly like ribs round the ship's empty stomach.

One has always a good deal to think about when one is taking one's family to the country. There is just as much to remember when, in addition to the family, one is taking five archaeologists, a doctor, a photographer, a crew of fifteen, a ship containing spare parts, special equipment and a year's meals for everyone. One feels like a conductor busy eating macaroni while trying to drive an orchestra through a Hungarian rhapsody by Liszt. My writing table was a complete chaos of passports and papers and licences and photographs and letters. The furniture was covered with charts and tables and samples of all kinds of gear. This madness soon spread all over the house. The telephone and the front door bell rang in chorus, and anyone trying to answer them in a hurry had to climb over cases and parcels and bundles of field equipment.

I was sitting in despair on the lid of a tape recorder with a sandwich between my fingers and the city telephone on my lap, trying to put through a call of my own. But that day it was hopeless, for I had just advertised for a first officer for a voyage to the South Sea Islands, and the telephone was never silent. I had got a skipper. At last I got through to one of the Oslo wholesalers.

"I want three tons of dental plaster," I said.

"Has somebody got toothache?" a voice answered drily.

A trunk call from Stavanger interrupted the conversation before I could explain that it was to make a cast of an Easter Island statue and not a denture.

"Hullo," said the new voice, "Hullo! There's a message from Olsen, your engineer. The crank shaft is worn out. Shall we regrind it or get a new one?"

"The crank shaft," I said. . . . Drrrrrrrr! The front door bell this time.

"Ask Reff," I shouted into the telephone. "He knows about all that."

Yvonne rushed in, buried under parcels.

"I've been through the steward's list," she said, "and cut down pepper and cinnamon by 5 lb. each. And Dr. Semb says that we can borrow his field medicine chest."

"Splendid," I said, and I remembered the man who thought I wanted plaster for dentures.

"Will you ring him up?" I said, and handed Yvonne the receiver just in time for her to get caught by an incoming call.

"This must be a mistake," she said to me. "Mustads are asking where they are to deliver 200 lb. of mixed fish-hooks, but we're taking two tons of frozen beef, aren't we?"

"The hooks are not to fish with," I explained. "They're to pay native diggers with. You don't think we're taking 1000 yards of coloured material to dress ourselves up in?"

She did not think so: she was, however, able to tell me that the second engineer had just telegraphed crying off; his wife had refused to let him go when she heard that the voyage was to the South Sea Islands.

I dashed out to the dustbin, which was empty.

"What were you looking for?" asked Yvonne.

"The other engineers' applications," I whispered.

"Aha!" Yvonne understood the situation.

There was more ringing—front door bell and telephone simultaneously. In came the intended frogman of the expedition with two companions and his arms full of webbed feet and air-tubes; they were to demonstrate the difference between French and American diving equipment. Behind them stood a queer little man, turning his hat in his hands. He had come about an important matter, quite confidential. He looked so peculiar that I dared not let him in farther than the front hall.

"Have you seen the statues on Easter Island?" he whispered, looking from side to side to see if anyone was listening.

"No, but I'm going to have a look at them now."

He stretched out a long index finger and whispered with a cunning smile:

"There's a man inside them."

"Is there a man inside them?" I asked unsuspectingly.

"Yes," he whispered mysteriously. "A king."

"How did he get in?" I asked politely, slowly and amiably steering him and myself back towards the door.

"They put him in. Just as in a pyramid. Break one in pieces
and you'll see." He nodded cheerfully and raised his hat politely
as I thanked him for his advice and shut the door on him in
bewilderment.

I was beginning to be accustomed to queer people where
Easter Island was concerned. There was no end to the strange
proposals which came by post after the newspapers had published
our plans. I heard almost daily from people in the most different
quarters of the world who were able to tell me that Easter
Island was the last remnant of a sunken continent, a sort of
Pacific Atlantis. It was on the bottom of the sea round the island
that we must seek for the key to the mystery; not on land.

There was even a man who proposed that I should abandon
the whole expedition. "It is a waste of time to travel so far,"
he wrote. "You can sit in your own study and solve the whole
problem by vibrations. Send me a photograph of an Easter
Island statue and a photograph of an old statue from South
America, and I'll tell by the vibrations if they originate from
the same people." He added that he had once made a model of
Cheops' pyramid in cardboard, with raw meat in it. And after
a time it vibrated so horribly that he had to send the whole
family to hospital.

I should soon begin to vibrate myself if I did not get
rid of all these lunatics. I made a rush to try to catch the frogmen, who had disappeared upstairs, but Yvonne stopped me
regretfully with the telephone at arm's length. And while I was
talking on the telephone she slowly pushed towards me a tottering
little pile of unopened letters—the morning post. I delayed
putting back the receiver for fear of the telephone ringing
again.

"That was from the Foreign Office," I said. "Ask the others
to wait upstairs; I must take a cab at once. The British Colonial
Office wants an answer to some questions about Pitcairn
Island, and Costa Rica has given permission to dig on Cocos
Island if I sign an agreement not to search for a hidden
treasure they think is buried there."

"Take the post with you," Yvonne called after me. "You
may find a late application from another engineer."

I doubted this, but I snatched up the pile as I ran. The
people who wrote asking to be allowed to come were usually

painters, writers and jacks of all trades. I had even had a letter from a German who wrote that though he was a baker by profession he had been working in a cemetery for the last few years, so he thought he was the right man to be taken for digging.

"Remember you're to see the sailmakers too, they've put up all the tents on the Bergslands' lawn," cried Yvonne, on her way up the stairs.

I ran to the door and nearly knocked over the postman, of all people, who was just about to deliver the afternoon post. I was just going to hand him my own bundle instead of taking his, but ended up with both bundles in the car with me.

"Majorstuveien," I said to the driver.

"That's here," he answered quietly.

"Foreign Office, then," I said, and began to tear open my letters as the cab moved off.

There were no engineers. The nearest approach was a watchmaker who wanted to come as cook. I had a cook already. But there was a letter from the archaeological section at Oslo University—from one of the two archaeologists who were to come with me. He had got a stomach ulcer and the doctor forbade him to make the journey.

One of the foundations of the expedition had collapsed. To set out without enough archaeologists would be making poor use of the expedition's striking power. It would not be easy to find at short notice another who would bind himself for a year. The only thing to do was to start again and write to archaeologists at home and abroad.

September came. A stream-lined Greenland trawler, shining white like a yacht, with the bearded face of the sun-god Kon-Tiki painted in brick-red on her funnel, was suddenly lying at pier C in front of the city hall. Forward, on the high bows, strengthened against ice, a curious blue emblem was painted, the meaning of which only the initiated knew. It showed two of the sacred bird-men of Easter Island, half bird and half human, copied from one of the rare pictures with undeciphered hieroglyphics on the island. Now there was heat in the funnel, and the ship lay full-loaded in the fjord water right up to her blue-painted waterline. There was hectic activity on board, and such a dense crowd ashore that it was almost impossible

for motor-trucks and trolleys, delivering bundles and parcels
at the eleventh hour, to get through.

Had we remembered everything? Of course we had food and
digging gear and all that we knew for certain that we should
need. The danger lay in the unforeseen. Suppose we found,
contrary to our expectations, a skeleton under water. Had we
the right chemicals to prevent it from dissolving? Suppose
we had to go to an inaccessible rock or ledge, had we the means
of reaching it? Or how should we tackle problems of contact
and provisioning if the camp was on one side of the island
and the ship had suddenly to go round to the other side on
account of bad weather? What if the cook burnt a hole in a
saucepan, the propeller was damaged by a block of coral, or
a sailor put his foot on a poisonous sea urchin? And what about
all the food if the refrigerator ceased to work? Had we all
imaginable special equipment and spare parts? Now there was
no more time to think it over. Now we must be prepared to
meet all conceivable reverses, for the Greenland trawler was
lying vibrant, ready to sail for Easter Island, the loneliest spot
in the world, which had not a single workshop or store.

The captain was in action on the bridge, and the crew were
running about the deck battening down hatches and hauling on
ropes, while a gigantic mate stood, carpenter's pencil in hand,
checking off items on a long list. At all events, everything he
had been told about had come. Even the skipper's Christmas tree was packed away in the refrigerator. The list was in
order.

The ship's bell rang for the last time. Orders rang out from
captain to first officer, and there was a fierce blast of exhaust
from the funnel behind the sun-god's shining head. Farewells
and the last good wishes were exchanged over the ship's rail
while a score of cheerful, expectant faces looked up from their
tasks on board to receive the last impression for a year of
wives and sweethearts, glimpsed here and there amid the
crowd on shore, their faces expressing every shade of sorrow and
happiness. Brusquely the gangway was rolled away, there was
a splashing of cables and creaking of winches, and the engineers
down below caused a miracle to happen: the ship began to
go of herself. A cheer rose from the long wall of figures on the
pier; hands were waved and handkerchiefs fluttered like a

forest in a gale, while the captain made the siren utter a few heart-rending howls.

But this chaos was the end of chaos, its climax and full stop.

I was left waving in the turmoil on the pier. It was not that I had forgotten to embark myself, but I had first to fly to the United States, whence three archaeologists had agreed to come, and after that I had to pay a courtesy visit to Chile before I went on board our ship when she came through the Panama Canal. H.R.H. Crown Prince Olav had most kindly offered to be patron of the expedition, and the Norwegian Foreign Office had obtained permission from the Chilean Government for the expedition to begin digging on Easter Island so long as we did not damage the monuments. Both Great Britain and France had given permission for their islands, so we had the green light for everything we could stumble upon in the Eastern Pacific.

When the ship turned her white stern towards us and slid slowly away from the quay a solitary deck boy stood high astern, as bright as the evening sun with sheer joy, proudly hauling in the end of a dirty mooring cable, while his class stood on shore shouting hip hip hurrah for Thor junior, who was being let off school for a whole year.

Then the little craft slipped behind a big ocean steamer and was lost to sight. She was in a hurry; she was to go half-way round the world with detectives on the track of other seafarers who had a start of several centuries.

CHAPTER II

WHAT AWAITED US AT THE WORLD'S NAVEL

How quiet!

What perfect peace. The engine had stopped. The lights had been put out. The whole starry firmament had suddenly escaped from the glare and was swinging to and fro, or in a slow circle, clear and glittering round the masthead. I leant far back in my deck chair and enjoyed this complete harmony. It was as though the plug of an electric line to the mainland had been slowly pulled out, the ceaseless stream of impulses from disturbing stations all over the world had gone, so that nothing remained but the moment and naked reality. Fresh air, black night and twinkling stars behind the masthead. Almost imperceptibly, sight and hearing opened wide again and let a breeze blow right through my soul.

There were here no impressions to be washed away or suppressed, no city racket with dazzling advertisements, restless competition and noisy amusements which, as though in a race with time itself, strove to force their way in through every opening at the risk of jolting to pieces the sensitive human soul. Here there was quiet so complete that time itself ceased to roll on: it too stopped, stood motionless and waited. One almost hesitated to cough, as if to do so would wake the sleeping elements of unrest. Far off towards the land a faint rushing noise was sometimes heard in the darkness, as of wind or waves breaking at short intervals against a cliff. All on board were curiously silent; the stillness must have given them a feeling of reverence. Only from the cabin hatchway did I hear now and again a short hushed exchange of words accompanied by the washing of water in finely graduated tones against the ship's side, and then a quiet rhythmical creak, creak, creak, like a contented grunting from the little vessel as she rocked so peacefully and discreetly in the silence of the night.

We had come under the shelter of the land.

We had done with the hurried panting beat of the engines and the seas which thundered against our bows in endless lines and rolled us up and down and sideways before they hissed past us. We had crept into the protecting embrace of a lonely coast before night fell over us and the sea. There, in the darkness, lay Easter Island.

We had stolen up under the land just in time to catch a glimpse of rolling grey-green ridges, steep cliffs along the coast, and, far away in the interior, statues standing scattered up the slope of an extinct volcano like black caraway seeds against the red evening sky. We had made our way in by echo and ordinary sounding as far as we dared go, and then the skipper had dropped anchor.

Not a soul was to be seen on shore, only a deserted, petrified world with motionless stone heads gazing at us from their distant ridge, while other equally motionless stone men lay prostrate in a row at the foot of a long terrace right in the foreground, on the lava blocks along the coast. It was as though we had anchored with a hovering space-ship off the shore of an extinct world, where beings had once lived of another kind than those on our own earth. The shadows were long, but nothing moved: nothing but the fiery red sun as it descended slowly into the black sea and drew the night down over us.

Strictly speaking we ought not to have anchored there. We ought really to have tumbled on through the seas right round the island and announced our arrival to the governor, who lived with the whole population in a little village on the other side. But it would have been no pleasure either to him or to the native inhabitants of the island if we had arrived just at dusk, at a place where a call from any ship is one of the greatest events of the year. Better to ride out the night here under the lee of the cliffs, even if the bottom was of the worst kind for anchoring. Then we could arrive at the village of Hangaroa early next morning with all flags flying.

The door of our cabin was cautiously opened and a strip of light was thrown across the boat deck for a few seconds as Yvonne stole out. In the cabin little Anette lay sleeping as peacefully as the night sky itself, with a nigger doll under one arm and a teddy bear under the other.

"We ought to have a little celebration today, even if we

haven't arrived officially," Yvonne whispered, nodding cheerfully towards the land.

It was the first time for fourteen days of rolling that she had been on her legs and able to think of anything of the kind. I was able to tell her that the steward had had his orders and that the captain was going to assemble all hands on the boat deck in a few minutes. Yvonne remained standing at the rail staring in enchantment landward into the darkness. We could actually feel a few light breaths of mother earth, a curious dry scent of hay or grass which now and then mingled with the clean salt sea breeze.

The men began to arrive. Newly shaved and smartened up till hardly recognizable, they sat down on chairs and forms which had been placed in a ring between the two ship's boats on the upper deck. There was Dr. William Mulloy, alias Bill. He came swinging along, broad and thickset, and flung the stump of a cigarette into the sea as he sat down and stared thoughtfully at the deck. Close behind him came tall, thin Dr. Carlyle Smith, alias Carl. He lit up and remained standing, half hanging from a stay and looking at the stars. They were both professors of archaeology, at Wyoming and Kansas Universities respectively. Then there was our old friend Ed, or Edwin Ferdon, from the Museum of New Mexico, the only one of the three American archaeologists I had known before. Round and smiling, he leant over the rail beside Yvonne and sniffed happily towards the contours of the land.

The skipper came tripping down from the bridge with his humorous face, a little man like a bouncing ball. Captain Arne Hartmark had been sailing to distant lands for twenty years, but he had never seen anything like Easter Island through his telescope. Behind him stood the gigantic mate Sanne, a cheerful jovial fellow, hanging on to a stay with each hand, looking like an amiable tame gorilla: and there were the shining teeth of second officer Larsen, the most good-natured man in the world, who would find something to laugh at and enjoy even in the electric chair. And now too he was sitting between two inexhaustible humorists, the stout chief engineer Olsen, his face wrinkled with perpetual smiling, and the skinny second engineer who, with his newly acquired chin tuft, had made himself look like a cross between a lay reader and a conjuror. The doctor, Dr. Gjessing, came up the ladder, bowed and sat down, and behind him gleamed the spectacles of the expedition's photographer, Erling Schjerven, who lit a small cigar on such special occasions. Thor junior had found room for his lanky boyish figure between two stout sailors up in a ship's boat, and the cook and steward were sitting there too, side by side, after having silently placed the most exquisite dishes on the table between us. No sea could prevent Gronmyr the steward and Hanken the cook from performing their culinary miracles on board. Then came the boatswain, the motor-man, the deck boy and the galley boy, with Arne Skjölsvold and Gonzalo. Arne was an archaeologist and head of the new state museum at Elverum. He had taken part in the Galapagos expedition as well. Gonzalo Figueroa was a student of archaeology at Santiago University and the official representative of Chile on the expedition. We were ready for anything, as I had invited him without seeing him, but Gonzalo came up the gangway at Panama cheerful and in high spirits, an athletic aristocrat with a chameleonic gift of adapting himself naturally to the most variable conditions of life.

So we were twenty-three in all, a most versatile party containing specialists of the most different kinds. These in the weeks on board had become a band of friends with a common desire to set foot on that very island that lay in there in the darkness. Now that all were assembled, and the engine had stopped, it was natural to tell them something about other people's experiences on Easter Island before us, so that they might all have a little background for what we ourselves had to expect.

"No one really knows the name of that island," I was able to tell them. "The natives call it *Rapanui*, but research workers do not think that this was its original name. In its most ancient legends the natives always call the island *Te Pito o te Henua*, or *Navel of the World*, but even that may be an old poetical description rather than the island's real name, for later the natives called it also *the Eye which sees Heaven* or the *Frontier of Heaven*. The rest of us, who live thousands of miles beyond all the island's horizons, have elected to place the name *Easter Island* on the map, because it was on the afternoon of Easter Day, 1722, that the Dutchman Roggeveen and his companions came here as the first Europeans to sail into these waters, and perceived that unknown people ashore were sending up smoke signals to attract attention. When the Dutchmen came nearer with their two sailing craft and dropped anchor at sunset, they had a glimpse of a strange community before night fell. They were first received on board their ships by tall, well-built people who, so far as can be judged, were fair-skinned Polynesians such as we know them from Tahiti, Hawaii, and the other eastern islands of the South Seas. But the population did not seem to be absolutely pure and unmixed, for among their visitors some were conspicuous by their darker skins, while others again were 'quite white,' like Europeans. A few were also 'of a reddish tint, as if somewhat severely tanned by the sun.' Many had beards.

"On shore the Dutchmen saw gigantic figures thirty feet high with great cylinders on the top of their heads like a kind of crown. Roggeveen himself narrates that the islanders lighted fires before these giant gods and then squatted down before them with the soles of their feet flat against the ground and their heads bent reverently. Then they began to raise and lower their arms alternately with the palms of their hands pressed together. Behrens, who was on board the other ship, tells us that when the sun rose next morning they could see the natives on shore lying prostrate and worshipping the sunrise, while they had lighted hundreds of fires which the Dutchmen thought were in honour of the gods. This is the only time that anyone has described active sun-worship on Easter Island.

"Among the first who came on board the Dutch ships was a 'completely white man' who had a more ceremonious air than the others. He was ornamented with a crown of feathers on his head, which otherwise was close-shaven, and he had in his ears round white pegs as large as fists. This white man showed by his bearing that he was a prominent person in the community, and the Dutchmen thought that he might be a priest. The lobes of his ears were pierced and artificially lengthened so that they hung down to his shoulders, and the Dutch perceived that many of the islanders had ears artificially lengthened in this manner. If their long ears got in their way when they were at work they just took out the pegs and tied the long ear-flap up over the upper edge of the ear.

"Many of the islanders went about stark naked, but with the whole body artistically tattooed in one single continuous

pattern of birds and strange figures. Others wore cloaks of
bark-cloth coloured red and yellow. Some had waving crowns
of feathers on their heads and others queer reed hats. All were
friendly, and the Dutchmen saw no weapons of any kind.
Curiously enough there were hardly any women to be seen
although the place swarmed with men; but the few women
who showed themselves were all the more ingratiating towards
the unknown visitors, without the men showing the smallest
sign of jealousy.

"The inhabitants lived in long, low huts made of reeds:
they looked like boats turned bottom upwards, with no windows
and a door opening so low that one could only just creep in.
Evidently masses of people lived in these without any furniture
but a few mats on the floor and a stone for a pillow. Fowls
were the only animals they kept: they cultivated bananas,
sugar canes, and above all sweet potatoes, which the Dutch
call the island's daily bread.

"These lonely islanders could certainly not have been active
seafarers, for the largest craft the Dutchmen saw were canoes
eight feet long, so narrow that one could only just force both
legs into them and so leaky that one spent just as much time
bailing as paddling. They were still living in Stone Age fashion,
with no metals, and their food they just cooked between glowing
stones in the earth. It must have seemed to the Dutchmen that
there was, in their own century, scarcely any place in the world
so backward in technique. It was, therefore, only natural that
they were utterly astonished to find, in the midst of these poor
people, gigantic statues towering upward, larger than any they
had seen in Europe. First they were amazed at the problem
it must have been to erect these tall statues; they saw no solid
wood or thick rope in the inhabitants' possession. They
examined the worn surface of one of the weather-beaten
colossi, and solved the whole problem to their own satisfaction
by declaring that the figures were not of stone, but were
modelled from a kind of clay which was afterwards stuffed
with small stones.

"They rowed back to the ships, which had already dragged
two of their anchors, and sailed away from the newly-dis-
covered island after a single day's visit. They noted in their
log-book that the inhabitants they had found were cheerful,

peaceful and good-mannered, but were all expert thieves. Through a misunderstanding one native visitor was shot on board one of the ships, and a dozen others were shot ashore, while the Europeans got off with the loss of one stolen table-cloth and a few hats which were stolen while they had them on their heads.

"The natives were left on the shore with their dead and wounded, staring after the great sails disappearing westward. Nearly fifty years were to pass before the next visit from the outer world.

"Next time it was the Spaniards who came. Led by Don Felipe Gonzales with two ships, they appeared over the horizon of Easter Island in 1770, and they too were summoned with smoke signals sent up by the natives. They went ashore with two priests and a large party of soldiers, and marched in ceremonial procession to the top of a three-humped height on the east coast, while great crowds of cheering natives came dancing after them, full of curiosity. They planted a cross on each of the three hummocks, sang, fired a salute, and declared the island to be Spanish territory. As a proof that all these proceedings were legal they wrote out a declaration addressed to King Charles of Spain, under which the boldest of the natives who stood round were allowed to sign their names 'with every sign of joy and happiness,' in the form of birds and curious figures which the Spaniards accepted as signatures. So now the island had an owner, the King of Spain, and it received a new name: *San Carlos Island.*

"The Spaniards were not deceived into thinking the monuments were of clay; they struck one of the statues so hard with a hoe that sparks sprang from it and thus it was abundantly clear that they were of stone. How these colossi were set up was a mystery to the Spaniards, and they even doubted whether they could have been made on this island.

"Both gifts and stolen goods disappeared so completely that the Spaniards suspected the inhabitants of having secret underground hiding-places, for the whole country was open and treeless. No children were to be seen anywhere; the whole population seemed to consist of multitudes of grown men and only a few women, but these few decidedly unrestrained.

"The Spaniards met on the island tall, fair men; two of the

biggest were measured and were respectively 6 feet 6½ inches and 6 feet 5 inches tall. Many had beards, and the Spaniards found that they were quite like Europeans and not ordinary natives. They noted in their diaries that not all of them had black hair; the hair of some of them was chestnut brown, and in other cases it was even reddish and cinnamon-coloured. And when they actually got the inhabitants to repeat clearly in Spanish 'Ave Maria, long live Charles III, King of Spain,' all the Spaniards agreed that they were teachable, intelligent people who would easily be domesticated, and, full of satisfaction, they left their new subjects, never to return.[1]

"It was the English next time, under the command of no less a person than Captain Cook, and after him came the Frenchman La Pérouse.

"The people of Easter Island were now beginning to have enough of these foreign visitors. When Cook landed, astonishingly few people were to be seen, only a few hundred in all, and these were all under middle height and in a miserable state. They were humourless and uninterested. Cook's guide thought that some misfortune must have befallen the island since the Spaniards' visit, so that the inhabitants were dying out. But Cook himself suspected that the population had gone into hiding underground, for in particular there were quite astonishingly few women to be seen, although patrols were sent all over the island. At several places the Englishmen found heaps of stones with narrow descents to what they thought might be underground caves, but every time they tried to investigate these their native guides refused to admit them. The Englishmen, plagued with scurvy, left Easter Island in despair and disappointment, having obtained for themselves nothing but a supply of sweet potatoes, the only important product they saw. But even over these they were cheated, for the cunning natives had filled the baskets with stones, and laid only a few potatoes on the very top.

"Only twelve years had passed since Cook's visit when the Frenchman La Pérouse paid a similar lightning visit in 1786. This time people appeared again all over Easter Island:

[1] An English translation of old log-books and original letters in connection with both Roggeveen's and Gonzales' visits to Easter Island is contained in Vol. xiii of the Hakluyt Society, Cambridge, 1908.

as before, some had light hair, and nearly half were suddenly grown-up women. There were, moreover, swarms of children of all ages, as in any normal community. It really seemed as though they had been spawned up from the interior of the earth into the treeless lunar landscape of the little island. And that was just what had happened. They came crawling up out of subterranean passages, and the Frenchmen obtained free admission into some of the narrow stone tunnels which the English had not been allowed to enter. They confirmed Cook's suspicion that the population had made themselves secret retreats in dark underground chambers. Here the aristocracy had sheltered itself from Captain Cook, and here the children and most of the women had been hidden even when the Dutch discovered the island. La Pérouse understood that it was because Cook and his men had behaved so peacefully that the population of the island now took courage and crept out into the light of day, a couple of thousand in all.

"Even if the greater part of the people were hiding under the earth while Cook was going about on the island, and even if they had hustled all their most important possessions down underground with them, at any rate they had not taken the huge stone figures with them: they stood on their posts as stubbornly as ever. Both Cook and La Pérouse were in agreement that these were relics from earlier times: they were in their eyes already very ancient monuments. Cook was not a little impressed by the masterpiece of technique achieved by those unknown builders, who had once raised their colossi on the top ledge of terraced walls, without any mechanical contrivances. However it had been done, Cook held it to be proof of intelligence and energy in the people who had lived on this desolate island in ancient times, for he was sure that the existing population had had nothing to do with it; they had not even attempted to maintain the foundations of the walls, which had long ago begun to fall into decay. Nor even did all the statues stand upright in their original places; many had fallen and lay prostrate on the ground at the foot of their own platforms, with every sign of active devastation.

"Cook investigated a few of the great wall terraces on which the statues stood, and was vastly impressed at finding that they were composed of huge stone blocks, so precisely cut and

Above: The expedition ship was a converted Greenland trawler from Stavanger.
Below: Lunch on board. From left: Gonzalo, Bill, author, Yvonne, Anette, Skipper, Carl, Arne, Ed.

Above: Thor junior at the wheel: released from school for an adventurous voyage as deck boy. Anette on a South Sea beach, singing in Polynesian and dancing the hula.
Below: The camp in Anakena Bay was King Hotu Matua's old site by the sea.

polished that they fitted together without mortar or cement. Cook had never seen more perfect mason's work in any wall, even in the best buildings in England. Yet, he added, 'all this care, pains and sagacity had not been able to preserve these curious structures from the ravages of all-devouring Time.'

"A genuine Polynesian from Tahiti was on board Cook's ship, and he understood some of the dialect spoken by the population of Easter Island at that time. From the scrappy information thus obtained the Englishmen got the impression that the statues were not regarded as ordinary images of the gods, but as monuments to earlier *arikis*, memorials of deceased persons of holy and royal birth. Parts of skeletons and bones showed that the platforms on which the statues stood had been regularly used as burial places by those who now lived on the island. It was obvious that they believed in a life after death, for on various occasions they made the clearest signs and demonstrations to explain that while the skeleton lay lifeless on earth the person's real *ego* had disappeared up in the direction of the sky.

"An effort to influence the local culture of Easter Island was attempted for the first time when La Pérouse landed pigs, goats and sheep, and sowed a quantity of seed, in the few hours he lay off the coast. But all this was eaten up by the hungry natives before it had time to propagate itself, and the island remained unchanged.

"No one else visited lonely Easter Island till the beginning of the last century. Then our own race suddenly reappeared, and the natives assembled in crowds on the cliffs along the coast and no longer tried to crawl down into their shelters. This time it was the captain of an American schooner, paying a short visit to look for colonists for a proposed sealing station on Juan Fernandez, the Robinson Crusoe island off the coast of Chile. After a fierce struggle he succeeded in kidnapping twelve men and ten women and put to sea with them. After three days' sailing he let his prisoners loose on deck. The men immediately jumped overboard and began to swim across the sea in the direction of vanished Easter Island. The captain took no notice of them, but put the ship about and carried out a fresh raid on the island.

"The next ships which passed were unable to land men on

the steep coast because they met an impenetrable wall of native stone-throwers. A Russian expedition at last succeeded in forcing a landing with the help of powder and shot, but a few hours later they also had to retreat and re-embark.

"Years passed. At last the natives' confidence was slowly regained, and at intervals of many years some passing vessel made a brief call. There was gradually less and less stone-throwing, and more and more women emerged into the daylight and charmed the visitors. But then there was a disaster.

"One day a flotilla of seven Peruvian sealing ships anchored off the coast. A crowd of natives swam out and boarded the ships, where to their gratification they were allowed to inscribe a few flourishes at the foot of a sheet of paper. Thereby they had signed another contract, this time to go as labourers to the guano islands off the coast of Peru. When, contented and unsuspecting, they wanted to go ashore again, they were bound and taken below. Then eight of the slave-hunters rowed ashore with clothes and bright-coloured presents and threw these down on the shore. Numbers of curious natives who had assembled on the rocks round the bay began slowly to come nearer to admire these tempting objects. When at last several hundred stood crowded together on the beach the slave-hunters attacked. The natives who were kneeling down and picking up the presents were seized and their hands tied behind them, while those who tried to escape over the cliffs or swim out to sea were fired at. Just as the last of the ship's boats was ready to put off, loaded to the gunwale with prisoners, one of the captains discovered two natives who had hidden in a cave. When he could not persuade them to go with him, he shot them down.

"So it was that on Christmas Eve of 1862 Easter Island lay desolate and depopulated. All who were not lying dead on the rocks by the shore, or below decks out in the bay, with their hands bound behind them, had crept down into their subterranean catacombs and rolled stones in front of the openings. An oppressive silence reigned on the treeless island; only the breakers murmured threateningly. The expression of the giant gods remained unmoved. But from the ships there was cheering and shouting: the visitors did not weigh anchor till they had celebrated Christmas.

"The population of the World's Navel, having now experienced the white man's Easter Day as well as Christmas, were next to see a little more of the outside world. The ships sailed away with a thousand slaves, who were landed to dig guano on the islands off the coast of Peru. The bishop of Tahiti protested, and the authorities decided that the slaves should be taken back to their own island immediately. But about nine hundred had died of illness and unfamiliar living conditions before the ship was ready to fetch them, and of the hundred survivors who embarked eighty-five died on the voyage, so only fifteen returned to Easter Island alive. They brought with them small-pox, which at once spread like wildfire and made an end of almost the whole population, even if they hid themselves down in the deepest and narrowest caves. Scarcity and misery prevailed till the population of the whole island fell to 111 in all, adults and children.

"In the meantime the first foreigner had settled on the island with the best intentions. This was a solitary missionary, who honestly did his best to alleviate the misery he found there, but the natives stole from him everything he possessed, even the trousers he was wearing. He got away in the first ship, but returned with several helpers and set up a little mission station. A few years after, when all the surviving islanders had consented to be baptized, a French adventurer came and set them against the missionaries. The natives drove out the missionaries and killed the Frenchman, and went on singing hymns on their own account while all other traces of the missionaries were obliterated.

"At the end of the last century the Europeans found that there was excellent grazing for thousands of sheep round the statues on Easter Island, and at last the island was annexed by Chile. Now there are a governor, a priest and a doctor on the island, and no one lives in caves or reed huts. Civilization has displaced the old culture on Easter Island, just as it has done among Eskimos and Indians and the inhabitants of all the other South Sea Islands.

"So we haven't come here to study the natives," I concluded. "We've come to dig. If the answers to the riddle of Easter Island exist today, they must be down in the earth."

"Has no one been here and dug before?" someone asked.

"No one thinks there is any earth to dig in. No trees grow
on the island. If there was no woodland in old times either,
much earth cannot have been formed from withering grass
alone. So no one believes that anything can be hidden in the
ground."

In fact there had been only two archaeological expeditions
to this strange island, and no others had made any plans to go
there. The first was a private British expedition headed by
Katherine Routledge. She came to Easter Island in 1914 in
her own sailing yacht and surveyed and mapped everything
she saw above ground: in the first instance wall terraces, old
roads and over four hundred gigantic stone statues which lay
scattered about all over the island. She had her hands so full
with this pioneering work that there was no time for any
systematic excavation, apart from clearing up round some of
the statues which had been partly covered by slow earth
subsidence. Unfortunately all the scientific notes of the Routledge expedition were lost, but in a book on her voyage round
the world she writes that the whole island is instinct with
mystery and unsolved problems. Each day she had been
filled with continually increasing wonder at the strange
unsolved problems which lay behind it all. "The shadows of
the departed builders still possess the land," she says. One
cannot escape from them. They are more active and real than
the living population of the island, and reign supreme with their
silent giant constructions as vassals. Impelled by motives
unknown to us, they had hacked their way with crude stone
picks into the mountain-sides and altered the shape of a whole
extinct volcano, just to obtain raw material for the fulfilment
of their fanatical desire to see gigantic sculptures in human
shape erected round about, in all the bays and landing places.

Everywhere is the wind of heaven; around and above all are
boundless sea and sky, infinite space and a great silence. The dweller
there is ever listening for he knows not what, feeling unconsciously
that he is in the antechamber to something yet more vast which
is just beyond his ken.[1]

Such was Mrs. Routledge's view of Easter Island. She freely

[1] Mrs. Scoresby Routledge: *The Mystery of Easter Island: the Story of an
Expedition*. London, 1919. Pp. 133, 165, 391, etc.

recognized the mystery, soberly presented her own facts, and left the solution to those who should come after.

Twenty years later a Franco-Belgian expedition was landed by a warship and picked up again later by another. One of the archaeologists died on the voyage; and while the Frenchman Métraux collected oral information from the natives for a large-scale study of the island's ethnography, the Belgian Lavachery was more than fully occupied in examining thousands of rock carvings and other strange stone-works which were to be seen everywhere on the treeless island. So no excavation was done this time either.

The Franco-Belgian expedition had, generally speaking, set itself other problems on the island than the British, and the statues were not their main object. But Métraux thought the mystery was exaggerated: ordinary natives from the islands farther west could have come there with the idea of making figures, and because there were no trees to carve they attacked the mountain rock.

Other research workers and numerous circumnavigators have landed on Easter Island both earlier and later: their vessels have waited for a few days, or most often a few hours, and meanwhile they have collected legends and wood-carvings from the poor population, or live creatures and plants from its equally poor fauna and flora. The little island east of the sun and west of the moon has been slowly stripped for the benefit of the world's museum cases and souvenir cabinets. Most of what could be taken away has been taken away. Only the giant heads stand on the slopes with a stony supercilious smile and say how-do-you-do and good-bye to the Lilliputians who come, stare and go again as the centuries roll by. A veil of mystery has continued to lie about the island like a haze.

These were the main features of Easter Island's history.

"Isn't it possible that the natives themselves have any more traditions?" the skipper asked quietly.

"Optimist," I said. "Tomorrow you're going to meet people who are as civilized as you and I. The first person who collected legends among them was an American, Paymaster Thomson, in 1886. At that time the original population was still alive which had grown up before any white man had settled on the island. They told him that their forefathers had come over the sea from the east in big ships by steering directly towards the sunset for sixty days. Originally two different races had lived together on the island, 'long-ears' and 'short-ears,' but the 'short-ears' had slaughtered almost all the others in a war, and then they ruled on the island alone.

"What ancient legends there were you can read in books today," I added. "There isn't much left of the old South Seas."

"Least of all on Easter Island," Gonzalo put in. "A handful of white people live there now, and even a school and a small hospital have been built."

"Yes, the only benefit we can get from the inhabitants is the extra help we shall need for digging," I added. "And perhaps they can get us a few fresh vegetables."

"Perhaps there are some vahines who can teach us a bit of hula," muttered one of the engineers, and there was a lively burst of laughter and approval from one of the ship's boats.

Then we suddenly heard a hoarse remark which no one would stand for, for everyone looked round in astonishment. Who had said what? The mate flashed a light over the dark deck. No one was there. Everyone looked rather silly. The engineer tried a new joke about hula girls, but at the same moment we heard the voice again. Was it someone overboard? We ran to the rail and pointed a torch down towards the black water. There was no water there; the light of the torch played straight into a mass of staring faces, the faces of the worst gang of pirates we had ever seen. They were standing close-packed in a little boat and gazing up at us.

"*Ia-o-rana,*" I tried.

"*Ia-o-rana,*" they replied in chorus.

So they were Polynesians. But upon my soul they were a mixture of everything possible as well.

We flung a ladder down to them, and one by one they came clambering up the ship's side and jumped on board. Most of them were strongly built fellows, but almost all conspicuously ragged and tattered. With a red cloth round his head and a bundle hanging between his teeth, the first man appeared in the light at the top of the ladder. He heaved his bare toes over the rail and scrambled on board, wearing a ragged singlet and the rolled-up remains of a pair of trousers. Behind him came a big, pock-marked fellow in an old green army winter overcoat and bare legs, with a large wooden club and a bundle of carved sticks over his shoulder. He was closely followed by the goggle-eyed grinning head of a wooden figure with a goatee beard and projecting ribs, which was manoeuvred up the ladder by a native in a white sailor's cap. One by one the ragged fellows jumped down on to the deck, shook hands with everyone they could get near, and produced bags and sacks full of curious things. The most bizarre wooden carvings began to circulate from hand to hand, and soon attracted more attention than their owners.

There was one particular weird figure with sloping shoulders which reappeared in all the men's wood carvings. It had a strikingly curved aquiline nose, a goatee beard, long hanging ear-lobes, large deep-set eyes and a face convulsed in a devilish grin. The spine and naked ribs stuck out, while the stomach was completely drawn in. The figure was always exactly the same, whether it was large or small. There were a few other curious wooden figures, notably one of a human being with wings and a bird's head, there were elegant clubs and paddles adorned with staring masks, and there were moon-shaped breast ornaments decorated with mysterious hieroglyphs which no person now living can interpret. All the carvings were masterly, faultlessly executed and so highly polished that they were like porcelain to the touch. There were also some copies, a good deal less successful, of the great stone statues, and a handsome feather crown with a dress belonging to it made of feathers artistically bound together.

I had never seen any such productivity on any of the other Polynesian islands, whose inhabitants prefer to take life very calmly. Here indeed we had been received by a whole team of admirable wood-carvers. It looked, moreover, to an uninitiated person as if these fellows with their bizarre works of art must be possessed of untameable imagination and creative joy. But on closer inspection one quickly perceived that the same curious things reappeared all the time, quite unchanged. There was no variation from certain predetermined norms.

I had just studied Dr. Mosny's collection of modern popular art from Easter Island in the National Museum in Chile, and when the natives began to produce their wooden figures they were most astonished at my recognizing all the different types both by appearance and name. In reality they were all perfect copies of belongings which the earliest Europeans found among the natives on Easter Island, and which now exist only in museums. The originals are today immensely valuable, but as they are no longer in the market the natives see that the trade is kept going with good copies.

The wood-carvers pointed with apologetic smiles to their ragged trousers and bare legs, and wanted to barter their goods for clothes and shoes. In a few seconds business was in full swing all over the deck. The crew, impelled both by acquisitiveness and charity, plunged down into the cabins and came up again with all they could spare in the way of shoes and clothes. Little Anette suddenly appeared in pyjamas. She stood in the middle of the throng, tugging, quite enthralled, at the leg of a grotesque bird-man which one of the worst piratical types held under his arm, and when he saw that she liked the figure he gave it to her at once. Yvonne hurried off to fetch a parcel for him.

The photographer came up and nudged my arm.

"I say, there's a chap standing here and holding something queer under his shirt; he says it's very, very old, goes back to his great-great-grandfather. . . ."

I smiled, but accompanied him to an almost thin, pleasant-mannered man who looked more than anything like a pale Arab with a Hitler moustache.

"*Buenos dias*, señor," he said, and drew from his breast with an air of mystery a little flat stone with a bird-man obviously quite freshly cut on one side. Before he had time to mention his great-great-grandfather again, I said enthusiastically:

"No, did you really do that yourself?"

He was rather taken aback for a second and his face was contorted in a struggle between a smile and disconcertment. Then he blushed proudly and looked at his masterpiece as if he thought, after all, it would be a great pity to give anyone else the credit for it.

"Yes," he said proudly, and was now visibly basking in the consciousness of his own talent. He had no need for regrets, for the photographer liked the stone and took it.

Another boat had suddenly come alongside, and I was told

that a white man was on his way up the ladder. It was a smart young naval officer, who presented himself as the governor's assistant and had come to welcome us on his behalf. We invited him into the saloon for a drink and explained why we had anchored here. He was able to tell us that in any case the weather had made it impossible to anchor off the village at the moment, but proposed that we should move next morning under the lee of another cape which was nearer the inhabited area, and then they would try to help us ashore on to the rocks. We were told that it was just six months since the last ship had called; she was, as might be expected, a Chilean man-of-war. The year before they had had a visit from a big luxury liner. The governor had been asked whether there was a lift in the hotel and if there was a tram to the landing-stage, and when he replied that there was no hotel and no landing-stage the passengers were refused permission to go ashore. Instead, some of the natives were allowed to go on board and sell souvenirs and do a hula dance on deck, and then the ship went on to see more of the Pacific.

"Well, we're going ashore if we have to swim for it," we laughed, without a suspicion how nearly true this was going to be.

On his way to the ladder the naval officer proposed that we should keep one of the natives on board as a local expert when we made the trip round next morning. "They steal like magpies," he added; "it might be best for you to keep the mayor; have you been introduced to him?"

I had not. The mayor was fetched by his proud subordinates. The man they led up to me was no other than the one with the stone; his shirt was now crammed with the photographer's barter goods.

"There's no chief any longer, but this is the mayor of Easter Island," the naval officer said, clapping the man with the moustache genially on the shoulder, "and he's the best wood-carver on the island as well."

"*Si*, señor," said the mayor, blushing and laughing and so proud that he did not know whether to look up or down, while his friends crowded round so as not to be deprived of their share of the honour of having their own mayor elected by themselves. Many of the fellows looked extremely sharp, and there were several robust leader types among them.

B*

"*Si*, señor," the slightly built man repeated, and drew himself up so that one leg of the photographer's old trousers stuck out of the breast of his shirt. "I've been mayor for twenty-eight years. They elect me again every time."

"Queer that they elect such a fool," I thought. It looked as if there was better material to choose from.

The naval officer had to use all his authority to get all the men to go with him when he left the ship. Only the mayor remained. Little did I suspect that he would play the chief part in the strangest adventure I had ever had.

I was awakened early next morning by the rattling of the anchor chains. I jumped into my trousers and went out on deck. The sun was already beginning to play over the island, which looked green and yellow and friendly now that its night silhouette had been obliterated and the colours wakened to life again by the morning sun. The unchangeable statues stood far away on the slope. But no one was lighting a fire, no one worshipping the marvellous sunrise, no one was to be seen at all: the island lay there as lifeless as if we had been taken for a slave-ship and everyone had gone underground.

"*Buenos dias*, señor."

There stood the everlasting mayor again, raising his hat. One of our hats. For he had been bare-headed when he came on board the night before.

"*Buenos dias*, mayor, there's not much life to be seen ashore."

"No," he said. "This isn't our country any longer, we live in the village on the other side, this is only for the Navy's sheep. Look there—" and he pointed to a round-backed down on which I now saw clearly a multitude of sheep, moving across it like a grey carpet.

The ship was moving all the time and the bay was shut off. We were gliding along a perpendicular cliff where foaming breakers had eaten their way into the volcanic formation till the coast was sheer and immensely high. There were gleams of reddish-brown and yellowish-grey in the layers of a cut cake, and high up on the crest over our heads we could see green grass and ancient walls which seemed on the verge of tumbling down the precipice. Mile after mile of inaccessible cliffs, till the surface of the island changed shape and rolled its stone-strewn fields down towards the sea from round grassy hummocks and hillocks in the interior. The green never came right down to the surf, for there a tumbled barrier of black lava blocks lay like a protecting wall all round the island. Only at once place did the landscape really open up, and there the island smiled at us, revealing a broad sunlit beach. The whole effect was wonderfully beautiful and inviting.

"Anakena." The mayor inclined his head reverently. "Here at Anakena the kings lived in old times. It was on this beach too that our first ancestor Hotu Matua landed."

"Who lives there now?"

"Nobody. The shepherds have a hut there."

I called to the skipper and pointed, and he agreed that this was an excellent camping ground.

The bay closed again, and the same savage lava coast, with precipices and loose blocks, continued right round the island till, right at the western end, the interior at last ran down in a gentle slope towards the sea, and here lay all the houses in the village of Hangaroa. Little white-painted houses in well-kept gardens, sometimes surrounded by solitary palms and scattered trees, and on the ridges behind there were even some fields planted with eucalyptus. A fence ran right round the village: the rest of the island was the Navy's sheep farm.

"That's my home," said the mayor, glowing with pride. And it was pretty. The mayor could quite justly note that we were all standing and staring landward in enchantment: even Anette sat motionless on Yvonne's arm, gazing as though hypnotized at the little doll's village under the great blue sky. The whole place suddenly began to move: everywhere people were running or galloping on horseback, all in one direction, the same as ours.

"Did you ever see such a place?" cried Thor junior. "It's like the theatre."

The captain had hoisted all our flags, and the whole ship was bright with bunting in all the colours of the rainbow and all the items of the code of signals from cholera to mail. We saluted both by siren and flag, and someone replied by running up a Chilean flag on a solitary mast on shore.

The mayor dried his eyes with his shirt-sleeve.

"Señor," he said. "This is Hotu Matua's country. This is my country. I have been mayor here for twenty-eight years.

What would Easter Island have been without me? Nothing. Easter Island, that's me. I am Easter Island." It came with violent emphasis while he struck his chest.

I thought I saw Hitler behind the little moustache, but no, I was wrong. This fool was infinitely nicer. He was contented with what he had, absolutely contented. He did not even want to take back the land from the sheep on the other side of the fence.

"Señor." More rhetoric followed. "We two are the only famous people on this island. Everyone knows me. Who knows the governor? People have come all the way from Germany to take blood samples from my ear, and letters have come from Glasgow and Austria ordering wood-carvings from the mayor of Easter Island. The world knows me. Señor, give me your hand as friend!"

When I had done this, he asked politely if he might call me Señor Kon-Tiki.

We rounded a fresh cape with precipitous sides, and the village had disappeared behind a chaos of perpendicular crags and wild little islands of lava, which lay like ruined castles and black steeples as sharp as awls at the foot of the great black cliff. There were foaming breakers now, and the ship was rolling where currents met in a race, with a fierce backwash from the cliffs. The mayor was seasick and tottered to a deck-chair, but managed to mutter something about its being just there that the bird-men had been active. He pointed to the grotesque wooden figure which Anette had laid in a doll's bed.

Once past the unquiet cape we came to a kind of open bay in which the cliffs no longer reached to the sky, even if the coast was both high and precipitous. The riders and the crowd of people on foot had taken a short cut across the cape farther inland, and the green slope above the drop to the beach was packed with horses and people. It looked as if some of the swarm had run on down a narrow promontory in the cliff descending to some black lava rocks in the foaming breakers, where they were launching a boat. There came the first boat to fetch us, dancing in the seas. The captain went as far in as he could and anchored. The mayor was very busy.

"In our own dialect 'good day everyone' is *ia-o-rana-kurua*," he whispered to me. "Call it out when you get ashore, and they'll like you."

It was a rough trip in through the foaming seas, and only a few elect were allowed to go ashore. A frothing crest lifted us up and hurled us in round a huge lava-block; here the native coxswain made a masterly turn and got us more or less into shelter before the next cascade came rushing on. There was no harbour, no breakwater, only Nature's wild fantasy. Behind the farthest protecting blocks stood a solid line of motionless natives, waiting for us at the top of a narrow ridge in a mass of lava which descended from the plateau as a kind of natural stair."

"*Ia-o-rana kurua*," I shouted at the top of my voice as we swung into their world.

"*Ia-o-rana kurua*," came an avalanche of voices all the way up the height, and all were in movement to help us ashore. They were a mixed assembly to greet: it looked as if most of the island's nine hundred inhabitants were there. They were Polynesians, but of very mixed blood, and they had all come in some combination of garments which had a mainland origin. I had hardly got out of the dancing boat when a bent old woman with a kerchief on her head caught hold of me.

"A secret, señor," she whispered hoarsely and produced a basket of sweet potatoes. She pushed a large potato aside and eyed temptingly the corner of a cloth which lay just under it.

"Thanks for letting me see it," I said, and went on. I had not seen anything, but no great secret was likely to be disclosed when the whole cliff-side was packed with staring people. Many of the men on the ledges of the cliff had wooden figures and bags, but no one tried to show anything. One by one they muttered "*ia-o-rana, ia-o-rana*" as we clambered past them.

The crest above us was black with waiting inhabitants, and in the midst of them stood a solitary white form in a fluttering gown. I guessed at once who he was. He was the most powerful man in the whole island, Father Sebastian Englert. He had written a book on Easter Island. I had heard him spoken of in Chile as the uncrowned king of the island. If one made friends with him all doors were opened, but woe to the man he did not like, someone had said to me.

Now he stood before me. Broad and straight-backed he stood,

with his legs apart, in a long white cloak with a cord round
the waist and long, brightly polished boots. He was like an
apostle or prophet in his white gown, bare-headed with hood
thrown back and flowing beard, against an incredibly blue
sky.

I looked into a ruddy face with searching eyes and shrewd
wrinkles, and held out my hand.

"Welcome to my island," were his first words.

I noticed the possessive adjective.

"Yes, I always say *my* island," he added, smiling all over his
face, "for I reckon it as mine and would not sell it for millions."

I understood that, and we were prepared to place ourselves
under his command.

He laughed.

"Do you like natives?" he suddenly asked, and looked at me
searchingly.

"The better the more genuine they are," I replied.

His face grew sunny.

"Then we shall be good friends."

I introduced Gonzalo, the captain, the doctor and one or
two others who had come ashore with me, and then we sauntered off to a jeep which was standing out in the open, among
lumps of lava and grazing riding-horses. We bumped off across
country on a zigzag course till we came to some wheel-tracks
farther inland, which led us down to the village. We turned
off inside the fence and at last stopped before the governor's
solitary bungalow.

A wiry little man in a khaki uniform came out and received
us cordially, and all formalities were quickly and easily disposed of in his office. Now we sat before the two chief people
of the island; the old sage Father Sebastian and the young
commandant Arnaldo Curti, the military governor. The first
had been there for twenty years and would remain there till
the end of his days, the other had come in the last warship to
run the island for two years for the government on the South
American continent. Which held the threads, experience or
power? We soon learnt that they formed an indivisible whole:
they put their heads together daily and solved the queerest
problems, which can only arise in a most unusual community
on the world's loneliest island.

When the captain had submitted the list of the ship's company, and the doctor a certificate of good health, there were no more formalities.

"Good luck with the digging," the governor said, and shook me by the hand. "We only impose on you two restrictions: you must not give the natives arms or alcohol."

That was all fair enough.

"One thing more," he said, scratching his neck. "You're by no means an unknown person among the natives, and you've created something of a real problem for us here on the island."

The priest smiled and stroked his beard.

"Well, your ship can take over the guard duties now," he said, laughing.

We did not understand, but were given an explanation. When the news reached Easter Island that the *Kon-Tiki* raft had drifted past and come to land safely in the South Sea islands, the natives had been interested. Since their forefathers had been able to survive such adventures, why should they themselves be any worse? There was no timber for a raft on the almost treeless island, but some fellows knocked together a little open plank boat and went far out to sea to fish. The current took them, and Easter Island was gone. They drifted involuntarily on the same course as the *Kon-Tiki* and landed five weeks later, starving and worn-out, on an atoll in the Tuamotu group, whence they made their way to Tahiti.

This whetted appetites. Some other men also built an open boat and were going out to sea, allegedly to fish. The governor had found the boat full of water-cans and smelt a rat. It was dangerous to let them go in such a craft and he ordered the boat to be hauled up on to the shore. When the natives tried to get away to sea in spite of this, he was obliged to set another native as armed guard over the boat. The only result was that another man took part in the voyage: the guard had put out to sea with the others at dead of night. This boat drifted still farther west than the first, and the natives on board did not see land till they jumped ashore in the best of spirits at Atiu, a long way beyond Tahiti. Now a regular travel fever set in on Easter Island. Two crews built boats, and these were now ready far inland. The whole village knew of the intention, and although there were only a handful of white men on the island,

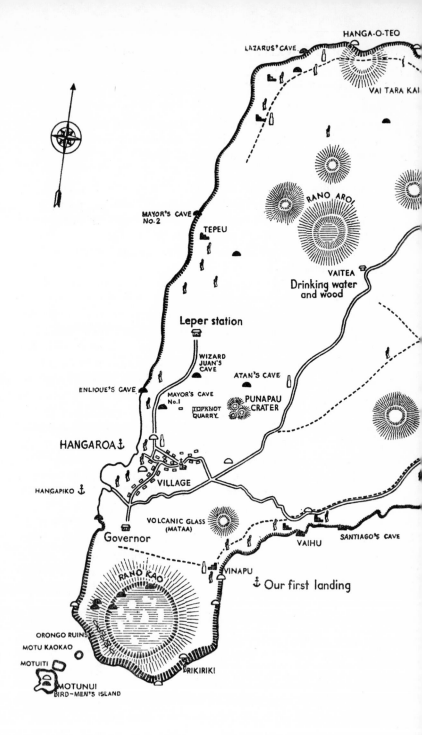

HANGA-O-TEO

LAZARUS' CAVE

VAI TARA KAI

MAYOR'S CAVE
No. 2

TEPEU

RANO AROI

VAITEA
Drinking water
and wood

Leper station

WIZARD
JUAN'S
CAVE

ATAN'S CAVE

ENLIQUE'S CAVE

MAYOR'S CAVE
No. 1

TOPKNOT
QUARRY

PUNAPAU
CRATER

HANGAROA ⚓

VILLAGE

HANGAPIKO ⚓

VOLCANIC GLASS
(MATAA)

Governor

VAIHU

SANTIAGO'S CAVE

VINAPU

⚓ Our first landing

RANO KAO

ORONGO RUINS

MOTU KAOKAO

MOTUITI

MOTUNUI
BIRD-MEN'S ISLAND

RIKIRIKI

Moje Wolter

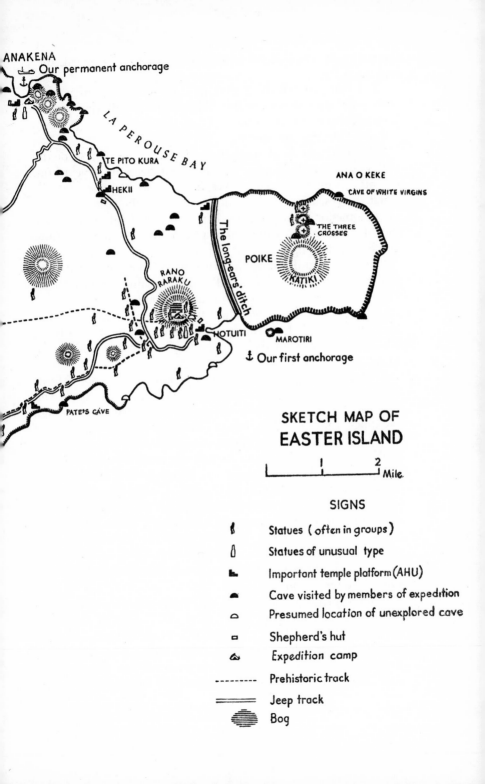

ANAKENA
⚓ Our permanent anchorage

LA PEROUSE BAY

TE PITO KURA

HEKII

ANA O KEKE
CAVE OF WHITE VIRGINS

THE THREE CROSSES

POIKE

RANO RARAKU

KATIKI

The long-ears' ditch

HOTUITI

MAROTIRI

⚓ Our first anchorage

PATE'S CAVE

SKETCH MAP OF
EASTER ISLAND

	1	2
Mile

SIGNS

🔱   Statues (often in groups)

◊   Statues of unusual type

🔳   Important temple platform (AHU)

⬤   Cave visited by members of expedition

◠   Presumed location of unexplored cave

▭   Shepherd's hut

⌂   Expedition camp

--------   Prehistoric track

═══   Jeep track

◉   Bog

the governor was obliged to keep one of them on guard, day and night.

"If I can just tell them that now we can fetch them back with your ship if they start, I'll be free of all this watch-keeping," said the governor.

I gave him my promise.

"We need guards at other places instead," he said. "For the natives steal anything up to two thousand sheep in the year from the other side of the fence. We have a sort of prison for the worst thieves, but it doesn't help much, for the prisoners have to go home for all meals. If we began to serve food in the prison they'd all think of some crime just to be put in prison and get fed for nothing.

"They're grand fellows in other ways," he continued, and Father Sebastian nodded. "If only one understands them. There's never any serious disturbance or fighting: stealing has always been their worst quality, but one must remember that they give away just as readily as they steal. Property is a thing which passes through their hands very easily: it doesn't mean so much as it does with us."

Father Sebastian promised us to pick out some good fellows as extra diggers. He would think out a suitable rate of pay and rations daily. Our selection of barter goods had a very high exchange value compared to all kinds of gold and notes, for there was no shop or cinema on the island, not even a barber's.

We agreed that Anakena Bay on the other side of the island was the best place for the main camp of the expedition. There were many reasons for this. It was the prettiest place on all the coast. It had the only decent sandy beach on the island, where we could land all the gear by raft. It was as far as possible from the village, with the minimum risk of thieving and incidents. Moreover it was the valley of kings, famous in story, where the legendary Hotu Matua had first landed. We could not desire much more.

After a splendid celebration meal in the governor's bungalow we returned to the ship. There were still swarms of natives on the cliffs, and to Father Sebastian's great pleasure all who wished to take a look round on board were allowed to do so. I thought they looked rather better turned out today, clean, and above all not so ragged as when they first came on board.

I mentioned this casually to the mayor, who had been home and put on a whole shirt. He gave me a crafty smile.

"That's an old trick of ours," he giggled. "If we put on old rags we get much better paid for the wood-carvings."

The sea was so rough that not many came out to the ship, and we promised to repeat the invitation another time. Just as we were about to send the last visitors back to the shore the skipper came hurrying up with the visitors' book.

"We must have the names of people who have been on board," he proposed, smiling. He gave the book to one of those who looked the brightest, and asked him to get them all to write their names. The fellow took the book and pen and wandered off to the others with a thoughtful look on his face. They put their heads together as though in profound reflection and muttered rapidly to each other. Then he returned gravely with the book, without one signature in it.

"Isn't there anyone who can write his name?" the skipper asked.

"Yes, many," the man said, "but they won't."

Gonzalo heard what was said. He took the book and went up to the crowd, explaining that he was a Chilean and that they might therefore understand his Spanish better. But when he tried to give further explanations there was more and more disturbance around him and at last there was such a row that it seemed to be blowing for a regular brawl—one of the men wanted to throw the visitors' book overboard. I had to use all my authority to get Gonzalo out of the crowd, and he came back with the book, untidy and dishevelled.

"It's quite incredible," he said. "But they refuse to sign. They declare that was how their ancestors were tricked into going to be slaves in Peru!"

"It isn't possible that they can still have traditions about that," someone said.

But when we began to calculate we realized that it was these people's grandfathers who had experienced the slave raid, and the fathers of some of them might already have been born at the time.

The visitors' book was hurriedly removed, and I explained to the visitors that they must go ashore now, for we were going to sail. No one went, and blowing the siren and starting the

engine, with as much shrieking and general racket as the
engineers could produce to order, was quite ineffective. Finally
I had to accompany several of them to the ladder to make them
clamber down into the two native rowing-boats which were
waiting. When I ordered the others to be rounded up I saw
that one boat was rowing away already, towing the other, which
had suddenly become full of water. I shouted to them and
asked them to take the others who were on board too, and they
replied that they would come back for the others as soon as
they had been ashore and got rid of the passengers and the
water. Time passed, but no one came back for all our blowing
of the siren. We were obliged to shift our anchorage before
darkness fell, and did not know those waters well enough to
land people between the lava blocks in our own boat. Finally
we had to weigh anchor and go, with all our new passengers
on board. None of them reacted in any way; they all took it
quite naturally. When our own supper was ready the cook
served food to our sixteen new passengers, who made a hearty
meal and then rushed to the rail overcome with seasickness,
for the ship had begun to roll.

We anchored under the lee of the same cliff as the night
before, but not even here did we get rid of our passengers, and
night fell. It began to rain a little. We should be thoroughly
robbed in the night if we let that gang of pirates into the
cabins. Accordingly I gave them the choice of sleeping on the
hatch on deck, or paddling themselves ashore on the ship's
aluminium raft in two batches. They chose the raft, and we
launched it. But then of a sudden they all insisted absolutely
on going in the second batch, and at last we had to give up all
idea of getting rid of them. Happy and well-fed, they now
produced a guitar and began to do a hula dance on the foredeck. This turned out to be a good move. The crew had not
been ashore or seen a show for a long time, and they were all
enlivened by the suggestive music. Now that we had them on
board whether we liked it or not, why not make the best of it?
Song and exciting string music, with rhythmical hand-clapping,
filled the whole ship, and in the surrounding darkness the ship's
lantern had the effect of footlights to the festive scene.

Te tere te vaka te Hotu Matua. . . .

The broad humour of our care-free pirates was so infectious

that scientists and seamen alike had no choice but to surrender and join in the dance and sing as best they could.

Then the mayor suddenly appeared out of the darkness, wet and frozen. He sat in a little boat with three other natives. After some discussion we quickly agreed that his party of four should come on board on condition that they rowed the sixteen others ashore. To make everyone happy I said that the two parties could remain on board and play for another hour. The mayor agreed and came on board delightedly, accompanied by his friends. He asked immediately if his party also could not have a meal such as the others had had.

"Yes," I said diplomatically, "but not till you've taken the other sixteen ashore."

He sauntered cheerfully up to the musicians and clapped in time for half a minute. Then he came hurrying back and said that the others must definitely go ashore at once, otherwise they would get wet and cold on the way home.

All my pleading for them was of no avail, and the fact that the hour had just begun made no difference; he began to shout to stop the music. So I altered my tactics.

"For that matter you can quite well have a meal now," I said.

The mayor rushed straight into the cook's galley without giving the musicians a further thought. He just stuck his head out, with his mouth full of food, to see if the three others were following him.

But he kept his word, and when the hour was over the native rowing boat, full of laughter and music, was tossing about on her way towards the dark coast. It had been a successful party. *Ohoi! Te tere te vaka te Hotu Matua. . . .*

So it happened that we arrived at the valley of the kings early next morning, with the mayor of the World's Navel himself asleep on the saloon table.

CHAPTER III

IN VOLCANIC GAS TUNNELS

THERE was not a soul in the Anakena valley when our first little patrol went round on the plain inside the beach looking for the best place to put up the tents. But as we walked a single rider appeared over the ridge, and a native shepherd jumped off his horse and came up and greeted us. He himself had a little white-washed stone cottage on the western side of the valley and was responsible for the sheep in that part of the island. When he heard we had come to live in the Anakena valley he immediately pointed to a little gully with several good-sized caves in it. He told us that they were Hotu Matua's caves. The first king and all his companions had lived there when they landed on that shore, the real discoverers of the island. Afterwards they had built large huts of fresh-water reeds. He talked of Hotu Matua as naturally as an Englishman would talk of Queen Victoria. It was unthinkable to him that there were people who did not know about Hotu Matua; he was the alpha and omega in the conceptions of Easter Island, a sort of hybrid between the Adam of religion and the Columbus of history.

When I told him that we had no need to live in caves because we had with us ready-made huts of watertight cloth, he at once pointed in the opposite direction.

"If you've got canvas you can sleep just across the beach on Hotu Matua's old site," he said. He accompanied us over the plain to a flat terrace at the foot of a little dome-shaped hill. Everywhere were traces of vanished greatness. In the middle of the bay, and on each side, were three temple-like terraces built up of colossal blocks of stone facing the sea. They lay just above the sandy beach and would have had the appearance of a fortress protecting the plain against attack from the sea if several large yellowish-grey human forms in stone had not lain prostrate in the sand beside it, showing that the terrace had served as a foundation for them. All these colossi had fallen face downwards and with the tops of their heads pointing inland, which showed that before they fell they had stood with their backs toward the sea looking inwards across an open temple square. By the central terrace a whole row of fallen giants lay side by side, and huge cylinders of rust-red stone which had once been balanced on the tops of their heads had tumbled off and lay on the plain.

The lofty and imposing terrace in the easternmost corner of the bay had had only a single statue, but lying where it did with its face buried in the earth this appeared much more broad-backed and bulkier than its slender relations on the next terrace, and it was just inside this broad giant that King Hotu Matua himself had lived. The shepherd pointed reverently to the solid foundation wall of the king's old house still visible on the ground, and just behind it was a curious five-sided stone oven which indicated the king's own kitchen. Here, of course, we should dig, so we marked out the camping ground close beside it, on the flat temple square in front of the crown of the fallen giant's head.

The shepherd looked on with great interest and went on repeating that this was the king's old site, till he was sure that we all completely understood where we were. Then he got a packet of cigarettes and rode on well pleased.

Soon after this we began to land the equipment. We first rowed about the bay in the little aluminium raft with a couple of natives to study the rocks and breakers. In the middle of the bay there were no stones and the surf was slight, so we landed the photographer first with all his camera outfit. Then we rowed out again towards the landing boat, which was waiting farther out, halfway between the ship and ourselves. When we were well under way we saw a great roller toss the ship's boat high in the air as she made off seaward with her engine at full speed to avoid the clutches of a still bigger sea which was just rising. We rowed after her as hard as we could and weathered the first sea, but the second came rolling towards us ever higher and steeper, and in a moment we were flung up against an absolutely perpendicular rock wall and felt the raft whirling round bottom uppermost. I got a violent blow on the head, but dived to the bottom as quickly as I could to avoid a still harder blow from the pontoons. I kept my eyes shut to keep out the whirling sand and swam as far and as

deep as I could before I had to come up for air. By that time
the others were already clambering up again on to the bottom of
the capsized raft, and the seas outside were as normal as before.

This was a valuable lesson before we had begun to land
indispensable equipment. Even if the biggest seas were rare,
we had always to be on the watch for unexpected huge breakers
which now and then came rolling in through Anakena Bay
when we least wished it. To avoid them we anchored our
largest life-saving raft out in the bay like a kind of floating
pier, well outside the danger zone of the breakers. The landing
boat could safely go in as far as this pier with equipment from
the ship, and here everything was transferred to a small
pontoon raft, which could be allowed to ride with the breakers
right on to the beach so long as none of the worst seas were
in sight. The whole transport of personnel and equipment
between ship and shore was effected in this manner; the
landing boat was ordered by blasts of the siren from the ship
and flag signals from the shore. On the last stage through the
surf there was always cursing and laughter and wet trousers,
and it was often so rough that the cook and the steward had
to swim ashore with their newly-baked bread in watertight
rubber bags. But if the water was rather cool the sandy beach
inside was warm and pleasant, and we were all of us happy
in the sun-soaked valley of the kings. Soon one green tent
sprang up beside another, and formed a peaceful little village
in the temple square between the old fallen giant and the
house in which Hotu Matua's dynasty had begun. Our native
friends who helped with the landing of the equipment were
vastly impressed when they came up behind the great wall
and saw where we had pitched our tents. The mayor drew
a deep breath and said solemnly:

"Señor, Hotu Matua built his first house just there: see,
there is the foundation wall and there the kitchen."

We had this again thoroughly driven into all our heads, but
no one seemed to object to our choice of a site, and they
willingly helped us to pitch the tents. Before night fell one of
them had gone and caught some unsaddled horses. They
thanked us and rode off in the direction of the village.

I was late getting to sleep that night. I lay gazing at the
moonlight on the thin green tent-cloth over my head and

listening to the surf on the beach where Hotu Matua had landed. I wondered what sort of craft he had had, what language he had spoken.

What did this valley look like when he came? Were there woods here then, as on all the other South Sea islands? Was it perhaps Hotu Matua's descendants who had cut timber and burnt logs, and finally destroyed all the woodland till the island became what it is today, without a single tree to give shade in all those rolling downs? I was a little uneasy when I thought of this complete lack of trees and shrubs. Perhaps it was right after all that it was useless to go to Easter Island and dig in the earth. Perhaps it had always looked as it did today, when there were no plants to rot and make the soil rise year by year into strata. But for the sand-dunes on the shore and the sheep's dung among the stones it looked as if the ground had lain there unchanged from Hotu Matua's day, dry and grudging. In fact, since Hotu Matua's own foundation wall lay visible and was pointed out as a regular tourist attraction above ground, the soil was obviously meagre, and the chances of new discoveries equally so. Louder thunder-peals came from some of the breakers on the shore, and I stroked the bump on my head. Now that we had managed to get here we must certainly not give up without at least attempting to dig, before we went on to the other islands on our programme.

During our first days ashore the archaeologists went out on reconnaissance tours to east and west, while the rest of us brought the equipment ashore and planned the further conduct of the expedition. There was not a brook in the whole island, but down in the craters of three of the old volcanoes there were marshes and partially open water full of reeds. We should have to carry both wood and drinking water four miles from Vaitea, the sheep farm up on the high ground right in the middle of the island. Here a little eucalyptus spinney had been planted, and here there was drinking water in a pipe from the volcano Rano Aroi. The governor lent us a stout home-made lighter which the natives rowed out to the ship, and one calm day we succeeded in getting the expedition's jeep brought into the village. Thereby our wood and water supplies were secured.

There were ancient remains of prehistoric roads on Easter

Island, and the network of roads had been increased by the
manager of the sheep farm having picked away the worst of
the stones so that one could bump along in a jeep right across
the island, which is about ten miles long. Father Sebastian and
the governor helped us to obtain plenty of horses and home-
made wooden saddles. Even the poorest natives had at least
one riding horse each on this island; nobody went on foot
because fragments of lava lay strewn all over the ground like
great lumps of reddish-brown and black coke, often so close
that only a horse's hoof could find room between them. Easter
Island children learn to ride as soon as they can walk, and we
often saw the tiniest tots galloping over the stony fields bare-
back, three at a time, each clinging to the next and the one
who sat in front holding tight to the horse's mane.

Along the coast there were a number of wells of great antiquity, dug in masterly fashion and lined with cut stone. The
original population had accustomed themselves to drinking
brackish water, which they obtained by intercepting subterranean streams where they had noticed that they came out
into the sea. Windmills had now been erected there, which
pumped the brackish water up to the sheep, and there we
watered the horses and fetched water to the camp for washing.

Meanwhile the boatswain, who was also carpenter, had
made shelves and tables for the big mess tent, where walls of
mosquito netting enabled us to eat and work undisturbed by
dense swarms of imported flies which whirled round us.

"We'll have to let down the tent wall on the side the wind
comes from," said Yvonne. "There's dust coming in through
the mosquito net."

"Dust here on the island?"

"Yes, look here," she said, and made a distinct streak along
the bookshelf with her forefinger.

I looked on with the greatest satisfaction. In a hundred
years or so there would be a pretty thick layer to brush away.
Perhaps it would be worth while to dig on Easter Island after
all! Just because there was no woodland, perhaps wind and
weather got a firmer grip on the hills and sent a shower of
fine dry earth over the lowlands like a fall of snow. No doubt
most of it drifted into the sea, but some of it, perhaps, up on
to the grass slopes.

The archaeologists came back from their reconnaissance tours with interesting reports. They had seen old walls which they wished to examine later, because there were possible indications that two different civilizations had built on the island before the Europeans came. But in order that they might get to know local conditions better, it was decided that they should first undertake some minor excavations near the camp at Anakena before setting about their main tasks.

The first choice was Hotu Matua's five-sided kitchen oven and the boat-shaped foundation wall just beside it. Excavation of this kind is done not with pickaxe and spade, but with a little mason's trowel with which one scrapes one's way down into the ground, a fraction of an inch at a time, so as not to injure what is found. The earth which is scraped away is shaken through fine-meshed netting so that everything of interest is left lying on the top of the sieve. The depth beneath the turf is noted exactly, for, of course, the deeper one goes the older the things one finds.

Just beneath the turf lay a fragment of an old stone bowl, with spear-heads and other sharp implements of black volcanic glass, and as the archaeologists scraped their way down they found bits of fish-hooks made both of human bone and of prettily polished stone. When they had got a foot down into the earth beside Hotu Matua's oven, the trowel scraped against some stones, and as soon as they had cleared the earth away they saw that it was another five-sided oven, of exactly the same type as that which lay above ground. If the uppermost one was constructed by Hotu Matua, the first ancestor of the island, who had been here before and cooked his food in just the same way? The natives did not understand at all: they themselves and all visitors had accepted the ruins above ground as Hotu Matua's, for this was quite certainly the place where he had lived.

We scraped our way farther down and found many fragments of fish-hooks, shell, bone splinters, charcoal and human teeth, till we were far down in the earth beneath the lower oven. We must be far back in antiquity now. Then Bill dug up a pretty blue Venetian pearl, and recognized it as a type Europeans had used in dealing with the Indians two hundred years ago. So we had not got so deep down as to be beyond the scope of the first European visits. The earliest date at which the pearl could have been brought to Easter Island was that of its discoverer Roggeveen: we had, therefore, not yet dug farther down than the year 1722. We looked up Roggeveen's log-book on the discovery of Easter Island, and found that the first native who boarded his ship had been presented with two strings of blue pearls, a small mirror and a pair of scissors. Nothing was more natural than that some of these pearls should have found their way to the king's house at Anakena. We dug a little way farther down, and then we came upon mere rubble without a sign of human activity.

One thing was certain now: it would be worth while to dig on treeless Easter Island. We could start in earnest now. We should have to enlist native diggers, for one or two of the projects we had in mind required more men than we ourselves could spare.

We had seen very little of the natives in these few days. To avoid thieving and intrigue Father Sebastian had expressly asked us to keep the camp closed to natives who had no special duties. It was no use trying to prevent the boys from becoming acquainted with the merry vahines of the island. It was impossible, and that he fully realized. But if the boys wanted to amuse themselves they would have to ride over to the village, otherwise the whole village would soon move over to us. We agreed to this arrangement, and put up a rope all round the camp as a kind of symbolic frontier of the taboo area. It was on the whole surprisingly effective. Moreover, no one but a handful of shepherds really had any occasion to roam about on that side of the island. For if the natives got through the fence on their side they always saw an opportunity of stealing a sheep or two. But such restricted freedom of movement was, of course, not easy to live up to on a small island.

On one of the first nights two water-cans were stolen from outside the camp area, and the thin rope which marked off our taboo ground was cut and carried off as a valuable prize. Father Sebastian thought it was stolen as gear for one of the small boats which was preparing to get away. Then the governor sent Kasimiro and Nicholas to patrol in the neighbourhood. They were the village's two native policemen. Old Kasimiro was as tall and thin as Nicholas was fat and round:

he had, moreover, a striking resemblance to the shambling, round-shouldered, weird figure in the Easter Island collection of wood-carvings. If the figure had not already been known in Captain Cook's time, Kasimiro might have been suspected of having sat for it. Kasimiro had a big leather holster at his side containing an old-fashioned revolver, and if he caught sight of any of his countrymen, irrespective of sex or age, he howled and yelled and brandished his revolver till they disappeared over the downs in a cloud of dust. Then he came back, stooping and swaying, and sat down on taboo ground in the shelter of the tent.

We liked old Kasimiro. He seemed a little weak in the head, but was extremely good-natured and modest. Nicholas was a good fellow too, but no one seemed to feel sorry for him. The daintiest remains from the cookhouse always went first to the skinny old man, who ate as he had never done in all his life and loafed about with his trousers pockets full of valuables in the shape of our cigarettes. Kasimiro was in the seventh heaven, and grew lazier and lazier as he lay in the shade of the tent playing with his big revolver. But one day he thought he must do something in return for all our hospitality. He came creeping into my tent and confided to me in a low voice that there was a cave with "important things" in it out on the bird-men's island. He had been out there when quite a small boy with his father and a few other children, and his father had asked the children to wait while he disappeared behind a rock, where he had crawled into a secret cave. Kasimiro had never seen the opening, which was blocked by stones, but if I would take him out there in our boat without anyone in the village knowing about it, he would point out the spot where he himself had stood waiting, and if I found the cave myself we would share the treasure. The old man's eyes shone.

I did not take this too seriously. Both the Routledge expedition and Father Sebastian had received similar offers. When they had gained the natives' confidence there was always someone who knew of a region in which there was a secret sealed-up cave. In caves such as these their ancestors had hidden ancient tablets of wood marked with hieroglyphics, *rongo-rongo* in the island language. These *rongo-rongo* tablets were worth a real fortune, for there were only a score of them in all the world's

museums put together. The natives knew that quite well. But
when someone agreed to take a party to such a secret *rongo-
rongo* cave, the only result was a lot of futile searching, for it
was always impossible to find the concealed entrance. A pity,
they said, now the opening had gone, covered up by a landslip
or subsidence.

Our first Sunday came.

Father Sebastian had hinted that we should be welcome at
the church if we would like to hear the natives sing. I called
all the men together, scientists and sailor alike, and explained
that church was something very special down here in the
South Sea Islands. It was not merely the only stable element
in the natives' world, a centre where they found a longed-for
replacement for their old belief in Tiki and Make-make, but
it was also the only social meeting place where the whole
population came together in their best clothes, because there
was no assembly hall, cinema or market place on the loneliest
of the South Sea islands. If one stayed away on that day one
could stay away for the rest of the week too: the natives were
often trained up to be fanatics for their own church, and if
people did not come it was interpreted as a demonstration, an
attack from a hostile quarter. On some of the islands the
natives were Protestants, on others Catholics or Mormons;
it all depended what missionary had come to the place first
and built a church. It was easy for an unsuspecting visitor to
put his foot in it.

"I'm an atheist and never go to church," said one of the
archaeologists. "But if you think it has any importance I'll
come with pleasure."

So off we went in a crowd over the downs, atheists, Protestants and Catholics at a gallop on the camp horses with the
jeep bumping along in the midst, to assemble outside Father
Sebastian's little village church.

The church square shone with white and coloured dresses:
the whole village stood waiting in newly washed and ironed
Sunday clothes. We walked into the little towerless church
among reverent men and vahines, children and adults, aged
people, and new-born and unborn babies. The village lay
empty in the sun; inside there was such a crowd that those

who sat at the end of the rows could get only half of themselves on to the wooden benches. But there was sunshine in Father Sebastian's church too. Bright colours, bright faces; the sun itself sent pencils of light through the gaps between roof and walls, and by the same route a few little birds had crept in, which flew about fearlessly and twittered and sang among the rafters.

Father Sebastian had put on a large cloak of spring green outside his white gown and stood there solid and cheerful, like a kindly grandfather with a big beard. The atmosphere in the church was that of an operatic performance. The climax of the service was the singing. The hymns were sung to a Polynesian text and most of them to old native tunes. Every single voice in the church took part except our own. We only used our ears, for this was an experience: the singing was perfectly practised and had a rhythm and colour which only South Sea natives can achieve.

Father Sebastian's ceremony was simple, and what he said was wise and clearly put. And around us our friends, the bandits and pirates and all their lively vahines, sat squeezed close together and followed his words, as enthralled by what they heard as children watching a cowboy film. There was a special word of welcome for all of us strangers: that all should go well for the expedition, and all the men and women on the island should do everything in their power to help us, for even if we had not all the same creed as they, we were all Christians with the same ideals.

From that day we became, so to speak, more welded together with the whole population: if Father Sebastian accepted us we were certainly all decent people.

After the service all the members of the expedition were invited to a splendid dinner at the governor's. Here, besides our hosts and Father Sebastian, we met the tiny white colony; two of the nuns who managed the leper station north of the village, the Chilean Air Force captain who was preparing plans for a future trans-oceanic airport on the island, and the governor's own two assistants. The only persons not there were the village doctor and schoolmaster. These two we had never seen, not even in church, and I noticed that our own doctor was specially asked to attend the governor, who had heart trouble.

When we were going home in the evening we were stopped
by a little thick-set fellow with jet black eyes and stiff black
hair. It was the village doctor, and he invited us all to a hula
dance. This was so popular that it was useless to say no.
The dancing was in the little native house of the mayor's sister,
which was so packed when we arrived that people had to climb
out of the open windows for us to be able to get in at the door
at all. To my alarm I saw that a large mug was going round
containing a whisky-coloured liquid with which glasses were
being filled to the brim, but it proved to be *aqua pura*, "pure
water," collected from the roof. The prevailing atmosphere
was none the less cheerful and lively, and roars of laughter and
jokes in four languages shook the roof when the vahines dragged
shy sailor lads and stiff-legged scientists out on to the dancing
floor and made them wriggle like eels on a hook. There was a
fearful racket, and such a crowd that the walls would almost
have bulged out if there had not been still more people outside
pushing and trying to get a glimpse through the packed
windows. Four men were playing the guitar and singing,
and in the midst of it all the village doctor pressed up to me
and wanted to initiate me into deep political problems.

"My aim is to open the window of the world for these
people," he said.

A good thing too, I thought, for there would soon be no air
left in the room. But he did not mean it like that, and I had
to resign myself to going outside and listening to his earnest
words.

He and the schoolmaster were in opposition to the other
white people on the island.

"We have Indian blood in our veins," he said, pointing to
two flashing black eyes. "We want the natives to get away
from the island and learn how to know the world on the mainland."

And Father Sebastian doesn't want that, I thought. For he
is afraid that they will drink themselves to death when they
get to a place where they have unrestricted access to alcohol.
He is afraid of their being exploited and going to the dogs.

"We want to raise the standard of living to a modern level,"
the doctor continued. "We want those who now go barefoot
to wear shoes."

To measure an Easter Island head one must be a good climber. The skipper is 20 ft. above ground, but how much of the head is under the soil?

Above: Father Sebastian Englert was the uncrowned king of Easter Island and the natives' best friend. Captain Arnaldo Curti was the Chilean governor, who ruled his happy little community, the loneliest in the world, with wisdom and skill.

Below: Two of the old Pakarati brothers narrating legends to the author by the crater lake in Rano Raraku.

And Father Sebastian thinks that's a mistake, I thought. For I had once heard him say that natives who had never worn shoes fared best, both ashore and at sea, on this island, where footwear was quickly worn out by the sharp lava stones. Those who had begun to wear white man's shoes got thin skin under their leathery feet, and cut themselves to ribbons every time their shoes gave way. No, I thought, there are two sides to all these questions, and Father Sebastian has had a generation in which to think the matter over, while the young doctor came with the last warship.

"Before you go you must give the musicians a thousand pesos or preferably fifteen dollars in cash. They expect it," he added.

"But they're all sitting there smoking our cigarettes and eating our chocolate, and they're enjoying themselves just as much as we are, if not more," I said.

"Don't you pay a dance band in Europe? If you don't give them a present just because they're natives no one will ask you to a dance again."

I quietly collected our fellows: we thanked our hosts and went home. We did not pay a halfpenny. But invitations to hulu dancing at Hangaroa continued to come all the time that we were on the island.

We had now secured a large body of native workers. Some lived at home in the village and rode over every morning, others moved into caves near the excavations. To free as many of our own people as possible we had engaged four vahines to help us with camp work and washing. One of them, Eroria, was a first-rate woman and a tremendous worker. She looked like a rising thunder-cloud to those who did not know her, but it was easy to conjure up her broad smile, and then the cloud vanished like morning dew and all her rough face lit up with dazzling sunshine. She had been Father Sebastian's housekeeper for years, but was lent to us to look after the camp on account of her complete reliability. Eroria and her old grey-haired sister-in-law Mariana were curiously enough the keenest cave-hunters on the island. They criss-crossed the hills with a pocket full of candles, searching for old dwelling caves, where they dug in the floor with a little iron bar to

C

discover their ancestors' stone and bone tools for Father
Sebastian's little collection.

"It's only in the caves it's any use looking for things," said
Father Sebastian. "Take Eroria and Mariana and get them to
show you all the old caves they've found."

When the rest of our party were well under way with the
excavations, we saddled four horses, and the photographer
and I, with Eroria and Mariana, rode off to reconnoitre old
caves. On the first day we were in and out of dark caves from
morning till night. Some were quite open, so that one could
bend down and walk in. Others were carefully blocked up
with stones, so that only a little rectangular opening was left
through which one could crawl in on all fours. But most of them
were mere rat-holes, into which you could neither walk nor
crawl, but had to push your legs in with stiff knees and keep
your arms outstretched over your head while wriggling your
body like a snake down a long and horribly narrow shaft. The
shaft always had neat walls, often of skilfully cut blocks; in
some caves it went in through the rock like a horizontal
channel, or sloping downwards, but in others it went down
into the ground perpendicularly like a chimney-pipe, so that
one had to brake with thighs and shoulders till one came down
through the roof into one corner of the pitch-black cave. In
most of these caves the roof was so low that one had to stoop,
and in some one could only stand doubled up or sit.

Here the old-time population of Easter Island had lived, at
any rate in uneasy times when they did not feel themselves
safe in the reed huts up in the fresh air. Here they had taken
cover when our own race came. Most of the holes were of the
size of an average bath-room, and it was so dark that one could
not see one's own hand without stretching it out into the
mouth of the narrow shaft. The floor was cold earth, deep and
rich from ancient refuse and as hard as a motor tyre from the
contact of a thousand crawling hands and knees. Roof and
walls were naked rock, often improved here and there with
artistic masonry.

At one place we crawled down into something which
resembled a huge open well with walled sides. Down at the
bottom we had to creep into a narrow hole, and beyond that
three spacious caves lay aslant one above the other in storeys.

Eroria treated this cave with special reverence. Her own grandfather had lived there; it was her family seat. The floor here had been thoroughly turned up by the two vahines' work with their iron rod. I picked up from the loose earth a sawn-off piece of human bone, bored through at the end as an amulet to hang round one's neck.

A little farther down towards the coast Mariana pointed out an overgrown foundation wall, the remains of one of the old boat-shaped reed huts of which we saw traces everywhere. Her own father-in-law, Eroria's father, had been born there. There he had lived during the last generation till the whole population of the island had moved to the village of Hangaroa to be Christianized.

So it's no longer ago than that, I thought, and looked bewildered at the two trousered vahines, who from their appearance and manners might have been civilized since the time of Noah. The foundation wall was of the shape and dimensions of the rail of a fair-sized rowing boat, pointed at both ends and composed of perfectly cut and often prettily curved stones of hard basalt, with rows of deep holes on the top into which pliant boughs had once been stuck to form the criss-cross foundation of the curved reed hut itself. If all the reed huts whose walls we found all over the place had been in use at the same time, Easter Island must once have had a quite considerable population.

The two vahines had found an immense number of old dwelling caves. In most of them they had already wrought havoc with their iron rods, but they also showed us the way to some holes which were not yet "opened"; that is to say, no one had visited them since the last inhabitant had moved out and rolled lava blocks in front of the opening. Once when I had rolled one of these blocks out of the way to creep down into the narrow hole, a motionless colony of fourteen scorpions lay under the stone. Another time the opening was so narrow between the rocks that I had to empty my pockets and have several tries, without my shirt on, before I was able to force my body through. Down in the darkness my torch shone on human bones and a snow-white skull. I tilted the skull cautiously, and under it lay a glistening black obsidian spear-point and an old wasps' nest. I thanked my stars that the nest was not inhabited, for it it were I should have been badly caught and swollen before I managed to squeeze myself up through the needle's eye.

On our way home in the afternoon we rode over a stony plateau on the high ground west of the camp. The ground was flat and thickly covered everywhere with a mass of lava stones strewn thickly all over the earth, often in low, compact heaps. We dismounted at one of these heaps, for Mariana's son had told her that he had found there the descent to a dwelling cave of "the other kind." How anyone could find the right heap of lava in that large stone-strewn area was more than I could understand, especially as Mariana had only been given the "address" of this dwelling by word of mouth. But, on the other hand, she might never have been able to find her way about the labyrinth of a city's streets.

By this time the photographer and I had been trained by the two descendants of the cave-dwellers to be regular experts in slithering in and out and up and down through narrow shafts. We followed blindly their advice always to work our way into the shafts feet first, with our arms stretched over our heads, and, if the shaft was not perpendicular, always on our backs with our faces turned upwards. But this time old Mariana first shone her light carefully down through the rectangular shaft, which was solidly lined with smooth stones to form a narrow perpendicular funnel. Then she asked me to look in a particular direction while working the lower part of my body down into the hole. The force of gravity drew me slowly down while thighs and shoulders braked against the stones as I desired, for it was so narrow that my arms had to be stretched straight up and held close together over my head. This time the funnel came to a dead end and I stood immured at the bottom, with my arms helplessly jammed together pointing upwards. There was a rectangular hole at the base of one wall, and I manoeuvred my legs into it while I slowly let my body sink down into a stiff-legged sitting position, with heavy masonry above my lap and closely surrounding my head and chest. Next my body had to follow the stiff knees into the narrow side-channel, and I wriggled down, with my arms still squeezed behind my, till at last I lay stretched on my back in a narrow horizontal funnel.

Give me a modern home with a lift! It is a horrible feeling to lie closely walled-up down in the earth with the rock in your face and your arms forced back over your head so that you cannot use them. With arms trapped above the head one feels especially helpless down in a rat-hole like this: the solid rock walls seem to press more closely than ever round one's head and cry "hands up, you're a prisoner." One ought not to hear this cry, nor ought one to try to free one's arms, for it can't be done; one ought to think of nothing and only shove oneself along backwards by twisting the shoulder-blades and dragging with the heels till one notices that one can bend the knees and kick about in an empty space, or that one cannot get any farther along the shaft because the soles of one's feet meet solid rock. If this is so, it means that the funnel makes another right-angled turn, and a man lying there with his arms over his head has to turn over on to his stomach and grope along feet first between the narrow rock walls into a new perpendicular shaft which ends in a last cunning turn. Here he remains immured in a hideous grip until he manages to twist himself round by force to enter the last horizontal funnel, where he notices the sudden disappearance of floors and walls. Then at last he is about to creep into the cave, and a moment later he can pull his arms down, he is free, he can brush away the sand round his eyes and do what he likes, so long as he does not bump his head against the roof before he turns on his torch.

I had been in two or three of these caves before I learnt to tow a pocket torch along with me. Then I could see the narrow shaft behind me as I went along. The shaft was always neatly walled with smooth stone blocks without mortar, and was built square like a narrow chimney. Some of the stones had symmetrical holes bored in them, and proved to be polished stones taken from the foundation walls of old reed houses, showing that the builders of these cave entrances had pulled down the idyllically pleasant reed houses of their predecessors to construct these wretched rat-traps instead.

On this first wriggle down into Easter Island's dark underworld I had not even taken a match with me, and the floor was slippery and full of surprises, so that I simply remained where I was, waiting in the dark like a blind man. I listened, and could hear someone coming after me down through the shaft. In a few minutes old Mariana stood beside me and lit her trusty candle-stump. It was of little use. The darkness was so intense down in the black rock that all I could see was Mariana's flashing eyes, surrounded by deep, shadowy wrinkles and fluffy cobwebs of ashen-grey hair, like a grotesque face pressed against a window-pane. She gave me another candle-stump and lit it from her own. When we held the lights with our arms stretched out we could gradually make out bulges and projections in the wall. Some obsidian lance-heads lay on the floor. Now Eroria too arrived: it took some time, with a good deal of scuffling and panting in the shaft, but she came. They were able to tell me that this was not an ordinary dwelling: it was a refuge for use in war-time, for no enemy could reach people here. If so, the wars must have been many and of long duration, to judge from the thickness of the hard-trodden layer of refuse at the bottom of the cave. I never understood how anyone dared to crawl down into these rat-traps in war-time; the enemy had only to fill up the shaft with stones and they were hermetically sealed up for good and all. But perhaps the trick was to keep these refuges secret; if they did that, and rolled a stone over the little opening behind them, it would be a hard task to find the fugitives.

I found a little hole between the stones in one of the walls, and I crawled in with Mariana and Eroria at my heels. We came into another and larger cave, and after wriggling through a little hole in the back wall of this we came into a large room, so high that we could not see the roof with our candles. We continued on our way through the rock; some places were as high and wide as a railway tunnel, elsewhere we had to crawl among stones and rubble, and at other points we had to lie flat on our stomachs and shove ourselves along till the roof rose again in a large room.

Each time I looked round to see if the others were following, I saw Mariana's wrinkled face close behind me; she would not let me get an inch away from her. She taught me to look out for loose blocks in the roof and holes and cracks in the floor. In one of the rooms there was underground water. It was running across our route and trickling down a side-passage, and into this we crept too. Ancient people had been at work here and cut a narrow gutter in the floor of the cave to keep the water collected, and the gutter led down into several artificially cut depressions like washing-tubs. I washed my hands in the lowest depression, filled them in the uppermost one and drank. Compared with spring water this tasted like the choicest wine—cold, clear and full-flavoured. I wondered if the old cave-dwellers had not known more about the grading of water than we who only get a third-class quality out of a metal pipe.

Far inside the rock the cave split into branches several times, and the innermost passages took the form of narrow catacombs with a level floor, and roof and walls arched in a pretty curve without a sign of projections or unevenness. Again and again it looked like the work of man, but these were only channels made by gas and streams of hot lava forcing their way through the molten rock at the time when Easter Island was just an erupting volcano. For long stretches the apparently smoothly polished archways shrank and became so narrow that they closed round my body as though tailor-made to fit a person lying flat on his stomach. Some of them terminated far into the rock in small bell-shaped domes, while others were blocked up with stones or became so narrow that it was useless to go on.

We visited several of these huge caves with room after room like pearls on a string running down through the underworld. Their entrances were all skilfully walled up, so that one could get down only through narrow funnels cut with sharp angles or zig-zags, in which any assailant would be completely helpless. There was water in some of the largest caves; two of them had regular subterranean ponds, and right down at the bottom of a third we found a walled well of ice-cold water, surrounded by a pavement and a well-built terrace some ten feet high.

These great refuge caves could have accommodated the whole population of Easter Island, but everything indicated that each cave entrance had belonged to a separate family or group of families at a time when bloody civil wars had raged on the island, so that no one could sleep securely in his old reed house. I thought, as I walked about in these great pitch-dark refuges, that it had been foolish of these people living on a sunny South Sea island to choose this way of life in preference to keeping the peace with their neighbours up in the sunshine. But then I came to think of the twentieth-century world, in which we too have gradually begun to bury ourselves and our most important installations in shelters deep down in the earth, frightened because we ourselves and our neighbours have begun to play about with the atom bomb. Then I forgave Eroria's and Mariana's primitive grand-parents, and as visions of past and future combined to haunt the darkness around me I began to wriggle up the long zig-zag shaft. I felt profoundly happy when I escaped into the dazzling sun of today, surrounded only by grazing sheep and horses dozing in the salt sea breeze.

It had taken us eighty minutes to crawl and walk through all the passages in this first great cave, and when we came up again through the last shaft we found the photographer, who had been seriously frightened. Halfway down the shaft he had had a touch of claustrophobia among all those stones, and had preferred to struggle up again and wait. Till then it had never taken us more than a few minutes to look at a cave dwelling, as we were not going to dig for the time being. After waiting patiently for three quarters of an hour he became uneasy and put his head down the shaft and called to us. When no one answered from below he became really anxious. He had yelled and shouted down the hole so that the shaft resounded, but the only person who heard him at last was old Kasimiro, who came hurrying up from a long way off with his revolver and stood waiting faithfully at the photographer's side when we crawled out of the hole.

Mariana came up too and picked up her big straw hat from a stone. She begged us always to take a hat with us, or some-thing else which we could leave behind on the ground if we crept down into these holes alone. Some Chilean treasure-seekers had once been down in one of the caves with a native, she told us, and while they were deep down below their lamp went out. Their last match was soon used up. They had lost their way completely in the dark among the rock walls and could not find their way back to the entrance shaft. Their lives had been saved by their caps and jackets which they had thrown off up above, for a native found these and realized that the men were underground.

The archaeologists dug up the floor in a number of caves. The inhabitants had dropped all their rubbish where they sat, and the floor, therefore, had often risen dangerously towards the roof. Fish-bones and shells lay there in masses, mingled with knuckle-bones of fowls and an occasional turtle. Even rats and human beings had figured on the menu, baked among glowing stones in the earth. Cannibals had lived in these caves: apart from the little native rat their two-legged enemies were the only quarry they could capture on land. Sitting in the dark round their primitive stone lamps they had dropped quantities of fine needles made of human bones among the waste on the floor. All they had left behind in their dark dwellings were, in fact, primitive implements of human bone, stone and volcanic glass, and some simple amulets of bone and shells. Nothing else.

There was something about this that did not make sense. Could these primitive cannibals have been the masters who wrought the classical giant sculptures of aristocratic ruler type which dominated the countryside on this same island? How could a people of hunted cave dwellers have bred such unique engineers and ingenious artists as the creators of those gigantic monuments? And how could monolithic work have been organized among people who did not even live together in a village, but hid here and there down narrow underground shafts scattered about the island?

I crept into the narrow funnel leading to a cave where Bill was sitting in the light of a paraffin lamp digging carefully with a mason's trowel. He had a bag beside him full of burnt human bones.

"The same primitive culture," he said, scraping two molars out of the earth at his feet. "Look here, these dirty bastards have been sitting eating each other and spitting the teeth on the floor."

It was not only on ceremonial occasions that human flesh had been devoured on this island. The natives had legends to this very day of ancestors who would rather eat their own race than fish or fowl. They had also persistent legends of a still earlier time of greatness on the island when another people, the "long-ears," had lived at peace with their own ancestors, the "short-ears." The long-ears had demanded too much labour of the short-ears, and the consequence had been a

C*

war in which nearly all the "long-ears" were burnt in a ditch. From that day no more statues had been made, many of those which were standing had been pulled down with ropes, and civil war, family feuds and cannibalism had marked the years which followed, right up to the time when Father Eugenio landed in their own parents' childhood and collected the inhabitants peacefully round him in the village of Hangaroa.

Father Sebastian was convinced that two different races with different cultures had come to Easter Island, and the natives were unshakeable in their affirmation that this was the case. He had also pointed out that the population differed in many respects from ordinary Pacific natives: among other things, they contained unmistakable remnants of a white race.[1] It was not only Roggeveen and the first discoverers who had noticed this. Father Sebastian pointed out that according to traditions of the natives themselves many of their own ancestors in olden times had white skins, red hair and blue eyes. And when Father Eugenio settled among them, as the first European, and assembled all the people at Hangaroa, he was surprised to find many entirely white people among the brown ones. As recently as the visit of the Routledge expedition fifty years ago the natives still divided their ancestors into two categories according to the colour of their skins, and they told Mrs. Routledge that even the last king had been a quite white man. The white branch was looked up to with admiration and respect, and just as in the other South Sea islands some leading personalities had to undergo special bleaching processes to be as much like their deified ancestors as possible.

One day Father Sebastian came to take us with him to *Ana o Keke*, the holy bleaching place of the *neru* virgins. *Neru* was the name given to specially chosen young maidens who in old days were confined in a deep cave to become as pale and white as possible for special religious festivals. For a long, long time they might see neither the light of day nor other people, and their food was carried to the cave and pushed through the opening by women appointed for the purpose. The natives could still remember that when the small-pox epidemic raged

[1] P. Sebastian Englert: *La Tierra de Hotu Matu'a*. Chile 1948. Pp. 203–5.

all over the island after the slaves returned from the mainland, it did not reach the *neru* maidens, but they died of starvation in their cave because there was no longer anyone to bring them food.

The entrance to the virgins' cave *Ana o Keke* lay at the most easterly point of the island, and the name means "Cave of the Sun's Inclination." To get there we passed the island's most easterly volcano, Katiki, behind which lay the three hummocks where the Spaniards had once set up their first crosses. There was a cave dwelling there too, and beside it a frightful diabolical giant's head carved in the rock wall itself, where the rain-water was led into an open mouth so large that I climbed in and concealed myself behind the under-lip with the greatest ease.

But Father Sebastian led us farther right out to the edge of the fearful precipice which falls into the sea all round this lofty peninsula. Here he began to walk along the very edge of the cliff in such a casual way that we four who were with him called to him and begged him to keep farther in, for an unusually violent east wind was thundering at the cliffs and tearing at our clothes, so that anyone might feel himself unsteady and insecure. But our white-clad friend in his long cloak and big black boots only went rapidly along the outermost edge in his fluttering gown; he was searching for the place and did not know exactly where it was. Suddenly his face lighted up and he threw up his arms: ah, here it was! He broke off a piece of the loose yellowish-brown rock to show us that it was quite worn away by weathering, so we must step carefully. Then he went straight to the very edge, a thundering gust of wind took hold of his cloak, we gave a yell, and Father Sebastian had gone.

Carl sat down and clutched at his hat in sheer bewilderment. I crawled cautiously out and looked over the edge. Far below I saw the foot of the cliff, on which white surf was slowly breaking, with the sea behind it stretching away white-crested into infinity. The air was full of thunder from the wind and sea. On a narrow shelf to my left I saw Father Sebastian's white cloak: the wind was tearing and pulling at it as he pressed himself close to the face of the cliff and moved downwards sideways. It was blowing furiously that day: the sea below was covered with white caps and the wind hammered at us in violent gusts, now from one direction, now from another because of the steep barrier that flung it back. I suddenly conceived an unbounded admiration for this old priest who climbed with such perfect confidence, and who identified reality with his own faith to such a degree that he had no fear of physical dangers. I almost believe he could have walked on the water. Now he turned towards me and smiled, pointed lower down beneath his feet and raised his fingers to his mouth as a sign that I must bring our parcels of food, for we were going to have lunch down there. I felt so unsteady in the uneven gusts of wind that I crawled farther away from the cliff and pulled off my shirt before I fetched the parcels of food and plucked up courage to follow Father Sebastian on the ledge. When I began to clamber down he had gone; I could not see a trace of his cloak, yet I could see six hundred feet straight down into the breakers below. Mountaineering is not my strongest point, and I did not feel very bright as I carefully lowered myself on to the ledge, pressed my stomach against the face of the cliff, and with my heart in my mouth set off in Father Sebastian's wake, feeling my way forward step by step to see if the rock would hold. The worst part of it was the wind. I arrived at a slight corner in a cliff where the only support was something which looked like a hard lump of earth, separated from the actual cliff by a crack. If it had borne Father Sebastian it would bear me. I kicked it cautiously, but dared not kick too hard.

I put my head round the projection and met Father Sebastian again. He was lying with only his head and shoulders pushed out of the entrance to a cave in the face of the cliff, half the height of the door of a dog-kennel, and laughing. I shall always remember him thus, like an Easter Island Diogenes in his tub, with rimless spectacles on nose, wide white sleeves and flowing beard. When he saw me, he raised his arms in a sweeping gesture and cried:

"Welcome to my cave!"

I could hardly hear what he said for the noise. Then he lowered his beard towards the narrow shelf and pushed himself in backwards through the crevice so that there should be room for me too, for under the opening there was a sheer drop. I got across to the shelf in front of the cave and squeezed myself in after him. Noise, wind and light disappeared; inside it was very small and narrow, but soon the roof became higher and there was an inviolable peace and security within the belly of the cliff. A scrap of light found its way in so that we could soon make each other out, and I could see with my pocket torch that the curved walls were covered with curious signs and figures.

This was the virgins' cave. Here the poor little girls had sat for weeks, perhaps for months, waiting till their skins should become white enough for them to be shown to the people. The cave was less than five feet high, and there was not room for many more than a dozen children if they sat in rows along the walls.

After a while the opening was darkened by someone forcing his way in. It was our native friend who had followed us. Father Sebastian sent him out again at once to fetch the other two; he would not have them drawing back when he, a man of sixty-eight, had led the way. We were soon all sitting together enjoying our lunch, while Father Sebastian pointed to a small hole in the back wall and said that if we crawled in there we could get four hundred yards farther into the rock. But it was the worst trip he had ever made, and he would never do it again. Halfway in, the passage for a long stretch was so narrow that it was only just possible for a man to force his way through, and just inside teeth and remnants of human bones were lying about as in a burial cave. It was a mystery to him how anyone could have carried a dead person in there, for it was impossible to push him in front, and if one dragged him behind one would bar the way back for oneself in the narrow passage.

I put on my shirt and wanted to see the rest of the cave, but Father Sebastian only roared with laughter at the thought of what I was going to encounter; I would turn back quickly when I saw what it was like in there! Only the native was willing to come with me when I crept in through the hole. The cave forked, but the branches met again immediately in a narrow passage in which we had to crawl. Then the roof rose and we found ourselves in a long tunnel, so high and spacious that we could run to save time. The torch was miserable and shone with only half its strength; the batteries had been damaged in the camp, and for safety's sake I had a stump of candle and a box of matches in my trousers pocket. To save the batteries I was continually turning the light off, and we ran, walked and crawled in the darkness as far as we had seen ahead of us between the flashes. We could not help knocking our heads against the roof two or three times so that little drop-shaped particles tinkled down like glass through our hair and down our necks. A long way in we came to a place where there was mud and water on the floor. Here the roof grew lower and lower. We had no choice but to stoop down and crawl on our hands and knees in water and slush, but it became still lower, and at last we had to lie flat on our stomachs and wriggle forward under the rock while ice-cold slush poured in through our shirts and trousers.

"Nice road," I called back.

My companion lying in the mud behind me laughed politely. It was beginning to be unpleasant. Now I understood what Father Sebastian meant, but if *he* had managed it there was little reason for us to give up halfway. Just after this I almost regretted having started. Although I was lying with half my body in water and soft mud, the roof came down so low that I tried again and again without finding a passage. The electric torch was watertight, but it was hopeless to keep the glass clear of slush when I myself was lying flat, pressed down into the mire. The faint light the torch gave showed clearly that the passage was not only low, but also so narrow that there was obviously no choice of road. Father Sebastian had squeezed himself through here. I forced my chest in slowly, and felt that it was just possible if only it did not grow worse, and with the slush pushed aside and the hard rock pressing me both from below and from above, I squeezed myself in through the crack inch by inch. It was so grotesque that I could not help groaning "nice road" to the poor wretch who was following me, but now his sense of humour was no longer functioning.

"Bad road, señor," he groaned.

We had to squeeze ourselves forward for five yards through this vice which held our ribs in its hold: then we were through the needle's eye and reached the part of the cave where the remains of skeletons lay. Here it was dry again and the roof was higher, so that again we could alternately crawl on all fours and amble through the passages. The poor *neru* maidens, if they wanted to stretch their legs and get a little exercise during their long stay in the cave, had had no romantic moonlight walk. I was stiff and cold from the wet slush, and when I turned the light behind me to see if my brown friend was following, I found that I was pursued by a figure caked in mud, distinguishable from the colour of the cave which surrounded us only by the gleam of his eyes and teeth.

At last the cave ended in a smooth, steep earth slope which led up to a hole in the roof. After much helpless slithering I managed to scratch my way up and came into a little bell-shaped dome which had all the appearance of being made by man. But it was only an old gas bubble. Father Sebastian had left a candle-stump there. I still had mine in my hip pocket, and my back and hinder parts were comparatively dry. I tried Father Sebastian's candle-end: it would not burn, and there was something wrong with the matches too. Now I felt the sweat streaming down my face; the air was bad there. I hastily slipped down the earth slope to my mud-caked man who stood waiting for me, and then we hurried homewards as quickly as the wretched light and the height of the roof allowed. We looked like two creatures from the underworld as we crouched and crawled along, and we felt like it too, for when we came to the horrible needle's eye we flung ourselves down in the water and mud with jesting words and squeezed ourselves into the crack. The native followed with his head right at my heels, and we forced our way forward inch by inch, feeling our chests crushed in the inexorable mountain jaws which would not open one hair's breadth extra for two human bodies. It had taken a long time to get in, but it seemed to be taking longer to get out again. We still tried to joke a little, knowing we would soon be out now; but I felt unpleasantly wet and dirty, the sweat was trickling down my face, and I was rather tired. The air was bad. After a while we kept quite silent and only struggled to force our bodies on with outstretched arms, trying not to let the glass of the torch get down into the mire.

Had there been more space under the roof for a moment? If so, now there was less again. It was queer that this narrow passage still continued, that we did not soon emerge into the outer tunnel. My weary brain had been vaguely considering this for some time, while I shoved and shoved to get my body through the vice. Then I saw, in the faint glow of the electric bulb just in front of my nose, that there was a sudden little upward bend; and it looked as if it was impossible to get one's body up through it. Perhaps this bend had been much easier to pass in the opposite direction, so that I had not realized how difficult it would be to get through on the return journey. Queer that I did not remember anything about it. With all my might I forced my body a little farther forward and tried to look up through the hole in a cramped position, with millions of tons pressing on my back and chest, and saw to my terror that there was something wrong; it was impossible to get past this bend.

"We can't get any farther," I said to the man who was lying at my heels. The sweat poured from my face.

"Go on, señor, there isn't any other way out," he groaned in reply.

I forced myself another fraction of an inch farther, with my head twisted on one side to find room in the narrow gap between the rock surfaces and with my chest in a devilish squeeze. Then I saw, by turning the light upwards, that the hole above was much smaller than my head: it was absolutely impossible to get through.

In the same second I switched off the torch: now every spark must be saved, for we had trouble ahead of us. One could think in the dark. I suddenly felt that the whole mighty massif of the Poike peninsula was lying on my body and pressing hard. It was terribly heavy, and it was worse if I tried to press against it: the only thing to do was to relax altogether and make oneself as thin as possible, but even then the rock went on pressing, from above and from below.

"Go back," I said to the man who lay right at my heels. "This won't work."

He flatly refused and only begged me to push on: there was no other way out of this hell.

This could not be the case. I switched the light on again and examined the ground before my hands and chest, shoving myself a little farther back as I did so. On this little slope there seemed to be a mixture of earth and half-dry mud; the impression

Great top-knots of red stone were placed like wigs on the heads of the completed statues. The three which lie abandoned in the shallows were once carried along the coast in large vessels built from fresh water reeds.

Easter Island, the isle of a thousand mysteries, had never before been excavated. What secrets lay hidden under the soil? What mysterious navigators had found their way to the world's loneliest island, what had happened, and when and why and how? At the foot of the extinct volcano Rano Raraku stone giants stood silently side by side guarding their ancient secrets.

Above: Proud features on old portraits. What race provided the models for these great heads?
Below: On the top of the volcano Rano Kao lay Orongo, the ruined village of the bird-men. Ed and the doctor study strange bird-men carved in the lava outcrops of the crater ruin. The entrance to an underground ceremonial house begins in the hole on the left under Ed's feet.

of my shirt and buttons was plainly visible just in front of my chest, and my finger-prints too as far forward as I then had my hands, but immediately ahead was muddy earth and rubble, untouched by man or beast. I switched the light off again. The air was heavy. My chest was in that beastly squeeze. My face and body were dripping with perspiration. Had we caused the old cave passage to collapse by talking or squeezing through on the way in? If a fall from the roof had blocked the whole passage ahead of us, how could we dig ourselves out into the daylight when there was no room to push earth and stones past us backwards? How long could we hold out in that bad air before the others realized what had happened and were able to dig their way in to us? Or could we have made a mistake in crawling and got into another passage which was a blind alley? How could we have done that, when the entire virgins' cave was one single narrow tunnel, hardly wider than a man's body in the part where we were?

The native imprisoned me completely from behind and tried to force me on; my whole body was caked with mud, and the cliff weighed me down with all its millions of tons, harder and harder the more I thought about it.

"Go back!" I shouted.

Now he was beginning to be desperate and press upon my heels; he had not seen the little hole and I could not let him past so that he could see for himself.

"Go back! go back!"

Now it seemed that the squeezed man behind me was working himself up into a mad panic. I raged at him "Go! go!" and kicked out with the sole of my foot. That had some effect: he shoved himself back inch by inch, and I followed. We went slowly, one little backward movement at a time; we must not get stuck fast or caught by the head between the rocks. I was most afraid of placing the head wrong, for it would not yield to pressure as the chest did.

Suddenly there was more space above us. I understood nothing: I was quite muddle-headed from the bad air. Could we have got right back to the skeleton place? I used my torch again and saw two openings in front of me: the right-hand one went slightly uphill. This was where we had gone wrong: we had crawled to the left instead of up to the right. I called to the native, but he only went on quite mechanically shoving himself backwards.

"Here it is!" I cried, and crawled forward again into the left-hand entrance, the native following me automatically. Our voices sounded very queer in the cave. The passage grew narrower and narrower again. This was ghastly. At last I used my torch and saw ahead of me just the same impossible little hole as before. Then I realized that my brain was no longer functioning clearly: I had crawled into the wrong hole for the second time, although I now knew perfectly well that it was the other hole I should have taken.

"Go back!" I groaned.

And now all our actions seemed purely mechanical. We forced ourselves out again backwards and I thought of only one word: right, right, right. When we saw the two passages again I crept mechanically into the right-hand opening, and soon we were able to raise ourselves up, we felt gusts of cold fresh air in the tunnel, we were able to crouch and crawl and soon we came out of the last hole and into the snug cave with the inscriptions on the walls where our friends were sitting waiting for us. It was heavenly to squeeze oneself out of the cliff, out into the roaring wind. Heavenly to meet again the blinding sunshine and the limitless space stretching from the precipice sheer below us into the unbounded blue immensity of sea and sky.

"Did you give it up?" Father Sebastian asked eagerly, laughing heartily at our appearance.

"No," I said. "But it's understandable that skeletons may be left in a cave like that."

"Have you been in the bleaching cave?" Yvonne asked when I came back to the camp. That was certainly not obvious from our appearance.

I went straight down to the shore and flung myself into the salt surf with all my clothes on.

CHAPTER IV

THE MYSTERY OF THE EASTER
ISLAND GIANTS

ANYONE who is dreaming of a trip to the moon can get a little foretaste of it by climbing about on the dead volcanic cones of Easter Island. Not only has he completely forsaken our own hectic world, which seems so immeasurably far away in the blue, but the landscape can easily give an illusion of being on the moon: a friendly little moon hung between sky and sea, where grass and ferns cover the treeless craters which lie gaping sleepily towards the sky, ancient and moss-covered, lacking the tongues and teeth of their fiery days. There are a number of these peaceful volcanoes here and there in hummocks all over the island. They are green outside and green within. The time of eruptions is past and so remote that at the bottom of some of the largest craters sky-blue lakes with waving green reeds mirror clouds flying before the trade wind. One of these waterlogged volcanoes is called Rano Raraku, and it is here that the men in the moon seem to have been most busily at work. You do not see them, but you have a feeling that they have only hidden themselves away in sealed-up holes in the ground, while you yourself walk about in the grass at your ease and survey their interrupted tasks. They have fled in haste from what they were doing, and Rano Raraku remains one of the greatest and most curious monuments of mankind, a monument to the great lost unknown behind us, a warning of the transience of man and civilization. The whole mountain massif has been reshaped, the volcano has been greedily cut up as if it were pastry, although sparks fly when a steel axe is driven against the rock to test its strength. Hundreds of thousands of cubic feet of rock have been cut out and tens of thousands of tons of stone carried away. And in the midst of the mountain's gaping wound lie more than a hundred and fifty gigantic stone men, finished and unfinished, in all stages, from the just begun to the just completed. At the foot of the mountain stand finished stone men, side by side like a supernatural army, and one feels miserably small in approaching the place, whether on horseback or driving in a jeep along the ancient roads which the vanished sculptors laid down, leading to their gigantic workshop.

Dismounting from one's horse in the shadow of a great block of stone, one sees that the block has features on its underside: it is the head of a fallen giant. The whole expedition could creep under it and find shelter in a rain-storm. On going up to the foremost figures, which are buried in the earth up to their chests, one is shocked to find that one cannot even reach up to the colossus' chin. And if you try to climb up on to those which have been flung down flat on their backs, you feel a regular Lilliputian, because often you have the greatest difficulty even in getting up on to their stomachs. And once up on the prostrate Goliath you can walk about freely on his chest and stomach, or stretch yourself out on his nose, which often is as long as an ordinary bed. Thirty feet was no uncommon length for these figures: the largest, which lay unfinished and aslant on the side of the volcano, was sixty-nine feet long, so that, counting a storey as ten feet, this stone man was as tall as a seven-storey house. That was a burly giant, a regular mountain troll.

In Rano Raraku you feel the mystery of Easter Island at close quarters. The air is laden with mystery; bent on you is the silent gaze of a hundred and fifty eyeless faces. The huge standing figures look down at you with an enigmatic stare: your steps are watched from every single ledge and cave in the mountain, where giants unborn and giants dead and broken lie as in mangers and on sick-beds, lifeless and helpless because the intelligent creative force has left them. Nothing moves except for the drifting clouds above you. It was so when the sculptors went, and so it will always be. The oldest figures, those which were completed, stand there proud, arrogant and tight-lipped; as though defiantly conscious that no chisel, no atomic power will ever open their mouths and make them speak.

But even though the giants' mouths were sealed seven times over, anyone going about in the chaos of uncompleted figures up the mountain slope could learn a good deal. Wherever we climbed and wherever we halted, we were surrounded, as in a hall of mirrors, by enormous faces circling about us, seen from in front, in profile and at every angle. All were astonishingly alike. All had the same stoical expression and the most peculiar long ears. We had them above us, beneath us and on both sides. We clambered over noses and chins and trod on mouths and gigantic fists, while huge bodies lay leaning over us on the ledges higher up. As our eyes gradually became trained to distinguish art from nature, we perceived that the whole mountain was one single swarm of bodies and heads, right from the foot up to the very top of the precipice on the uppermost edge of the volcano. Even up here, five hundred feet above the plain, half-finished giants lay side by side staring up into the firmament, in which only the hawks were sailing. But the swarm of stone phantoms did not stop even up here on the topmost edge, they went on side by side and over one another in one unbroken procession down the side of the crater into the interior of the volcano. The cavalcades of stiff hard-bitten stone men, standing and lying, finished and unfinished, went right down to the lush green reed-bed on the margin of the lake, like a people of robots petrified by thirst in a blind search for the water of life.

We were all equally overwhelmed and impressed by the gigantic enterprise which had once been interrupted in Rano Raraku. Only little Anette took it all quite calmly.

"Look at the dolls," she said enthralled, when I lifted her down from the pommel at the foot of the volcano.

But when we went closer the dimensions became too great for her imagination also. She played hide and seek round their necks without suspecting that heads rose into the air on top of them. When her mother helped her up a ledge she could not climb, she did not realize that she was being lifted from the upper lip of a recumbent giant on to the tip of his nose.

When we began to dig the impression was no less astonishing. The famous Easter Island heads were large enough already, standing on the slope at the foot of the volcano, but when we dug our way down along the throat the chest appeared, and under the chest the stomach and arms continued and the whole of the huge body right down to the hips, where long thin fingers with enormous curved nails met under a protruding belly.

Now and then we found both human bones and remains of fires in the strata of earth down the front of the statue. The heads looked quite different standing there with bodies and arms beneath, instead of as head hunters' trophies, as we are accustomed to see the Easter Island statues in encyclopaedias and travel books. But this uncovering solved none of the problems of Easter Island; it was merely a fascinating sight which the Routledge expedition once experienced before us. We had the greatest difficulty in throwing a line over the highest heads, and only the best climbers attempted to struggle up the rope, for when these statues were completely excavated some of them stood as much as forty feet high, or as high as a four-storey house. The last bit, from the eyebrows upwards, was the worst, for here the rope was pressed tight against the giant's forehead and did not afford a decent grip.

It was difficult enough for a rope-climber without encumbrances to ascend the skull of one of these standing giants, but it was more difficult to understand how it was possible to carry up a large hat which was to be placed on the very top of the head, especially considering that the hat too was of stone, and could have a volume of 200 cubic feet, and weigh as much as two elephants. How can one lift the weight of two elephants to the level of the roof of a four-storey house, when there are no cranes and not even a high point in the neighbourhood? The few men who could find room for themselves up on the figure's skull could not possibly have dragged an enormous stone hat up to the small flat space which was their only foothold. And although a crowd of men could stand on the ground at the foot of the statue they were mere Lilliputians, who could not stretch their arms more than a fraction of the way up the lower part of the giant. How then could they have pushed the weight of the two elephants high in the air, right up past the chest, and on past the towering head up to the very top of the skull? Metal was unknown, and the island was practically treeless.

Even the engineers shook their heads resignedly. We felt like a crowd of schoolboys standing helpless before a practical conundrum. The invisible moon-dwellers down in their holes seemed to be triumphing over us, asking: "Guess how this engineering work was done! Guess how we moved these gigantic figures down the steep walls of the volcano and carried them over the hills to any place in the island we liked!"

There was little use in guessing. We must first have a really good look round, to see if the mysterious old-time genii had been careless enough to leave behind something which could give us even the smallest hint.

To tackle the problem at its root we first studied the numerous uncompleted figures which lay on the ledges in the quarry itself. It was clear that all the work had been broken off suddenly; thousands of primitive unpolished stone picks still lay in the open-air workshop, and as different groups of sculptors had worked simultaneously on many different statues, all stages of carving were represented. The ancient stone-cutters had first attacked the bare rock itself and made the face and front part of the statue. Then they had cut alley-ways along the sides and made giant ears and arms, always with extremely long and slender fingers, curved over the belly. Next they had cut their way underneath the whole figure from both sides, so that the back took the shape of a boat with a narrow keel attached to the rock.

When the façade of the figure was complete in every minute detail it was scrubbed and thoroughly polished: the only thing they took care not to do was to mark in the eye itself under the overhanging brows. For the present the giant was to be blind. Then the keel was hacked away under the back, while the colossus was wedged up with stones to prevent it from slipping away and sliding down into the abyss. It was a matter of utter indifference to the sculptors whether they carved the figure out of a perpendicular wall or a horizontal slab, and head upwards or downwards, for the half-finished giants lay all over the place and leaning in every direction, as on a battlefield; the only thing that was consistent about them was that the back was the last part to remain attached to the rock.

When the back also had been cut loose the breakneck transportation down the cliff to the foot of the volcano had begun. In some cases colossi weighing many tons had been swung down a perpendicular wall and manoeuvred over statues on which work was still proceeding on the ledge below. Many were broken in transport, but the overwhelming majority had come down complete—that is to say complete but for legs, for every single statue ended in a flat foundation just where the abdomen ends and the legs begin. They were sort of lengthened busts with complete torsos.

At the foot of the cliff lay a thick layer of gravel and decomposed rock, often piled up into ridges and regular hillocks. This was the result of thousands of tons of stone splinters which had been carried away from the quarry by the sculptors. Here the giant men had been temporarily raised up into a standing position in holes which had been dug in the rubble. Not till now, with the statues standing thus, did the sculptors set to work on the unfinished back, and the neck and hinder parts take shape, while the waist was decorated with a belt surrounded by rings and symbols. This little belt was the only piece of clothing the naked statues wore, and with one exception they were all men.

But the mysterious progress of the stone colossi did not end here among the rubble. When the back also was finished they were to go on to their wall-less temples. Most of them had gone already: only comparatively few were still on the waiting list for transportation from their holes at the foot of the volcano. All the fully completed giants had moved on, mile by mile over the whole island: some had finished their journey up to ten miles from the quarry where they had first taken human shape, and the very smallest weighed from two to ten tons apiece.

Father Sebastian acted as an outdoor museum director in this deserted lunar landscape. He had climbed about everywhere and painted a number on all the statues he could find, and there were over six hundred in all. All were of the same greyish-yellow black-grained stone: all had been hewn in the same gigantic workshop in the steep face of Rano Raraku. It was only there that this special colouring of the rock was found, and knowing this one could recognize a statue simply by its colour even if it was lying prostrate among other huge boulders a long way off.

The strangest thing was that the colossi had been carried about not as shapeless lumps which could stand a knock or two, but as perfectly smooth human forms, scrubbed and polished front and back, from the lobes of their ears to the roots of their nails. Only the eye-sockets were still lacking. How had it been possible to move the complete finished article across country without rubbing it to pieces? Nobody knew.

At their destination the blind stone men were not erected just by dropping them down into a hole: on the contrary, they were lifted up in the air and placed on the top of an *ahu*, or temple platform, where they remained standing with their base a couple of yards above the ground. Now at last holes were chiselled for the eyes; now at last the giants might see where in the world they were. And then came the top of the macaroon cake. Now they were to have "hats" put on the tops of their heads—"hats" which weighed from two to ten tons and in the latter case could tip the balance against two elephants.

Actually, it is not quite correct to talk about "hats," even though everyone does so nowadays. The old native name for this gigantic head decoration is *pukao*, which means "topknot," the usual coiffure worn by male natives on Easter Island at the time of its discovery. Why did the old masters lift this *pukao* up on top of the giant in the form of an extra block? Why could they not simply cut it out of the same stone with the rest of the figure? Because the important detail was the *colour* of the topknot. They went to the opposite end of the island, seven miles from the stone quarry in Rano Raraku, and here they had hewn their way down into a little overgrown crater where the rock was of a very special red colour. It was this special red stone they wanted for the statues' hair. So they had dragged yellowish-grey statues from one side of the island and red topknots from the other, and had placed one upon the other on top of more than fifty raised temple platforms all round the coast. Most of these platforms had a couple of statues side by side, a great many had four, five or six and one had no fewer than fifteen red-haired giants standing side by side, with their base twelve feet above the ground.

Not one of these red-haired giants stands in his old place on top of the temple platforms today. Even Captain Cook, and probably Roggeveen also, arrived too late to see them all standing in their old places. But our first explorers were at any rate able to testify that many of the statues were still standing at their posts with red *pukaos* on their heads. In the middle of the last century the last giant crashed down from his temple, and the red topknot rolled like a blood-stained steamroller over the pavement of the temple square. Today only the blind hairless statues in the rubble-filled holes at the foot of the volcano still stand with heads raised defiantly. They stand so deep in the earth that no native enemy has succeeded in pulling them down, and a single attempt to cut off one of the heads with an axe was totally unsuccessful because the ancient executioner had not managed to cut his way more than a hand's breadth into the giant neck.

The last statue to fall was dragged down from its *ahu* about 1840 on the occasion of a cannibal feast in a cave near by. It had a topknot 200 cubic feet in size on the top of its thirty-two-foot tall body, which in turn stood on a wall almost the height of a man. We have all the measurements and also the density of this fallen giant; it weighed fifty tons and was transported two and a half miles from the quarry in Rano Raraku. Let us imagine ourselves taking a ten-ton railway truck and turning it upside down, for the wheel was unknown in Polynesia. Next we capsize another railway truck alongside the first one, and tie the two firmly together. Then we drive twelve full-grown horses into the trucks, and after them five large elephants. Now we have got our fifty tons and can begin to pull, and we have not merely to move this weight, but drag it for two and a half miles over stony ground without the slightest injury being done to it. Is this impossible without machinery? If so, the oldest inhabitants of Easter Island mastered the impossible. One thing is certain: this was not the work of a canoe-load of Polynesian wood-carvers, who set to work on the bare rock faces when they landed, merely because they could find no trees to whittle. The red-haired giants with the classical features were made by seafarers who came from a land with generations of experience in manoeuvring monoliths.

Now that we have got our fifty-ton load to the right place, the four-storey stone man must be got up on to a wall and made to stand upright, and then the topknot has to be put on: it alone weighs in this case ten tons, and has been carried seven miles as the crow flies from the topknot quarry. Seven miles is a long way in country like this, and thirty-two feet in excess of the stone platform is a good height anywhere when the object to be lifted weighs ten tons, as much as twenty-four full-grown

When the first Europeans visited Easter Island several of the statues still had their red stone wigs balanced on top of their heads. Old illustration from the visit of La Pérouse. (Note the native hat thief.)

horses. But it was done. And the whole thing was pulled down
again in 1840 by cannibals, who undermined the foundation
stones in the wall and celebrated their deed by eating thirty of
their neighbours in a cave.

I stood on the top of the crater of Rano Raraku and had a
magnificent view all round over the grass-clad island. Behind
me there was a fairly steep slope down into the overgrown
interior of the volcano, where the little sky-blue crater lake lay
as clear as a mirror in a broad framework of the greenest
reeds I ever saw. Perhaps it seemed a brighter green in contrast with the grass all over the island, which now, in the dry
season, was beginning to turn yellow. In front of me there was
a steep drop down the terraced wall of the quarry to the flat
ground at the foot of the volcano, where the members of the
expedition were working like ants, excavating the brown earth
around the gigantic figures. Their horses stood tethered here
and there, looking pitiably small alongside the burly giants.
From here I had a good survey of what had happened in the
past: this was the focal point and centre of Easter Island's most
conspicuous problem. This was the statues' maternity home: I
was standing on a sturdy embryo myself, watching the swarms
of others all down the descent both before and behind me. And
on the slope at the mountain's foot, both outside and inside the
crater, the new-born stood erect, blind and hairless, waiting in
vain to be hauled away on their long transport.

From up here I could see the course the transport had taken.
Two of the figures which were completed inside the crater had
been on their way when all work suddenly ceased. One had
just come up on to the edge of the crater on its way out, the
other was already on its way down through a gully on the outside, when the transportation had suddenly stopped and there
they lay, not on their backs, but on their stomachs. Along the
old stoneless grass tracks over the plain, as far as the eye could
see, others lay singly and in irregular groups of two and three.
They were blind and hairless, and all the indications were that
they had never been set up where they lay, but had been
abandoned just anywhere along the route, while being transported from Rano Raraku to the platforms that awaited them.
Some had gone right away, beyond the hindmost hills and
ridges. And there, beyond the horizon, far away to the west,

lay the little volcano Puna Pau with the topknot quarry. I could not see it from where I stood, but I had been down into its blood-red interior and seen half a dozen topknots lying like giant stone cylinders down in the precipitous little crater, while the old master hairdressers had conveyed a number of the largest up over the steep slope. These now lay in a dump outside, waiting to be conveyed further. Others had evidently been abandoned while under way to their future owners, for here and there a solitary topknot lay on the plain. I measured the largest topknot which had been carried up out of the red crater. It was 650 cubic feet in size and weighed roughly thirty tons, or as much as seventy-five well-grown horses.

My own comprehension was insufficient to grasp this far-reaching Easter Island engineering scheme, and I turned resignedly to the native shepherd who stood by me in silence, gazing at the abandoned giants which lay about on the plain.

"Leonardo," I said, "you are a practical man, can you tell me how these stone giants could have been carried about in old times?"

"They went of themselves," Leonardo replied.

But for his grave and reverent air I should have thought he was joking as he stood there in his newly-washed trousers and shirt, for Leonardo was no less civilized, and more intelligent, than the average man in the world outside.

"But, Leonardo," I said, "how could they go when they had only heads and bodies and no legs?"

"They wriggled along like this," said Leonardo, and gave a demonstration by working himself along the rock with feet together and stiff knees. "How do you think it happened?" he asked indulgently.

I was silenced at once, and as I was certainly not the first white man who had shown Leonardo that he had no comprehension whatever of the mystery, it was really quite reasonable that he should accept the practical explanation of his own father and grandfather. The statues had walked of their own accord: why set ourselves unnecessary problems when the answer was so simple and efficacious?

When I got home to the camp I went over to the kitchen tent to old Mariana, who was sitting peeling potatoes.

"Have you heard how the great *moai* were carried about in the old times?" I asked.

"*Si*, señor," she said with conviction. "They went of themselves."

And old Mariana began to tell a long story about an old witch who lived at Rano Raraku at the time when the sculptors made the great figures. It was her magic which breathed life into the stone giants and made them go where they should. But one day the sculptors had eaten a big lobster, and when the witch found the empty shell, none of the contents of which had been given to her, she was so angry that she made all the walking statues fall flat on their noses, and they have never moved since then.

Fifty years ago the natives told Mrs. Routledge just the same story about the witch and the lobster, and I found to my astonishment that all the natives I talked to still accepted this easy solution of the mystery. And unless someone could give them a more plausible explanation, they would stick firmly to the witch and lobster version till Doomsday.

In general the natives were certainly not naïve. With or without lawful grounds, they were always thinking of cunning excuses for leaving the village and coming over to the camp to sell wood-carvings. Nearly all of them could carve; several of them were real masters, and the best of all was the mayor. Everyone wanted his figures, for even if all men invariably offered the same subjects, his graceful lines and perfect polish showed that no one could shape a piece of wood better than he. He had far more orders in the camp than he could execute.

American cigarettes, Norwegian fish-hooks and bright-coloured English materials ranked highest on the list of barter goods. As on so many of the other islands, the people of Easter Island were absolutely crazy about cigarettes. Those who came on board the ship and had obtained a few packets by barter the first night had not smoked them themselves. They had galloped off to the village and gone from house to house there waking up relations and friends so that everyone should taste a cigarette, for the supply which had come with the last warship had been consumed months ago.

Among the elegant wood-carvings there appeared now and then a very inferior stone figure, either a naïve copy of the great statues or a shapeless head with nothing but eyes and nose casually indicated. At first the owners tried to make us believe that these were old figures found on the ground or in temple walls. But when we laughed at them most of them gave it up, and only a few of them tried to be still smarter.

A woman came riding up and fetched me away, saying that she had found something curious right in the middle of a heap of stones. When we came to the place she began carefully to remove the stones, and right down among them I saw the light fall on a little, newly-made model of a statue.

"Don't touch it," I said to the woman; "it's new, someone has put it there just to play you a trick!"

The woman's face grew very long, and neither she nor her husband tried to fool us again.

Then there was a fellow who came panting up after dark to tell us that he had found a baby statue buried in the sand while he was fishing in the sea by torchlight. If we wanted to have it we must come along right now in the dark, even if we could not see very well, for he was on his way home to the village. He was visibly surprised when we manoeuvred ourselves to the spot in the jeep and turned the headlights full on. There on the grass lay a badly executed little figure, carefully plastered with sand, but otherwise brand new. While the rest of us stood by laughing, the owner had to pack his miserable production away in a sack and lug it back to the village. A sailor in the next warship will probably get it.

A third variation came from a native who wanted to show me a little open grotto with a water-hole and some curious sculptures in the roof. The figures in the roof were genuine enough; there were old bird-men and great staring eyes, and I was really pleased. While I was studying the roof my innocent-looking guide stood and amused himself by casually dropping lumps of earth into the water. Suddenly he gave a shout. I saw a piece of earth slowly dissolving, and a little doll-like stone figure peered out down in the water, like a chicken coming out of an egg. It was so surprisingly comic that I laughed more than the sinner deserved, and he never tried any more games with me.

But in their zeal to secure our popular barter goods some of them really did find old things in the ground. One day a

young married couple came and took me to see four curious
heads that they had found. The place was surprisingly close
to the sheep fence east of the governor's land, and when we got
there we were met by an old woman and a virago of a daughter
who I thought was going to scratch our eyes out. They were
beside themselves with rage and shouted and shrieked at a
rate which is only possible in Polynesian. If our two guides
tried to get in a word a shower of abuse was almost spat in
their faces. The photographer and I sat down and waited
for the steam to blow off. The old lady cooled down a little.

"Señor Kon-Tiki," she said. "These two are thieves and
rascals. These are my stones; no one may dare to touch them.
I am descended from Hotu Matua and this has always been my
family's land."

"It isn't now," one of our two guides interrupted. "It's
the Navy's sheep farm now. The stones are ours because it was
we who first found them!"

The old woman was mad with rage again.

"First found them? Liars, thieves! The stones belong to my
family, you thieves!"

While the two parties were quarrelling savagely over the
ownership I suddenly realized from their gesticulations what
stones they were talking about. The old woman and her
daughter had now each sat down on one of them, I was
unconsciously sitting on a third, and our two guides were
standing by the last. They looked like ordinary boulders. I
thought of the wise man Solomon, who, when two mothers
both laid claim to the same child, took a sword and prepared
to cut it in half. I could have done the same now with the help
of a sledge-hammer. The young couple would just have agreed
and said yes if I had raised the hammer to strike. The old
woman would have gone out of her mind.

"Let us have a look at your stones, and then we won't
touch them," I said to her.

She did not say a word in reply, but let us roll the great
round stones over so that they lay bottom upwards. Four
grotesque faces with round eyes as large as tin bowls stared
blindly up into the daylight. They were not in the least like
the great classical statues, but rather suggested the round
gods' heads in the Marquesas group, terrifying and devilish.

Great naked stone bodies appeared down in the earth when the heads were
dug out. Centuries of blown sand and subsiding gravel had formed a deposit
covering the old giants' bodies.

A man feels very small when digging his way down along the body of an Easter Island statue. But how had the unknown sculptors of antiquity transported and erected these giants with no technical equipment?

The two owners of the stones looked desperate, while the two who had found them were triumphant, thinking that they were going to do a good stroke of business. Both sides looked equally tense when we rolled the grotesque heads back into their place, with their faces buried in the earth. Then we thanked them all and went away. The young couple were left behind, open-mouthed. Time would show that the old woman did not forget this.

In the meantime something else happened which puzzled us a good deal. Pottery, or ceramics, was as unknown on Easter Island as everywhere else in Polynesia when our own race came out into the Pacific. This was curious, for the art of pottery was at an early date an important cultural feature in South America, and it was still older among the peoples of Indonesia and Asia. We had found vast quantities of fragments of South American pottery in the Galapagos, because that group of islands lay within range of regular calls from the old sea-going rafts of the mainland, and furthermore, because there was hardly any earth to cover old remains. On Easter Island the conditions were the opposite. It was unlikely that prehistoric voyagers had often found their way from the continent out to Easter Island with their jars, and the little they might have broken after their arrival would today lie hidden deep under the grass-roots. But in any case I had brought a fragment of pottery with me, meaning to ask the natives if they had seen anything like it, for single fragments can tell the detectives of archaeology as much as a written book.

Our first surprise was that several of the old natives, independently of one another, immediately called the fragment *maengo*, a word which was not even in Father Sebastian's lexicon. One of them had heard from his grandfather that *maengo* was an old thing which people had in earlier times. A man had tried to make *maengo* of earth many years ago, but he did not quite succeed. Eroria and Mariana thought they remembered having seen some such fragments in a cave, and they went about for two days trying vainly to find them. The governor's wife had seen them while digging in the garden. And then a native came and told us with an air of mystery that he had a fragment like it at home.

The man, whose name was Andres Haoa, took several days

D

to bring us his ceramic fragment. To our great surprise we saw at once that it was hand-moulded in characteristic American Indian fashion and not turned with the help of a potter's wheel, as among Europeans. I promised to give him a wealth of cigarettes if he could show us the place where he had found the fragment, so that we ourselves could find more and confirm that the place of discovery was genuine. He then accompanied us to a great *ahu* with a row of fallen statues and a gigantic stepped wall which was strikingly similar to the classical Inca walls in the Andes. He pointed down into the pavement of the upper platform, saying that he had found three pieces of the kind just there several years ago. We carefully raised a number of the slabs with the help of native labour. In one place inside the stone terrace we uncovered two complete skeletons stretched out side by side, a quite unusual form of burial to find on Easter Island. Just beside them we found a descent to two dark chambers each covered by a gigantic beautifully cut stone plate, and in both chambers quantities of old skulls lay about higgledy-piggledy. But we found no fragments of pottery, and Andres did not get his full reward.

Next day Carl went back to the place with archaeological equipment and an excavation crew: *Ahu Tepeu* was obviously a building which in any case deserved closer study. An old native who was with him digging suddenly began to pick up fragments of pottery from the ground: he was the only person who found any, and the bits were so miserably small that it was strange that he had seen them. Then Arne and Gonzalo came galloping from the village. They had heard from a native woman that the old man had received fragments of pottery from Andres Haoa to help him get his full reward. We compared the new small pieces with the big piece I had formerly got from Haoa, and saw at once that one of them was only a corner broken off the big sherd. Haoa was furious at our having discovered his swindle, and would not tell us where he had really found the big piece. He went defiantly to Father Sebastian, who was astonished when three whole ceramic jars were placed on the table before him.

"Look here," said Haoa indignantly. "I'm not going to show these to Señor Kon-Tiki because he says I'm a liar. I'm not a liar."

Father Sebastian had never seen any such jars on Easter Island, and asked Haoa where he had found them.

"My father found them once in a cave and said they were nice to have water in," said Haoa.

This was obviously a fresh lie, for Haoa had no water in the jars, and he did not even have them in his house: the many friends who had wandered in and out and knew every corner of their neighbour's little hut could testify to that.

The three mysterious ceramic jars promptly disappeared without trace, just as they had come, after Father Sebastian alone had had a sight of them, and so we had yet another mystery to chew over. The jars did not return to Haoa's house: where did he hide them, and what was actually going on?

In the meantime we had acquired one more problem to tax our brains. I had decided to accept the old policeman Kasimiro's invitation and make a trip out to the bird-men's legendary island to look for his father's secret *rongo-rongo* cave. There was so much whispered gossip among the natives of ancient wooden tablets covered with hieroglyphs which were still hidden in sealed caves that everyone who was long enough on the island was bound gradually to be infected with curiosity.

"We have been offered 100,000 pesos for a *rongo-rongo* tablet, and so it's worth at least a million," the natives said. And I knew in my heart that they were right. But I knew also that if any of them found the entrance to a *rongo-rongo* cave they would scarcely dare to go in. For every *rongo-rongo* tablet had in their ancestors' time been a sacred possession, and the old learned men who had hidden their sacred *rongo-rongo* in caves at the time when Father Eugenio introduced Christianity had put a ban upon these hieroglyphic boards and made them taboo, so that all who touched them should die. This the natives fully and firmly believed.

There were only some twenty specimens of these wooden tablets in all the museums of the world combined, and none of the world's scholars had so far been able to make out the inscriptions. They were artistic written symbols of a type not found among any other people: the signs were prettily cut in a row according to a continuous serpentine system in which every other line was upside down. The tablets which are preserved today were nearly all taken from the island while

they were still in the possession of their native owners. But Father
Sebastian was able to tell us about the last which left the island,
for it was found in a taboo cave. The native who found it had
let himself be tempted to take an Englishman with him to a
place near by. The Englishman had been told to wait there,
and the native had laid a semicircle of small stones before him,
which he must not cross. Then the native disappeared and
came back with a *rongo-rongo*, which the foreigner bought.
A short time afterwards the native had suddenly gone out of
his mind, and a little later he died. This had done much to
increase the natives' old fear of breaking the taboo of a *rongo-
rongo* cave, Father Sebastian said.

Whatever the reason may have been, old Kasimiro too
drew back when at last I accepted his own offer to take me to
the cave. He said he did not feel very well, but proposed
instead that old Pakomio should show us the place: he had
been there too when, as small boys, they had had to stand and
wait while Kasimiro's father went to the cave alone. Old
Pakomio was a son of the prophetess Angata, who had started so
much trouble and superstition when the Routledge expedition
was there fifty years earlier. I approached him through Father
Sebastian, and he actually persuaded Pakomio to show us the
way. Old Pakomio reverently climbed on board our motor
launch, and we went out to the bird-men's rocky island,
Motunui. Behind our backs we had the highest precipice on
Easter Island hanging over our heads. On its sharp topmost crest
lay the deserted stone ruins of the ancient cult centre Orongo.
Ed was digging and surveying up there with his men. We could
barely pick them out as white dots, and they saw the boat
below them as a little grain of rice floating in the blue.

As lately as the last century the mightest men in the island
used to sit for weeks on end in the half-subterranean stone
houses up on the lofty cliff watching for the year's first migration
of sooty terns, which settled on the little rock island of Motunui
down below. It was an annual competition to swim out to that
island on a reed float and find the very first egg that was laid
there. The man who became owner of that egg was exalted
to a kind of divinity: he had his head shaved and painted red,
he was led in procession to a sacred hut among the statues at the
foot of Rano Raraku, and there he had to remain indoors in

the shade for a year, without contact with the common people. Food was taken to him by special servants, and he was designated the sacred bird-man of the year. The surface of the whole rock face by the ruins where Ed was now working was decorated with one confused masss of arch-backed men with long curved birds' beaks, carved as relief sculptures in the rock.

When we leapt ashore on to the legendary bird island not so much as a feather was to be seen. All the birds had moved to another precipitous rocky island farther along the coast: when we passed in the motor launch a swarm of birds rose above it like a smoke-cloud over a volcano.

But on Motunui we found at once the entrances to a number of half overgrown caves. In a few of them human bones and skulls green with age lay along the walls, and in one place a diabolical red-painted head with a goatee beard was thrust forward, like a trophy head carved in the roof. Mrs. Routledge had been in two of these caves. Pakomio stood waiting impatiently outside. He remembered Mrs. Routledge well. But it was not these caves he was to show us. He took us halfway up the cliff and stopped suddenly.

"It was here we baked the chicken," he whispered, pointing to the ground just in front of him.

"What chicken?"

"Kasimiro's father had to bake a chicken in the earth to bring good luck before he went into the cave."

We did not quite get the point, and all Pakomio could add was that this was the custom, and that only the old man had been allowed to stand where he could smell the baked chicken, the children had to keep to the other side of the hearth so that none of the odour could enter their nostrils. They had not even been allowed to see the things that were in the cave, but they knew they were immensely valuable. It had been an experience for Pakomio and Kasimiro just to be allowed to stand near by and know that the old man was inside inspecting all that wealth.

Of course we did not find the secret cave. When we had made a long and thorough search for the secret entrance among ferns and boulders, Pakomio suggested that the old man might have gone that way just to trick them, and that the cave was sure to be in the opposite direction. When we had clambered about for a while in the opposite direction too, our interest began to flag. The sun was broiling hot, and one by one we gave up the search. Instead we went and flung ourselves head first into a cleft brim-full of crystal-clear sea water pumped in by the ocean through a crack in the rock. We dived to the bottom after violet sea urchins, which Pakomio ate raw, and we bumped noses with queer fish gliding about in all the colours of the artist's palette. One by one they came gaping out of their hiding places to examine these new additions to Motunui's open-air rock aquarium. Glittering rays from above kindled a glowing firework display of colour on the marine life down in the sun-filled cleft, where the clear water was so pure that we felt like bird-men hovering among whirling autumn leaves. It was fantastically beautiful, a Garden of Eden under the sea. We could hardly bring ourselves to climb up on to the dry hot rocks again, knowing that all the priceless beauty down in the pool would be abandoned, perhaps for ever, to eyeless sea urchins and colour-blind fish.

But we had a good deal of use for our eyes on shore also, not least on Easter Island itself, where picks and spades were beginning to expose to the sunlight things which not even any native had seen for hundreds of years. People began to gossip in the village. The natives interpreted what was happening with a slight infusion of superstition. How could a foreigner know that old things lay hidden under the turf unless he was in direct contact with the island's own past with the help of *mana* or supernatural power? At first no one said it in so many words, but one or two came and asked me if I was not really a *kanaka*, a local native, and not a foreigner. My light skin and fair hair meant nothing, for some of their ancestors had been white and red-haired, and the fact that I knew just a few words of Easter Island's Polynesian dialect only signified that I had been so long in Tahiti and in Norway and other foreign countries that I had forgotten most, but not all, of my old language. At first none of us dreamed for a moment that they meant what they said; we took it as a kind of Polynesian compliment. But the more the archaeologists discovered under the turf the more evident it was to the natives that there was something queer about Señor Kon-Tiki.

It began with Bill's excavation team. Bill had chosen an

exciting task. He was the first archaeologist to set to work on the most famous ruin on Easter Island, the great *ahu* at Vinapu. All explorers and tourists who have seen this unusual piece of stone-mason's work have been struck by its remarkable resemblance to the grand mural constructions of the Inca empire. There is nothing like it on the tens of thousands of other islands in the vast Pacific. But Vinapu stands as a mirrored reflection of the most classical masterpieces of the Incas' predecessors, and this is all the more striking because it appears on the very island that is nearest to the Incas' own coast.

Could it be the master masons from Peru who had been busy out here too? Could it be scions of their guild who had first landed and begun to chisel gigantic blocks for the Easter Island walls?

The evidence spoke for it. But there was indeed another possibility, which science hitherto had preferred. Technical similarity and geographical proximity could be purely accidental, the result of mere coincidence. The people of Easter Island *could* have produced this masterly and most intricate type of architecture as a result of independent evolution on their own little island. If this was correct, the classical wall at Vinapu was the last phase of a local development, and theoretical research had till now accepted this view without investigating the ruins.

Bill worked at Vinapu for four months with twenty men. But the first few weeks provided the general answer we were eagerly awaiting. The central wall at Vinapu, with the classical stone masonry, belonged to the very oldest building period, contrary to all previous theories. The *ahu* had twice been rebuilt and added to later by far less capable architects, who were no longer masters of the complicated Inca technique. Ed and Carl, who had been working separately on other *ahus* rebuilt in prehistoric times, came independently to exactly the same conclusion as Bill.

It was discovered for the first time that there were three clearly separated epochs in Easter Island's enigmatic history. First, a people of highly specialized culture, with the typical Inca masonry technique, had been at work on Easter Island. Their classical buildings had no parallel in the later history of the island. Gigantic blocks of hard basalt were cut like cheese and fitted carefully to one another without a crack or a hole, and these mysterious constructions, with their elegant steep walls, stood for a great length of time, looking like altar-shaped and partly stepped fortresses all round the island. But then the new epoch had begun. Most of these early classical structures had been partially pulled down and altered, a paved slope had been built up against the inland wall and giant figures in human form had been brought from Rano Raraku and erected with their backs to the sea on the top of these rebuilt edifices, which now often contained burial chambers.

It was just while this gigantic mass labour was at its height in the second epoch that everything came to a sudden and unexpected standstill, and a wave of war and cannibalism swept over the island. All cultural life came to an abrupt end, and the tragic third and last phase of Easter Island's history began. No one chiselled great stones now, and the statues were pulled down without reverence. Boulders and shapeless blocks were flung together to make funeral mounds along the walls of the *ahus* and the great fallen statues were often used as improvised roofs for new burial vaults. The work was makeshift and utterly lacking in technical ability. As the archaeologists dug and scraped, rents were gradually appearing in the veil of mystery. The history of Easter Island was for the first time beginning to have depth. And one riddle was solved, one piece in the great puzzle placed. We knew now that the specialized Inca technique on mural construction was brought to Easter Island in a fully developed form. It was used by the people which had first landed on the island.

Serious natives came in crowds to look at the excavations at Vinapu, where Bill took care to uncover the concealed back wall of the *ahu* so that the stratification of all three epochs was clear to everyone. While this was going on, Bill stumbled one day over an unusual red stone on the plain behind the excavation ground. He called me and asked if I shared his impression that the stone had two hands with fingers. It was a long brick-red stone shaped like a four-sided column, and only one side of it just protruded from the turf. It was not at all like the statues, either in shape or substance. It was not even Rano Raraku stone. Nor did the stripes which suggested fingers appear at the very base of the column as in all the six hundred figures known on Easter Island. The natives smiled politely and explained that this was nothing but a *hani-hani*, nothing but a red stone.

The first thing which struck me was that what lay before us in the earth recalled strikingly the pre-Inca red column statues in the Andes. I had copied the bearded head on the sail of the *Kon-Tiki* raft from just such a four-sided column representing a man, and it too was hewn from a choice red and rough-grained stone exactly like this.

One-two-three-four-five: yes indeed, those could be fingers. But no head or other human characteristic were to be seen.

"Bill," said I, "we must dig. I've seen four-sided red columns like that in South America on the shore of Lake Titicaca!"

Father Sebastian had once stopped at this stone when he was going round with Eroria and painting numbers on all the standing and lying statues on Easter Island. Eroria had pointed out the stripes that looked like fingers, but Father Sebastian had shaken his head and gone on with his paint-brush. All the statues on Easter Island were of one type, and none of them looked like the four-sided red stone down there in the earth.

We carefully dug a deep trench in the thick turf all round the stone, and worked our way slowly in towards the sides of the column with the masons's trowel. Were those meant to be fingers or was it only a stone with accidental furrows? I was so excited that I held my breath as I proceeded to cut away the first strip of turf which covered what ought to be a hand. A hand it was! Fore-arm and upper arm came to light too. continuing all up one side of the statue, and it was the same on the opposite side. It was a statue of a type hitherto quite unknown on Easter Island; only the head had been knocked off and a deep hole bored in the chest where the heart ought to be. The figure even had short legs.

We patted Bill on the shoulder and shook him by the hand. Father Sebastian, the commander of Easter Island's silent old stone guard, was more shaken than anyone else by this unexpected addition to his mighty force of a beheaded, red and four-sided soldier.

"Dr. Mulloy, this is the most important find which has been made on the island in our time," he said. "This statue abso-

D*

lutely does not belong to Easter Island, it belongs to South America."

"But it's been found here," Bill laughed, "and that's what counts."

We raised the red statue with lifting tackle and twenty men to pull, till it stood upright with its short clumsy legs buried in a hole in the earth. The natives who hauled and struggled with the ropes had still more cause for astonishment. It was not a mere *hani-hani* after all, but how could we foreigners have known?

This was only the beginning. Soon afterwards Ed dug a curious little smiling figure up out of the earth in a quite unknown temple he had uncovered near the bird-men's ruined village on the top of Rano Kao. Father Sebastian, the governor and crowds of natives made a pilgrimage up there to see. And where Arne's team were working, at the quarry in Rano Raraku, other peculiar things came to light down in the earth. The most impressive was a bulky giant with a figure as foreign to Easter Island as the red statue at Vinapu. An innocent little corner of a rock with two eyes was all that was visible when Arne began to dig, and thousands had gone past without seeing that the stone was staring at them, and without dreaming that there was more under the soil. The eyes belonged to a burly troll weighing ten tons, who lay hidden underground with the turf as a quilt and with his eyes just peering up out of the grass.

A thick layer of fine rubble and masses of worn-out stone tools from the abandoned quarry above had buried this giant, and when we brought him to light he had not a single feature in common with his stiff, blind and legless neighbours. Both archaeologists and natives stared in equal amazement, and Father Sebastian and the governor had to be fetched again. Everything was different. This figure had a fully-developed body with complete legs; it was sculptured in a lifelike kneeling position with a fat backside resting on its heels and with its hands placed on its knees instead of on the belly. It was not naked, like the others, but was wearing a short cloak or *poncho*, with a square opening for the neck. The head was quite round with a peculiar goatee beard and strange eyes with pupils, and the figure stared straight forward with an alien expression which no one had ever seen before on Easter Island.

It took us a week just to raise this giant with the help of jacks and tackles and crane and jeep and multitudes of sailors and mystified natives. But one day it was there, in its humble kneeling position, staring dreamily up to the sky. It seemed to be straining its eyes for other planets, for a world which had gone. What had it to do with us, uninitiated aliens; where were its faithful old servants? and who were those stiff, long-nosed figures up above, whose birth rubble had buried his own person?

When the newly-raised figure stood there, as an alien among aliens, the men took their hats off, one by one, and wiped the sweat from their foreheads. Then they drew themselves up to gaze at the figure, as if expecting that something would happen. But nothing happened; the figure just stood there motionless and ignored us all.

Old Pakomio suggested quietly that it was now time to give the island a new name: it was now no longer Rapanui or Easter Island. Everything was changed, he said. Kasimiro and the whole team of excavators agreed, but the mayor added that in that case they would have to find new names for Orongo Vinapu and Rano Raraku as well, for nothing was as before. I proposed that they should keep the old names, for the only change was that old sights were now being seen again.

"Old sights are new to us, Señor Kon-Tiki," said Pakomio. "When one has lived on Easter Island all one's life one remembers every little thing one sees. Now we don't remember all that we see round us, and so it isn't Easter Island any longer."

"Then you can call the island the World's Navel, *Te Pito o te Henua*," I said in fun.

They all brightened up, nodded and laughed as they recognized the name.

"That's what they called our island in old times; so you knew that," said the mayor, with an inquisitive smile.

"Why, everyone knows that," I said.

"Everyone doesn't, but you're a *kanaka*." This from an old man who was standing behind the statue and nodded slyly to show that he had realized the source of my knowledge.

The natives had never seen anything like this new giant brought up out of the earth to remain for ever among them, kneeling in the hillside. But to Gonzalo and myself it was almost an old acquantance. We had both been at Tiahuanaco, the oldest pre-Inca cult centre by Lake Titicaca, and there we had seen similar kneeling stone giants which could easily have been cut by the same master, so like they were in style, features and position. They had knelt at Tiahuanaco for over a thousand years, along with the bearded red figure and other stiff four-sided columns depicting mysterious men, surrounded by the most enormous and best cut blocks of masonry which the whole Inca realm can offer. Indeed, in the whole of ancient America there is nothing to equal this imposing megalithic work. Archaeologists have discovered that the largest cut blocks weigh over a hundred tons, the weight of ten railway trucks drawn together, wheels uppermost. And they too were transported for mile upon mile across the plain. Gigantic blocks have been carried about all over the neighbourhood, stood up on end and lifted up on top of one another as if they were empty cardboard boxes, and in the midst of these ruins of unroofed walls and terraces the old masters placed all their strange statues in human form. The largest is twenty-five feet high; the many others are considerably smaller, even if they are of superhuman dimensions. Tiahuanaco lies there in the mountain plains, mysterious and desolate with all its statues and cut blocks of masonry, and the Incas say that these were lying there equally deserted and ownerless when the first Inca came to power. At that time, they say, the master sculptors had already migrated into the open Pacific, and left the field to the primitive tribes of the Uru and Aymara Indians. Only the legend of the vanished creators of Tiahuanaco lived on. But for the moment we left the legends alone. We were digging in the earth for bare facts, and what we found were mute stone men. Tribal memories may be called upon later, like a living breeze to blow life into the nostrils of the dead stone figures.

One of the mysterious things about the Easter Island statues had been that all were of the same type; one was astonishingly like another, and all were quite characteristic of Easter Island and nowhere else. Outside this one island there was nothing in the whole world which harmonized exactly with them. Before the dawn of history unknown civilizations had abandoned large stone statues in human form all the way from Mexico down to

Peru and Bolivia, and on the very nearest islands where the ocean current from Peru reaches the easternmost outposts of Polynesia. But none were precisely of the Easter Island style. And on the neighbouring islands to the west, towards Asia, there were no statues of any kind whatever. How could Easter Island's giant figures have been inspired from outside, when there was nothing quite like them anywhere else? Most research workers, therefore, had been led to believe that the idea once arose on this little oceanic island, independently of the outside world, gigantic and incomprehensible as the whole undertaking was. The more imaginative took refuge in the theory of a sunken continent: similar statues must be found on the bottom of the sea.

But now statues of different types were beginning to appear in the soil of Easter Island. Furthermore, inside the walls of several of the *ahus* we found a number of unusual figures, some of which had been smashed to pieces and only used as building stone and filling during the second cultural epoch, at the time when the classical walls had been rebuilt and the gigantic statues from Rano Raraku had been placed as huge monuments on top of them. Father Sebastian also suddenly recollected having stumbled upon a couple of figures the size of a man made of hard black basalt. One of them he had seen walled-in as foundation stone in the façade of an old *ahu;* only the broad back projected. And right in the actual village area Father Sebastian and the natives helped us to put a stout fellow on his legs: this too proved to be a primitive type the like of which no one had seen on the island, and it was of the same kind of red stone as the headless figure at Vinapu.

Now we were a long way nearer our goal: the second piece in the puzzle was soon in its place. We had discovered that the men who had built the beautiful Inca walls in the first period had made statues unlike the famous stone giants from Rano Raraku which had made Easter Island so renowned. These different figures left from the first epoch were generally not much larger than a man. They had round heads, short faces and large eyes. They were sometimes of red tuff and sometimes black basalt, but also of the yellowish-grey Rano Raraku stone which became all-important to the sculptors of the subsequent period. These earliest island statues had few peculiarities in

common with the famous Easter Island giants except that they
too usually held their arms flexed with both hands in a stiff
position on their stomachs so that the fingers pointed towards
one another. But this one special feature was also a peculiar
characteristic of a large number of old pre-Inca stone men and
of the statues on the neighbouring islands in Polynesia.

Now at last we were on speaking terms with the taciturn
statues of Easter Island. It was the abased and humiliated
walled-up specimens that first loosened their tongues, and they
set the haughty, defiant fellows up on the top gossiping too,
right up to the quarry in the mountain. The family tree of the
stone men had begun with a gust from the other world which
brought ideas and technique to the island along with the classical masonry. The stumpy figures which were later pushed into
the wall, the headless red pillar statue on the plain at Vinapu,
and the large kneeling one which lay buried under the rubble at
the foot of Rano Raraku, belonged to this early period. Then
came another epoch in which local sculptors had invented a
more elegant and exclusive style of their own, and bulky
colossi with red hair were carved and carried up to the top of
the numerous rebuilt walls. As the sculptors gained experience
the new colossi steadily increased in size: they became larger
and larger, ever larger. Those which had already been erected
on the *ahus* were big enough, but many of those which were
left under way were bigger, and some of those which stood at
the foot of the volcano waiting to have their backs finally
chiselled were bigger still. And the biggest of all was the giant
seven storeys high who lay unfinished in the quarry itself with
his back as part of the solid rock.

How would this local evolution have ended? Where would
the limit of the possible have been ultimately fixed? No one
knows. For before the limit was reached the catastrophe came
which halted the advance of the marching stone giants, and
they were all flung flat on the ground. All because the witch
did not get her lobster, the people of the island believed today.
But the fight was probably for stronger meat, for the march of
the stone giants ended just when the third epoch began, and
the cannibals suddenly took the stage.

The population of the island today is the freshest shoot sprung
from the victorious warrior tribe of the third epoch. It was no

peaceful affair when their Polynesian ancestors arrived from the palm islands to westward. Of the battles which followed their arrival, of the statues which fell, of the time when adzes cut their way into men of flesh and blood instead of men of stone, we were soon to hear stories from the living population of the island. For during this epoch their own forefathers had really been present and played the leading part. The third epoch was not dead yet, although peace and tolerance now reigned on the island.

CHAPTER V

THE LONG-EARS' SECRET

IN the camp at Anakena life followed its usual round. The
sun shone on the gleaming white paint of our ship anchored
outside the rocks in the bay. It seemed to have become a part
of Easter Island, a landmark like the bird islands round the
coast. No ship had ever remained at the island for so long—
none but those which had been washed up against the rocks
once and for all and still lay at the bottom of the sea with the
tops of their masts many fathoms beyond the grasp of the trade
winds.

When the on-shore wind thundered too loud on the tent
walls the steward hurried out to the ship and brought ashore
an extra supply of provisions, for it might happen that the
skipper would sound the siren and tell us on the walkie-talkie
that he must say good-bye. Then the ship went off round the
coast and found shelter under the cliffs behind the cape where
we had first anchored, at the foot of Rano Raraku. For a day
or two the bay in front of the camp looked painfully empty,
like a familiar picture in which something essential was suddenly
lacking. But then one morning when we crawled out of our
tents, woken as usual by the steward's hammering on a frying-
pan, we saw the ship lying there, pitching in the morning sunshine, just in her usual place.

The sunny camp with all its tents had become a home
for us, a firm anchorage among shifting scenes of activity
on the island. When we saw the white ship behind the black
rocks, with the green tents on yellow grass and yellow sand in
the foreground, and a vault of blue above us and reaching out
of sight, we were at home. Then the day's toil was over, the
breakers called aloud to us to come and bathe, the steward
hammered on his frying-pan and invited us to a tasty dinner.
When evening came we lay in groups on the grass and talked
under the stars or in brilliant moonlight; some of us sat near
the lamps in the mess tent, reading and writing or listening to
the gramophone, while others jumped on to horses and dis-

appeared at a gallop over the ridge. The seamen had become regular cowboys on shore, the second mate was stableman, and when the men were starting for the village of Hangaroa the old temple square in front of the tents was a real circus ring full of neighing and rearing horses. Only the mess boy broke an arm through taking a short cut through the scree, and the doctor had to set it. But what sacrifices will a man not make to arrive quickly in a distant village when a real hula dance is the attraction?

We soon knew most of the people in the village. But the black-eyed village doctor was rarely to be seen even by those who went to the hula dancing, and his friend the schoolmaster we never saw. They did not attend with the rest of the population in Father Sebastian's little church, and so were never present at the Sunday dinners which followed, either at the nuns' house or with the governor and his wife. This surprised us, for irrespective of religious belief, something of Easter Island was lost, both to eye and ear, if one was not there when Father Sebastian threw open the church door for the simple Sunday talk and strangely beautiful Polynesian singing. The atmosphere the natives created was infectious: this was their great getting together, the event of the week, and even the laziest folk who sat on their door-steps the whole week long, all indeed who could walk or crawl, put on their best clothes and sauntered slowly and ceremoniously up to the church square when the native sexton Josef began to pull the bell-rope.

But one day fate unexpectedly brought the schoolmaster into the picture. The governor had asked several times on behalf of the school if the school-children might make a trip round the island in the expedition ship: it would mean so much to them all. They could go ashore at Anakena and have a picnic lunch in front of the camp, and go on round the island in the ship in the afternoon so as to get back to the village the same evening. I was not greatly taken with the idea, but the nuns pleaded for the children, and when Father Sebastian told me that none of them had ever seen their own island from the sea, except from the village bay, I promised to ask the skipper to bring the ship round to the village. The whole of the main deck was admirably suited to children in that it had high sides curved inwards which no child could climb over; and, as everybody said, the native school-children could swim like fish anyhow; they began to lark about in the bay long before they started school.

We dropped anchor off Hangaroa village early one morning in fine weather, and 115 native school-children were taken on board: they were an eighth part of the population of the whole island. The schoolmaster himself, the village doctor and his assistant, the governor's assistant, three nuns and seven adult natives went along to look after the children. The governor and Father Sebastian did not want to come on this trip. There were cheers and shouting all over the deck, the children sang and were wildly excited. They fought for places right up in the bows to watch the seas being ploughed aside. But when the anchor was raised with a clatter and crash, and the siren sounded a farewell to the village, most of them seemed to become quieter and looked almost sadly shoreward towards their homes, as if they were going on a voyage round the world instead of a day trip round Easter Island. Lonely Easter Island —well, of course, that was the whole of their world.

When the ship began to pitch gently in a long, shining swell they were all seasick without exception. A native came and asked us to hurry up so as to get home sooner; then he tottered off and lay down on one of the hatches, which was already covered with children trying to sleep. Soon they lay strewn all over the deck like motionless bundles of washing; and if anyone went to the rail it was not to look at the pretty coast.

The only one of the guests who was in top form was the schoolmaster. He had been full of activity from the moment he came on board, thick and round, a portly figure amid the crowd of children. He declared that he had never been seasick, though he had made countless sea voyages in all kinds of weather. With his raven hair and flashing black eyes the schoolmaster reminded one in a way of his active friend the village doctor, and he immediately displayed the same political enthusiasm. The natives were Chilean citizens, but did not possess Chilean rights unless they could go to Valparaiso in the warship and settle down on the mainland among other Chileans. His aim was to help the natives to get to the mainland. But even if his black eyes were as hard as coals when he was preaching his politics, something gentle came into his face when he took out his pencil to draw the rolling contours of the coast in his diary, or when he saw a chance of patting one of the children on the head. He stumped about, a solid sturdy figure, consoling his seasick pupils in their own Polynesian language. Now he was sitting with some of them and giving them pills, now he was dancing off to the rails dragging a long weedy lad whose signs and gestures made it clear to everyone that he must get out of the way, for a clear road was wanted.

When we rounded the cape the sea was so quiet that the bigger children came to life. Instead of following our advice and remaining amidships, they all wanted to go forward into the bows, where there was most movement. Soon the school-master had to step in and drag them back, green and gaping, to a horizontal position on the hatch. There was no gaiety or go in the school-children till we entered Anakena Bay. Then they suddenly woke up, and Polynesian singing and cheering started while the deck hands swabbed down the ship, which now looked like the cliffside under a seagull's nest.

When the ship again lay in her usual place off the camp at Anakena all the children were brought ashore and shown the tent village on Hotu Matua's old site. Then their guardians took the whole party down to a temple terrace, where they encamped in the grass at the foot of the wall. A few natives had come over the island on horseback to help, and six lambs were baked in Polynesian fashion between hot stones in the earth.

The day was declining. Up by the fire nothing but sun-dried bones were left, while the bay was full of bathing children, and the air as full of song and shouting. The nuns had assembled a group up on the beach, singing enthusiastically their ancestors' old song of Hotu Matua, who had come here to Anakena Bay.

Then the schoolmaster looked at his watch, clapped his hands and told his people to get ready to leave; the children must go on board again. The sea was quiet with a gentle rolling swell, and the motor launch lay as usual moored to the large anchored raft a little way from the shore. The children had been using it as a diving-board. The engineers went out with the first boatload to get everything ready on board, and when the launch came back the schoolmaster stood on the beach again rounding up pupils for another trip. The chosen ones were rowed out to the large anchored raft in the little landing raft, and some of them treated themselves to an extra farewell plunge by swimming alongside. When the launch had gone for the second time some rowdy boys swam out on their own account and crawled up on to the anchored raft to wait for the next trip. The schoolmaster therefore went out to the raft himself to exercise better control, and when the launch went he was in it himself. The other grown-ups in charge of the children remained ashore to divide the rest among the last trips.

Then the accident happened, like a bolt from a clear sky. While the launch was chugging peacefully round the outermost point on her way to the ship, the children began to move about. Everybody suddenly wanted to go forward and see the bow wave. Everybody wanted at the same time to push their way forward to Thor junior, who sat right in the point of the bows with the mooring rope. The schoolmaster tried with all his might to keep order among the children, but now they did not obey or even listen to Polynesian. The carpenter who was steering put the engine astern, and he and Thor bellowed at the children at the top of their voices, but at the same second the catastrophe came in the shape of a quiet leisurely wave. The launch, with a capacity of two tons and only half loaded, ran her bow deep into the side of the slow surge and filled in an instant. All that was to be seen was the stern and a mass of swimmers' heads.

On board the ship a boat was immediately swung out, while the expedition doctor and I jumped on to the landing raft on the beach. All the others ran out to the far end of the point, which was only about eighty yards from the scene of the disaster. I turned my head as we hurriedly rowed out and saw that some of the children were swimming in towards the point, but most of them were bobbing up and down in one place round the stern of the boat. We were soon there. We went straight for the carpenter and a native schoolboy who were swimming side by side supporting two helpless creatures. When we hauled them up on the raft I saw that one was the mayor's thirteen-year old daughter, a pretty little girl with a strikingly white skin and red-gold hair. Then I dived in, while the doctor stayed on the raft to row about and haul children on board. Now the first swimmers from the point had arrived too, headed by the skipper. We picked up the children one by one and shoved them up on to the raft. Most of them were quite apathetic and only let themselves bob up and down without making any attempt to save themselves. When the raft was packed full the skipper and carpenter came swimming up with the schoolmaster, whose huge body floated of itself. It took several men to heave the upper part of his body up on to the float, and this threatened to capsize when three bewildered natives, who also had swum out, began to climb on board. Swimming nearby I had to bellow like a madman before I could get them to jump into the sea so that the raft righted itself. Two of them jumped straight for me and clung on, so that I was forced under again and again, and at last had to dive to get free of them. Now all our own sailors from ashore were on the spot, as well as the village doctor's assistant and half a dozen natives. These swimmers began to push the raft in towards the point while the doctor rowed like fury with all the children on top of him.

The skipper and I went on swimming round among a mass of floating objects to see if there was anyone we had overlooked, and three fresh natives had come swimming out to us. The water was brilliantly clear, and by diving I could see a quantity of shoes and clothes lying spread over the sandy bottom some twenty-five feet below. And to my alarm I saw something which looked like a doll down on the bottom. I flung up my legs and swam down as far as I could, down, down, while the doll increased in size. I am not a top-class swimmer, and now I was dead beat to start with. When I was twenty feet down I was completely done for, could not manage a moment longer, and had to kick myself up desperately, heartbreaking as it was to be forced to give in just short of what I now saw so clearly. Directly I got my head above water I saw Josef, the native sexton, just beside me. I knew he was the best diver on the island: he had once been chosen to show us two sunken wrecks off the village. I gasped a few words to him while pointing down and in a twinkling Josef was gone. A few seconds later he was up again, shook his head, took a deep breath and disappeared again. Now he came up holding a boy in front of him with his arms at full length. We got the boy up on to a drum and were swimming to shore with him when we saw that the ship's boat too had come and was being rowed round with the engineers diving from her. But now there was nothing left on the bottom but clothes. Forty-eight children were on board the ship already, and the lists of names of those on board and those ashore showed that no one was missing.

When we reached the point all the children from the raft had already been carried ashore on to the rocks, where our own doctor was conducting artificial respiration with the help of the village doctor's assistant and all the bystanders. The village doctor himself, who had been standing on the point receiving those arriving on the raft, had jumped on board to take it right in to the beach, as it proved impossible to haul the heavy schoolmaster up on the sharp lava rocks where all his pupils had been brought ashore. In the dreadful hours which followed, while night sank over the island, the village doctor worked on his friend the schoolmaster on the beach, helped by our biggest and strongest men, while all the rest were working on the children out on the point. Nearly a dozen were in need of treatment. Everywhere people were running about with paraffin lamps, carrying blankets and clothes: up in the camp Yvonne had thrown all the tents open and was serving hot food to old and young. And as riders began to stream in from the village, people swarmed all around us in the dark.

It was a night of dread which I shall never forget. An atmosphere of horror hung over the Anakena valley and was emphasized by a grey, quite colourless rainbow which stretched itself gloomily over the black night sky, just where the moon was hidden behind the ridge. The children came back to life one after another and were carried into the tents and put to bed. But the hours passed, and two of them did not move. One was the little red-haired girl. The mayor sat motionless by her side and said in a calm voice:

"She's well off, she's always been good, she's with the Virgin Mary."

I have never felt grief at such close quarters. I have never seen people take it more quietly. Those who had lost their children took our hands silently in both of theirs as if to show us that they knew that we, the owners of the boat, could not

help what had happened. Those whose children had been
saved flung themselves on our necks and wept. For several
hours every tent, and the space outside them, was packed
with school-children and their parents and others who had
come to look on. But when the night chill descended they began
to pack their bundles and mount their wooden saddles in
family groups of two and three to a horse. A couple of the
children had dysentery and remained in the tents with their
nearest relatives. Loneliness came upon the Anakena valley
as the riders moved off in the dark with over a hundred children
on their saddle-bows.

The last to come up from the beach were eight men carrying
the schoolmaster on a stretcher. The sky was black and the
grey arch of the colourless rainbow still lay across it as a frame
of sorrow above the eight lanterns swinging in the night.
The village doctor looked at me with quiet coal-black eyes.
He said:

"The island has lost a good man, señor. He died at his post
and his last words were: '*Kau kau, poki!*—tread water, boys!' "

The next time I saw the village doctor was in Father
Sebastian's little church. He was standing motionless with bared
head beside his friend's bier. The two children had been buried
the day before with a simple and beautiful ceremony, with
palm leaves and quiet singing, and the whole village walked
in the funeral procession singing gently of the two who had
gone to heaven. Today Father Sebastian's address was short
but warm.

"You have loved your pupils," he ended. "May you meet
again."

When we saw the schoolmaster disappear for the last time,
we heard the village doctor muttering:

"Tread water, boys, tread water."

The natives forgot the whole disaster incredibly quickly.
The relatives at once began to slaughter cattle and sheep for the
great feasts which they always held when they lost their dear
ones. They even came riding over to us with whole haunches
of oxen and large quantities of other meat. But what surprised
us most were the conditions inside the tents after everything had
been tidied up. For two centuries the most notorious characteristic of the natives of Easter Island had been thieving, the

pilfering of everything they could lay their hands on. On that dark moonless night there was no control, all the natives went in and out of the tents just as they liked, and everything we owned lay there openly. We did not expect to see a single thing again. But we were completely wrong. Nothing had gone: not a hat, not a comb, not a shoelace. And all the dry clothes and blankets which were lent to the children when they went away on horseback, came back from the village, washed and ironed, in neat piles. Nothing was missing.

However, one of the expedition's men threw his watch into his hat on shore when he dived in to the rescue. That watch was stolen by a native out on the point while the owner was in the water saving children. It was a shabby action, but of little importance. Therefore I had a shock when I met Father Sebastian in the churchyard for the first time after the disaster.

"It was terrible about the children," was all I could say.

"It was worse about the stolen watch," said Father Sebastian without blinking an eyelid.

"What do you mean?" I asked, quite shocked at the monstrous answer.

Father Sebastian laid his hand on my shoulder and said calmly:

"We all have to die. But we don't have to steal."

I shall never forget those words and my struggle to understand until I suddenly realized once more that I had met here on Easter Island a great personality, perhaps the greatest I had ever known. His teachings were to him as real as life itself, not just edifying words reserved for Sundays. To him beliefs and teachings were completely at one.

He said no more, and silently we walked together back to the village.

A few days later I met Father Sebastian again. I had knocked off all work during those days, but the natives did not like that. When the sun had risen and set and risen again, yesterday was yesterday, and today today, and then they wanted to work for more rations, more daily pay and more goods. The mayor sat on his steps and carved a bird-man out of a large chunk of wood while the shavings flew thick and fast, and he smiled and waved and showed his work as the jeep passed. We stopped outside Father Sebastian's little white-washed house behind a glowing flowerbed next to the church, and I jumped out of the jeep and let myself in through the low garden gate. I saw Father Sebastian through the window: he beckoned to me to come into his little study, where he sat at a table thickly covered with papers and letters. On the wall behind him was a shelf with books in an impressive number of languages. They formed an erudite and colourful frame for the big, bearded old sage who sat behind the little table in his white cloak with turned-down hood. The only thing I missed was a large quill pen in an inkstand on the table. Father Sebastian had a fountain pen. But to make up for that an old stone adze lay there as a paper-weight.

This old priest was something exceptional for the twentieth century. While on the one hand he was completely at home among us, yet he could just as well have been a student monk in a mediaeval painting, a bust of a Roman sage, a portrait of a scholar on an ancient Greek vase or on a clay tablet from Sumeria. Father Sebastian could have lived and been himself for thousands of years, and still the joy of living and the energy of youth shone from the blue eyes in which a smile was always lurking. That day he was full of eagerness; he had something particular in his mind. He wanted to ask me to start excavating at a very special place on the island, a place which figured more than any other in the traditions of the natives.

I heard for the twentieth time the legend of Iko's ditch, or the long-ears' earth oven. Everyone who has landed on Easter Island has heard the legend; everyone who has written about the mystery of the island has dealt with it. The natives had shown me the marks in the earth where the ditch had once been, and all had been eager to tell me the story. Father Sebastian had written down the tradition in his own book; now I heard it from his own lips, with a request that I would set a team to dig in the ditch.

"I believe in the legend," he said. "I know that science has claimed that the ditch is natural, but scientists can make mistakes. I know the natives. The tradition of the ditch is too living to be mere fancy."

The story of the long-ears' defence ditch begins far back in the recollections of the present population. It begins where the march of the statues ends. It begins in the blue mists of antiquity

and describes the catastrophe which put an end for ever to
Easter Island's golden age.

There had been two peoples on the island, and they lived
side by side all over it. One of these peoples had a peculiar
appearance: their men and women pierced their ears and put
heavy weights into the lobes till the ears were artificially
lengthened right down to the shoulders. For this reason they
were called *Hanau eepe*, "long-ears," while the other people
were the *Hanau momoko*, "short-ears".

The long-ears were an energetic people who always wanted
to work, and the short-ears had to moil and toil and help them
to make walls and statues, which led to jealousy and dis-
satisfaction. The long-ears' last idea was to rid the whole of
Easter Island of superfluous stone, so that all the earth could
be cultivated. This work was begun on the Poike plateau, the
easternmost part of the island, and the short-ears had to carry
every single loose stone to the edge of the cliff and fling it into
the sea. This is why there is not a single loose stone on the
grassy peninsula of Poike today, while the rest of the island is
thickly covered with black and red scree and lava blocks.

Now things were going too far for the short-ears. They were
tired of carrying stones for the long-ears. They decided on
war. The long-ears fled from every other part of the island and
established themselves at the easternmost end, on the cleared
Poike peninsula. Under the command of their chief Iko they
dug a trench nearly two miles long which separated the Poike
plateau from the rest of the island. This trench they filled with a
great quantity of branches and tree-trunks till it was like a
gigantic far-flung pyre, ready to be set on fire if the short-ears
on the plain below tried to storm the slope leading to the
plateau. Poike was like a huge fortress, with a sheer drop of
600 feet all round the coast, and the long-ears felt themselves
secure. But one of the long-ears had a short-eared wife: her name
was Moko Pingei and she was living up on Poike with her
husband. She was a traitress and had arranged a signal with
the short-ears down on the plain. When they saw her sitting,
plaiting a large basket, the short-ears were to steal in a long
file past the place where she sat.

One night the short-ears' spies saw Moko Pingei sitting and
plaiting a basket right at one end of Iko's ditch, and the short-

A long-ear from Easter Island with beard and feather crown, drawn on the spot during Captain Cook's visit.

ears stole one by one past the place where she sat, at the very edge of the cliff. They sneaked on along the outer edge of the plateau till at last they had completely surrounded Poike. Another army of short-ears down on the plain marched openly up towards the ditch: the unsuspecting long-ears lined up to face them and set fire to the whole pyre. Then the other short-ears rushed forward from their ambush, and in the bloody fight which followed all the long-ears were burned in their own ditch.

Only three of the long-ears succeeded in leaping through the fire and escaping in the direction of Anakena. One of them was called Ororoina and another Vai, but the name of the third is forgotten. They hid in a cave which the inhabitants can point out to this day. There they were found, and two of them were stabbed to death with sharp stakes, while the third and last, Ororoina, was allowed to remain alive as the only surviving long-ear. When the short-ears dragged him out of the cave he shouted *orro, orro, orro*, in his own language, but this was a language which the short-ears did not understand.

Ororoina was taken to the house of one of the short-ears who was named Pipi Horeko and lived at the foot of the hill called Toatoa. There he married a short-ear of the Haoa family and had many descendants, among them Inaki-Luki and Pea. They in turn had a number of descendants, the last of whom are still living among the short-ears on the island now.

This was the tradition of the long-ears' ditch in its most complete form, and now Father Sebastian would have me dig in the ditch. I knew that the two expeditions before ours had heard variations of the same tradition and had been to look at the remains of the ditch. Mrs. Routledge had been doubtful, but was inclined to think that the ditch itself must have been a natural geological depression which the long-ears might have used in self-defence. Métraux went still further. His conclusion was that the whole ditch was merely a natural formation which had tempted the natives to make up a story: the whole legend was inspired by the natives' urge to explain a geographical peculiarity, and the whole story of the long-ears and short-ears was therefore certainly no more than an invention of the people of the island in fairly recent times.[1]

[1] A. Métraux: *Ethnology of Easter Island*, Honolulu, 1940. Pp. 72-4.

A professional geologist had also been up to have a look at the long-ears' ditch, and he established once and for all that the ditch was a natural formation caused in pre-human times by a flow of lava from the centre of Easter Island having run into an older congealed flow from Poike; where they met a kind of ditch had been formed.

When the specialists had given their verdict the natives were bewildered and could not understand. But they stuck to their guns; this was Iko's defence ditch, the long-ears' earth oven. And Father Sebastian believed in their version.

"It means something to me personally if you will dig there," he said, and he almost leapt with excitement when I agreed.

Carl was to direct the excavation of the long-ears' ditch. We jolted off next day with five natives in the jeep, along a cleared track through the stony plain at the foot of Poike. Above us Poike's smooth slopes lay like a grass carpet without a single stone, but round us and behind us lay the scree like a covering of black coke. Up on Poike we could have driven freely where we liked with the jeep. But we stopped at the foot of the slope, where all the grass began. All along the hillside from north to south we saw a faint depression in the ground, like a filled-in ditch. In some places it was fairly deep and clear, in others it disappeared for short stretches and then would become clear again, continuing right out to the precipices on both sides of the peninsula. Here and there we saw a hummock like a bulwark of earth on the upper side of the ditch. We put on the brakes and jumped out. This was *Ko te Ava o Iko*, Iko's ditch, or *Ko te Umu o te Hanau eepe*, the long-ears' earth oven.

Carl wanted to test the ground at a few points first before we began to dig in earnest. We strolled along the depression and stationed each of the five natives at wide intervals along the ditch: each of them was told to dig a rectangular hole straight down through the soil. Never had I seen natives take up pick and shovel with greater zeal, and as no damage could be done we went for a short turn along the plateau. When we came back round the crest to look at the first experimental hole, the old man who had begun to dig had disappeared without trace, and his tools with him. But before we had time to wonder where he had gone, a shower of earth came sailing up out of the dark hole. And when we went up to it the old fellow was standing a good six feet down in the ground, hacking and digging as the sweat ran down him. And in the mustard-yellow earth wall we saw a broad red and black stripe slung round the digger like a coloured sash. Charcoal and ashes in thick layers! There had once been a great fire down in this earth, and Carl was able to say that the heat had been intense, or else the fire had burnt for a long time; otherwise the ash would never have become as red as this. Before he could say any more I was off across the hillside to look into the next hole.

Carl hurried after me, and we saw the sexton Josef's smiling face sticking up out of the earth farther on. He had found the same remains of a fire down in the earth and showed us his hand full of carbonized boughs and pieces of wood. All round us not a bush was to be seen. We ran on to the next hole, and the next. Everywhere we were met by the same sight, the flaming red band of ashes surrounded by black carbonized remains which wound round the walls of the hole.

Father Sebastian was fetched, and ran from hole to hole in his fluttering white gown to look at the red ash. His face was all radiant as we jolted home round the taciturn statues of Rano Raraku on our way to a good dinner at Anakena. He looked back on the great triumph of the day and forward to good food and good Danish beer, for now we must go to the camp and strengthen ourselves for the exciting adventure of the next day, when real digging would start on Poike.

Next morning a team of diggers was set to uncover an exact cross-section of the depression, and in the days that followed Carl started excavations which revealed the whole secret of the ditch. The topmost part of the depression was, indeed, merely the work of nature and followed the border of an old lava flow. But deeper down industrious men had been at work. They had hewn their way farther down into the rock and constructed a deep and artificial defence ditch with a rectangular bottom, twelve feet deep, about forty feet wide and nearly two miles long across the hillside. It had been a gigantic construction. Sling-stones and carved slabs were found down among the ash. Sand and rubble cut away from the bottom of the ditch had been used to build a rampart along the upper side of the ditch, and the deposit of rubble in the rampart revealed that it had been carried up from the ditch in large plaited baskets.

We knew now that Iko's ditch was a defence work superbly laid out by man, and down in the ditch, all along the hillside, great quantities of wood had been collected and a huge pyre lighted. We looked at the natives. Now it was our turn to stare: they had known all this; from generation to generation they had been told that this filled-in depression was the remains of Iko's defence work and the scene of the final slaughter of the long-ears.

One of the easiest things for a modern archaeologist to put a date to is charcoal from an old fire. Its age is fixed within certain limits by measuring its radio-activity, which diminishes at a known rate from year to year. The great fire in the long-ears' earth oven had burned three hundred years before our own time, perhaps a little earlier, perhaps a little later. But the whole of the elaborate defence works in the ditch had been built by men long before this final catastrophe, for the ditch was half filled up with sand when the defence pyre against the short-ears was constructed and burnt. There were remains of fires farther down, and the original makers of the ditch had flung up their rubble over a hearth on the ground above which dated from about 400 A.D. This was the oldest date which had been established so far in any part of Polynesia.

Fresh life had now been breathed into the story of the long-ears, both in the village and in the camp at Anakena. There seemed to be more meaning in the curious profiles of the giant statues: they all had curiously long ears which hung down the side of the head like a beagle's.

One evening I was sauntering about alone among the long-eared statues at the foot of Rano Raraku. I had so much to think about, and one thinks best alone under the stars. One does not really know a place properly till one has slept there. I have slept in the queerest places—on the altar stone in Stonehenge, in a snowdrift on the top of Norway's highest mountain, in adobe chambers in the deserted cave villages of New Mexico, by the ruins of the first Inca's birthplace on the Island of the Sun in Lake Titicaca: and now I wanted to sleep in the old stone quarry in Rano Raraku. Not because I was superstitious and believed that the spirits of the long-ears would come and betray their secrets, but because I would like to assimilate fully the peculiar atmosphere of the place. I clambered over

huge stone bodies lying up on the ledges until I came right up
into the swarm of figures at a place where one giant had been
removed from his birthplace. The bed in which he had been
born lay empty, like a theatre box with an overhanging roof.

From here I had a splendid view over the countryside, and
here I should keep dry if it poured with rain. For the moment
the weather was superb. The sun was about to descend behind
the silhouette of Rano Kao's steep volcanic wall at the other
end of the island, and red, purple and lilac cloud-banks had
rolled up as a screen before the bed of the retiring sun-god.
Nevertheless the sun managed to thrust some silver rays
through and down on to the distant lines of glittering breakers
which slowly and noiselessly moved shoreward in their eternal
attack on the distant corner of the island. I had not seen them
in the daytime, so far away they were, but the rays of the evening
sun filled the foaming crests with gleaming silver, and the
silver dust hung in the air at the volcano's foot. It was a sight
for the gods. And among a multitude of giant gods I sat, a
solitary little human being, up in the mountain stage box
watching the great spectacle of Nature.

I tore off a few stiff tufts of grass and swept the foot of the
giant's forsaken bed clear of sand and sheep's dung. Then in
the last paling rays of the sun I made myself a good bed of
grass and ferns. Down on the plain below me I heard two girls
singing tender Polynesian love-songs. They came along on
horseback, going nowhere in particular, with nothing to do
but send laughter and South Sea song out into the evening
air, while the horses ambled aimlessly round in a circle. But
when the man up on the mountain had crept to bed alone and
the sun was beginning to draw the darkness down after it over
the sky like a dark curtain, the two vahines suddenly became
silent, and as if afraid of magic they both set off at a gallop
towards a lonely shepherd's hut down by the bay. The shepherd
also had gone down towards the same hut. I had seen that he
stopped continually and set fire to the grass as he moved
across the plain. The dry season had long since begun: showers
were extremely rare and the grass was yellow and stiff. It now
had to be burnt away so that new grass might come through
fresh and green for the sheep. As long as it was light I saw only
the smoke from the grass fires which lay like a grey fog over the

Above: Native swimmers with reed floats in the Rano Raraku crater lake.
Below: A reed fishing boat was an incredible craft. It had the raft's advantage of being unsinkable, and rode the sea like a swan.

Above: All the stone giants which once were completed and set up at their final destinations all over the island now lie with their noses in the sand, overthrown in civil war. The red top-knots have rolled into the temple squares.
Below: We went to work like Snow-White's dwarfs at the foot of the quarry. Here the statues were only temporarily erected for their backs to be completed before their transport began.

Above: A niche in the quarry with an uncompleted figure (end view). The old sculptors had hewn their way into the hard rock with stone picks as if it were cheese.
Below: A half-finished giant left in the mountain wall. The whole rock face had been cut away by small hand picks. Work in the quarry had stopped quite suddenly, so that unfinished statues in all stages had been left there.

Above and below: A giant on a keel. Unfinished statues in the quarry showed that the back was the last part to be cut loose from the rock. The sculptors' stone hand picks lay where they had left them, and showed what primitive tools they had used on the iron hard rock.

plain. Then the night came and the smoke was swallowed up by the darkness, but not the fire. The darker it grew the brighter the flames shone out, and an innocent grass fire spreading in all directions looked like a thousand red pyres in the pitch-black night.

There was a cold breeze up on the cliff-side, and I pulled the sleeping-bag well up under my chin as I lay listening to the silence of the night, drinking in the whole atmosphere of the long-ears' quarry, which now appeared in an entirely new setting. I felt again that I was in a theatre as I lay under the roof of my box. This was the long-ears' big show. The silhouettes of the burly giants round me looked like black sets framing a stage against a starry black-cloth. Now the action was transferred to the pitch-dark plain below, where it glowed and flickered, fire continually springing up in new places till it looked as if a thousand invisible short-ears came stealing in on a wide front, torch in hand, to storm the quarry. Time had again ceased to exist. Night and the stars had always been there, and man who played with fire.

I was just dropping off to sleep with this impression burned into my mind when I suddenly woke up again. I clearly heard something prowling quietly and cautiously in the dry grass. Who could be feeling his way about so carefully up here in the quarry? Natives looking for what I had put down beside me in the dark? There was a pattering noise close by my head, and I twisted myself round and switched on my torch. Not a soul. The light blazed up and died down to a murky red glow. These cursed damp batteries! All I could see behind my head in the faint beam thrown by the lamp was a giant statue on its way down from the ledge above me: it lay like a huge arch over the shelf I lay on, and was broken off at the neck. Monstrous eyebrows and a couple of gigantic noses stuck up out of the grass on the ledge next to me, and threw queer shadows on the rock. It had clouded over and was beginning to rain a little, but not where I lay. I turned off the light and tried to sleep, but now the pattering noise around me began in earnest: and when I shook the torch till it gave a faint glow I caught sight of a brown cockroach as big as my thumb. I fumbled about and got hold of a clumsy stone pick of the type which lay strewn about everywhere in the quarry. But before I got in a

E

blow at the creature I saw another sitting motionless beside it, and another, and another. I had never before seen such large cockroaches on Easter Island. Now I threw the feeble light round me on all sides and discovered that fat cockroaches were sitting about everywhere: they sat in groups on the rock wall beside me, on the roof over my head; a couple were actually sitting on my sleeping-bag w,aving their feelers at me. They were loathsome to look at, sitting there and staring at me with large dumb round eyes: but it was worse when I switched the light off, for then they began to move in all directions. One bold spirit even came over and tweaked my ear. Outside the rain poured down. I took the stone pick and killed the largest ones nearest to me, and swept off those which were on the sleeping-bag. Then the torch went out altogether, and the next time I had a faint light I saw that there were just as many as before, and a few big brutes were making a cannibal feast of those I had killed. Suddenly I caught sight of two fearful eyes staring right into my face, with a grinning toothless mouth beneath them. This was sheer nightmare. The horrible face proved to be a rock carving of a terrifying *make-make* spirit which had, in the remote past, been carved on the wall just by my head. I had not seen it in daylight, but the feeble side light of the torch threw shadows into the furrows and made the grotesque traits of the face stand out from the wall.

I killed a few more cockroaches with the stone pick, but finally decided to yield to superior numbers, otherwise I should sit there murdering the whole night. As a scout in my boyhood I had learnt a wise saying: all creatures are pretty if one looks thoroughly at their details. I looked straight into the stupid round chocolate eyes of a straddling, six-legged cockroach, pulled the hood of my sleeping-bag well down over my head and tried to doze off. But the rock was hard and I had time to think another small thought. I thought how appallingly hard this rock really was, not to lie on, but to hew. I grasped the stone pick once more and hit the wall of the quarry as hard as I could. I had done it before, and knew well that the pick sprang back from the wall without making any mark but a light dusty patch. In fact, the skipper had been up here with me once and tried his luck with hammer and chisel in the statues' quarry, and it took him half an hour to chip off a bit the size of his own fist. At the same time we had calculated that over 700,000 cubic feet had been hewn out of the solid rock of the visible ledges where we stood, and the archaeologists thought that this estimate could safely be doubled. It was incomprehensible. I felt again the fabulous magnitude of the long-ears' project here in the mountain, and an idea that I had been toying with for a long time forced its way back into my mind. Why not start an experiment? The stone picks still lay where the sculptors had flung them down, and the last of the long-ears still had living descendants in the village. Work could actually be started in the old quarry again in our own day.

The cannibals' torch procession down on the plain was quenched. But up on the mountain ledge among the giants a swarm of tiny cannibals were feasting on their own kind who had fallen to a long-ear's stone pick. And while they crawled and scrabbled all over me I fell into a sleep without foothold in time and space, like a Gulliver among the busy cannibals and a dwarf among the dreaming giants: and the great starry sky spread itself over the whole mountain.

Next morning the sun was spreading gold all over the yellow plain, and only a mass of wings and bent legs lay around me to show that the invasion of cockroaches had not been a dream. I saddled my horse and galloped along the ancient grass-grown track which led in the direction of the village bay.

Father Sebastian gave me a roguish smile when I told him where I came from and what I had in mind. He was at once in favour of the plan, so long as we chose a secluded corner of the quarry and did not spoil the impression of Rano Raraku as seen from the plain below. But I would not have just anyone to help me make a statue. I knew that Father Sebastian was the leading authority on the local family trees, and had published a genealogy of Easter Island. I told him that I was looking for natives who were descended from the last long-ear.

"There's only one family left today which is descended in a direct line from Ororoina," said Father Sebastian. "It's a family which chose the surname Adam when Christianity was introduced in the last century. Or Atan, as the natives of this island pronounce it. You know the eldest of the brothers: he's Pedro Atan, the mayor."

"The mayor!" I was not a little surprised and could not help smiling.

"Yes, he's rather a buffoon, but he's by no means stupid, and he's a good-natured fellow," Father Sebastian assured me.

"But he doesn't look like a native at all," I said. "His thin lips, his narrow sharp nose, his light skin . . . ."

"He's of pure blood," said Father Sebastian. "And there are only eighty or ninety of the native population we can guarantee as of pure blood today. Not only that, but he's a genuine long-ear in direct descent on his father's side."

I was on my horse in a twinkling and rode up the rough village road to the garden fence where the mayor's little white-painted cabin lay, half hidden among bushes and trees.

The mayor was sitting working at a pretty little set of chessmen which took the form of statues—bird-men and other familiar Easter Island subjects—instead of the traditional pieces.

"This is for you, señor," he said, proudly displaying his little masterpieces.

"You're an artist, mayor Don Pedro," I said.

"Yes, the best on the island," was the glib reply.

"Is it true that you're a long-ear too?"

"Yes, señor," said the mayor with the utmost gravity. He jumped up and stood at attention like a soldier who has been called out of the ranks. "I'm a long-ear, a genuine long-ear, and I'm proud of it," he said dramatically, striking himself on the chest.

"Who made the great statues?"

"The long-ears, señor," he replied emphatically.

"I've heard some of the other natives say it was the short-ears."

"That's an absolute lie, señor, they're trying to get credit for what my ancestors did. The long-ears made everything. Haven't you seen that the statues have long ears, señor? You don't think the short-ears made statues of long-ears? The statues are in memory of the long-ears' own chiefs."

He was so excited that his chest was rising and falling and his thin lips trembling.

"I believe that it was the long-ears who made the statues," I said. "Now I myself want a statue made, and I will only have long-ears to do the work. Do you think you can do it?"

The mayor stood motionless for a few moments, with trembling lips: then he drew himself up sharply:

"It shall be done, señor, it shall be done. How long is the statue to be?" he added.

"Oh, medium-size, fifteen to twenty feet long."

"Then there must be six of us. We are only four brothers, but there are several others who are long-ears on their mother's side; will that be all right?"

"Quite all right."

I rode up to the governor and got Pedro Atan temporarily released from his duties as mayor, and he and his relatives obtained permission to go to Rano Raraku and carve a statue.

The day before the work was to begin I had been asked to keep a little food ready for the long-ears; I had ordered the statue and I must give the food, that is old custom. The day passed and no one had collected the rations. One after another our people began to go to bed in the camp, first Yvonne with Anette in the tent beside the fallen giant, and soon the lights were put out in the tents all over the camp. Only Gonzalo, Carl and I sat in the mess tent writing.

Then we heard a curious, quite faint humming and singing. It grew louder and louder, it was right in the camp, and now a rhythmic thumping on the grass began. What we heard was something completely strange and prehistoric. Gonzalo rose, looking bewildered, Carl opened his eyes wide, and I myself listened quite enthralled: I had never heard anything like it during all my experiences in Polynesia. We opened the zipper of the tent and went out into the darkness. The photographer was just coming out of his tent in pyjamas, and the lights were coming on in one tent after another.

In the faint light which showed through the mosquito net of the mess tent we saw a group of humped figures sitting in the middle of the open space between the tents and striking the ground with curiously carved war clubs, dancing paddles and stone picks. Each of them had a feather-like crown of leaves round his head, and two small figures on the edge of the group had large paper masks drawn over their heads to represent bird-men, with large eyes and huge projecting beaks: they

bowed and nodded while the others swayed and sang and beat
time on the ground with their feet. But the tune was more
hypnotic than anything we could see: it was a direct greeting
from a vanished world. One single shrill grotesque voice in the
deep male choir had an indescribably strange effect: it was the
finishing touch to this unearthly chorus. When I grew accustomed to the light I saw that the voice came from a very old
woman, as thin as a rake.

They were all deeply serious, and the singing went on and on
till one of our fellows came out of a tent with a lamp. Then the
chorus stopped abruptly, and they all murmured "no" and
hid their faces in their hands. When the light disappeared the
song began again; one man started, and then all the rest
joined in, the old woman last. I felt far away from the South
Sea Islands; I had heard singing which reminded me of
this when I was among the Pueblo Indians in New Mexico,
and all the archaeologists said the same.

When the singing was over I fetched a dish of sausages which
the steward had put out in the kitchen tent, and the per-
formers rose and retreated into the darkness with the dish. We
now saw that the two masked bird-men were little children.

The mayor came back with the empty dish, profoundly
serious, and with a wreath of ferns round his head. I joked and
laughed and complimented him on the astonishing performance, but the mayor did not move a muscle of his face.

"It was a very ancient custom, it was the old song of the
stone-cutters," he said gravely. "They sang it to their most
important god, Atua, to pray for good fortune in the work they
were about to begin."

There was something peculiar about the mayor that night,
something about the song and the whole way in which it was
presented, which made me feel confused and uncertain. This
had not been just a show: it had not been done for our enter-
tainment: it had about it the flavour of a ceremony. I had
experienced nothing like it in Polynesia since I lived with the
old hermit Tei Tetua in the Ouia valley in Fatuhiva, nearly
twenty years before. Everywhere in Polynesia the inhabitants
have given up all that is old, except when they appear in straw
skirts for tourists. If they play and sing, it is more or less
imported *hula* music, and if they tell stories these are most

often legends they have heard quoted from white authors' books. But there was something or other about this little night ceremony which was not meant for us alone: we were only accidentally involved because it was we who had asked them to make the statue.

I deliberately tried to joke with the mayor and his people, but now it did not fall on good soil. He took me quietly by the arm and said that in a way it had been "a bit serious," because it was an old song to God. "Our ancestors knew no better," he continued: "they thought God was called Atua. We know better today, but we must forgive them because no one had taught them what we know now."

Then the whole party, old and young, moved off across the temple square with all their dancing equipment and vanished into the darkness on their way to one of Hotu Matua's caves in which they were to spend the night.

Next morning we went up to the quarry in Rano Raraku. There we found the mayor and five of his long-ears, who had been up the cliff for a long time, going round collecting old abandoned stone picks. They lay on the ledges literally in hundreds, on the ground and under it, looking like gigantic eye-teeth with sharp points. Up on the balcony where I had slept was a large flat side-wall which was not visible from below: it was a wide gash in the cliff-face where the old-time sculptors had carved their way in. It was through this anciently cut side-wall that we were to proceed further into the rock, where old cutting grooves still stood like huge claw-marks on its face. Our friends the long-ears knew from the very first exactly what they would have to do. They spread a supply of stone picks along the mountain wall where they were to begin, and each of them had a calabash of water standing beside him. The mayor hurried about with yesterday's wreath of ferns round his head, making sure that everything was ready. Then he took a series of measurements along the rock face, now by means of outstretched arms, now by spreading out his fingers. He obviously knew the relative proportions from his own wooden figures. With a stone pick he cut marks at different places on the rock face. But instead of beginning he politely asked us to excuse him, and disappeared with all his men behind a projecting rock.

A new ceremony was evidently in preparation, and we waited eagerly to see what would happen. But then they came slowly back with set faces, and all six drew themselves up along the wall, each holding his stone pick in his hand. It looked as if the required ceremony had been held on the other side of the rock. They held their picks in their clenched hands like daggers, and at a sign from the mayor they burst into the stone-cutters' song of the day before, each man lifting his arm and striking against the rock face in time with the rhythm of the tune. It was fantastic to see and to hear. I missed the old woman's second, but the echoing blows of stone against the rock were a good substitute. It was so gripping and infectious that all of us who saw it stood quite hypnotized. And now the singers warmed up, they smiled broadly, they sang and hewed, hewed and sang. One tall old man at the end of the line was so inspired that he danced and swayed his hips as he sang and hewed. Stroke followed stroke, clink-clink, clink, clink-clink-clink, the rock was hard, stone against stone, the little pick was the hardest and the rock must give way: clink-clink-clink, the blows of the picks must have been heard far out over the plain. For the first time in centuries the clink of the stone was heard in Rano Raraku.

The song died away, but the strokes continued, steady and unbroken: six long-ears had taken up the tools and the craft their forefathers had been compelled to abandon. Not much of a mark was made by each blow, hardly more than a grey patch of dust, but with another blow, and one more, and still another, something was gained. And at intervals the men grabbed the calabash and splashed water on the rock face where they cut.

So the first day passed. Wherever we went in the neighbourhood we heard clinking and hammering up on the cliff among the motionless giants. When I went to bed in the tent the rippling brown backs and the sharp stones cutting into rock were still present to my eyes, and the blows resounded in my ears although all had long been quiet in the quarry. The mayor and his friends now lay asleep dead tired in Hotu Matua's cave. The old woman had been over in the camp to fetch a large dish of meat and a sack full of bread, butter and sugar, so the long-ears slept with full stomachs.

Next day, and the day after, the work went on in the quarry: the men hewed and the sweat streamed down. On the third day the contours of the giant were clearly visible on the rock wall. The long-ears hacked and cut parallel depressions down the face of the rock, then they cut across the edge left between the furrows, breaking it off into pieces. They cut and cut and flung on water. And continually they changed their picks, for the point soon blunted. Earlier investigators had thought that when a stone pick was worn out it was just thrown away, and that this explained the astonishing number of picks which lay about the quarry. But this proved to be wrong. When they were worn the mayor grasped one after another by the end like a little club and struck it against another stone pick on the ground: the splinters flew through the air like sharp flakes and he produced a new fine point, as easily as a clerk sharpens a pencil.

This taught us that the greater part of the unbroken picks in the quarry had been in use at the same time, but that every sculptor had had a series to work with, one after another. There were not many sculptors to each statue. An average figure of about fifteen feet would take six men. That was why it had been possible to work on so many statues at once. A couple of hundred men were enough to keep the work going on a considerable number. Moreover, work on many of the statues in the quarry had been given up on purely technical grounds before the general stoppage came. In some cases the sculptors had found a disastrous crack in the rock, in others a black stone, hard as flint, had defied the sculptors' tools, and the statue was left unfinished with a great wart on its nose or chin.

Now we had seen the details behind the sculptors' technique. But what interested us most was to know how long it would take to carve such a statue. According to Mrs. Routledge's calculations fifteen days were all that was needed. Métraux too thought that the work on the "soft stone" went more quickly than people believed, even if fifteen days was an under-estimate. They had certainly made the same mistake as we ourselves and many others—that of judging the hardness of the rock by the outer surface of a statue. We were all too respectful to do what the first Spaniards did when they thought the statues were made of clay. They struck a figure with a pickaxe
E*

with all their might till the sparks flew. The figures are as hard
as bone inside the outer surface, and so is the rock where the
rain has not reached it.

After the third day the tempo of the long-ears' work slowed
down. They came to me with crooked calloused fingers and
said that they were indeed wood-carvers who worked with
adze and chisel all day long, but they were not trained *moai*
men, statue sculptors, therefore they could not keep the tempo
going week after week as their ancestors had done. We sat
down quietly on the grass and each of us made his calculations.
The mayor came to the conclusion that it would take twelve
months to complete a medium-sized statue with two teams
working all day in shifts. The tall old man worked it out for
himself and said fifteen months. Bill made an independent
study of the rock and arrived at the same result as the mayor:
the work on one statue would take a year, and then the problem
of removing it would arise.

The sculptors amused themselves by making fingers and
features on the unfinished product, and polished the surface
with flat-rubbed pumice stone, left behind in the quarry by the
old stone-masons.

That evening I took little Anette on my shoulders and, with
Yvonne, went over to the long-ears' cave on the other side of
the Anakena valley. They had seen us a long way off and when
we came they were sitting, each man occupied with his own
task, smiling and swaying their bodies rhythmically while singing
a quiet song about Hotu Matua. This was an ancient and well-
known song on Easter Island, with as catchy a tune as any
popular hit. It was pleasant to hear among the hula singers in
the village, but it sounded still better here in Hotu Matua's
own cave. Even Anette, only three years old, knew the tune
with all the Polynesian words. She began to sing and dance
with two little Polynesian children who came out of the cave,
while Yvonne and I crawled in and sat down on the reed mat
on which the long-ears made room for us, delighted at having
visitors in their cave.

The mayor beamed and, with hands on his stomach, thanked
us for the good food they got from the cook daily, and especially
for all the cigarettes; they were the best of all. He and two
other men were sitting with little adzes carving at their tradi-

tional wooden figures: one of them was putting eyes of white sharks' vertebrae and black obsidian into the grotesque head of his bearded spook. The old woman who looked after the men sat plaiting a hat: the others lounged and chewed straws and looked out at the evening sky. A black cooking-pot stood sputtering on a fire outside.

"Don't you ever rest?" I asked the mayor.

"We long-ears like working. We work all the time. I don't sleep many hours of the night, señor," he replied.

"Good evening." The words came from a man we had not noticed because he was lying on a fern mattress up in a dark pocket of the cave wall. "Aren't we comfortable here?"

I had to admit that they were. But I was astonished at their realizing it themselves. Outside it was beginning to grow dark: through the mouth of the cave we saw a recumbent crescent moon appear in the sky. The old woman produced an old can with a dent in the bottom. In the dent were sheep's fat and a home-made wick, and this imitation of an old-fashioned stone lamp, when kindled, gave a surprisingly good light. The thin old man explained to us that in the days of their ancestors no one used a light at night for fear of being seen by the enemy.

"What's more, the warriors had to accustom themselves to see clearly in the dark," the mayor added. "Nowadays we're so used to paraffin lamps that we're almost blind in the dark."

One remark led to another.

"And in those days they never slept like this." The old man lay flat on his back with his mouth open and his arms stretched out and snored like a motor cycle. "They slept like this." He rolled over on to his stomach and curled himself up like a ball, resting with his chest on his knees and his forehead on two clenched fists, with the top of his head pointing towards me. He held a sharp-pointed stone in his hand.

"Then they could spring up to meet the enemy and kill him as soon as they were awake themselves," the old man muttered. And to illustrate the action he was describing he suddenly shot forward like an arrow and flung himself upon me with a canni-balistic howl which made Yvonne utter a scream, and the cave resounded with laughter. The children rushed in to see what was happening, but soon went on dancing round the fire, while the long-ears continued to revive the tales their grand-parents had told them.

"They didn't eat much either in those days," said the old man. "And they never ate hot food. They were afraid of growing fat; they always had to be ready to fight in the time we call *Huri-moai*, or the 'Statue-overthrowing' time."

"It's called so because that's when the warriors threw down the statues," the man up on the ledge added by way of explanation.

"Why did they, when the long-ears had been burned already?" I asked.

"The short-ears did it against each other," the mayor told me. "They owned everything then, and each family had its particular area. Those who had great statues on their land were proud of having them, and when they went to war one family pulled down the statues on another's land just to annoy the owner. We long-ears are not so warlike. I've a motto, Señor Kon-Tiki: take it easy."

He laid his hand on my shoulder in a pacifying gesture as if to show his peaceful temperament.

"How can you be so sure that you're a long-ear?" I asked cautiously.

The mayor raised his hand in the air and began to count on his fingers.

"Because my father Jose Abrahan Atan was son of Tuputahi who was a long-ear because he was son of Hare Kai Hiva who was son of Aongatu, son of Uhi, son of Motuha, son of Pea, son of Inaki who was son of Ororoina, the only long-ear who was left alive after the war at Iko's ditch."

"That's ten generations," I said.

"Then I've left one out, for I'm number eleven," said the mayor, and he began to count on his fingers again.

"I'm of the eleventh generation too." The words came from the man up on the shelf. "But I'm only a junior. Pedro is the eldest and knows most, that's why he's the head of our family."

The mayor pointed to his forehead and said with a sly smile: "Pedro has a head. That's why Pedro is chief of the long-ears and mayor of the whole island. I'm not really old, but I like to think of myself as a very old man."

"Why?"

"Because old men are wise, they're the people who know something."

I tried to find out a little about what had happened before the short-ears exterminated the long-ears and the "Statue-overthrowing time" began. But nothing was to be learned. Their line began with Ororoina, and what lay behind him no one knew. The long-ears had come with Hotu Matua when the island was discovered: that they knew, but they added that the short-ears said the same of their line, just as they tried to get the honour of having made the statues. But whether Hotu Matua came from east or west no one remembered any longer. The man up on the shelf suggested that Hotu Matua had come from Austria, but as he got no support from the others he soon gave way and added that he had heard it from someone on board a ship. They all preferred to talk about the "Statue-over-throwing time," which to them was something quite real. When the mayor talked of the treacherous woman with the basket who had betrayed the whole of his race he became so furious that tears came into his eyes and he had to swallow. That story would live on from father to son for another eleven generations, even with the motto "take it easy."

"There were handsome people among our ancestors." said the mayor. "There were two kinds of people on this island: some were dark and some were quite fair-skinned like you from the mainland, and with light hair. They were white people, but they were genuine Easter Islanders, quite genuine. In our family there were many of the fair type, who were called *oho-tea* or the light-haired. My own mother and my aunt had much redder hair than Señora Kon-Tiki."

"Much redder," his brother on the ledge agreed.

"There were many of that type in our family, all the way back. We brothers are not like that. But my daughter who was drowned had a milk-white skin and completely red hair, and so has my grown-up son Juan. He makes the twelfth generation after Ororoina."

This was quite correct: both of them had hair as red as the topknots on the thin-lipped, long-eared statues which had adorned the *ahus* of the island in the second cultural epoch. Their race was burnt on Poike and the statues were pulled down, but the red hair can be traced from the great stone

pukao, through living individuals described by the first discoverers and the first missionaries, down to the last descendants
of Ororoina, the mayor's nearest relatives.

We almost felt like fair-haired long-ears ourselves when we
crept out of Hotu Matua's cave and strolled home to the dark
camp on the other side of the plain. This had been much too
late for Anette.

A few days later I was standing with the mayor looking at
the row of fallen statues on the temple square in front of the
camp. Bill had just reported from Vinapu that his native
diggers had used a curious method to lift a stout block into its
place in the wall. This raised afresh the century-old mystery
of the transportation and handling of the giant statues.
The men had taken the simple method they had employed at
Vinapu quite as a matter of course. Perhaps it was a dodge
they had inherited from their ancestors? Who knows? I
remembered that I had once asked the mayor how the statues
were moved from the quarry. The answer was the same as that
given by all the others: the statues had walked of their own
accord. I now took my chance and asked again:

"You're a long-ear, mayor, don't you know how these giants
were raised?"

"Yes, señor, I do know. There's nothing to it."

"Nothing to it? It's one of the greatest mysteries of Easter
Island!"

"But I know it: I can raise a *moai.*"

"Who taught you?"

The mayor grew solemn and drew himself up in front of
me.

"Señor, when I was a very little boy I had to sit on the floor,
bolt upright, and my grandfather and his old brother-in-law
Porotu sat on the floor in front of me. They taught me many
things, just as in school nowadays, I know a lot. I had to repeat
and repeat it until it was quite right, every single word. I
learnt the songs too."

The mayor seemed so sincere that I did not know what to
believe: he certainly had shown in the quarry that he was no
mere light-weight, but at the same time he had a lively imagination and knew how to draw the long bow.

"If you knew how the statues were raised, why didn't you

tell all the people who have been here and asked, long before us?" I hazarded.

"No one asked *me*," the mayor answered proudly. He clearly thought any further explanation unnecessary.

I did not believe him. I coolly offered him a hundred dollars on the day when the biggest statue at Anakena stood in its place up on the temple wall. I knew there was not a single statue standing in its place on its old *ahu* in all Easter Island, and I was sure that I would never see one either, except the blind figures which had been temporarily raised down in their holes at the foot of Rano Raraku.

"It's a deal, señor," the mayor said quickly, and gave me his hand. "I'm going on a trip to Chile with the next warship, then I shall need dollars."

I laughed and wished him luck. The mayor was a bit of an oddity anyway. Soon afterwards the mayor's red-haired son came riding from the village with some notes on a scrap of paper. His father wanted me to talk to the governor and arrange that he himself and eleven other men should be allowed to go back to Hotu Matua's cave at Anakena to raise the largest statue. I rode in to the governor: both he and Father Sebastian laughed at the mayor and said, what I too suspected, that it was just empty brag. But Don Pedro the mayor stood before us hat in hand, with his lips quivering, and I held to my words. The governor gave his blessing on a piece of paper. Father Sebastian was much amused and thought it would be interesting to see anyhow.

Then the mayor came with two of his brothers and a chosen party of relatives who were all long-ears on their mother's side, the steward served out rations, and they moved into Hotu Matua's cave again. They were twelve men in all.

Just before sunset the mayor came over and dug a deep round hole in the ground between our tents, and then he disappeared.

When it was pitch dark and the camp was all quiet a queer uncanny music began, as the time before, but this time a curious thumping increased in strength together with a humming chorus which grew loud and shrill, led by the old woman's cracked voice. Lights were kindled all over the camp, and all the tents shone a ghostly green, like great paper lamps.

But we all came creeping out into the darkness without bringing our lights, for we had learnt the time before that the song must be sung in the dark.

This was quite a different performance. All the men had decked themselves with leaves and boughs: some of them swayed and danced and stamped as if in ecstasy, while the old woman sat as chief singer with closed eyes and led the choir with her queer second. The mayor's youngest brother stood with both legs down the newly-dug hole, in which we saw later that a container had been placed with a stone slab over it. He was stamping rhythmically with bare feet to produce a hollow drumming noise which helped to increase the underworld atmosphere of the whole performance. We could only just make out the ghostly group in the faint green light from the tent walls: but then a slender figure emerged from the dark background, and made all the boys open their eyes wide.

She was a young girl with bare legs and long flowing hair, wearing a light, loose-fitting dress. She came hovering into the green circle like a fairy nymph, and light-footed she danced before the drummer without any swaying of the hips or hula rhythm. It was such a pretty sight that we hardly dared breathe: she was so serious, a little shy, supple, slim and graceful, and she seemed scarcely to touch the grass with her bare feet.

Where did she come from? Who was she? When the sailors slowly realized that they were standing on solid earth, that this was not a dream, they began to whisper questions to one another, and to old Mariana and Eroria. They had thought for a long time that they knew every single beauty on the island: had the long-ears kept this nymph hidden in a bleaching cave? We were told that she was a niece of the mayor's; she was so young that she had never been out to a hula party with the others.

Meanwhile the singing and dancing went on, entirely fascinating. We heard and saw the whole performance three times. We understood only the refrain, which was about a *moai* which was to be erected at Kon-Tiki's command on an *ahu* at Anakena. The tune was quite unlike the stone-cutters' song, but just as catchy and rhythmical. When the drummer had crawled up out of his hole and all the rustling leaf-clad dancers were preparing to go, they were again given food to carry off to their cave. One of our men asked if they could not sing and dance some of the ordinary hula melodies as well, but they all refused to do that. The mayor consented to their singing the stone-cutters' song as an extra number, but said it was not seemly to sing any other kind of music, for these two songs were serious and would bring us good luck in our work. The other songs they could sing on other days, when they would not by so doing profane their ancestors and destroy the good luck which they were now seeking. So we heard the stone-cutters' song again, before they rustled off across the temple square and vanished into the darkness with the fairy nymph among them.

The sun had just begun to shine on the tent wall when I was woken by people moving about outside. It was the twelve long-ears who had come over from the cave to look at the statue and the problem that faced them. The largest statue at Anakena was the broad fellow who lay with his nose in the soil just beside our tent. He was a strapping sturdy giant, nearly ten feet wide across the shoulders and weighing between 25 and 30 tons. That meant more than two tons to lift for each of the twelve men. It was not surprising that they stood in a circle round the giant scratching their heads, but they seemed to have confidence in the mayor, and he walked about and looked at the colossus and took the situation with the most perfect calm.

Chief engineer Olsen also scratched his neck, shook his head and laughed.

"Well, if the mayor can manage that devil, he'll be a helluva fellow."

"He'll never do it."

"No, never!"

In the first place the giant lay at the foot of the wall with his head far down a slope, in addition he lay with his base four yards from the great slab on which he had originally stood. The mayor showed us some nasty little stones which he said had been wedged under the slab by the short-ears when they upset the statue.

Then he began to organize the work, as surely and calmly as if he had never done anything else. His only implements were three round poles, which he later reduced to two, a quantity

of boulders and a few big stones which the men had collected in
the neighbourhood. Even though the island is treeless today,
apart from a few newly-planted clumps of eucalyptus, trees
have always grown round the crater lake down in Rano Kao.
There the first explorers found woods of *toro miro* and hibiscus,
so the three wooden poles lay well within the scope of the
permissible.

The figure had its face buried deep in the earth, but the
men got the tips of their poles in underneath it, and while
three or four men hung and heaved at the farthest end of each
pole, the mayor lay flat on his stomach and pushed small
stones under the huge face. Occasionally we saw a faint
suggestion of movement in the giant when the eleven men got
an extra good heave on the ends of their poles, but otherwise
nothing happened except that the mayor lay there on his
stomach grubbing about with his stones. But the hours passed,
and the stones he moved out and shoved in became larger and
larger. When evening came the giant's head had been lifted a
good three feet from the ground, while the space beneath was
packed tight with stones.

Next day one of the poles was discarded as unnecessary,
and five men assembled at each of the others. The mayor set
his youngest brother to push the stones in under the statue:
he himself stood up on the *ahu* wall with arms outstretched like
the conductor of an orchestra, beating the air in time as he
shouted concise orders to the men.

"*Etahi, erua, etoru!* One, two, three! One, two, three! Hold
on, push under! Once more! One, two, three! One, two,
three!"

Today they had pushed both poles under the right side of the
giant. He tilted imperceptibly: but the imperceptible became
millimetres and millimetres became inches which became feet.
Then the two poles were moved over to the left side of the
giant: this was treated in the same way as the right, and
it too tilted up slowly, while all the time countless stones were
carefully pushed in and arranged underneath. After that they
turned back to the right side, then to the left again, and the
right, and the left. And the statue rose steadily, still lying in a
horizontal position on an ever rising heap of stones.

On the ninth day the huge figure lay stretched on its stomach on the top of an elaborately built tower the highest side of which was nearly twelve feet above the slope. It was quite uncanny to see this giant of nearly thirty tons lying stretched out up there, a whole man's height above the tops of our heads. The ten men could no longer reach the poles on which they hauled: they just hung dangling from ropes which were made fast to the ends. And still the giant had not begun to tip towards a standing position: we had not yet had a glimpse of the front of the figure as it lay on its stomach with the whole of its front hidden in the compact stone tower.

This looked deadly dangerous. Anette was no longer allowed to push her pram up to the statue with pebbles for the mayor. Now only the big strong men came staggering along barefoot like Neanderthal men with heavy boulders in their arms. The mayor was extremely careful, checking the position of every stone: the weight of the colossus was so great that some of the stones cracked under the pressure like lumps of sugar. A single careless placing could mean catastrophe. But it all had been thoroughly thought out, every little move was precisely and logically calculated. We stood with our hearts in our mouths as we saw the men pushing their bare toes in between the stones while clambering up the tower with more big blocks to be placed in position. Every single man was on the alert, and the mayor did not relax for a second. He held all the threads together and did not utter an unnecessary word. We had not known this side of him: we knew him in everyday life as a rather tiresome buffoon, a boaster and a bore, by no means popular among the men in the camp on account of his bragging and the shameless prices he put on his woodcarvings, even though admittedly they were by far the best in the island. But now he was calm and sensible, a born organizer and something of a practical genius. We began to see him with different eyes.

On the tenth day the statue lay at its highest. Imperceptibly the long-ears began to jerk it, feet foremost, in the direction of the *ahu* on which it was to stand.

On the eleventh day they began to raise the giant into a standing position by building the stones up even higher, but only under the face and chest.

On the seventeenth day a shrivelled old woman suddenly

appeared among the long-ears. Together with the mayor she laid a semi-circle of stones as large as eggs at a certain distance in front of the statue's foot, on the great slab on which the giant was now beginning to fumble for a foothold. This was preventive magic. The statue was now standing at a dangerously sharp angle and there was imminent danger of its slipping forward of its own weight and rolling down the steep wall of the *ahu* towards the beach. Quite apart from a slip of this kind, it could also capsize in any direction when it was suddenly tilted off the tower and on to its own base. Accordingly the mayor tied a rope round the giant's forehead, and this was made fast to stakes in the ground on all four sides.

Then the eighteenth working day came. While some hauled on a rope down towards the beach and others held fast to another twisted round a post in the middle of the camp, the last cautious jerks with a wooden pole began. Suddenly the giant began to move quite visibly and the orders rang out:

"Hold on! hold on!"

The giant rose in all his might and began to tilt upright, the tower was left standing without a counterpoise, a rumbling and sliding of stones began, and great blocks came crashing down on top of one another in a cloud of smoke and dust. But the colossus only wobbled and came quietly to rest in an upright position. There it stood, stiff and broad-shouldered, gazing out over the camp, unaffected by the change of scene since last it stood on the same foundation looking across the same temple square. The giant bulked so huge that the whole landscape was changed. The broad back was a landmark which could be seen far out to sea. We who lay in the tents at the foot of the wall and in the shadow of the giant's broad countenance no longer felt ourselves quite at home on Hotu Matua's old site. Wherever we went we saw the broad head close to us, towering over all the tent-tops like an old Norse mountain troll. When we moved about in the camp at night, the burly ogre seemed to come rolling forward out of the starry sky ready to strike over the green glowing tents in the darkness.

For the first time for hundreds of years one of the Easter Island giants stood in his place on the top of an *ahu*. The governor with his family, and the priest and the nuns came over by jeep. Horses' hoofs clattered outside the tents, everyone who could come from the village made a pilgrimage to Anakena to look at the mayor's work. The long-ears proudly removed the heap of stones, and the mayor basked placidly in the universal praise. He had known that he could provide the answer to one of Easter Island's oldest riddles. Had anyone expected anything less of him, Don Pedro Atan, a sage of long standing, mayor of the island and senior long-ear? If only he was paid for it he would put up every single statue in every single *ahu* on the whole island, and everything would be as in the good old days. What he earned now he shared with his friends, but if he were allowed to go to Chile when the warship came, he would get the President in person to throw wads of notes on to the table so that all the statues could be raised. He had raised this giant in eighteen days with eleven helpers and two poles: what could he not do with more men and more time?

I took the mayor away to a quiet spot and stood him up ceremoniously in front of me, with a hand on each of his shoulders. He stood there like a good little schoolboy, looking at me eagerly and expectantly.

"Don Pedro mayor," I said, "now perhaps you can tell me how your ancestors moved the figures round about on the island."

"They went, they walked," the mayor replied glibly.

"Rubbish," I said, disappointed and slightly irritated.

"Take it easy! I believe that they walked, and we must respect our forefathers who have said that they walked. But the forefathers who told me that had not seen it with their own eyes, so who knows if they did not use a *miro manga erua*?"

"What's that?"

The mayor drew on the ground a Y-shaped figure with crosspieces, and explained that it was a stone sledge made from a forked tree-trunk.

"At any rate they used those to drag the big blocks for the wall," he added by way of a concession. "And they made thick ropes from the tough bark of the *hau-hau* tree, as thick as the hawsers you have on board. I can make you a specimen. I can make a *miro manga erua* too."

A few paces from the camp one of the archaeologists had just dug out a statue which had been completely hidden in the sand

and therefore had never been given any number by Father
Sebastian. It had no eyes, and consequently had been abandoned before it had been set up at its destination. I pointed to it.

"Can you draw that *moai* across the plain with your men?"

"No, the other people in the village will have to help, and
they won't. We haven't enough people, even with all your
diggers."

The statue was not at all large: it was if anything below
medium size. I had an idea. The mayor helped me to get hold of
two sturdy oxen in the village: they were slaughtered and baked
by the long-ears between hot stones in a large earth oven.
Then we sent out invitations to a great feast for the natives
from the village, and soon the whole plain beyond the tents was
swarming with life. The long-ears carefully dug away the sand
which covered the oven, and a steaming mat of juicy banana
leaves came to light. When this uneatable vegetable carpet
was rolled away the steaming, well-cooked carcases appeared,
and the savour of the world's juiciest beefsteak spread among the
admiring crowd. Men and women encamped in groups all over
the grass with their hands full of large steaming pieces of meat,
and the long-ears served out heaps of newly baked sweet
potatoes, corncobs and pumpkins which had all been baked
along with the oxen in the same air-tight underground oven.
All round the party black and brown horses stood close-packed
and grazed with their saddles on. Guitars were produced, and
there was song and laughter and hula dancing on the temple
square.

Meanwhile the long-ears had made preparations for the
moving of the blind statue, and a hundred and eighty cheerful
natives, sated and jubilant, took their places on the long rope
which was made fast round the statue's neck. The mayor was in
great form, with a new white shirt and striped tie.

"One, two, three! One, two, three!"

Pang! The rope broke, and there was wild cheering as men
and vahines rolled over one another on the ground in chaos.
The mayor gave an embarrassed laugh, and ordered the rope
to be doubled and made fast to the figure. And now the giant
began to move—first in short jerks, but then suddenly it
seemed to break loose. The colossus slid away over the plain so
quickly that Lazarus, the mayor's assistant, jumped up on to

the giant's face and stood waving his arms and cheering like a gladiator in a triumphal procession, while the long lines of toiling natives hauled patiently and yelled at the pitch of their voices with enthusiasm. It went as quickly as if each of them had been towing an empty soap box.

We stopped the whole cavalcade a little way out on the plain. We had established that 180 natives with full stomachs could draw a twelve-ton statue across the plain, and if we had only had wooden runners and many more people we could have drawn a much larger figure.

At last we had seen how water and stone picks could gnaw the statues out of the solid rock, if only one had sufficient time; we had seen how ropes and wooden runners could move the giants from place to place, if only there were enough hands and feet to help; we had seen how the colossi could heave themselves into the air like inflated balloons and raise themselves to the tops of walls if only one applied the right technique. There was only one practical mystery left: how was the huge topknot placed on the head of a standing figure? The answer had already presented itself. The stone tower which had helped the giant on to his legs was a made road up to the head, and the red topknot could easily be lifted up its wall with the aid of the same simple system. When both statue and topknot were in their place up on the wall, all the stones were taken away: the statue remained there silently awaiting the future, and the mystery was not created until the sculptors died: how had this been done, without iron, without cranes or any machinery?

The answer was simple. An industrious and intelligent people had come to this tiny island with its unlimited peace. Total peace with ample time and traditions of an old technique were all that was needed to raise the Babel towers of Easter Island. The island's discoverers lived for hundreds of years as a nation with nothing but fish and whale as their neighbours on this, the loneliest settlement in the world. Our excavations showed us that spear-heads, the local fighting weapon, were not made on Easter Island until the third epoch began.

Not far from the tents lay a gigantic cylinder of red stone. It had been trundled seven miles from the topknot quarry on the other side of the island. The mayor wanted to trundle it on moveable logs for the few hundred yards which separated it from the camp, and then to place it on the head of the giant he had just set up. But at the very time when the long-ears were raising the giant, a new Easter Island mystery began to develop in place of all those we had now solved. It interfered with the whole of our programme, and the red topknot was left untouched by us where it had taken its last breather before the final sprint across the king's own site.

We ourselves had something new to think about.

CHAPTER VI

SUPERSTITION AGAINST
SUPERSTITION

THE lamp hung by a string from the roof and threw long shadows on the thin tent wall. I turned down the wick till the light was half extinguished and was just going to bed. The whole camp was dark and silent: only the roar of the surf down on the beach was to be heard. Yvonne had already crept into her sleeping bag on a camp-bed along the far wall of the tent, and Anette had long been asleep behind a low canvas barrier which divided her little pen from the rest of the tent. Then I heard someone outside scraping with a finger on the tent cloth, and a faint voice whispered in broken Spanish:

"Señor Kon-Tiki, may I come in?"

I pulled on my trousers again and cautiously moved the zipper of the tent door till I got my nose and one eye outside. Out in the darkness I could just see a dim figure with a parcel under its arm, and behind him the bulky silhouette of our still recumbent giant who was towering towards the starry sky. This was at the end of the seventh day of the long-ears' attempt to raise him.

"May I come in?" the voice whispered again imploringly.

I slowly opened the tent door and reluctantly allowed the figure to enter. He slipped in and stood in a stooping attitude, looking round him quite enthralled, with an admiring and grateful smile. I recognized him: he was the junior member of the mayor's team, a so-called false long-ear, an unusually good-looking lad of twenty, Estevan Pakarati by name. The tent was so low that he could not stand upright, and I asked him to sit down on the end of my bed.

He sat for a few moments with an embarrassed smile on his face, searching vainly for words. Then he clumsily thrust at me a round parcel in crumpled brown paper, and said:

"This is for you."

I unfolded the paper, and out came a hen. A stone hen. It was quite realistically shaped, life-size and did not remind me

of anything which had ever been made on Easter Island.
Before I could say anything he hastened to add:

"Everyone in the village says that Señor Kon-Tiki has been
sent to us to bring good luck. That is why you have given us so
many things. All the people smoke your cigarettes and are
grateful."

"But where did you get this stone from?"

"It's a *moa*, a hen. My wife said I was to give it to you by
way of thanks, because it's she who gets all the cigarettes you
give me every day."

Yvonne leaned out of her sleeping-bag and took a length of
cloth out of a suitcase. But Estevan refused emphatically to
accept the cloth. No, this was not a barter deal, this was a
present for Señor Kon-Tiki.

"And this is a present for your wife," I said. He gave way
reluctantly, thanked me again for all the food and cigarettes,
and all that he and the other long-ears received every day, and
then he crept out of the tent and disappeared into the darkness.
He was going to the village for the night. But before he left he
begged me to hide the hen so that no one should see it.

I looked at the well-shaped hen again. It was a masterly
piece of work. The stone smelt a little of smoke. For the first
time I had seen a real artistic product of the natives which was
not merely one of the everlastingly repeated old wooden
figures, or a copy of the great statues. I put the stone hen away
under my bed and blew out the light.

Next evening, when all was quiet, the whispering voice was
there again. What did he want now? Today he had a new
stone with him, this time a crouching man with a long bird's
bill, holding an egg in one hand. The figure was carved in high
relief on a flat stone and was a variation of the sculptures in the
rock at the bird-men's ruins of Orongo village. It was an elegant
piece of work. His wife had sent the figure as a present because
she had received the cloth from us. The stone had been cut by
her father, but we must not show it to anyone. We sent him off
with a fresh parcel for his wife. When I was putting the stone
away I noticed that it smelt very strongly of acrid smoke: it was
still rather damp and had been thoroughly scrubbed with
sand. Something strange was going on. But what?

I puzzled my head so long over these stones which smelt so

peculiar and were so unusually well made that at last I could restrain myself no longer. Late the next afternoon I called the mayor into the tent and rolled down the walls outside the mosquito net.

"I must ask you something if you promise absolutely not to say a word to anyone."

The mayor was full of curiosity and promised to say nothing.

"What do you think of these?" I asked, pulling the two stones out of the case.

The mayor started back as if he had burnt his fingers: his eyes stood out of his head as if he had seen an evil spirit or the muzzle of a pistol, and he turned quite pale.

"Where did you get those? Where did you get those?" he burst out.

"I can't tell you, but what do you say to them?"

The mayor still sat staring, drawn back against the tent wall.

"There's no one on the island but myself who can make figures like those," he said, looking as if he had suddenly stood face to face with his own soul. As he sat staring at the figures something suddenly seemed to occur to him: he looked at them, I felt, more curiously, till he had reached some conclusion in his own mind. Then he turned quietly to me and said:

"Pack up both stones and get them on board the ship so that no one on the island can see them. If you're given any more, just accept them and hide them on board, even if they look new."

"But what are they?"

"They're serious things; they're family stones."

The mayor's eccentric behaviour did not make me much wiser, but I understood that I had involuntarily put my fingers into inflammable material. Estevan's father-in-law was engaged in some queer business.

Estevan was a naïve, friendly soul who was always grateful and willing to help. When he came creeping along in the dark again another evening I determined to find out what was really going on. I made him sit down on the edge of my bed and started a long conversation. But he was too eager to be able to listen to me: he had three stones in a sack, and when he rolled them out on to the sleeping-bag I was completely speechless.

One stone depicted three curious classical heads with moustaches and long beards, and the heads were carved in a circle round the stone so that the beard of one imperceptibly blended with the hair of the next. The second stone was a club with eyes and mouth, and the third was a man standing with a large rat hanging from between his teeth. Not only was this a choice of motif and a style of art which was alien to Easter Island: I had never seen anything like it from any part of the globe. I did not believe for a moment that Estevan's father-in-law had made it. There was something grim, almost heathenish, about these stones, and this was reflected in the way the lad looked at them and handled them.

"Why has the man a rat in his mouth?" I asked. I could not think of a more sensible question on the spur of the moment.

The lad became still more eager. He drew a little nearer and told me in a hushed voice that it was a mourning custom of his ancestors. When a man lost his wife or one of his children, anyone he was fond of, he had to catch a *kioe*, a native rat of the edible kind that lived on the island before the ships' rats came. Then he had to run all round the coast of the island without resting, with the rat in his mouth, and kill all the people who placed themselves in his path.

"This was how a warrior showed his grief," Estevan explained, with ill-concealed admiration in his voice.

"Who made the mourning man?"

"My wife's grandfather."

"It was her father who made the others?"

"I'm not sure, her father made some and her grandfather others. She has seen her father making some."

"Is her father working for me?"

"No, he is dead. These are holy, serious stones."

This was becoming more and more puzzling. I was told again that he and his wife had heard in the village that I was sent to the island by higher powers. The whole thing seemed completely nonsensical.

"But where have you and your wife kept these stones since her father died? In the house?"

He shifted a little where he sat, and then he said:

"No, in a cave, a family cave."

I said nothing. Then the confidence came. The whole cave was full of such things. But no one could find it, no one at all. Only his wife knew where the entrance was. She was the only person who could get in. He himself had never seen the cave. But he knew roughly where it was, for he had waited while his wife went in and fetched the stones. She had told him that the cave was full.

Now Estevan and I shared a secret. The next night he came it was easier to talk. Estevan proposed in a whisper that he should try to persuade his wife to take me into the cave with her. Then I myself could choose the stones I liked best, for there were such quantities that it was quite impossible to bring them all to me. But the worst problem, he explained, was that in this matter his wife was strong-willed and hard, as hard as rock. He himself had never been allowed to go into the cave. If she said yes, we must steal into the village in the middle of the night, for the cave was not far from the house, in the middle of the actual village area.

He told me that his wife had scrubbed the stones with sand and water before she sent them to me: she was afraid some native might see them and realize that she was taking old things from the family cave. The smell he thought came from the cave, until it occurred to him that they were dried over the kitchen fire after being washed. He would get this washing stopped, since I wished it. His wife had asked if there was anything special I wanted from the cave. But it was not easy for me to know what to ask for, when not even Estevan could tell me what there was. One thing was certain. Ethnographical art treasures of incalculable value had begun to emerge from a hiding-place on the island.

It was a simple matter for the mayor to notice which of his men disappeared from Hotu Matua's cave at night, and, for all I know, he may also have used his eyes well outside the tent in the dark. At any rate he took me aside one day and confided to me, with a knowing look in his eye, that Estevan's father-in-law had been a good friend of his till he died many years before. He was the last man on the island who had made "serious" stones, the mayor added: stones which they kept for themselves, and which were not for sale.

"What did they use the stones for, then?" I asked.

"They brought them out and showed them at feasts: they took them along to the dances."

Nothing more was to be got out of the mayor on that subject.

I had another meeting with Estevan later, and that night he came back with several stones from the cave. Then his nocturnal visits suddenly ceased. At last I sent for him late one afternoon, and when he came into the tent he looked crestfallen and disappointed. His wife had discovered that the two spirits who guarded her cave were angry at her having taken so much out, and she now flatly refused to take me with her into the cave. So Estevan had nothing more to bring me from her cave. He himself was willing to do anything in the world for me, but his wife could not be persuaded; she was so hard, the lad repeated, as hard as stone. It was just for that reason, he added, that her father had chosen her to inherit the secret of the family cave.

During the time in which Estevan was paying his nightly visits with the stones, a great deal else was happening on the island. The archaeologists were continually making new and surprising finds, and the natives were displaying more and more superstition. On the top of Rano Kao, Ed had discovered the walls of a hitherto unknown temple which he was excavating with a native team, and one day when I was visiting him two of his diggers went straight to the point.

"Confess that you are one of our family who left Easter Island many generations ago," one of them said.

"We know it, you may just as well tell the truth," said the other.

I laughed and told them that I was a genuine Norwegian and came from the other side of the globe. But the men would not give in: they had unmasked me, so why could I not admit it? They had heard the legend of a man who had left the island in ancient times and never came back. Besides, if I had never been on the island before, how could I have gone straight to Anakena and set up my camp exactly where Hotu Matua had settled when he first landed?

I just had to give it up and laugh the whole thing off: it was no use my saying anything.

On the same day Arne had got the natives to turn over a

A bird-man, *tangata manu,* and the long-eared ghost man *Moai
kava-kava.*

large square block of stone close to the path in Rano Raraku. He thought it looked rather queer. Everyone knew that stone, and most of the natives must have sat on it. But it had never been turned over till now, and to everyone's astonishment what appeared was an absolutely strange head with thick lips, a flat nose and large pouches under the eyes. The large square face had nothing in common with the known style of art of Easter Island: again something new had turned up, something that bewildered the natives. Who had given Señor Arne a tip that it was worth while to turn that stone over? The natives declared to Arne that they knew that Señor Kon-Tiki was in contact with the supernatural.

Then again, one evening Yvonne and I were over in Hotu Matua's cave with the mayor and his long-ears. They were lying there regaling themselves with thick slices of bread spread with butter and jam, and the coffee pot was simmering outside.

"We only get sweet potatoes and fish at home," said the mayor, patting his stomach with pleasure.

The tin with the wick in it was lighted, and again the talk was of old days, of the time when a king named Tuu-ko-ihu had discovered two sleeping ghosts at the foot of the red cliff down in the topknot quarry. Both ghosts were long-ears, with pendulant lobes down to their necks: they had beards and long hooked noses, and were so thin that the ribs stood out from their breasts. The king went home quietly and hastened to carve their portrait in wood before he forgot what they looked like. This was the origin of the *moai-kava-kava*, the weird figure which always recurs without variation in the wood carving of Easter Island. No sooner had the men finished their meal than they produced their chunks of wood and began to work on their *moai-kava-kavas*, while some of the older ones told stories.

This opened the door to ghost stories which might well have made anyone's hair stand on end, while flickering shadows danced round us on the uneven walls of the cave. We heard of cannibal ghosts which came at night and demanded intestines, of a female ghost which lay right out in the sea with an immensely long arm and drew solitary people to her from the cliffs, and of others which went about pushing folk into the

Above: Ready to be launched from the quarry. Even high up on the mountain complete statues lay wedged with loose stones, waiting to be transported down the steep slopes, often to a distant destination beyond the ridges on the horizon.

Below: An old fellow from the island's earliest period showed his face for the first time when we set him up near the village among a group of modern Easter Islanders. Father Sebastian and the skipper standing behind him are surrounded by typical inhabitants of the village.

Alien gods, unknown even to the natives, emerged from the bosom of the earth. This kneeling giant, sitting on his heels with his hands on his thighs, was unlike anything previously known on Easter Island.

An old navigator with a ship on his chest. A three-masted sailing vessel appeared when Arne uncovered the chest of one of the giants. The line on the right leads down to a turtle on the statue's stomach.

Above: The fish bite in the Pacific for those who know the ropes, and a good fisherman need never go hungry.
Below: Bill with his headless red pillar statue at Vinapu, and Ed with a stone head dug out when he discovered the old solar observatory at Oronga.

sea. Lazarus, the mayor's assistant, had a grandmother who had been pushed down a precipice by a malignant ghost, but there were also many spooks which were friendly and helped individual people. Most of them were friendly to one particular family and hostile to everyone else.

One ghost story followed another till they all suddenly recollected something which had happened to themselves that day. "You were present yourself," one of them said to me, "and you didn't look a bit surprised." Then they explained. They knew that their ancestors had supernatural help when they moved the statues about on the island, but when they erected them they had had to toil themselves with poles and stones, even if the supernaturals had been present then too and had done part of the work. But today they had all of them seen something they had never experienced before. An invisible *aku-aku* had been there and helped them in the work of raising the statue. They had had luck with them because of their singing.

They showed us, with a little figure and two sticks, how they had been working to push up one side of the statue. While doing this, they said, the giant's head had suddenly risen several inches of itself, without anyone having touched it.

"Very strange: it was very strange," the man up on the ledge assured us.

Thor junior had been sent as assistant to Ed on the top of Rano Kao at this time. The ruins up there were to be mapped. Ed and Bill were staying as guests in the governor's bungalow at the foot of the hill, and the governor's wife, who always showed us boundless hospitality, invited Thor also to stay in the house, as the camp was too far away. But Thor had a boy's longing for adventure: he had decided that he would like to live in the bird-men's ruined village on the top of the cliff. Several of the ancient stone huts were in a habitable state, and even if the floor was hard and the roof low he had shelter in all kinds of weather and a view the like of which could not be found in all the kingdoms of the world. The whole of Hangaroa village and the greater part of the island lay spread out at his feet, and the Pacific stretched beyond to the vault of heaven. The bird-men's half-subterranean stone huts lay closely side by side, against the curiously sculptured outcrops

F

up on the topmost knife-edge of the volcano: a few steps from
the threshold the cliff flung itself sheer for a thousand feet
down into the sea where the bird islands lay. And a few steps
away in the opposite direction another giddy drop fell just
as steeply into the gigantic crater of Rano Kao, which lay like
a huge bowl, a mile wide from edge to edge. The bottom far
down there was covered with a speckled green cloth, a dangerous
bog in which tarns and little open pools shone out everywhere.

When Thor went up with sleeping-bag and provisions
the natives were panic-stricken. They begged and prayed him
to come down for the night: they went to Ed and asked him
to order the boy down. I myself received a message at Anakena
saying that the boy must not sleep alone in the ruins of Orongo:
he would be taken by an *aku-aku*. But warnings were of no
avail. Thor had found the castle of his dreams: he would camp
alone at Orongo.

At the end of the day, when Thor remained on the top while
the others came down, Ed's native foreman was seriously
troubled, and finally sent up three volunteers to keep Thor
company during the night. When the sun set, and the trade
wind roared in the dark abysses round him, Thor had his first
fright. Three shadows came marching into the ruins—three
native girls had been sent to spend the night there. The girls
were terrified at being up in the ruins in the dark: one of them
was almost crazy with fear. For her the echo down in the black
crater was straightway an *aku-aku*. She saw another in a
twinkling star mirrored in a black pool at the bottom of the
giant bowl. There were *aku-akus* everywhere. When daylight
came the three girls were only too glad to hurry down to the
village again.

On the following nights Thor stayed up on the rim alone:
he was sitting there happily admiring the sunrise when the
others came climbing up from the valley. He had become a
hero in the eyes of the natives: they deluged him daily with
melons, pine-apples and baked fowls; accordingly the boy was
not to be got down from the cliff-top. The natives were now
reassured: Kon-Tiki-iti-iti was quite safe up in Orongo alone,
he had a protecting power on his side. Thor stayed up on the
top for four months. The *aku-aku* left him in peace.

This was not the end of superstition: quite the contrary.

The next approach came from Lazarus, just when I was worming the first secret of the family cave out of young Estevan. Lazarus was the mayor's right-hand man and they both agreed he was one of the most important on the island. He was one of the natives' three elected representatives, and according to the mayor an extremely wealthy person. The blood of long-ears as well as short-ears flowed in Lazarus' veins, with a slight infusion from casual European visitors. He was a physical masterpiece, but Darwin might have appropriated his features to support his theory of evolution, and if his skull is ever dug up people may suspect Easter Island of having been the cradle of mankind. But in spite of the low sloping forehead with projecting brows, the equally protruding lower face with small chin, large lips and a perfect row of teeth between them, a thick nose and an animal's watchful eyes—despite his whole appearance—Lazarus was no stupid ape. On the contrary, he was unusually smart and mentally alert, and he had a keen sense of humour. But he too was highly superstitious.

One day a report came from Ed that he had found several unknown rock paintings on a large slab in the roof of a ruined house in Orongo. At about the same time Arne had found a new statue, differing from those already known, buried in the earth at the foot of Rano Raraku. Late in the afternoon, when the long-ears had ceased work for the day and sauntered over to Hotu Matua's cave, Lazarus, with an air of secrecy, took me aside for a little talk.

"The only thing you need now is a *rongo-rongo*," he said, slyly studying my face to see the effect of his words.

At once I realized that something special was brewing, and pretended to be casual.

"There are none left on the island today," I remarked.

"Yes, there are *some*," said Lazarus cautiously.

"But they're rotten and crumble away if you touch them."

"No, my cousin has touched two."

I did not believe him. He saw it, and asked me to come with him behind the temple wall where the statue was abandoned for the day, lying on its stone tower. Here he told me in a whisper that he had two twin cousins, Daniel and Alberto Ika. Alberto had been born an hour after Daniel, yet it was he who had been chosen to inherit the secret of the entrance to their family cave, which was full of curious things, even some *rongo-rongo*. Two years ago Alberto had been in the cave and brought out two *rongo-rongo*, which he had taken home. They were of wood, and one of them shaped like a flat fish with a tail. Both were full of small figures, they were almost black and extremely hard, though they were very old. Lazarus and many others had seen them. But Alberto had broken the taboo by taking the tablets away from the cave, and in the night while he was asleep an *aku-aku* had come and had begun to poke and pinch him till he awoke. Then he had looked out of the window and seen thousands of tiny little men about to climb into his room. He was almost crazy with fear, and had gone straight back to the cave and put both the tablets back in their places. This *rongo-rongo* cave was somewhere near the Hanga-o-Teo valley, and Lazarus would do everything in his power to make his cousin summon up courage to go in and fetch the tablets again.

I gradually extracted from Lazarus the information that his family had more than one cave, Lazarus himself had access to another cave which also was near the Hanga-o-Teo valley: there were no *rongo-rongo* there, but many other things. I tried to get Lazarus to take me with him to this cave, but here his co-operation ended. He looked at me with a crushing magisterial eye and declared that it would be the end of both him and me. The family *aku-aku* lived in the cave; and there were also the skeletons of two of his ancestors. If an unauthorized person tried to enter unlawfully the *aku-aku* would take a fearful revenge. The entrance to the cave was the most sacred of all secrets. I tried to laugh at the *aku-aku* and make Lazarus, as an intelligent fellow, see reason, but it was like hammering at a wall. I got nowhere.

The only result I secured after persistent efforts at persuasion was to get Lazarus to promise to bring me something from the cave himself. But what would I like to have? A bird-man with or without an egg? The cave contained every possible thing except *rongo-rongo*. I proposed that he should bring several different things, so that I could see for myself and be able to choose. But this was no good. The cave was full of strange things, and he could only risk bringing one single item. Here the conversation was interrupted by a message to me, and Lazarus said good-bye and vanished.

Next day I was out watching the long-ears carrying stones to the tower they were building under the statue, when the mayor and Lazarus came up to me for a chat.

"The *aku-aku* is helping, you see," the mayor said in a low voice. "It would have been impossible for the twelve of us to manage this alone without supernatural help."

They told me how they had baked a fowl that day, in an earth oven near the cave, to make the statue rise more quickly.

I met a flood of protests from Lazarus and the mayor when I tackled them both at once and tried to kill their superstition. They looked at me as if I was a blind idiot when I maintained that there were no *aku-akus*. Of course there were. In old days the whole island was full of them: there were not so many now, but they could patter off the names of many places on the island where *aku-akus* still lived. There were both male and female *aku-akus*. Some were friendly and others were evil. People who had talked with them declared that they had shrill piping voices, and there was no end to proofs of their existence.

I could not even get in a word. I could as easily have persuaded them that there were no fish in the sea or chickens in the village. I was beginning to realize one thing. The air of the island was filled with some lunatic form of superstition, and this acted as an unforceable barrier to caves with contents hitherto unknown to the outside world.

I drove in to see Father Sebastian. No living person knew Easter Island and its natives as well as he. I knew too that what I told him would remain a confidence between us two. In his book about the island I had found the following passage:

> There were also secret caves which were the property of particular families, and only the most important persons in a family knew the entrance to their respective secret caves. These served as hiding-places for valuable things, such as inscribed tablets, *rongo-rongo*, or statuettes. The secret of the exact situation of the entrance is buried in the graves with the last survivors from the old times. . . .

I told Father Sebastian that I had reason to believe that secret family caves were still in use on the island. He started back in astonishment and tugged at his beard.

"Oh, no!"

I told him, without mentioning names, of the mysterious stones I had obtained. He was soon ablaze with eagerness and wanted to hear where the cave was. I could only tell him the little I knew, and that it was impossible for me to get to the cave because of the ghost stories. Father Sebastian had been walking quickly up and down the room in his long white gown. He stopped abruptly and clasped his head in despair.

"They are hopeless with their superstitions," he said. "Old Mariana came to me the other day and declared quite seriously that you were not a human being. Their superstition is so ingrained that it is no good expecting to get it all out of their heads in one generation. They have an immense respect for their own ancestors, and that of course one can understand. They are good Christians, but oh, their superstition!"

He told me quite resignedly that he had not yet been able to get out of his admirable housekeeper Eroria's head the belief that she was descended from a whale which had been stranded in Hotuiti bay. Eroria only replied that he could not possibly know anything about it even if he was a priest, for she had heard it from her father, who had been told it by his father, who had it from his father, and he was the one who ought to know best, for it was he who had been the whale!

We agreed that I should have a hard nut to crack: it was not so easy to get the natives to accompany one to places where they thought that devils and evil spirits barred the way. Father Sebastian proposed to lend me some holy water: the natives had a great respect for it, and perhaps they might pluck up courage if we sprinkled it at the entrance to the cave. The conclusion we arrived at, however, was that Father Sebastian must not come into the picture openly: he said himself that he was the last person to whom they would come with secrets of this kind. But we must keep in regular contact at all costs; I must come to him even in the middle of the night if I should obtain access to a secret cave.

The insane superstition of the intelligent people of Easter Island was hard to understand until I began to draw parallels with our own familiar world. I have heard of twenty-storey houses which have no thirteenth floor, and of aeroplanes in which the numbers of the seats jump from twelve to fourteen. Are there people who believe that an evil spirit watches over the number thirteen—a nameless spirit of disaster? All that is wanting to complete the parallel is that we should call it an evil *aku-aku*. I have heard of people who are afraid of spilling salt, of breaking a looking-glass, or who believe that a black cat crossing the road may affect your future. These people believe in an *aku-aku*, only they do not use the name. Is it then so strange that the natives of the world's most desolate island suspect their ancestors of wizardry and of walking as ghosts among their giant portraits, which our own race openly calls a mystery? Is there not more excuse for imagining an *aku-aku* among skulls and skeletons in the dark caves of Easter Island than in the skin of a friendly black cat strolling contentedly across the road on a sunny summer day?

Superstition on Easter Island had been ingrained in the people for generations. I had not taken this into account, nor had anyone done so before me. This oversight had been a major omission which had so far prevented all access to the real mind of the natives. It was no use trying to quench the flames of superstition with reason: all my explanations were received like water on a duck's back. Nor can a real forest fire be put out with water: one must start a counter-fire. Fire is fire's worst enemy provided it is kept under control. The natives had inherited the belief in evil spirits residing all over the place: there were certain areas where some of the natives never even dared go, least of all at night. The mayor and Lazarus confided to me gloomily that it was a real menace to the island.

I racked my brains over the problem, and came to the conclusion that superstition might be superstition's deadliest enemy, if kindled as a regular counter-fire. Those who believed that I was in contact with their ancestors ought to accept as well a message passed on from the same source, a message advising them to abolish all the old and dreaded curses and taboos. Why not? I lay and tossed about in my sleeping-bag all night. Yvonne thought it was a crazy plan, but agreed anyway: it ought to be tried.

Next day the mayor, Lazarus and I had a long meeting up in the rocks behind our camp. It was incredible what I was to learn when once I had begun to gossip with them. I told them first—what was quite true—that I knew very well the secret of the taboo, and that I myself was the first who had paddled a

canoe on the taboo waters of Vai Po, in an accursed underground cave on Fatuhiva. There too, without any evil conse-
quences, I had been down in the secret vault of a taboo *pae-pae*
wall. The mayor and Lazarus sat and listened with eyes wide
open: they did not know that there were other islands besides
their own which had taboos. I knew enough about the taboo
system to impress both of them beyond limits, not least
because I could quote stories I myself had heard from natives of
Fatuhiva, describing disasters of the strangest sorts which had
overtaken various people who had infringed their forefathers'
taboo.

The mayor sat pale and shuddering. He laughed shame-
facedly, and confessed that whenever he heard stories of this
kind he shivered with cold even in the baking hot sun, for they
had had exactly, just *exactly*, the same experiences of the taboo
on this island too. And now I was the one who had to listen
quietly to local examples of the dire effect of the taboo—of a
whole family who had become lepers, of a shark which had
bitten off an arm, of a fearful flood which had drowned all the
people in a reed house, and of many who had gone mad because
the *aku-akus* had poked and punched them night after night, all
because various attempts had been made to break the taboos
of family caves.

"What happened to you on Fatuhiva?" Lazarus asked,
greedily curious.

"Nothing," I said.

Lazarus looked almost disappointed.

"That's because you've got *mana*," he said. *Mana* is the term
for a kind of magical quality, a source of supernatural strength.

"Señor Kon-Tiki has not only *mana*," the mayor said slily to
Lazarus, "he has an *aku-aku* which brings good fortune."

I grasped this straw.

"So I can quite well go into a taboo cave without anything
happening," I declared.

"Nothing happens to you, but something will happen to us
if we show you the cave," said Lazarus, pointing to himself and
nodding with a wry grin.

"Not when I am with you. My *aku-aku* is too strong for
that," I tried to argue.

But Lazarus found this hard to digest: his family *aku-aku*

would take vengeance on him: my *aku-aku* could not prevent
that even if it protected *me*. And I could never in all my life
find the opening by myself, even if I stood as near to it as I was
to him now.

"Lazarus belongs to a very important family," the mayor
boasted on his friend's behalf. "His family has many caves.
They are rich."

Lazarus spat proudly.

"But I too have *mana*," the mayor declared, and went on to
boast of his own supernatural power. "It's my *aku-aku* which
helps us to lift the statue. I have three *aku-akus* inside a small
ahu in La Pérouse Bay. One is the figure of a bird."

Now we all knew that we were three important persons sitting
together up among the rocks. The two others began to brag
about who knew most about what brought "good luck" and what
brought "bad luck," and I realized that quite unknowingly I
had slipped through a narrow needle's eye that very day. The
mayor told me that he had been looking on when I was tying
a knot in the guy-rope of the tent that morning, and this
had confirmed his suspicion that I knew the secrets of "good
luck," for I had tied the knot from the right and not from
the left.

With this concession as a bridge-head I delivered my final
attack. I said that I knew their family caves had been declared
taboo by the ancestors only to protect the valuable contents.
The only thing that brought "bad luck" was to barter the
figures in the cave to tourists and sailors who might not realize
what they were and after a time might throw them away. But
it brought "good luck" to trade the same figures with men of
science who would preserve them in a museum. A museum
was somewhat like a church, a place where people could only
walk about quietly and look at the figures behind glass cases,
a protected spot where no one could break them or throw them
away. The evil spirits would depart from the caves together with
the figures, and so there would be nothing more to be afraid of
on the island.

I thought I detected that this made a special impression on
Lazarus, and I was not wrong. That night there was again some-
one whispering "Kon-Tiki," and scraping the wall of the tent.
It was not Estevan this time, but Lazarus. He gave me a sack

F*

containing an old flat stone head with the most peculiar
features and long thin moustaches. There were spiders' webs
in the holes, and the head had neither been washed nor
scrubbed with sand. I learnt a good deal about the cave Lazarus
had been in. It was full of sculptures: he had seen a stone bowl
with three heads, strange animals and human beings, and
models of ships. This cave near Hanga-o-Teo was inherited
from his great-grandfather, and he owned it together with
his three sisters. No "bad luck" had befallen him, and now he
was going to talk to his two eldest sisters, to get permission
to bring more things from the cave. There was no need for him
to say anything to his younger sister: she was only twenty and
did not understand such matters.

Lazarus felt himself a hero now that he had been in the cave.
His family had four caves. The *rongo-rongo* cave where Alberto
had been was supposed to be near the one from which he had
just come, but only Alberto knew the entrance. Then there was
one in the cliffs at Vinapu: Lazarus knew that one and would go
there another night. The fourth cave was in the very rock face
of the statue-mountain Rano Raraku. Three different families
each had their own section in this important cave; it was full
of skeletons, and he would never dare set foot in it; nor did he
know the entrance.

I asked whether, if three families knew the entrance to the
same cave, they never stole from one another. Oh no, he said,
that presented no problem: each family owned its own
well-defined section, and had its own *aku-aku* there to look
after it.

Lazarus received dress material for his two elder sisters and
disappeared into the night.

Next day the mayor was standing as calm as ever in his place
on the *ahu* wall, directing his long-ears as they hung and swung
at the end of their lofty poles. He had not betrayed by one
gesture that he too had a cave: he stood there as undisturbed as
ever, beating time with his arms and directing the work. All
that he had boasted of was his own helpful *aku-aku* and three
small colleagues in the spirit world who lived in an *ahu* in La
Pérouse Bay.

I watched him standing there calm and cool, organizing
the work like a trained engineer. It would be strange if

Lazarus' family had four caves, and the chief of the long-ears himself not a single one. But stronger medicine would be required to make the mayor talk.

Later in the day I saw a chance of getting the two men aside once more. I had no idea whether the mayor had a cave, but at any rate he must know a good deal about their existence on the island. I asked in the course of conversation if many families had secret caves. The mayor admitted that there were some who had, but said that hardly anyone got to know anything about other people's caves. Most of the caves had been lost, because usually only one member of the family at a time had the whole responsibility of knowing the entrance. Sometimes this person died before a successor had been initiated into the secret, and the system was so ingenious that no one could ever find the opening again. A great number of family caves had been lost in this way, and both the mayor and Lazarus stressed that such a loss brought "bad luck."

"That is just what ought to be stopped," I explained. "That is why the things ought to be moved to a safe museum, where no one can steal them and where they cannot be lost. A watchman is always there to look after them."

The mayor reflected a little. He did not feel quite convinced. Those who had made the things had said that they were to be hidden in secret caves, not kept in houses.

"That was because the reed huts of their day were not safe," I said. "The caves were the safest places they had, but they are not really safe, since everything is lost whenever the entrance is forgotten. There's no danger of anyone forgetting the location of a museum door."

The mayor did not entirely accept my way of reasoning. His forefathers' old commandments had more power than all the *mana* he attributed to me. After all, he had both *mana* and *aku-aku* himself, and he had not seen any sign of his forefathers having changed their view on the taboos.

I was stuck. Not even Lazarus looked quite confident now. Then I decided to carry out a crazy plan. It must be possible to show the superstitious mayor some impressive sign which would convince him that his forefathers had now at long last abolished their deadly taboo.

At the foot of the plain and right next to the camp lay an

old *abu* with fallen statues. The original classical wall had been sadly damaged during the rebuilding period of the second epoch: the work had never been completed, and later destructive hands had been at work: blocks and boulders in great numbers lay strewn about on the sand in front of the façade. Bill had been over one Sunday and looked at the damaged wall, and as he was brushing the sand away from a slab he saw something which he thought was a whale's nose cut in relief on the stone. A large block lay on top of it and covered the rest of the figure, but before riding back to Vinapu Bill mentioned the stone to me. The photographer and I went over to the heap of stones and searched till we found what Bill had seen, and when we turned the slab over a figure clearly representing a whale about three feet long rolled down on to the sand below us. It now lay with the shapeless back of the stone upwards, looking like all the other slabs and boulders which were strewn about in the neighbourhood.

This gave me an idea. No one had noticed what we had done. I asked the mayor and Lazarus to come to the camp about midnight when everything was dark and quiet: we would then hold a magical seance and get their ancestors to send a work of art made by them up out of the earth as a sign that they were no longer afraid to disclose their old secrets. The days of taboo were over.

The mayor and Lazarus were as keen as mustard, and when it was dark they came stealing to the camp. Just before they came Estevan had left my tent upon his last nocturnal visit. Yvonne was frightened at the thought of what might happen and was lying wide awake in the dark tent, listening. Everyone else was asleep. I explained to the two men that we must stand in a row and hold on to each other's shoulders. Then we would walk slowly in a wide ring, and next morning we should find within that ring something which their forefathers themselves had made and laid there as a sign that I was right in saying that no one would any longer be punished by *aku-akus* for breaking old taboos.

So off we went, I myself ahead with my arms crossed, then the mayor with his hands on my shoulders, and Lazarus behind him. I could not see at all where I was putting my feet, and was so convulsed with laughter that I nearly stumbled over every stone: but the two I had in tow were so solemn and absorbed by the ceremony that they might have been following me on a lead. When the round was completed and we stood before my tent again, we bowed deeply to one another without exchanging a word, and each of us disappeared quietly to his own sleeping quarters.

The mayor was on the spot as soon as daylight broke, and told me of two mysterious lights which had appeared outside Hotu Matua's cave in the night. They did not come from the jeep, so they were certainly some sign of "good luck." As soon as the day's programme had been organized for the rest of the expedition, I fetched the mayor and Lazarus and asked them to bring the best and most honourable man they had to help us search inside the ring we had made in the night. The mayor promptly chose his youngest brother, Atan Atan, a little fellow with a moustache and large innocent eyes, who naïvely told me in confidence that the choice was well made, he was a good fellow with a heart of gold: if I did not believe him I could ask anyone in the village. We took Atan over to the heap of stones and began to search. I asked them to turn over every single stone which lay strewn over the sandy ground to see if one of them was a work of art made by their own ancestors. To make it more dramatic we began at the opposite end of the circle so as not to find the whale immediately.

Atan happened to be the first to find something—a curious red stone object; then I myself found an old stone file and a pretty little obsidian adze. Soon afterwards came a shout from Atan, who had turned up a large slab and brushed away the sand from its underside. The mayor, Lazarus and I rushed up: on the slab was a beautiful relief figure of a whale. But it was quite a different whale from the one I knew of, so there must be two of them. All the long-ears from the stone statue had rushed over to see, and from the camp the cook, steward and photographer came running. The mayor's eyes were popping out of his head, and his chest was heaving as if he had just finished a hard sprint. Both he and Atan were filled with admiration and murmured praise of my aku-aku's power. Lazarus became very serious. He said with assumed tranquillity that this area had belonged to his own family and their aku-aku. The mayor shivered. All the natives looked at me as if

I were a strange animal. I knew myself that I had now a still greater surprise in reserve.

"Have you seen a sculpture like that before?" I asked.

No, nobody had, but this was an old picture of a *mamama niuhi*, a dolphin, they could all see that.

"Then I'll make another of the very same sort come up inside the circle," I said.

The mayor sent his men back to collect boulders for the statue, while we four went on searching. Stone after stone was turned over, and we were nearing the goal. Then the steward called out that lunch was ready. I ordered the others to wait till I came back: it was I who would make the whale appear.

While we were sitting in the mess tent eating we heard shouts and arguments from the distance, and the mayor came running to fetch me, quite desperate. Unseen by him, two of the younger men had gone inside the circle and searched on their own account: they had found the whale and were carrying it off between them to Hotu Matua's cave. They were going to sell it to me. The mayor was seriously worried. I stood rubbing my nose. What the devil could I do now? Those two fellows had carried off the honours of the day, and now I should not be able to conjure up the whale I had already guaranteed I would produce myself.

Lazarus had fetched the two men back: they came reluctantly, dragging the whale, and laid it down where they had found it. But surely they were laying it in the wrong place? I went up with the mayor, and now it was my turn to be puzzled and speechless. My own whale still lay there bottom upwards: no one had yet touched it. Those two fellows who now stood before us, frightened and with bad consciences, had found a third whale, a rather small one. I reassured them all: everything was all right, I said, and we would continue as soon as I had had my lunch: then I would produce a still larger and finer whale.

When we continued the search and came to the last sector of the circle I noticed that all three carefully passed by the right stone, while they turned over every single one of the others. At last the circle was completed.

"There were no more," the mayor said, a little astonished.

"You haven't turned over that one," I said, and pointed questioningly to the all-important stone.

"Yes, we did turn it over, don't you see it's lying with the pale side uppermost?" said Lazarus.

I suddenly realized that these children of nature could tell merely looking at a stone whether it was lying with its old sun-burnt side uppermost or not. This one lay with its pale shady side uppermost, and they thought they had turned it over themselves.

"It doesn't matter whether you've turned it over or not," I said. "Turn it over once more. You remember what happened when Señor Arne turned over the big stone you all knew so well up at Rano Raraku."

Lazarus helped me to get a good hold, and we rolled the block over together.

"Look!" was all Lazarus managed to gasp out; he simply stood staring and smiling foolishly, while Atan cheered loudly. The mayor seemed electrified and could only stammer:

"Very important—very important. What a strong *aku-aku!*"

Both the long-ears from the statue and our own people from the camp came rushing up to stare at the third whale. Even the two young rascals who had found a little whale of their own were vastly impressed, and the photographer and I, who had started the whole business, found it hard to keep a straight face, for this was the last word in queer coincidences.

Eroria just shook her head and told me calmly that I had good luck, real good luck. She gazed enraptured at the three whales, and I thought to myself that for her this was a regular family portrait gallery, for it was she who had learned from her father that she was directly descended from a whale. But old Mariana had something more to tell me. She lived with the shepherd Leonardo in a stone hut on the other side of the valley, and Leonardo's old brother Domingo had spent the last night with them. When the old man woke up that morning he told them of a dream he had had: he had dreamt that Señor Kon-Tiki had caught five tunnies.

"Then we're two short," the mayor said quickly, and before I knew what was happening the whole crowd began to turn all the stones on end once more: some of them in their eagerness undoubtedly went outside the circle. They were all absolutely

determined to find the two required to make Domingo's dream
come true. Late in the afternoon two obscure fish carvings
came to light: both were at once accepted as whales, and
the natives triumphantly laid the five figures in a row on
the sand.

The mayor took up a little stone and drew a curve in the
sand in front of the figures: then he made a little hole in the
middle of the curve and said:

"That's done."

He and Lazarus stood up by the curve and sang a snatch of
Hotu Matua's old song, their hips swaying rhythmically in
the hula fashion. They sang another snatch, then fell silent, and
continued in this manner with short breaks, until at last
evening came and everyone went off home.

Early next morning Lazarus was on the spot with a sack
over his shoulder. This he smuggled into my tent unobserved by
anyone outside. When he laid it down there was a clatter of
stones. From that day onwards Lazarus was a frequent night
visitor to my tent: he worked with the others in the daytime
and lay down to sleep with them in the cave when evening came.
But in the darkness of the night he crept out over sleeping forms,
got on to his horse and disappeared over the ridge to the west
. . . and next morning there was another sack on the floor of
my tent.

The mayor was on tenterhooks for three days, but then he
too could control himself no longer. We went up into the scree
and had a long talk. He told me he had a friend with a large
red statue hidden in his garden: it had no number on it, and
his friend had promised that I could take it on board ship
with me for "good luck." I explained that no one was
allowed to move monuments of this kind: they were protected. The mayor was visibly disappointed and ill at ease; his
contribution had not proved the success he had hoped.
He was clearly itching to win my favour, so at long last he
said quietly that he would talk to his own men. Several of
them had family caves, and he would try to persuade them.
But I must not allow myself to be misled if anyone brought
me strange stones which looked newly scrubbed, even if the
owners lied and declared that they themselves had found or
made them.

"For people are afraid to talk openly about these things," the mayor said. "Besides, they wash the cave stones and keep them clean."

I said emphatically that they must never do that; it ruined the stones.

Then the mayor made his first slip: his father had expressly asked him to wash the stones, he assured me.

"You must only blow the dust away," I explained, "or the surface will wear away."

The mayor thought this was a sensible idea. I knew a lot, he said, and he would pass on this information. But he was worried about small roots and insects' eggs getting into the porous lava stone. In caves which were not looked after there were many figures which were cracked and damaged. Before he realized what he had said he had revealed that he washed all his figures at monthly intervals.

I received this piece of information without any visible surprise, and as a result the mayor's tongue really started to wag. It took him fifteen nights to finish a washing ceremony, he confided, for as eldest brother he was responsible for four caves. His wife had to go fishing while he was busy with the stones: she could not help, as she belonged to another family. He always had to go into the cave alone and never make a sound while he was inside. He had to be quick and snatch up a few stones— one here, one there—and then hurry out to wash them. He had money too, in one of the caves. Iron money. But the caves were rather damp, so there were no wooden figures there. But he had inherited two caves of the other kind, too, *ana miro*, and they were full of wooden things. But so far he had not been able to find the concealed openings leading to the two caves. He had been right on the spot three times and baked a chicken in an earth oven so that the smell would help him to find the way to the hidden openings. So far it had not worked, but now he would have another try.

Finally he told me that his own *aku-aku* had recently been advising him to take things from the other caves and give them to Señor Kon-Tiki, in spite of his own father having told him never, never, never to take anything away from the caves. If I gave him a pair of trousers, a shirt, a tiny little scrap of cloth and just a few dollars he would hide them in the cave and take them out when a relative really needed them. And then we could await events.

The mayor got what he asked for, but for a time nothing happened. Meanwhile the work of raising the statue had reached its sixteenth day, and before long the giant would tilt into position. The long-ears were working against time now, for the governor had been notified by telegram that the warship *Pinto* was on her way to Easter Island. We were well into February, and the annual visit to the island was impending.

The mayor was most anxious to get the statue raised so that the captain of the warship would see with his own eyes that it was really standing. The captain acted as the supreme authority on the island from the moment he set foot ashore, and the mayor hoped he would give a favourable report to the Chilean President.

On the sixteenth day the mayor asked for rope to pull and support the statue at the moment when it was being raised. All the rope brought by the expedition was now in use in different parts of the island, and that evening we drove over in the jeep to see the governor and ask him if he had any rope to spare. When we got there, he told us a telegram had come saying that the *Pinto* would arrive the very next day: she had been ten days at sea. The mayor's face fell. Now he would not be able to complete the raising of the statue, for when the *Pinto* arrived everyone would be kept busy loading wool and unloading flour and sugar and certain sorely-needed commodities for the coming year. The governor was sorry; but the long-ears and all my native diggers would have to stop work and report to him next day.

We drove crestfallen through the village and on to Father Sebastian's, to give him the latest report on the progress of the work. I whispered in his ear that all efforts to get into a family cave were still of no avail, apart from the fact that I now had a remarkable collection of sculptures on board the ship.

On our way to the priest's the mayor had suddenly proposed that both of us should sit and concentrate on our respective *aku-akus*, and get them to help us to hold up the *Pinto*, so that he would have another day in which to complete the work. He sat on the tool-box, silent and reverent, between the photographer and myself, bouncing up and down and hanging on grimly to stop his head hitting the roof. Returning from Father Sebastian's we passed right through the village once again, and were about to turn left at the cross-roads where the jeep tracks ran off towards Anakena. There stood the governor in front of us in the light of the head-lamps, pointing to a sizeable coil of rope lying by the roadside. He had just received another telegram: the *Pinto* would not be arriving until the day after tomorrow.

I leant back in my seat, helpless with silent laughter. The photographer sat chuckling at the wheel. This was really the queerest coincidence of the lot. Only the mayor accepted it as a mere matter of course.

"There you are," he murmured in my ear.

Now I had nothing more to say. I merely sat shaking my head in sheer amazement as we bumped along across the island in the dark.

What no one knew as yet was that the long-ears required *two* more working days, instead of *one*, which completely ruined the mayor's plan. But he did not know that yet, as he sat rejoicing in the strength of our combined *aku-akus*. This complacent mood gave way, after a while, to a sneaking suspicion that, after all, it was probably my *aku-aku* which had really done the trick; for he began, quite unprompted, to whisper to me about all the incredible things he had in his caves. Never, never had he taken from the cave anything he had inherited, but now he was being tempted more and more by his own *aku-aku*.

The next day was the seventeenth working day on the statue. Everyone expected it to be raised that day. Now an ancient crone suddenly turned up and laid her magic half-circle of stones, each about the size of an egg, on the huge slab on which the statue was to stand. She came up and presented me with a large fish-hook of black stone, exquisitely shaped and polished as bright as ebony. She had "found" it that very day as a sign of "good luck." I had never seen this old grey-haired woman before. She was a bent and fragile little creature, but behind her wrinkles one could see traces of a truly handsome, aristocratic face, lit by two shrewd flashing eyes. The mayor whispered to me that she was the last surviving sister of his father: her name was Victoria, but she preferred the name *Tahu-tahu*, which meant sorcery.

She had been dancing for them all night in front of the cave
to bring them "good luck" and prevent the giant from falling
over when it was suddenly tilted free from the stone pile.

The giant did not capsize, but neither did it tip up into a
vertical position. When the seventeenth day was over, it still
stood all aslant: next day it would most certainly have tilted
into position, if only the long-ears had had time to complete the
work. But next day they all had to be in the village for the
great event of the year, the visit of the warship. To the disappointment of the mayor, the giant was doomed to remain in
his undignified position, reclining drunkenly, with the stone
pile up to his nose, when the ship's captain made his personal
tour of inspection.

When night came only our guards were left in camp. The
rest of us had gone on board, for at daybreak we were to put
to sea and escort the warship into the village bay. The natives
must have felt that the untracked ocean off their island, where
the horizon always hung suspended like a delicate spider's
thread between two shades of blue, was fast becoming a centre
of maritime activity. Tomorrow a fly and a midge would
suddenly appear on the thread, and later two ships would
anchor side by side off the village.

There was a third vessel too which in the last few days had
occupied the natives more than usual: she was not armoured
with steel, but plaited together with golden fresh-water reeds,
and the natives themselves had launched her at Anakena.
Now she lay on our ship's deck gleaming like gold in the sun.
She had been built as a practical experiment, but once she
was launched and lay rocking on the sea, she too sailed right
into the web of secrecy surrounding the family caves.

It began with Ed crawling about under the stone slabs in
the narrow ruins up on the cliff-edge in Orongo. Here he
discovered new wall paintings in addition to those already
known. The most curious finds were a typical American-
Indian weeping-eye motif, and several ceiling paintings of
crescent-shaped reed boats with masts. One of the reed boats
had lateral lashings and a large square sail.

It is known that formerly the inhabitants of Easter Island
had made for themselves the same curious one- and two-man
reed boats as the Inca Indians and their predecessors have used

along the coast of Peru from time immemorial. But no one had ever heard of the old Easter Islanders making reed boats large enough to carry sail. I myself had special reasons for being interested: I had sailed on Lake Titicaca in reed boats of this kind, with mountain Indians from the Tiahuanaco plain as my crew. I knew that they were splendid craft of incredible carrying capacity and speed. At the time of the Spanish conquests large reed boats of this kind were also in use on the open sea off the coast of Peru, and old drawings[1] on jars from pre-Inca times show that during the oldest period of Peruvian civilization people had built proper ships of reeds, just as the old Egyptians had built boats of papyrus. Rafts of balsa logs and boat-shaped vessels of fresh-water reeds were un-sinkable means of conveyance which the people of Peru preferred for all their sea traffic. I knew, too, that the reed boats would float for many months without getting water-logged, and a reed boat from Lake Titicaca which Peruvian friends had brought down to the Pacific took the seas like a swan and went twice as fast as a balsa raft.

And now reed boats had suddenly turned up in an old ceiling painting in Ed's ruined house No. 19, on the edge of the crater of Easter Island's largest volcano. We found not only a picture of the boat, but we also found the actual reeds. In the abyss beneath us, on one side of the bird-men's ruined village, the ocean spent its fury on the rocks, flinging up the salt spume, while deep down below us on the other side lay a silent overgrown crater lake, whose fresh water was covered with a peculiar giant reed. This was the reed the old Easter Islanders had used. Every single native could still tell of a little craft they called a *pora*, which each of the competitors made for himself in the race to the bird islands for the first egg of the year.

I also knew that this particular reed down in the deep crater was something of a botanical curiosity. It was in fact a speci-fically American fresh-water reed, the very same as the one growing round Lake Titicaca, and which it was most surprising to find down in a crater lake on Easter Island. It was of this very reed that the Peruvian Indians made their strange

[1] See plate lxxxi and figures on pp. 588–9 of Thor Heyerdahl's *American Indians in the Pacific*: Oslo, Stockholm, London. 1952.

vessels on the shores of Lake Titicaca, and it was this reed they cultivated in artificially irrigated swamps along the desert coast of Peru, so as to be able to make their traditional reed boats in areas where access to balsa logs was difficult. How had this American reed, a fresh-water plant, come all the way to Easter Island?

Father Sebastian and the natives had their own answer. According to tradition the reed was not originally a wild plant, like certain other plants on the island. This reed had been carefully planted down in the lake by their own ancestors. Legend gave the honour to one of the first natives, Uru by name: he had gone down into the crater with root-stocks and planted the first reed, and when it spread he had taken new root-stocks, first to the crater lake at Rano Raraku and then to Rano Oroi. The tall reed was one of the most important plants on the island: it was used not only to construct vessels, but also to build houses and make mats, baskets and hats. To this very day the natives go down regularly and cut reeds in the crater lake. And down in a shining pool in the middle of the swamp below us we saw through our glasses a large reed raft, which the children had made in order to bathe from.

I wanted to make a *pora*. Apart from a primitive old drawing no modern human being had ever seen what it was like and how it was used in the open sea off the island.

"The Pakarati brothers should be able to help you," said Father Sebastian, interested in the new problem I had brought him. "They're four amusing old chaps who know all about boats and fishing."

Yes, said Pedro and Santiago and Domingo and Timoteo, they could make me a *pora*. But I must give them good knives and enough time for the reeds to dry. The four old men were given their knives, and went down to the crater lake in Rano Raraku. But there were two kinds of reed boat, old Timoteo explained. One kind was for a single person setting out for the bird islands in search of eggs; the other was for two persons fishing in the open sea. I asked them to make one of each kind. The reeds, which were much taller than the men themselves, were cut off at the roots and laid to dry at the bottom of the inner statue quarry: then the four old fellows rode round the island looking for *mahute* and *hau-hau* bushes from whose

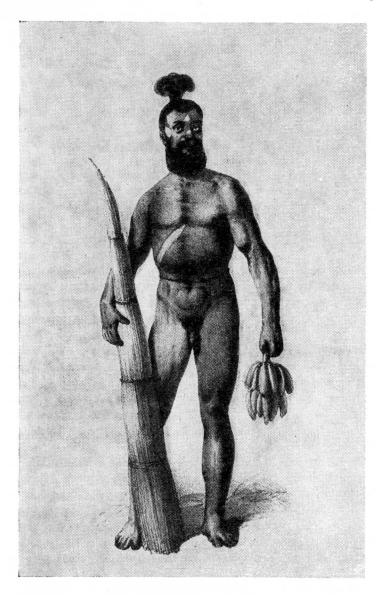

Old drawing of an Easter Island native with topknot and beard
who came swimming on a small reed *pora* to visit the ship of
Petit-Thoua.

bark they could make suitable rope-work, so that the reeds could be bound together in the old traditional way.

It was an eternity before the old men got their reeds ready, for no sooner did they leave the crater where they had laid them out to dry, than other natives went in with horses and rode off with large bundles. The reeds were popular for mats and mattresses, and it was so much simpler to supply oneself with reeds ready cut than from those still growing in the swamp. And so the old fellows had to set to work with their knives again.

One day, while the green reeds were still being dried in the Rano Raraku crater, I took a tent with me and went down into the other volcano up on the rim of which was the bird-men's ruined village. Thor had not yet moved up to help Ed, so he was with me when I clambered down the steep wall of the crater into the interior of the volcano. This was the wildest sight we had seen anywhere on the island. When we had descended by the only possible track down the wall there was not a single foot of flat ground to be found, apart from the vast oozing quagmire which lay like green spinach at the bottom of a giant cauldron whose walls rose steeply into the sky on every side. The photographer was with us too. He could tackle peaks and cliffs with the agility of a mountain goat, but he was not at his ease by the morass at the bottom of the cauldron. The slope on which we stood was very steep, and if we set foot on the bog either we put it down in open water or the whole surface swayed under us, so that it was like balancing on a tightly stretched rubber sheet.

At the bottom of the slope we had to build a small platform of boughs, carpeted with reeds, and make our tent fast to this, for otherwise we could not have lain down at a single spot without rolling into the bog. Where there was not a sheer precipice over our heads there were endless screes, so steep that any attempt to scramble up was liable to start a big rock-fall. In the few places where the slopes were not too steep for us to move, trees and bushes had got in ahead of us and formed a dense scrub. It was from the depths of this crater that the people of Easter Island had obtained their wood right up to our own time. For once, with plenty of firewood to hand, we enjoyed the luxury of a blazing camp-fire, a friendly spark re-kindled in an extinct volcano. When we finally retired to our tent for the night, we praised the unknown navigator Uru who had given us such a wonderful reed mattress.

Till now no one had carried out any test boring for a study of this gigantic swamp, and for this purpose we expected to be down in the volcano for several days and nights. After all, according to legend it was here that the boat-building reeds— which we knew had come from South America—had first been planted. The very first Spaniards who came to the island from Peru had recognized this important fresh-water reed as the *totora* of the Incas, and modern botanists have shown that they were right. It was now our intention to bore down into the marsh, as far as our special 8-metre bore could reach, for samples of turf. We knew that a bog like this was just the place in which all kinds of pollen would be hermetically preserved for all time, and on our return Professor Olof Selling of Stockholm was going to analyse the samples and determine the ancient vegetable life of Easter Island through the ages.

If we were lucky the pollen in the turf would tell us whether Easter Island had ever been covered with forests, and also when the South American fresh-water reed was first introduced into the crater lake. Anyone could see that it was a long time ago, for the great crater lake was over 300 acres in extent, and yet so thickly covered with green *totora* that it resembled a huge sugar-cane plantation, with occasional brown boggy patches of tangled dead reed. It looked as if any movement on this surface would be dangerous, but the whole thing was merely a question of habit. The natives, feeling their way for generations across the swamp, had got to know the safe places and the tracks leading to some of the open water-holes. When the villagers were suffering from drought they had to ascend this lofty volcano and climb down into the deep crater to fetch water from the marsh. The natives believed the marsh was bottomless, and Father Sebastian told us that someone had let down a 500 ft. line in one of the open pools without touching bottom.

The sun was late in waking us down in the depths of the volcano, and as we lay blowing at the smoking fire for our morning coffee Ed's native foreman, Tepano, came clambering down to guide us out into the quagmire. We wanted to reach a

series of areas which I had chosen for test borings. He took us
for a queer walk: as soon as we had set foot on the heaving bog
we had first to force our way into a regular jungle of giant reeds
standing as close-packed as the bristles of a brush and as high
as the walls of an ordinary room. These lush green reeds grew
up out of vast accumulations of dead reed-fibres, whose tough
coils wound about our limbs and seemed to pull us down into
an endless web of loose disintegrating matter, from which we
could only raise ourselves by pushing thick bundles of fresh
reeds beneath our bellies as we crawled.

When we got through this dense barricade, which skirted the
edge of the overgrown lake, we saw the whole crater marsh
spread out before us like a patchwork quilt in every possible
shade of brown, yellow, green, blue and black. At some places
we had to wade through surface water while the buoyant turf
beneath swung and heaved: at others we sank up to our knees
in moss and mud at every single step, and amid the gurgling
and seething around us we felt that we should be dragged down
into the unplumbed depths if we did not immediately put a
foot forward. Here and there were narrow cracks in the floating
turf, with open brown water in them, and the whole mass
heaved violently as we jumped across.

In many places patches of giant reed grew in small copses,
and when we forced our way out of one of these Tepano, Thor
and I disappeared into open water completely coated with
green slime. Tepano assured us that there was no danger so
long as we could swim. We soon looked like water-sprites,
covered with mud and slime: the sun blazed down fiercely into
that windless witches' cauldron, and at last even the dark open
water-holes tempted us to take a dip and clean up. The water
was quite tepid on the surface, but ice-cold farther down.
Tepano begged us insistently to keep our heads above water:
once a native had dived there and never found his way up again
because he had missed his direction under the floating turf.

We found no suitable places for boring. If we put the bore
in, it went straight through the turf and down into open water.
Often the turf was ten or twelve feet thick and consisted of a
tangled mass of dead reeds. If we sounded in the water-holes
we were able to record the most varying depths, but we never
got down to the bottom of the crater lake, for some underwater

tangle of turf was always in the way. Tepano told us that these open tarns were never in quite the same place: they shifted from year to year: everything was in motion down in the witches' cauldron.

Before evening Tepano went back over the edge of the crater, and the photographer left us too. Thor and I were to remain down in the crater a few more days, to see if we could get better borings. We now knew the secrets of the crater bog. We could tell, from colour and substance, what to expect when we put our feet down.

Next day we made our way right across the marsh to the crater face on the other side when we suddenly caught sight of a stone wall twelve feet high, built on the very edge of the swamp. It was overgrown with scrub and straggling wisps of greenery, and when we climbed up we were standing on an old man-made platform. From there we could see that four or five other walls continued as terraces one above the other along the side of the crater; and when we began to clamber about we found low rectangular openings giving access to underground stone houses of the type hitherto known only from the bird-men's ruined village up on the cliff at Orongo. We had actually come upon a group of ruins unknown even to the natives; at any rate they had never said a word about it to any white man. A number of the stones in the walls were covered with half-effaced relief carvings of human beings, birds and fabulous creatures, grotesque faces and magical eyes. The most conspicuous were a couple of bird-men and a four-legged beast with a human head. The terraces had once been built for agriculture, and at the foot of the lowest wall, at the edge of the swamp, we took numerous samples of turf and soil for pollen tests.

On our fourth day down in the crater we were sitting sealing up all our test tubes with melted paraffin wax when the skipper came clambering down into the volcano with the news that Arne had made a fresh discovery at Rano Raraku. He had dug out the body of a giant statue which had been standing with its head just above ground, and on the chest of the figure was a picture of a large reed boat with three masts and several sails. From the deck of the boat a long line ran down to a turtle carved on the giant's stomach.

We packed our things and left behind us the volcanic underworld of Rano Kao. While Thor went up to Ed's ruined village, I drove to Rano Raraku with the skipper in the jeep. Arne showed me his new find, surrounded by all his native diggers, who were beaming with pride and veneration at the ancient vessel catching a turtle on the *moai*'s stomach. They were all sure that this was Hotu Matua's own ship, for he had landed on the island with several hundred men on board two vessels so capacious that Oroi, Hotu Matua's worst enemy, had made the passage as a stowaway. There were no *honu* or turtles on the island today, but when Hotu Matua came one of his men had been injured trying to catch a big one on the beach at Anakena.

Stories of the great feasts of their ancestors began to well up again, and I was treated to fragments of well-known Hotu Matua legends which had actually been recorded by Father Roussel and Paymaster Thomson at the end of the last century. We could all see that this was an unusual ship and not a European craft, even though it was strange to realize that the old Easter Island statue-makers built themselves vessels so large that there was room to raise more than a single mast. And yet, who would have thought that the same people could have erected gigantic human figures as high as four-storey houses, but for the fact that these statues still remained, thanks to the imperishable stone in which they were carved? After all, it was obvious that these indefatigable engineering geniuses were not merely expert builders in stone: it was as mariners in the world class that they had found their way out to this tiny haven, the loneliest in the world, where for centuries they had been able to create their stone statues in peace. Since they had the *totora* reed, and used it to make small rafts, there was really no reason why, by lashing more and larger bundles together, they should not have been able to increase the size according to requirements.

When the first Europeans came to Easter Island they saw nobody building ships, but neither did they see anyone making statues. The only craft the Europeans saw were tiny narrow canoes which could just hold from two to four men in a smooth sea, and even smaller reed rafts. But the Europeans came to the island in the third, or barbarian, cultural period, when war and

schism had destroyed all the old culture and bloody feuds
prevented all collaboration between the various family groups.
In these chaotic conditions a divided people, spending most of
their time in and around their refuge caves, were hardly likely
to get together and build ships.

This explains why historic records of only two miserable
little types of craft in Easter Island have come down to us—a
little Polynesian outrigger canoe, the *vaka ama*, and a little
South American reed raft, the *pora*, both of them too small
ever to have brought man to the world's most solitary island.
But native tradition contained vivid descriptions of large
vessels used for long voyages by their ancestors in the golden age
of long ago. In the last century Father Roussel was told of
great ships which could carry four hundred passengers and had
a lofty prow raised like a swan's neck, while the stern, equally
high, was split into two separate parts. Many of the reed boats
we find depicted on ancient jars in Peru are just like this. But
Easter Island tradition also tells of other old types. Father
Sebastian had learned that there was a large vessel shaped like
a flat raft or lighter. It was called a *vaka poepoe*, and was also used
when the navigators set out on long voyages with many people
on board.

Now that Ed and Arne had each found a picture of a reed
boat we were on the alert every time we saw a boat-shaped
figure. We found several on the statues and in the quarry itself
with the bundles of reeds clearly separated, and Bill found one
with a mast and a square sail. On the underside of a fallen
statue over thirty feet long Carl found a reed boat with a mast
running straight up through the figure's round navel; and up
in Orongo Ed found a roof painting of another, with a little
round sail on the middle one of her three masts.

It so happened that we were to obtain yet more tangible
evidence that such large vessels had really existed. In many
parts of the island we had seen wide paved roads which disappeared straight down into the sea. These mysterious constructions had in the course of time stimulated a great number of
speculations and fantastic theories. They have been one of the
main supports for all who believe that Easter Island is the
remnant of a sunken continent. The paved roads, they
declared, undoubtedly continued along the ocean floor, and if

one could follow them one would reach the ruins of the sunken
continent of Mu.

We *could* follow them: we had a frogman with us on the
expedition. And with him we rode to the nearest track which
vanished down into the depths. It was a priceless sight to see the
frogman in his green uniform, with Martian helmet and
oxygen mask, marching down the road to Mu with his frog
feet flapping on the smooth paving stones. He swung in his hand
a flame-coloured camera container resembling a lantern, and
he waved a graceful farewell as he left the dry pavement and
strode on into the sea, bound for Mu. Soon we saw only the
oxygen containers on his back and two splashing feet, and then
the frogman disappeared entirely, and only scattered air bubbles
breaking on the surface told us which way he was going. But
clearly the frogman was not taking any short cut to Mu. Soon we
saw the bubbles moving to the left, then they changed direction
and struck off to the right; and as we watched the bubbles
wandered to and fro in rings and spirals till the frogman poked
his snouted helmet up out of the water to take a fresh bearing
from the road ashore. Then he continued his underwater
search, zig-zagging in a seaward direction, till he gave up and
swam ashore to report.

"Weren't there any proper sign-posts down there?"

"Didn't you meet a mermaid who could tell you the way?"

Questions rained down upon the poor frogman. He had seen
no road. The paving went no farther than the water's edge,
beyond which were only ledges and boulders, mushroom corals
and deep crevices, till the rocky ocean floor shelved steeply
into the hazy blue depths at a spot where he had seen some big
fish.

We were not particularly surprised. Oceanographers had
long since established, on the basis of deposits taken from the
bottom of the Pacific, that in the Polynesian part of that ocean
the land masses had neither risen nor fallen so long as man has
existed. Once again I had recourse to the natives. No one
could remember what the broad paved roads leading down to
the sea had been used for, but they had a name: they were
called *apapa*. *Apapa* means to "unload." This confirmed our
suspicion: they were unloading places or landing ramps where
large vessels coming in from the sea were drawn up. One

apapa ran down to a shallow inlet at the foot of a large temple platform on the south coast. The inlet was so full of boulders that the old navigators had had to clear a wide channel to enable craft to come alongside the landing stage. And in the shallows of this channel lay three gigantic red topknots, abandoned in the water. Two of the colossi lay so close together that they must have been on board the same boat, unless the ancient vessels were so large and sturdy that these stones could have been placed in the bow and stern of two ships lying stern to bow. This was the first evidence we had come across suggesting that the sculptors had sent some of their heavy cargoes by sea along the coast. We had now established that they actually had vessels which could transport twenty tons, and without a cargo they would have been able to carry a crew of nearly two hundred. Later we found proof that even individual statues had been carried by sea and landed at a spot where only a beamy reed- or log-raft, of very shallow draught, could have come in with so heavy a cargo.

While we were beginning, by fragments, to obtain a clearer picture of the remarkable maritime achievements of the prehistoric islanders, the four old men were working away with their *totora* reeds in the Rano Raraku crater. When the reeds were dried, each of them swiftly made his own *pora*. By using a special lashing, they achieved a curved, pointed shape, exactly like a huge tusk. It was strange to see them going down to the water, each with his own craft. And it was particularly strange because what they carried were perfect replicas of the peculiar one-man boat which had been a characteristic feature of the Peruvian coast for centuries. And as we knew, it was even made from the same South American fresh-water reed.

When the four old men were about to start building the larger two-man boat, Timoteo directed operations with complete self-assurance, while the other three seemed helpless without his orders. I therefore asked the reason and was told that Timoteo was the oldest, and therefore the only one who knew what the boat should look like. I was a little surprised at the reply, but it was not till some time afterwards that I began to suspect the reason.

When the canoe-shaped two-man boat was launched at Anakena she strongly recalled, in all her construction, the reed

boats of Lake Titicaca. The only difference was that the bow
and stern were drawn out in a long point sticking up into the
air at an angle, just as in the most ancient reed boats on the
coast of Peru. The two older brothers leapt aboard, each with
his paddle, and the reed boat danced over high foaming
breakers with the utmost ease, heading for the open ocean.
This curious flexible craft twisted its way across the waves and
mastered the seas like an air mattress on top of which the two
old men rode dry and safe. The other two plunged into the
breakers with their one-man *poras* and cheerfully faced the
sea. They lay with chest and stomach up on the thick end of the
stout tusk-shaped bundle of reeds, and pushed themselves
forward through the water by swimming with arms and legs.
The two-man boat farther out took the seas so safely and
gracefully that when she came back from her trial trip all four
brothers crawled on board and paddled out into the roughest
seas.

Father Sebastian and the mayor stood with me on the shore:
we were all three equally fascinated and excited. Just behind
us we saw the back of the long-ears' giant statue which had
begun to rise above the tops of the tents, but the mayor had
eyes only for the golden-yellow boat with the four men paddling
in unison out on the sea. He just stared and stared, with tears
in his eyes.

"Our grandparents have told us of boats like this, exactly
like this, but this is the first time any of us has seen one, and it
brings our ancestors so near to us," he said. "I feel it here," he
added, and struck his chest with emotion.

When Timoteo's two-man boat came in again with four men
paddling, one of our biggest sailors clambered on to the stern
without the craft showing a sign of sinking. If the little, hastily
built reed boat could carry five grown men, there could hardly
have been anything to stop the ancient local engineers from
cutting enough reeds in the three craters of the island to build
themselves sizeable ships.

Father Sebastian was quite fascinated. These strange boats
had been described to him before, by old people on the island,
but only now did he understand what they had meant. Now
he remembered that they had also shown him a picture of
such a craft painted in a cave on Poike.

Exploration underground. Both on Easter Island and on Rapaiti we found old shelters and burial caves running far into the rock as long tunnels and large rooms. The skipper carries the light for Carl, the South Sea girl Ruita and the author, who had been swimming in a subterranean lake surrounded by old tombs.

Above: In a nocturnal ceremony, the evening before they began to make a statue, the long-ears' direct descendants reveal for the first time the stone-cutters' strange old working song.

Below: For the first time for hundreds of years a statue is being made in the old quarry of the volcano. In the foreground lies a heap of old stone picks with some gourds of water. These were the sculptors' only tools.

"This is a fishing boat," said the mayor and pointed proudly to the golden vessel. "Think what sort of boats the ancient kings had for their long voyages."

I asked if he knew whether they were large enough to use sails, and to my astonishment he replied that they had sails of reed matting. Once more I was amazed at the mayor, who calmly began to draw in the sand a sail made of reeds which ran perpendicularly. It was easy enough to make such a sail, he said: one had only to bind the reeds together side by side, as Domingo had done quite recently when he made a mat for me.

I had myself seen how the *totora* boats on Lake Titicaca use reed sails to this very day, the only difference being that in them the reeds are sewn together horizontally instead of perpendicularly.

"How do you know the boats had reed sails?" I asked, rather puzzled.

"Aha, Don Pedro knows a lot," he replied with a proud, knowing smile.

This happened just at the time when Estevan was still bringing me his wife's cave stones, and it was on the previous night that Lazarus brought his very first head from the cave. He was so eager now that he could not restrain himself, and told me that among all the other things he had seen in the cave there were small models of ships. Some of them reminded him of those which Timoteo had built. Directly I heard this I took a chance and, having got Estevan to myself for a moment, fired a long shot at him. His wife had just asked me to say if there was anything special I wanted from the cave. I had not known what to ask for, since I did not know what was there. Now Lazarus had let out that his cave had models of boats, so I took a chance and told Estevan to ask his wife to give me the boats she had in the cave. Estevan stared at me round-eyed, but when the day's work was over he galloped off in the direction of the village. Late that night he was back again with five amazing sculptures in a sack. The first, which he unpacked from some dry banana leaves, was a pretty little crescent-shaped model of a reed boat. He added that according to his wife there was a still finer boat left in the cave: it had fine lashings and was high and pointed both fore and aft, and it also had a figurehead at each end.

G

I listened to him on tenterhooks, for this was the night when I expected Lazarus and the mayor to come and walk in a circle round the hidden whale. When Estevan slipped out into the darkness, I did not know that his wife, scared by the *aku-akus*, would stop him from bringing anything for many nights to come.

Lazarus himself did not get away to fetch a boat that night, for when he and the mayor had come back to their sleeping friends in Hotu Matua's cave after the nocturnal ceremony, the mayor just lay on the watch with his eyes open and saw mysterious lights and other omens outside the entrance to the cave. But the next night, after all the whales had been found, Lazarus saw his chance of stealing out over his sleeping friends. One of them had woken and drawn his legs up quickly, for on Easter Island it means bad luck to have a person step over you. He had asked what Lazarus was up to, and Lazarus had said that he had to go out to obey a call of nature. But he had his horse standing ready saddled behind a rock, and had ridden off towards the cave at Hanga-o-Teo.

Early in the morning Lazarus pushed a sack into my tent, and in a little while he came creeping in himself. He squatted down on the floor of the tent and proudly drew from the sack a stone model of a tusk-shaped one-man *pora* with lashings. Then came a monster resembling an alligator, and an elegant red stone bowl with three human heads projecting round the edge. He said there were three more boats in the same cave, but none of them were so like those which Timoteo had made as the one he had brought with him.

Lazarus was well rewarded for what he had brought, and I asked him to bring the other boats with him next time. This he did three nights later. One was a model of a regular ship with a broad deck and high bow and stern, and both deck and sides were made of thick bundles of reeds lashed together. The other craft was a *vaka poepoe*, as broad and flat as a raft or lighter, with a mast and sail carved in stone and two inexplicable domes side by side on the forward deck. The third was not a real vessel; it was more like a long dish, but it was carved as if made of reeds, with a hole for a mast in the middle. At each end there was a most curious head, placed inside the hull at bow and stern and staring towards the mast-hole. One of the heads had blown-out cheeks and pursed lips, looking like a real cherub sending a puff of wind into the sail. The hair was blended with the reeds on the outside of the vessel.

The sculpture was old, and both the subject and the style were completely foreign to Easter Island. When I questioned Lazarus closely about the stones he brought me, he just flung out his hands and was unable to give me any explanation. The stones were like that, he could say no more. But there were masses and masses of other queer things left in the cave, and as he had now seen that no disaster followed he would take me with him one day after the visit of the warship. His one condition was that not a soul in the village should know what we were doing, so long as I was on the island.

The mayor had so far not brought me anything, apart from his own eternally repeated wooden figures. On the last evening before the warship came I called him into my tent. This was my last chance. When the warship left the mayor was going with her, and no one else in the island, not even his own wife, knew the entrance to his secret caves. When he came into the tent I had prepared a really pleasant surprise for him, partly because he deserved an extra reward for all he had now taught us, but also in the egoistical hope that he might produce an equally pleasant surprise for me. I rolled down the tent walls, screwed down the wick till it was half dark, and leant towards him whispering. I already had the impression that his hair was beginning to stand up on his head: he clearly realized that something of a mystical nature was going to happen.

I told him that my *aku-aku* had said to me that the mayor needed a good many things for his first voyage from Easter Island, and I was going to take my *aku-aku*'s advice and give him just what it had told me he needed. Thereupon I brought out my best suitcase, which I presented to him, and in it I laid in due order a travelling rug, sheets, towels, a warm jersey, two pairs of new khaki trousers, shirts, various ties, socks, pocket-handkerchiefs, shoes and all kinds of toilet articles from comb and soap to toothbrush and shaving tackle. He also got a ruck-sack full of kitchen utensils and field equipment, so that he could fend for himself if he had lodging without board. Several cartons of his favourite cigarettes followed, and a wallet full of Chilean pesos, to keep him going if he struck hard times in the great unknown world. He received one of Yvonne's best dresses as a farewell present to his wife, and various children's garments.

The last thing I produced was a stuffed baby caiman or South American alligator a foot long, which a Panama native had induced me to buy for a small sum. Both Estevan and Lazarus had brought a similar reptile in stone from their respective family caves, and the same animal, referred to as *moko*, was also depicted in a well-known wood-carving on the island. The *moko* is known throughout Polynesia as a ferocious legendary creature, although the only things resembling it on these islands are tiny innocent lizards. This has led many people to believe that the legendary *moko* of Easter Island was a recollection of caimans which the old navigators had seen on the tropical coast of South America.

I handed the little stuffed beast to the mayor, saying: "You can put this in your cave as an *aku-aku* guardian while you yourself are on the mainland."

The mayor was so excited as the gifts were handed to him one by one that his eyes and teeth nearly jumped out of his head. He now went completely mad and hissed that he had a stone exactly like that creature in his cave, and he would bring it to me. Then he could find words no longer: he shook my hand with both his, and all he could say was to reiterate that my *aku-aku* was *"muy bueno, muy, muy, muy bueno."*

It was black night before he crept excitedly out of the tent, a very happy man, and called to his faithful friend Lazarus, who helped to carry the heavy spoils to the waiting horses. Then they dashed off to catch up all their friends on the way to the village.

So the cave mystery remained a confused and unsolved riddle, and the sturdy giant stood aslant by the tents, with a humiliating stone-pile up to his nose, when the Anakena valley was again emptied of people. After seventeen days on the statue, one day short of completion, the long-ears rode home to be ready for the next day's work and festivities, and we ourselves temporarily abandoned the tents and went on board our ship, which lay in the bay spick and span and freshly painted, ready to put to sea and meet the *Pinto*.

CHAPTER VII

MEETING THE CAVE'S DUMB GUARDIANS

THE big Chilean warship appeared on the horizon when the sun still hung low over the sea and bathed the cliffs along the coast in morning gold and haunting shadows. Broad and flat and all grey, with a tower of bristling technicality, she grew in size as she approached us—the first greeting from the world outside, the first reminder that there was still land beyond every horizon. The winds had filled in Iko's ditch, man had changed his weapons.

We met the *Pinto* just outside the bird islands. Decks at every level of the great ship towering above us were jammed with people lined up along the rails. As soon as we were alongside Captain Hartmark gave a blast of the siren and we welcomed our hosts by dipping our ensign. The warship replied by firing one of her guns and running up our own Norwegian flag on her mainmast. This was more friendly than we had ever dared to hope. We turned in a sharp half circle, putting on all the speed our engines would stand, and the little Greenland trawler escorted the peaceful grey giant in to her anchorage off Hangaroa village. The whole population was on its legs and down at the pier. The *Pinto* fired twenty-one salutes, and then the launch came out from the shore, bringing the governor to bid the captain welcome to his naval protectorate.

Twenty minutes after the governor had gone on board I went over, as agreed, in our own launch with the skipper and expedition doctor. We had a most cordial reception. A bugler sounded a fanfare when the launch came alongside, and the captain and the governor stood at the head of the gangway to receive us. Up in the captain's cabin we also met a Chilean surgeon-admiral and the American naval attaché with his wife: he was to examine the possibility of constructing a large-scale airfield on Easter Island, to open an air route between South America and Australia. Over a cocktail I gave thanks in a little speech for the wonderful hospitality the governor and his people had shown us during our stay, and the captain most cordially followed up by wishing us as good fortune in the future as we had hitherto had on the island. He offered us supplies if there was anything the expedition lacked, and he sent for two large mail-bags on which the skipper and doctor laid eager hands. The formalities were thus disposed of and the foundation laid for pleasant social intercourse.

Soon after the door opened again, and in came the mayor in a freshly ironed shirt and tie, marching ahead of Lazarus and half a dozen native representatives. The mayor rushed straight up to the grave gold-braided captain, shook him by the hand, and in a loud voice and with vehement gesticulations announced to us all that this was the right kind of captain, he knew how things ought to be done, he was the first who had fired a salute when he came to the island. Then he drew himself up as straight as a ruler, with his fingers stuck down along the side of his trousers, and, with his men standing stiffly at attention behind him, he sang the Chilean national anthem with full bravura right under the captain's nose. The very second this was over all the men relaxed utterly, and like a regular dance band, with swaying shoulders and giving at the knees, they burst out into their own rhythmical royal song about Hotu Matua's landing at Anakena. The mayor had hardly finished the last verse when he caught sight of me. He stiffened like a cat about to spring, pointed and exclaimed:

"*Mi amigo*, Señor Kon-Tiki!"

As if on a signal he and all his friends stuck their hands deep into their pockets and pulled out packets of American cigarettes of different brands, which they held up right under the captain's nose. Here he could inspect samples of the good things Señor Kon-Tiki had brought to the island: that was how it ought to be done!

The captain listened patiently and with stoical calm, and when the cocktail tray came in again, drinks were offered to the new arrivals too. The mayor's eyes shone with pleasure: this captain was a damned sensible fellow after all; it didn't matter if the cigarettes he brought were not as good as Señor Kon-Tiki's. I saw with anxiety how the cocktail disappeared into the mayor at a single gulp. He gave me a sidelong look of pride and satisfaction and said with a reassuring nod that I need not be alarmed, he knew what it was to drink good wine. Then he and his colleagues strolled cheerfully out of the captain's cabin to inspect the ship.

The next time I saw the mayor he was surrounded by an admiring crowd down in the bar of the officers' mess. There were a number of selected passengers on board this trip, including the two professors, Wilhelm and Peña, and a party of Chilean students of archaeology who had come out to look at our excavations. I knew both the two friendly professors from Chile, and was heartily embraced in southern fashion. Both they and the students heard with great interest of the discovery of Easter Island's different epochs, and of the statues of alien type which we had dug out of the earth.

I dared not say a word in the bar about the curious sculptures I had obtained from secret caves: a single careless word now would ruin all my chances of solving the riddle of the family caves. The whole project of getting into one of them still hung on a thread, and if anything leaked out to the natives now, they would be frightened and keep their mouths shut, and their caves, with seven unbreakable seals.

But when I rose to go, I had a real shock. From the bar counter I heard a new and peculiar note in the mayor's bragging voice, and when I saw the manner in which he put down his empty glass I realized that the counter was somewhat out of focus. Then I heard the mayor say, loudly and clearly:

"My friends, I'm a rich man. I have a cave."

I stood for a moment or two as though riveted to the floor to hear what would happen next. Nothing happened. The others went on talking and drinking and the mayor said no more. This can hardly have been the first time he had given himself away over a glass. But either no one had heard him, or it had been taken just as a drunken man's talk; if in fact anyone understood there was anything special about having a cave. It looked as if the mayor had woken up and been frightened at his own words, for no sooner had I returned to our own ship than he was on his way to the shore in another boat.

This year a poor stock of wood-carvings was offered to the crew and passengers of the *Pinto*. The best had been bartered to the members of the expedition long ago. Accordingly Professor Peña went straight up to the mayor's own hut,

where he found an ample choice of finished and half-finished
wooden figures of the best quality. But the mayor refused to sell:
all had been made for Kon-Tiki, and he had more orders from
Kon-Tiki's ship than he could deal with.

Peña had to accept this. The next thing he heard was about
Kon-Tiki's "good luck," that whenever Kon-Tiki's men turned
over a stone or stuck a spade into the earth something strange
came to light. Peña listened patiently to this too, but when the
garrulous mayor got going, still not free from the influence
of the day before, there was absolutely no end to all the things
the Kon-Tiki people had found in the earth. At last Professor
Peña began to be a little worried. The mayor's description
was bound to give anyone the impression that the grass of
Easter Island grew upon a solid mass of art treasures: he quite
forgot to mention that all we had found of real value underground were ruins and giant figures, all of which were still left
in place. Peña could not but believe that our ship was full of
excavated treasures and museum pieces, which we had discovered because we were the first to dig in the earth on the
treeless island.

Later in the evening Professor Peña came ashore for the
second time, and now he went round with a telegram in his
hand. Some who had seen it came to me in dismay to tell me
that it was from the Chilean Minister of Education, who was
now authorizing Peña to confiscate the expedition's archaeological discoveries and take them back with him in the warship.
The governor was extremely disturbed, the captain was
equally unhappy but had no power to intervene, and Father
Sebastian was completely bewildered. If indeed this was
direct authority from the Minister no one on the island could
stop Peña. In that case the expedition would have to surrender
every splinter of bone and every sample of charcoal which the
archaeologists had laboriously excavated in the past few months.

Our despairing Chilean friends would do all they could to
clear the matter up, and it was decided to hold a round table
conference with Professor Peña in Father Sebastian's little
study. Everyone sincerely hoped that the affair would be settled
in such a way that the expedition's material would not be
confiscated. In the meantime the news had spread to the natives.
They came to me trembling with anger and assured me that

no one could take from me what I had bought from them; they could do what they liked with their own property. Estevan and Lazarus in particular were in mortal fear for their cave stones, but Lazarus added that if I sought help from my *aku-aku* it was certain that no one could touch a thing on board my ship. The mayor was profoundly distressed and realized that it was all his fault. He would go straight back to Peña, he said, and explain that the only things of value I had taken on board the ship were personal property I had bought from the people in the village, and that I had looted nothing from the earth.

"We can give or sell our own things to whom we like," said the mayor, and he went off to find Peña.

In the meantime it was decided that the captain of the *Pinto* and his party should drive round in the jeep and inspect the work of the expedition throughout the island. Not until a few days later were we to meet at the conference which had been arranged. The *Pinto* would remain for over a week. Gonzalo would conduct Peña and the students on horseback round the island, and later, under the professional guidance of Bill, they were to begin their own excavation of an ancient reed house site on the Tepeu plain.

Next day the sea was rough and the breakers thundered in towards the coast. The *Pinto*'s passengers could not come ashore, and those who were ashore had to stay there and had recourse to Father Sebastian, of whom they had all heard as a legendary personality and the uncrowned king of the island. At last Father Sebastian grew so tired of questions and photography that he left the house and came to ask me if we could not go out to our ship, where we could sit by ourselves undisturbed by this swarm of people. Father Sebastian did not worry about the surf so long as someone who knew the reefs would take us out. Down at the pier, where steep breakers came frothing in one after another, the mayor stood with a sad face and asked humbly if he might come too: he must speak to me now.

"Don Pedro may come with us," Father Sebastian said kindly, and crawled on board the dancing launch in his long gown, with a helping hand from the skipper.

On board the ship the others had finished dinner, so the steward laid a cold *smörgåsbord* for Father Sebastian, the mayor,

G*

the skipper and me. Father Sebastian loved good food, and a *smörgåsbord* with beer was the best thing he knew. I too have an excellent appetite and count a good meal among the great material pleasures of life. In the two guests now on board I had the most congenial company: they ate and ate, and spread themselves and ate again, and enjoyed life till they were in a regular glow, while the ship rolled slowly in the swell, to and fro, to and fro.

We had canned beer on board, and Father Sebastian gave a friendly nod as a sign that the mayor might have a can too: we both knew that anyway he could now buy wine from the *Pinto*. The mayor was overjoyed and went on eating, filling his glass from the can. But Father Sebastian was beginning to chew more slowly: then he smiled awkwardly and asked us to excuse him, the swell was rather heavier than he had thought. The skipper went out with him to the rail to get a breath of fresh air. The mayor, quite unaffected, went on to consume a fresh helping of the good things from the table.

As soon as we were alone he leant towards me munching and began to talk *aku-aku*. I need not be afraid of anyone taking anything from me: why, our combined *aku-akus* had held back that great warship out there for a whole day. I picked up the thread and whispered that my *aku-aku* had now revealed to me what the mayor had hidden in his secret cave, in addition to the *moko* he had told me about himself. I described in the most cautious terms the appearance of some of the cave stones which had proved to be common to both Estevan's and Lazarus's caves. I assumed that features common to both of them were likely to be found in the mayor's cave also.

The mayor stiffened in his chair and forgot to munch. Had my *aku-aku* been in his secret cave? He had to admit that I was right, and went on chewing feverishly while questioning and fishing to find out what else I had got to know. I had not asked my *aku-aku* about anything more, for now I counted on the mayor being willing himself to show me the cave before he sailed with the *Pinto*. That calmed him down and he said no more, only ate. The steward came and filled the dishes. The mayor loaded his plate afresh, and devoted himself once more to the unaccustomed joys of the *smörgåsbord*. He raised the beer can and looked at me sadly: it was empty, and so

were the others. I had just thought I would go out and ask
Father Sebastian how he was, when I saw the steward had put
down a newly-opened can of beer on an oil drum beside the
door. In one action I stepped over the coaming on my way out,
grabbed the new can, leaned back to place it before the voraci-
ously eating mayor, tossed the empty one into the sea and went
out of the saloon.

While I was standing at the rail talking to Father Sebastian,
who felt better in the breeze, we suddenly heard a terrified
bellow from the mayor. I was at the door in a trice: there he
sat as though transfixed, pointing to the beer-can with his face
convulsed and his eyes popping out of his head!

"Who put it there? who put it there?" he yelled like a
madman.

It occurred to me that there might have been something
wrong with the can. Some had fermented: perhaps the mayor
thought we were trying to poison him. I smelt it.

"Who put it there? All the cans were empty when you went
out," he continued, as hysterically as if surrounded by spirits.
I suddenly realized that he might not have seen me make
the exchange.

"Has no one been here since I went out?" I asked cautiously.

"No! not a soul!"

"Well, then it must have been my *aku-aku*."

The mayor did not doubt it for a moment. He had never seen
such an *aku-aku*: he looked at me quite enviously, the owner
of an invisible servant who could fetch beer whenever I sat
down feeling I should like some. He slowly calmed down and
went on eating, keeping a sharp look-out for any more
mysterious happenings. He wrapped the last pat of butter in
his paper napkin and put it in his pocket. Then he had had
enough, and came to join the rest of us outside. The skipper
had weighed anchor and was carefully moving the ship closer
under the land, where a tiny cape gave us more shelter.

The episode with the beer-can had made a greater impression
on the mayor than the stone whales or anything else he had
seen till then. When we rode in again with the breakers
late in the afternoon, he took me aside on shore and whispered
that his own *aku-aku* was now begging him all the time to go
to the cave and fetch something for me. He too wanted to do

so, but he must get his grandmother's consent first. I had no idea that he had a grandmother, and asked where she was.

"Up there, above Hanga Piko, close to the road and under a block of cement," he replied.

I started, and for a fraction of a second I had a vision of an old woman sprawling helplessly under something which had been overturned: but then I realized that she was dead and had been buried up there. The mayor confided to me in a whisper that he could not ask her in the daytime or by moonlight: it must be pitch dark. But he was going to ask her now, and if she agreed he would go to the cave as his *aku-aku* proposed.

Next day we weighed anchor and returned to the camp at Anakena, while the *Pinto* began to unload. Gonzalo set out on his tour with Professor Peña and the students, and the archaeologists of the expedition, who now had no diggers, were at their posts and showed the visitors over the excavations. These were sociable days, with dinner for us on board the *Pinto* and for the captain and his staff both at the governor's and with us at Anakena. When Peña and the students reached the camp on horseback there was another lively party, and they stayed the night with us. One of the students was a Bolivian archaeologist, and his enthusiasm knew no bounds when he saw the red pillar statue at Vinapu and the kneeling giant at Rano Raraku: he had dug at Tiahuanaco himself and immediately recognized both these types from his own country. Peña was in the highest of spirits: he was wildly excited over all that he had seen, but he whispered to me that unfortunately he had a "disagreeable mission": he had been looking for me in vain to arrange a meeting in connection with a very unpleasant telegram. I told him that the meeting was already arranged. And we remained as good friends as ever.

A couple of days later I had a message from the mayor asking me to send the jeep over to the village to fetch "a heavy sack with important objects." The skipper drove over, he was going anyhow to fetch the three nuns who were to sail in the *Pinto* and were anxious before they left to see the statue which the mayor had almost set up. When the jeep came bumping back again the mayor and Lazarus, with queer poker faces, were sitting on the top of a large sack in the back of a vehicle crammed with nuns and a priest from the *Pinto*. While the others were taken sight-seeing the two natives came into my tent with the sack between them. The mayor had cracked at last. He had been in the cave with his own grandmother, and was so profoundly agitated that he seemed almost irritable. Lazarus, on the other hand, was obviously relieved: I felt that he breathed more freely now that he was no longer the only man who had removed stones from a family cave. They had both been terrified when they had got the infernal sack on to the jeep and the skipper had told them that he was going on to fetch the nuns. But all had gone smoothly: they had had "good luck."

In the sack was a large parcel containing five stones: they came from Lazarus' second cave, which was at Vinapu; from this cave he was now bringing stones for the first time. All the other thirteen stones were from the mayor's own cave. They were the most exquisite sculptures I had yet seen on the island. One figure was a gaping, snarling dog's head with bared teeth and slanting eyes, so wild that it suggested a wolf or fox rather than a domesticated dog. It was a perfectly classical piece of sculpture: I never grew tired of looking at it. There were several dogs or dog-like animals; the snout, body and tail of one were so long that it would have resembled a crocodile but that it stood clear of the ground on four short legs. There was also a crawling *moko* with a broad head, huge jaws and a dentated ridge along its back, a genuine reproduction of a caiman. And there were birds and bird-men and a very curious stone head. Lazarus also had a number of queer figures, among them a flat stone with two copulating snakes in relief.

In the natives' eyes I was bound to know all the answers beforehand, and I had to be extremely careful not to reveal that I was a complete outsider by asking stupid questions. But now I was so absorbed that I blurted out a question about the purpose of these stones. My friends too were so deeply engaged that my blunder aroused no suspicion.

"They give power to actual things," the mayor whispered eagerly. He produced a very realistic sculpture of a lobster, or to be more correct, a Pacific rock lobster with its legs drawn under as in nature and its antennae flat along its back.

"This gives power to the lobster, so that they multiply along the coast."

Then he pointed to the two snakes and explained that double figures gave double power. I knew that the snake was a completely unknown animal on all these islands, and to try them I asked if this gave double power to the "eel." But this did not work, for these were not eels, they said; the eel had no slender neck behind its broad head as these two had; these two were land creatures similar to what the Chileans called a *culebra*. A gigantic one of the same kind was carved in the live rock on the way to the Hanga-o-Teo valley.

I suddenly remembered that Father Sebastian had once told me this, and had asked me to go and look at it with the archaeologists. Eroria knew where the place was, but so far I had not managed to make the trip.

Suddenly Lazarus confessed contentedly that this was the first time anyone had talked openly with anyone else about things like these. He had admitted first to the mayor that he had been in his cave several times to get figures for me, and then the mayor had said that he had decided to do the same. They had confided in one another, and found that much of what they had in their caves was common to them both.

I knew that in Polynesia magical power had once been attributed to human hair, and this knowledge of mine enabled me to impress the mayor and Lazarus, both of whom said that they themselves knew all about it. I now learned that in a stone bowl in the cave the mayor kept locks of hair from all his dead relatives, even from his little red-haired daughter. Then he made a fearful grimace and, shuddering, confided that there was also a *head* in the cave, a real *head*. There were masses of skulls in every possible hiding-place on the island, so I realized that he did not mean a skull, and asked if he meant a stone head. Oh, no, this was a proper head, a human head, he added, shuddering afresh, as with a horrible grin he plucked at his own hair. Could he have a mummified head in the cave, as on some other Polynesian islands?

Lazarus admitted that he himself had neither hair nor heads in the two of his family caves in which he had been: he had only skulls and bones of his own forefathers.

The mayor confided to me that there must be at least

fifteen family caves on the island still in use, and many, many more which had been lost. To the best of his knowledge it was only the descendants of long-ears, and people who had some long-ear blood in them, who had such caves. He did not think that genuine short-ears had caves. He had inherited his own most important cave in the direct line from Ororoina, the only male long-ear who had survived the war at Iko's ditch. The mayor had taken over the cave on the death of his father, to whom it had been handed down from his ancestors going right back to the war, when Ororoina and the other long-ears had to hide all their treasures in secret caves so as not to be robbed by the short-ears. Since the age of five he had worked to learn old customs from the elders of his family, but his father had no confidence in him and found him unworthy of seeing anything till he was fifteen. Then he was allowed to accompany him to a point near the cave, where he waited while his father entered it to fetch some special objects which the boy was allowed to see. That had been the practice for eleven generations.

The mayor paused. Then he said:

"This is the first time I have told this to anyone. But before I went in through the cave's entrance my father cut a lock of hair from my head."

He plucked at the hair up on the top of his head, and Lazarus followed the least of his movements so intently that I realized this was as new to him as it was to me. The mayor went on to describe how his father had rolled up the lock of hair in part of a banana leaf, tied outside with string, in which eleven knots were made. Then the little parcel was taken into the cave and laid in a stone bowl, on which another stone bowl served as lid. All the ordinary family hair lay in another bowl beside it, but in this special bowl there were until now only eleven small packets of hair, most of them red. The first had only one knot and belonged to Ororoina, the second had two knots and belonged to Ororoina's son, and so on down to one with ten knots which belonged to the mayor's own father, and the last with eleven knots which was his own.

After his own hair had been placed in the bowl he learned for the first time the secret of the cave's entrance. A ceremony was held in honour of the *aku-aku* who was guardian of the place and was now to be told that another person was properly

authorized to enter. And then he had for the first time been
allowed to go in and see Ororoina's own cave. For a whole
generation he alone had possessed the ancient secret, but
now an almost insoluble problem had arisen with serious
bearings on the future. His own red-haired son Juan was a
child of his time who no longer understood the old ways. He
was grown-up and married; nevertheless, he could not be
relied on in such serious and secret matters. If Juan found
out where the entrance was he would be tempted by money
and make himself a very rich man by selling the contents of
the cave to the first yacht that came by. The mayor added
sadly that he might therefore be compelled in time to let the
cave go to his youngest brother Atan Atan, who had a truly
good heart and respect for the teachings of their forefathers.

We were expecting guests from the warship to dinner and I
had to break off our conversation. The mayor concluded by
emphasizing that he and Lazarus and I were now united as
brothers, and it was the same with our *aku-akus*, which were
present at that very moment.

"Mine's there," the mayor said cheerfully, pointing down
his left-hand side to a spot on a level with his own knee. We
all left the tent in a crowd, presumably with the *aku-akus*
toddling between our legs, unless the invisible little things
went straight out through the tent walls. For these *aku-akus*
have their own ways of getting about: the mayor had told me
that his own could travel to Chile and back in two minutes.

Outside the tent the mayor gave Lazarus some practical
advice as to how the raising of the statue was to be completed
in one day when he himself had gone in the *Pinto* and Lazarus
had taken charge. Then the dinner guests arrived in jeeps,
ours and the governor's, and when evening came I accompanied
them back into the village: we were to have the meeting with
Professor Peña in Father Sebastian's little house. Father
Sebastian himself was in bed with a temperature, but his little
study was crammed full when all who were to take part in
the proceedings were seated.

The captain from the warship presided, as he was now the
highest authority on the island. Like the governor himself he
too was positive in his attitude from first to last, especially since
he had seen the work of the archaeologists. He now wanted to

Above: How did the old Easter Island sculptors raise a statue without modern apparatus? The long-ears' descendants at last agreed to disclose their old secret.
Below: This is how a statue was set up. It is first lifted into the air on a growing heap of stones, while the mayor stands on the wall directing the work. He possesses the whole secret, handed down for eleven generations.

With a heap of stones under its stomach the figure moves upwards and backwards until it stands in its old place on the wall. Twelve men with poles and
stones set it up in eighteen days.
On the last day the giant is held by ropes to prevent it from toppling off the
high wall when it is tilted into the standing position.

Above: A landmark visible far out to sea was erected at Anakena when the giant stood up in his former place behind the camp on the king's old site.
Below: A structure from the island's earliest epoch. Bill discovered that the *ahu* at Vinapu was the best preserved example of mural technique in the first cultural period. In the second period the statues grew to vast dimensions and absorbed the architect's interest: in the third everything was pulled down.

telegraph to the supreme command of the Chilean Navy and try to get us permission to take a whole statue away from the island. He knew that we had applied earlier and had been refused, because the statues were protected monuments, but he had seen that we had brought to light formerly unknown statues, and that there would thus be more statues when we left than when we came. Beside the captain and his adjutant sat the governor, Professor Wilhelm, Professor Peña and a student; also Gonzalo as the expedition's official liaison officer, Ed and myself.

Peña opened the proceedings by expressing gratitude and admiration for the expedition's work on the island, and then regretfully produced his authority to confiscate all our archaeological material.

Professor Wilhelm, who was an anthropologist of international reputation, rose immediately and defended our case. He explained that it would be impossible for the archaeologists of the expedition to complete their work if they could not take their own scientific material with them to the laboratories. And why, he asked, had nobody said this before? Heyerdahl had been in Chile himself to settle all problems before the expedition came to Easter Island to dig.

Peña admitted this, but said the whole thing was due to a deplorable blunder in the administration. The Foreign Department had given the permission, although the decision lay with the Department of Education.

I put in that I had also been to the Minister for Education in person: he had been extremely kind and told me to let him know if I came up against any problems and needed his help.

Wilhelm hastened to emphasize that everyone wanted to help, it was only a matter of finding a legal way of doing so. And that could be done, for he had himself been on the committee which had drafted the law in question, and there was a loophole in it.

Then Peña's student quickly rose and asked if he might speak. He declared that the lack of Easter Island material in Chilean museums made this confiscation necessary. "No country has so little from Easter Island as we who own the island," he assured us, and Peña nodded.

I replied, with support from Ed and Gonzalo, that the excavations had brought to light the monuments and ruins which they had all now seen for themselves. These finds we had merely exposed and partly reconstructed. What we had otherwise excavated were mainly bones and charcoal and fragments of old stone tools which were very little to put in a museum, but indispensable to our further archaeological study of the island's ancient history. All we had found would be recorded later in our scientific report, and if not included there it would be of no value anyhow. I therefore proposed that we should be allowed to take with us everything we had excavated, and let representatives of Chile choose what they liked after the studies had been completed and the material published.

Both Peña and the student seized upon this: some such arrangement was just what they had in mind, and all the better now that it came as an offer from me.

I added that although we had found no portable museum treasures in the earth, the natives themselves had brought me many curious figures which they claimed were their personal property.

"What the natives have brought you does not interest us," said Peña, "unless—," he moved closer to me, smiling slyly— "unless they should have brought you a *rongo-rongo*?"

"No, I haven't had a *rongo-rongo*," I said, "but they have brought me a lot of other things."

"That does not interest me," said Peña. "I haven't come here as a Customs official. The things you have bought from the natives we could all have bought: what concerns us is what you yourself have found in the earth, for no one has dug here before you."

Thereupon a contract was drawn up at once, by which I was merely deprived of permanent ownership of the archaeological material the expedition itself had found in the earth. I invited Peña to inspect all the expedition's material, both what we had found ourselves and what we had bought or been given, and the meeting then closed. While the others remained to make a fair copy of the contract I went out into the darkness, where the skipper and chief engineer were waiting in the jeep. As I crept into my seat I gave a start. There was a strange black shadow standing motionless in the dark beside me. It was Lazarus. I whispered to him that all had gone splendidly, but he quickly interrupted me.

"I know. I was standing at the window and listened to everything. If the fat little man had said that he would take anything from you, I'd have run to the mayor and we should have been back with two hundred men!"

I thanked Providence for my own sake and Peña's that we had come to a friendly understanding, and I tried to explain to Lazarus that he must never think of doing such a thing. Farther along the road we met the mayor, standing visibly nervous outside his garden gate.

"Take it easy, take it easy," he said warningly, as if he thought we were as agitated as he. "What happened?" he then asked, full of curiosity.

He straightened up and threw out his chest when he heard that they were not going to take from me as much as a single *moai-kava-kava*.

"Ha!" he said triumphantly, striking himself briskly on the chest. "Our combined *aku-akus*!"

He begged the skipper and the engineer in a friendly manner to remain in the jeep: he had a few words to say to Lazarus and me inside the house. In the sitting-room he had one round table, three chairs and a corner cupboard. He turned up the paraffin lamp and produced a newly bought bottle of wine, which he poured into three glasses. We had to pour a little on our fingers too and rub it in our hair for "good luck": then we drank toasts with the rest and strolled out to the others with our hair smelling of wine. The mayor had made a plan. The night was moonless and dark. Lazarus was to keep the two in the jeep company, while the mayor took me to see his grandmother. He wanted to ask her if I might go with him into the cave.

We drove on in the jeep to the cross-roads by the governor's bungalow, then turned a short way down the track towards the little jetty, stopped and turned off our lights, so that we had only the stars twinkling above us. Some native riders passed in the dark: I could barely make them out, although the horses' hoofs clattered by quite close to the open jeep. When they had gone, the mayor declared that he and I were going up the hill to study the stars, and both the skipper and the engineer pretended to believe him. I followed close on the mayor's heels for some distance away to the right of the track till we caught sight of something which in the darkness looked like the remains of a stone wall. Here he stopped and whispered that on the other side of the stones he would not be able to say another word to me, but only make signs.

He sneaked on in silence for another fifty yards, and I followed cautiously, hard on his heels. We came to something which looked like an irregular whitish stone slab: it could quite well have been a patch of cement smeared on the ground, it was too dark for me to see it properly. Here the mayor stopped dead. He pointed to the ground in front of him, made a tremendously deep bow and stretched out both arms before him with the palms of the hands turned downwards. I gathered that he expected me to do the same, so I moved up beside him and repeated the manoeuvre as well as I could. Then, tip-toeing noiselessly, he made a full circle round the light patch on the ground. I followed close behind him and could just make out that a regular track had been worn round the spot. When we had made the circuit, we both bowed deeply again with our arms stretched out before us. This was repeated three times, then he drew himself up silently against the starry sky with his arms folded, and I did exactly the same. I saw in the background all the lights of the great warship lying off the coast.

I was now thoroughly shaken by what I had encountered. This was no longer Easter Island: it was as though I had suddenly witnessed a heathen ceremony in some unexplored wilderness a hundred years ago. And yet I knew that the motionless black figure beside me was the peaceable mayor of the island, who in daily life had a little well-trimmed moustache and at the moment was actually wearing one of my ties. He did not move, he said nothing, but stood as if thinking intently of remote matters. We should never get anywhere with this unless my own *aku-aku* came to the rescue and negotiated a reasonable concession from the obstinate grandmother. I opened my mouth and began to mutter a few words. I should never have done this.

"That's all, there she went!" said the mayor, and suddenly dashed off. I followed as quickly as I could so as not to lose sight of him altogether. He stopped a little way down the hill beyond the stones and stood breathing heavily.

"She said yes," I said.

"She said no," he said, and he repeated what he had so often told me, that his own *aku-aku* said yes, yes. He took a box of matches out of his pocket and emptied the whole of the contents into one of his hands.

"You're to empty your cave like this for Señor Kon-Tiki, my *aku-aku* says, but my grandmother says no, no."

He had asked her three times and she just said no. But now she had said that he was to go to the mainland in the *Pinto* and when he came back he was to present one of the caves to Señor Kon-Tiki, complete, with everything that was in it.

We stood for some time discussing what his grandmother had actually said, and at last he agreed to ask her once more, but alone, and another night. There were not many days left, however, before the *Pinto* sailed.

Two days later I stopped the jeep outside the mayor's garden gate: I had heard nothing at all from him. I found him and Lazarus over a bottle of wine in the little room with the round table. The mayor hastened to assure me that this was a lucky day for Lazarus, for he had said that he would show me one of his caves two days before the expedition left the island. But for the mayor it was an unlucky day. His grandmother still said no: moreover his own brothers were sure that he would die if he took me to the cave, and since he was their chief he must not die. Besides, all the natives had gone on strike and would not unload the *Pinto* unless they received higher wages, and the mayor had just been told that if he did not succeed in stopping the strike he would not be allowed to travel in the *Pinto* on her voyage to the mainland.

The strike continued and spread to the Navy's sheep farm, where no one was any longer looking after the windmills which served to pump brackish water up from prehistoric wells for tens of thousands of sheep. The *Pinto*'s sailing was delayed. Meanwhile the Chileans on board did everything they could for the expedition. Professor Wilhelm saved the expedition's valuable blood samples by replacing a very special preserving fluid. It had run out when the heat had forced the rubber corks from the doctor's test-tubes. The

Pinto's radar experts revived our own radar, which had suddenly broken down after excellent service. And engineer and steward were able to solve many of the problems of their departments through fresh supplies from helpful colleagues on board the great warship. They reported cheerfully that everything should now go without a hitch for another six months. In spite of the delay the launch came in regularly from the *Pinto* with flour and sugar, and large bales of wool were loaded. Finally, the sailing date was fixed.

The day before the *Pinto* sailed we brought our ship round once more from Anakena and anchored alongside the warship. Peña came with us on this trip to inspect the archaeologists' cases on deck in peace and quiet. As soon as he came on board I took him into my cabin and gave him an envelope. It contained a detailed report to the Minister of Education of the results secured by the expedition up to the *Pinto*'s arrival. Peña himself was given a copy in an open envelope, and I asked him to read it. In the report I also described in detail the different types of curious cave stones I had received, which the natives declared to be inherited property kept hidden in secret family caves. Peña asked if I myself had seen such a cave. I said I had not, but that I expected to be taken to one after the warship had sailed. This did not interest Peña, but he thanked me for the report, and asked to be shown the cases containing the things the archaeologists themselves had found.

We went down on to the foredeck, where the first officer had assembled all the archaeologists' cases. When we had opened two, and Peña saw that these contained only plastic bags of charcoal and burnt and crushed fragments of bone, he had no wish to see any more. It was with great reluctance that he consented to come to the shelves in my little private store-room and look at the cartons containing what the natives had brought me. The *Pinto* was to leave the island next day, so I knew that virtually there was no longer any danger of anyone talking carelessly in the village. I took out a sculpture of a grotesque head with terrifying open jaws. Peña started, and excitedly grabbed the stone from my hands. He had never seen anything like it from Easter Island. Had we found any sculptures like that in the earth as well?

We had not. I told him it was always the natives themselves who brought me figures of this type.

Peña lost all interest at once and laid the gaping head back in the carton. He looked admiringly at a large wooden *moai-kava-kava*, and recognized the mayor's work. He regretted the strike which had now prevented that able wood-carver from making the voyage to the mainland, for he felt that the mayor could have given him more interesting information than most people on the island.

On no account would Peña inspect anything more; this did not concern him. In the meantime we had anchored alongside the warship, and the captain and all our friends from the *Pinto* came over in the launch to say good-bye. While I was standing talking to Peña, his own assistant and two other students approached us. I stood them in front of me and while they gazed at me expectantly I said, dramatically and with emphasis, that they must listen to me now and not forget what I said. Then I told them that there were natives on that island who possessed important secrets.

"The Pakarati brothers," someone quickly put in.

"Perhaps. But also the mayor and many others," I said. I told them that the secrets consisted of superstitious customs which were likely soon to disappear. Moreover, I was quite certain that the inhabitants of the island knew the entrances to secret caves containing small sculptures, although I had not yet been allowed to enter such caves.

One of the students interrupted me, saying that I must not pay too much attention to the natives' boasting or to their crazy legends; another said with a knowing smile that the natives were masters in making imitations.

I asked them again to remember what I had said: there were secret caves with sculptures, and I should do all I could to get into one, but if I did not succeed before I sailed, it was their duty to see that an ethnologist was sent to the island as soon as possible to carry on where I had left off. Some agreed, others smiled, and Peña clapped me on the shoulder, laughing indulgently. He had offered the natives 100,000 pesos, or 200 dollars, if they could get him a *rongo-rongo*, but it had been no good. One of the students put in that if only the *Pinto* had stayed another five days he would have got a *rongo-rongo* from a secret cave.

Soon the ship was full of visitors from both the *Pinto* and the village, and no more was said on the subject. Now I had laid all the cards on the table, and they could believe what they liked.

The *Pinto* sailed next day. On board was our frogman, who had dived to forbidden depths in his spare time and had split his ear drums. It was sad to see one of our own party go, but his place was filled by a splendid young Chilean student who had come out with the others in the *Pinto*. Eduardo Sanchez had studied archaeology in Chile and was now to join the expedition as assistant on shore and seaman on board. Gonzalo and he were old friends, and we could not have found better expedition members.

We followed the big grey ship a little astern on her port side for the whole length of the island. We had many friends now among the waving crowd that was closely packed on her wide afterdeck and towering upperworks. As the sun went down we bade her farewell with siren and flags. The little Greenland trawler turned off along the dark cliffs of the coast, and the warship glided on into violet evening clouds which lay in the east, sinister, like the smoke of a fallen shell, while the opposite horizon far to the west still glowed from the angry sun's last burst of fire. So we were left alone in the night with the strange little island, its living population going to bed in the village on the other side. Here only an *aku-aku* or two sat keeping watch over mystic stones on the dark mountain shelves, and far away came a faint glimmer of light from our own camp guard at Anakena.

When the *Pinto*'s last light disappeared, the ship itself passed away into unreality. The outer world does not exist for the natives of Easter Island except when it comes into their ocean for a visit. Many are attracted by stories of Tahiti's green palms and Chile's great houses, but life beyond the horizon, like life after death, is something remote and unreal which takes place quite out of sight, far beyond the blue vault of heaven. To its native population Easter Island *is* the Navel of the World. The cord of birth binds them to this lonely rock in the ocean, this speck which is the real centre of the world. Even great countries like Chile, U.S.A., Norway and Tahiti are located either in the east or the west. But the

Navel of the World is located right here, at the intersection of east and west and north and south—that is, in the centre of the world.

When the *Pinto* had gone life on the island quickly relapsed into normal grooves. The *cocongo* had not yet begun to spread in earnest. The *cocongo* was the natives' great terror—the annual influenza epidemic which always accompanied contact with the mainland. It came and went with the regularity of clockwork. After the ship's visit it always raged in the village for a month or two: it got into chests, heads and stomachs: everyone was ill, and there was always a toll of human lives before the *cocongo* passed and left the people in peace for the rest of the year. But this year the epidemic had been quite unusually mild so far. The natives found their explanation at once: the expedition ship had brought the island "good luck." That, of course, was the reason why no one had fallen ill when we had come to the island.

The Governor and Father Sebastian sent our native diggers back to us, and the archaeologists resumed their work where it had stopped. Ed returned to the top at Orongo where he had made a number of new finds before the *Pinto* came. When he dug out a small and badly executed *ahu* beside the bird-men's ruined village, he had discovered that it was built above the ruins of an older building with beautiful stones, classically cut in the Inca style. He had the turf and earth removed for a long way in front, and found that a series of stones had been placed in rows, connecting the newly discovered classical masonry with the smiling head he had previously found. Round about, on all the stones, carvings of large circular eyes stared at him like typical sun symbols; and when, in the middle of the whole complex, Ed also discovered a curious system of holes bored in the rock, he became suspicious. December 21st was the summer solstice in the Southern Hemisphere, and before the sun rose he and the skipper were standing ready on the top with a rod thrust into one of the holes. When the sun rose over the crater rim on the opposite side of the giant cauldron, a sharp shadow from the rod fell right into the hole where Ed had expected it. He had thus discovered the first ceremonial solar observatory known in Polynesia. The Governor promised to be on the spot at sunrise on the day of the winter solstice, for the expedition would

be gone by then. Ed pointed out the hole into which he then
expected the shadow to fall, and when the time came and the
governor was on the spot, the shadow did fall exactly according
to expectations.

At the summer solstice Bill too took his stand with surveying
instruments, but down on the great classical *ahu* he had
excavated at Vinapu. The sun struck exactly at a right-angle
to the mighty Inca-style wall. The Incas and their predecessors
in Peru were sun-worshippers, and once again these new
observations recalled to our minds the old cultures of South
America. And Bill discovered something more. The plain on
which the red pillar statue had been excavated was a gigantic
sunk temple square about 400 ft. by 500 ft., and formerly
surrounded by an earth wall which could still be clearly seen.
Charcoal from a man-made fire was found beneath the earthen
wall, which laboratory analysis, through radio carbon testing,
dated at about A.D. 800. The corresponding red pillar statue at
Tiahuanaco also lay in a similar rectangular sunk temple
square. And in front of the great stone wall Bill found the
remains of an ancient crematorium in which a great number of
people had been burnt and buried, some of them with their
own bone fishing gear. Cremation had till now been completely unknown in Easter Island archaeology.

Carl went about mapping and studying old stone constructions. In the *ahu* of the Pito te Kura, where the largest
statue on the coast lay overthrown, he excavated a small
burial vault in the elaborate wall. Among crumbled human
bones he found two of the long-ears' extremely beautiful ear
plugs, made from the thickest part of some very large shell.

Arne had several digging teams at work and made interesting
discoveries both inside and outside the crater of Rano Raraku.
Now he had started a trench through one of the round hillocks
which lay at the foot of the volcano. They were so large that
the natives had given them place-names of their own, and
science had hitherto regarded them as natural formations. We
were now to see that all these hillocks had been artificially
formed. They were rubble from the quarry which had been
carried down in large baskets and dumped on the plain, and
here good fortune gave us the only conceivable means of
scientifically dating the making of the statues. As we cut our

way down through the hillock we found broken stone picks and
charcoal from fires. Again the charcoal could be dated by
measuring its radio-activity, and we were to learn that this
particular pile received rubble from the sculptors in the quarry
until about 1470, or two hundred years before the fatal defen-
sive fire was lighted in the long-ears' ditch on Poike.

As work was resumed on various parts of the island, the chief
of the long-ears sat calmly on his front steps after the *Pinto* had
gone, polishing the hooked nose of a wooden figure. With the
aid of his motto, "take it easy," he did not worry much about
the sudden collapse of his dream of travel. The governor let me
promise him instead that he should accompany us to Tahiti,
Hivaoa and Panama when we ourselves left the island, and
this made the mayor the happiest man in the world. This was
indeed a sign of "good luck."

He visited his grandmother again with fresh courage, silent
and alone, but she was as stubborn as ever. That night he was
continually awakened and finally kept awake because his own
aku-aku would give him no peace: it kept on repeating "go into
the cave, go into the cave." At last he could stand it no more:
he rose and went into the cave. He had not seen a soul on the
way, and had not once needed to take cover. When a man was
going to his cave this was a sign of "good luck." When he had
passed through the opening he had grabbed the head of an
animal with long teeth, but the *aku-aku* had said "take more,
take more" and he finally brought a quantity of sculptures
out of the cave. These were now waiting in a hiding-place
outside the village. I must come with the jeep as soon as it
was dark.

This time the queerest animals were there to greet me. One
which continually recurred had a long raised neck and a snout
with three front teeth above and three below, its jaws being
otherwise toothless. But the prize specimen was a round and
broad reed boat, shaped like a regular ark, with three masts and
thick grooved sails which were placed in round holes along a
bulging deck. It looked like a baker's masterpiece made of
dried lava instead of dough.

"Now you see how I knew that the sails also were made from
reeds," said the mayor proudly, pointing to the perpendicular
grooves which gave the illusion of reeds.

That day I noticed that the mayor for the first time had begun to clear his throat; the *cocongo* was knocking at his door. The owner of the cake-ship said contentedly that he could never remember the *cocongo* being so mild as it was this year. But as long as he had the suspicion of a cough he could not visit the cave, for it was "bad luck" for anyone who was not quite well to enter such a place. A few old people had done so in the past, but it was on purpose to hide there and die.

When the long-ears came back to Anakena it was Lazarus who climbed up on the *ahu* wall and directed the work with certainty and vigour during the critical moment on the eighteenth working day when the giant tilted up and freed himself from the unwieldy stone pile, which instantly collapsed in a rumbling cloud of dust.

Soon afterwards a storm broke out and the skipper had to take the ship into shelter by moving round to the village side of the island, and anchoring there for a couple of days. When the storm abated and the ship returned to her old anchorage off our beach, I heard through the walkie-talkie that the skipper had with him a native from the village who insisted on showing me something he had with him on board.

I went out in the launch and found that the native was my young friend Estevan. The lad had evidently something on his mind. Today there was a boyish happiness about his smile which had been absent of late, since his wife had suddenly stopped the cave traffic. He asked politely but eagerly if I had a really dark place on board the ship, for he was now going to initiate me into a great secret. I took him to my own cabin and pulled down the blinds. This was dark enough for Estevan. He disappeared and came back lugging two large bundles. He carefully shut the cabin door behind him and asked me to stand in one corner and just watch what was going to happen.

It was so dark in the cabin that I could only just distinguish Estevan as a dim shadow when he bent over something he had drawn out of the bundles. My first thought was that some phosphorescent object would appear, as he had to have the cabin so dark. But no, what he took out was as black as the darkness around us, and I dimly saw that he was putting something on himself. So he was going to perform in a dancing mask or some other disguise. I was sure I could see two great long ear-flaps dangling down beside his head, but it was too dark to make out anything with certainty. At last he took two large dark objects out of the bundles: one remained on the floor, the other he laid on the seat beside my bunk. Then he squatted down and I could see that he laid a hand on each side of the object on the floor, as if he was about to enter upon a serious conversation with a dear friend.

And then he began to murmur a stream of Polynesian words in a low and reverent voice. His voice was soft and melodious, but grave and uncannily intense, and a curious feeling came over me. A few seconds passed before I suddenly realized that this was no mere demonstration for my sake: the handsome young man was busy performing a serious heathen ceremony. I saw that he was becoming more and more absorbed and moved by what was happening, and when he had finished with the object on the floor and put his hands round the other on the seat, he gradually became so emotional that the whole tone of his voice changed; soon he began to sniffle. It was impossible to hear what he was saying, but I gathered that I myself was mentioned several times. Towards the end he had increasing difficulty in suppressing his choking sobs, and at last he was weeping as bitterly as if he had lost a close friend for ever.

I was extremely uncomfortable. I felt an intense desire to talk to him and console him, and to find out what was going on. But I thought it wisest not to interfere for the time being. Finally Estevan pulled himself together and began to take off his costume in the dark. He asked me to let in the light. When the blinds went up Estevan stood before me with a grave smile on his face, his eyes red with weeping. I had to give him a handkerchief, which he needed for both eyes and nose: but behind it all he seemed as happy as if he had come to the end of a bad dream.

The clothes he had worn were a thick dark woollen jersey, and a regular black polar cap with long hanging ear protectors which he must have got from a passing whaler. On the floor sat a large red stone dog, so thoroughly worn by scrubbing that it looked like a half-melted chocolate figure, and up on the seat there lay outstretched a diabolical creature like Satan himself in the shape of a beast, with a hump-back and a goatee beard under an evil grin. It was made of a harder grey stone and was perfectly preserved, in contrast to the overwashed dog on the floor.

Estevan pointed reverently, almost affectionately, to the object on the seat and said that according to his wife it was the more powerful of the two. These were two of the four *aku-akus* who guarded his wife's cave. The other two, which were still in the cave, were large heads with strange figures on the top. It was these two guardians now lying before me who had been angry because his wife had taken so much from their section of the cave. She had been suffering from stomach trouble ever since, and she had now decided that the best thing to do was to send the two angry guardians over to me in the hope that they would be pacified when they recovered their sovereignty over their own stones. Estevan had with him five ordinary cave stones which belonged to the same group: one of them was a double-headed monster which looked much more terrifying than the innocent dog sitting quietly on the carpet before the bunk. There were several more figures in the cave which belonged to these two guardians: one was the big boat with figure-heads fore and aft of which he had told me before. Now it was all to be mine.

I asked if I could not visit the cave myself and fetch these things, since they were going to be mine anyhow. Estevan suggested that we should make a joint effort to persuade his wife. I promised to pay them a visit in the village one evening, and said I would bring the doctor to find a remedy for the mysterious illness she had contracted. Then Estevan turned to his friends the dog and Old Nick on the seat, and emphatically declared that these two guardians were now legally transferred to me. He had done everything his wife had said he should do, for this was the way her father had acted when she took over the cave, and her grandfather had done just the same when handing it over to her father.

Now the whole responsibility was on me, and when some day I should hand over the two guardians to another person I must act exactly as he had done, preferably in clothing that was not visible in the dark. I could show the guardians to anyone on board, but not to a single person on the island. I must wash them for the first time after three months, and from then on they should be attended to four times a year. It was not enough to wash them clean of dust and growths: I must carefully pick out some white webs which appeared like cotton in the holes of the stone, and every year I must smoke out insects which laid eggs in the pores.

When the two guardians and their stone subjects had been packed away a heavy responsibility seemed to have been lifted from Estevan's young shoulders. He gave me to understand that he himself was a good Christian, but his ancestors knew no better than to hold converse with devils and had bequeathed a fearful responsibility to those who had to take over the devils and could not escape from their whims.

I asked Estevan if the two creatures he had given me were devils, and he had to admit that in Spanish that would be the name for them, even if his forefathers called them *aku-akus*.

So now I had two *aku-akus* on board the ship. It was nice to know. Estevan gave me clearly to understand that if the decision lay with him I should get the two which were left in the cave as well, and all the others in the island. It would be best if every single *aku-aku* was put on board our ship and taken away from the island for ever; then there would be no need to worry about such things again. For all the people on the island today were good Christians and would never have had anything to do with this business if it had not been forced upon them to the danger of their lives and health.

Estevan had been to school, and he could write. In beautiful characters he wrote down for me what he had said in the dark, and explained that I must hand on the same text to the person who some day would take the two guardians from me. I read on the scrap of paper:

Ko au Ko Kon Tiki he Atua Hiva
Hua viri mai te i Ka uru atua na Ki te
Kaiga Einu Ehoraie Ehiti Ka pura Eurauraga
te Mahinaee. Ka ea Korua Kakai Kahaka
hoa ite umu moa ite umu kokoma ote
atua hiva.
Ko Kon Tiki mo hatu O Ko ia
To Koro Va Ka Tere Ko haho Kogao Vari
one ana Kena O Te Atua hiva Ko Kon Tiki.

Estevan was unable to give me a proper translation, but the

gist was that I, a lord from the outside world, had come from there to here with my party, and here I had caused the four *aku-akus* named Einu Ehoraie, Ehiti Ka pura, Eurauraga and Mahinaee to eat the intestines of a cock baked in an earth oven before the entrance to the cave O Ko ia, while my ship lay swinging at anchor off the sands at Anakena.

I realized that this business with the intestines must have been something Estevan and his wife had already arranged on my account before the opening to her cave.

The doctor and I took the first opportunity of going into the village a couple of days later, and we slipped into Estevan's little hut unseen. A small table with a bowl full of flowers, together with two stools and two benches, made up the whole inventory of the hut, and we guessed that there was a bed behind a curtain along one of the walls. Everything was painted white and light blue and all was spotlessly clean.

When Estevan's wife came out from behind the curtain, she turned out to be a real beauty. She was pale and well-shaped, with long black hair, grave intelligent eyes and a quiet, modest bearing. There was complete poise about the sick girl as she came forward and greeted us, bare-footed, with the dignity of a queen. She did not talk much Spanish, and Estevan helped when we had difficulty in understanding. They apologized for having no chairs, but we were happy to sit down on the benches. I looked at the quiet girl sitting erect with her hands in her lap. She was not the idea I had formed of Estevan's strong-willed wife; I had expected a regular amazon. She answered all the doctor's questions clearly and placidly: she proved to have developed an abdominal trouble, the curing of which would be a simple matter if she would go into the little village hospital for treatment.

Estevan himself raised the matter of the cave. His wife's gentle, quiet answers to my questions were given as calmly and confidently as ever. Her father had said that if a stranger was let into the family cave some near relative of hers would die. She did not want to die, and she did not want anything to happen to Estevan. So she could not take me to the cave. She was completely inflexible on this point. Estevan added unhappily that the first time he had tried to persuade her she had wept for two days and nights, and when I saw how desperately

The only giant at his post Hundreds of statues once stood on walls all round the island: all of them were flung down during the civil wars in the third period. Lazarus and the author standing before the newly erected giant, the only one which today stands in his place, gazing across the old temple square.

Above: The mayor was a pure-bred long-ear and the strangest personality on the island. He possessed great funds of old knowledge, fine abilities and vivid imagination, but he was highly superstitious. From the left: the mayor's brother Atan Atan, the mayor, Hei, the mayor's redhaired son Juan, Lazarus, Enlique.

Below: A giant on the move. The mayor organized the dinner guests in the Anakena valley to pull a newly excavated statue on a trial run.

serious she was about the whole thing I decided to drop the matter.

I asked instead if she would take a photograph for us in the cave if we taught her how to do it. But no. If she did that, strangers could see the cave in the photograph, and it was the cave which was taboo.

This was a real disappointment. Finally I asked, without much hope of consent, if she could bring the rest of the things in the cave to the house so that we could photograph them there. To my astonishment she agreed without a moment's hesitation. I was still more amazed when Estevan proposed to her that they should put all the stones in an ordinary cave they had in the garden, which had a secret entrance but was not taboo. Then I could simply photograph everything there. His wife immediately agreed to that too, with two exceptions—the two guardians which had to remain in the family cave.

They looked quite crestfallen when I shook my head and explained that the cave interested me only if it was the actual family cave. We finally agreed that the contents of the cave should be brought to the house, and they would let me know when everything was there.

As we were taking our leave I asked if it was her father who had made the stones. Oh, no! He had only helped with a few of them. Her grandfather, who had received the name Raimundi Uki when Christianity was introduced, had made almost all of them before he died at the age of 108. She could remember him working to teach her father when she herself was quite a little girl. She had been told that her great-grandfather had originally helped her grandfather with "advice." When the cave was first brought into use she did not know, but some of the things were really old, even though the bulk of them came into the cave in her grandfather's time.

We now knew that at any rate one of the strange caves on Easter Island had been a growing institution, part of the local life, and not only a sealed-off chamber with treasures stored away since the island wars. Estevan's wife's cave may have been the last on the island which had still been growing: and it was the first to lose any of its contents to the outer world. But I realized when the young couple let us out into the night that this particular cave I would never see.

H

CHAPTER VIII

INTO THE SECRET CAVES OF EASTER ISLAND

ONE evening at sunset Lazarus and I were riding side by side along the old grassy road that led from the statue quarry in Rano Raraku to the camp at Anakena. Behind us the volcano glowed red in the evening sun, before us stretched the stone-covered plain on which the shadows were beginning to lengthen. The quiet of the evening lay over sea and sky: all that met the eye breathed of peace. Only two deformed caricatures of riders followed us in every slightest movement, our own long shadows. I felt once again as if Lazarus and I were riding alone on the moon.

Then I stopped my horse and turned round: the two grotesque shadows had suddenly become three. An unknown horseman had appeared close on our heels; lanky and pale, he sat on his horse and stared at us with as grave a mien as death himself. He stopped like a shadow the moment we stopped, without saying a word: but directly we jogged on this third shadow followed us. There was something mysterious about the man and the whole of his demeanour.

Lazarus muttered to me over the horses' bobbing heads that the man who was following us was the sexton's brother. The other day he told Lazarus that if he got him a job with me he was willing to work without pay. This made the man even more mysterious: I felt no urge to have this gloomy horseman among my nearest workers. I felt his eyes on the back of my neck: he did not overtake us if we slowed down, and if we quickened our pace he did the same. Out of the corner of my eye I saw the gaunt, spidery shadow of him and his horse following us, mile after mile, right down to the camp, where shadows of men and tents blended into one as the sun set behind the ridge and night fell upon us.

Lazarus did not think that the rider had heard what we were talking about. I had said that some time in the future it would be possible to find the secret caves and tunnels of the island by going over the ground with a kind of cavity detector. This had made a strong impression on Lazarus. As we rode along he pointed out several areas in which such an apparatus would be effective because there were supposed to be secret caves below, of which the openings had been lost. He declared with dismay that the first person to bring the apparatus to the island would get rich simply by walking among the houses in the village. A secret cave three hundred yards long, which had belonged to one of the last kings, ran underground to the sea from an unknown spot near the most northerly houses. It was found by a man who brought up some gigantic spear-heads from the cave, but the *aku-akus* bit and pricked him night after night until he died.

As soon as I came out of the tent next morning I saw the pale, skinny man again. He was lying motionless in the grass just outside my tent, gazing at me from the other side of the rope boundary. The policemen, Nicolas and Kasimiro, had long since ceased to keep watch, for no one touched a thing in the camp any more. All day I had the impression that the thin man was following me like a faithful dog, always at a distance and without having anything to do or a word to say.

When night fell again, and all the rest of us went to bed in the camp, I saw him sitting in the dark on the temple wall outside my tent.

There was a regular cloudburst over the island that night. The natives were delighted, for the water-tanks in the village were bone-dry and people had begun a laborious search for water in caves and up in the great crater swamp. Now the water poured down in streams, to them a sign of "good luck" in the very middle of the dry season. But for us in the tents it was a veritable deluge. After the rain had stopped a frothing brown chocolate-covered brook came rolling down the jeep track from the high ground and turned the camp area into a lake.

I was awakened by Anette calling out excitedly in Polynesian "Look, mummy, look!" and pointing in delight to her potty, which had begun to move and sail about among the camp beds. I was less enthusiastic when I saw that the trunks and all our belongings were awash and foundering. Outside there was a whirling, gurgling stream, and I heard a beautiful mixture of

laughter and swearing from the different tents. The roof of the
kitchen tent had collapsed, the Primus screens were full as wash-
tubs, and the food was afloat. The cook and steward stood in a
porridge of flour and sugar striking the floor with an iron bar
to make an outflow into the sand, the cameraman was piling
films and gear into his bed, and the sailors were baling out
their tents with mugs and buckets as if they were on board
a sinking ship.

We quickly diverted the rest of the flood by making a ditch and
a dam across the track. Amid all our misery and chaos the long-
ears came over jubilant from their dry cave and congratulated
me: this was "good luck!" Now there would be water enough
on the island for both man and beast for a long time to come.
The skipper reported happily from the ship that they had
collected several tons of rain-water: the fresh-water tanks had
been filled to the brim in a single night. The winds died down
with the heavy rain which put an end to the unstable weather
of the last few days.

But over in the long-ears' cave a solitary man lay writhing
in agony. He was back from a night visit to his family cave,
fetching stones for the first time, when he was caught by the
cloudburst. I knew nothing about it till late the next night,
when the doctor and I came home from our meeting with
Estevan and his wife. It was long past midnight, and before I
crept into my tent I stood for a moment to look at the silhouette
of the newly erected giant against a southern sky ablaze
with stars. Then Lazarus appeared out of the darkness, and
I saw by the grave expression on his face that something
was wrong. He told me that the sexton's brother, the gaunt
rider, lay dying in Hotu Matua's cave. Could the doctor
come?

We stopped the doctor from crawling into his sleeping-bag,
and all three of us hurried across the plain to the cave. Lazarus
told me on the way that the sick man had confided to him that
he had a cave: he had been there the night before and fetched
a number of things, which he had hidden in a sack among some
rocks up on the ridge above the Anakena valley. But early
in the morning, back in Hotu Matua's cave, he had suddenly
been taken ill: he grew worse as the day passed and was now
lying doubled up and retching, with a fearful pain in his

stomach. He had told Lazarus where the sack was hidden, and asked him to bring it to me if he himself should die.

People were lying everywhere in the cave trying to sleep, and at the far end the lanky man lay, pale and hollow-cheeked, looking like death itself as he twisted in pain, groaning and panting. They all watched round-eyed while the doctor examined the skinny body fore and aft and gave him a meal of pills. As the night passed the patient became quieter, till it was evident that he was neither in pain nor in danger. When at last we left the cave the thin man was so far recovered that he was able soon afterwards to creep out and disappear into the darkness. He went straight up to the ridge for the sack, and hurried direct from there to the cave, where he rushed the contents of the sack back into their old places. Then he returned to the village, relieved and empty-handed, and told his friends that he had escaped death by a hair's breadth. The doctor told me that the man had only suffered a severe attack of colic.

The sexton's pale brother had come and gone almost like a shooting star in the night, but both the torrential rain and the healing of a dying man had made an impression on all his compatriots in the cave. When I returned to my tent in the small hours of the morning, a great snarling head lay in my bed, the head of a feline large enough to be a lion or a puma. When I struck a match and looked round in the flickering light I saw that Yvonne was wide awake. She whispered that a native had been there and pushed the great head in through the tent opening. She thought she had recognized the mayor's youngest brother.

She was quite right. Next day the little man with the moustache and the large antelope eyes came to me in the tent. It was young Atan, who had a heart of gold and had turned up the first whale along with the mayor, Lazarus and me. Lazarus, who now felt quite emancipated, had been trying for a long time to put courage into little Atan. Atan had disclosed to Lazarus that he too had a cave: he had even told Lazarus that he had thought of asking his eldest brother, the mayor, for permission to give Señor Kon-Tiki something from the cave.

When Atan had peered out of the tent and made sure that no one was listening to us, he replied freely to any questions, and told me all he knew. He was a long-ear of pure blood.

There were four brothers: the eldest, who was head of the family, was the mayor Pedro Atan, then came Juan Atan, Estevan Atan and finally himself, Atan Atan, who bore the additional name Hare Kai Hiva, after an old ancestor. Each of the four brothers had received a cave from their rich father. Atan, being the youngest, had the smallest cave with only sixty sculptures. Further, as the youngest, he had nothing to do with his brothers' caves, but they could take decisions about his. He had received the cave from his father, who had it from Maria Mata Poepoe, who had it from Atamo Uhu, who had it from Hare Kai Hiva, and it was he who had made the sculptures. I recognized the name of Hare Kai Hiva from the mayor's family tree: he was a direct descendant of the only surviving long-ear, Ororoina.

To a question from me, Atan replied rather hesitantly that the great head he had brought me represented a sea-lion; these animals sometimes appeared on the coast. I pointed out that a sea-lion had no ears. Atan agreed, but thought there might have been other kinds of sea-lions in Hare Kai Hiva's time.

Atan was genuinely distressed at the idea that some day people would be able to find his cave with a machine: Lazarus had told him this. If his brothers would allow him he would rather be rid of the whole thing, for he was a good Christian and thought it would be best if the whole responsibility was transferred to a protected museum.

Atan Atan was a simple candid soul and not very difficult to influence. He had seen more than enough and required no further persuasion: three evenings later I was invited to his own little hut on the outskirts of the village. There he confided to me in a whisper that both his old aunt Tahu-tahu and his two brothers Pedro and Juan had given him a free hand to make over the cave to me: only one brother remained, Estevan Atan, and I must help to persuade him. While I sat alone, waiting by the burning candle, Atan stole over to the next hut and fetched his brother.

I saw at once that this was a man I had never met. He was the only one of the four brothers who had never worked for me. Atan naïvely confided to me that his brother was captain of the gang who had built a boat to clear off to Tahiti as soon as the expedition ship was no longer there to keep an eye on them. The new arrival looked rather annoyed, but admitted that this was true. He had never been to sea, but he had learnt all about the stars from old islanders, and knew how to find his way across the ocean.

So here was the next village skipper to push off for Tahiti. He was an unusually fine looking fellow in his thirties, with thin firm lips, honest eyes and a good bearing. As with the other brothers, there was nothing of the native in his appearance: he would have passed unnoticed in any street in Northern Europe. But he was a genuine long-ear, a direct descendant of Ororoina.

Estevan Atan, the "village skipper," was a man of enquiring mind. He asked about the drift of the *Kon-Tiki* raft and the outside world below the horizon. The night was well advanced before little Atan managed to change the subject to families and caves, but it went quite smoothly. Late at night it was disclosed that the village skipper himself had about a hundred sculptures in his own cave: formerly there had also been a jar of *ipu maengo* among them, but this tiny coffee-coloured vessel had been broken. His finest treasure was a "book" with *rongorongo* written on all the pages. No one in the island had seen it but himself. I was also told that the family cave-chief was old aunt Tahu-tahu: she was something of a sorceress and had dealings with the devil. She had an immensely important cave, which their cousin would certainly take over at some future date. Old Tahu-tahu had friendly feelings towards me, for I had once given her cigarettes and black dress material when she came to Anakena to dance for "good luck" before the men in Hotu Matua's cave.

A few days later things began to move. Rumours first reached the camp that little Atan had suddenly developed blood poisoning and was in the village hospital. My heart sank. He was sure to think that this was punishment for having taken the feline head from his cave. Soon afterwards Lazarus brought news that the village doctor had lanced Atan's finger: he had "good luck," for all was going well. And then came a message the concealed purport of which was that Atan awaited me at his hut. To attract as little attention as possible I went by jeep to the church late in the evening and stepped in to see Father Sebastian. He was ablaze with excitement when he heard what was brewing. His dearest wish had been to see one of the secret caves of which he had heard so many rumours, and which he thought were now lost. He realized that it was useless for him, as a priest, to come with us. But I had to promise to report to him as soon as I had seen anything. I was just to come in and wake him up at any time of night if I was passing.

For the last stretch from Father Sebastian's house to Atan's, down a rocky path, I groped my way along a stone wall in pitch darkness. I found the gate and went in and knocked at the low wooden door. Atan, with his arm in a sling, opened it cautiously and let me squeeze in. He shut the door carefully behind me, and we sat down on each side of a little table with a lighted candle. Atan removed a cloth and disclosed a grinning death's head on the table between us. The head was of lava with horribly realistic features, bared teeth and jaw-bones and deep dark holes for eyes and nostrils. On the top of the skull were two strange cup-shaped cavities the size of a thumb-nail.

"That's for you," exclaimed Atan, pointing to the skull. "There is the key to the cave. Now the cave is yours."

I was so surprised that I did not know what to do, but little Atan was at least as excited as I was. Before I could say anything stupid he pointed to the two little hollows on the cranium and confided to me that they had been full of powdered bones from an *aku-aku* which would have killed anyone who touched this "key." But old aunt Tahu-tahu had been in the cave and removed all the bone-meal so carefully that I could feel quite safe. Throughout, Atan referred to his stone skull as a "key" and said I must keep it under my bed until we went to the cave together two days later. Then I must take the "key" with me.

I shall never forget the sight of Atan with the flickering candle beside the grey skull, and I shuddered inwardly as I saw myself and my shadow grasp the grinning stone "key" which now was mine. Both the light and our voices were so faint that they scarcely reached the walls, but outside I heard the clatter of horses as solitary riders passed up and down the alley. The amount of activity in the village at night was puzzling.

Atan begged to come to the camp for a special meal, a *curando*, for "good luck" as he put it, on the day he fixed for our nocturnal visit to his cave. When I asked to be allowed to take a friend along, he was at first very reluctant. But his second thought was that the cave was mine now, and if I was going to empty it anyhow another person might not do much harm. He was relieved when I suggested Ed, for his brother Juan had worked for Ed at Orongo and said he was a good fellow. But three was an unlucky number, so Atan wanted to take his own brother Estevan, the village skipper. Finally I managed to wangle in the photographer as well, but then Atan wanted to have another of his people too so that we should be six; for two, four and six were good numbers. But he asked me meekly not to take more, for we might unintentionally annoy the *aku-aku* of the cave.

On the great day our captain drove over to the village to fetch Atan Atan, and came back bringing also Atan's brother, the village skipper and a young friend, Enlique Teao, who had been working all the time with the mayor's team of long-ears. Dinner was over when they arrived, so we were alone in the mess tent where the steward served a plain *smörgåsbord*. The village skipper asked me quietly to give a little "good luck" present to brother Atan today, and another to aunt Tahu-tahu, who had agreed to his handing over the cave. She had even gone to the cave early that morning and had baked a hen for the *aku-aku* near the entrance.

When we sat down to table the natives first made the sign of the cross and murmured a little grace. Afterwards Atan looked up at me innocently and explained that this was *otra cosa aparte*, "another thing apart." Then he leaned over the table towards the rest of us and said in a whisper that before we began the meal each of us must repeat aloud in Polynesian:

"I am a long-ear from Norway. I am eating from the earth oven of the Norwegian long-ears."

When everyone had said this in turn, all further conversation was conducted in whispers. Only afterwards did I realize that the meal was in honour of the *aku-akus*, to whom our mutual relationship had just been made known. I knew that Atan had abandoned his former idea that the original inhabitants of the island had come from Austria: both he and the other long-ears were now certain that at least their own tribe had come from Norway. We had on board our ship a big sailor with flaming red hair who was specially enlisted in support of this idea. So

H*

now, during the ceremonial *curando*, the *aku-akus* were initiated into this rather complicated relationship.

When Ed came into the tent with a message I asked if he might participate in the "good luck" meal since he was to visit the cave with us. Then Ed had to repeat in Polynesian, with a broad American accent, that he too was a long-ear from Norway, who was eating from the earth oven of the Norwegian long-ears. Then the meal continued, profoundly serious, with all conversation in hoarse whispers. The table talk about spirits and caves was as strange to us as the *smörgåsbord* dishes were to our guests. Atan liberally helped himself to butter with a cheese-scoop and laid slices of lemon on his bread instead of in his tea, but everything tasted equally good, and they all thoroughly enjoyed the meal. When the three natives were full they went into an empty tent to rest; it was a long time before the hour when we could set out on our secret mission.

A couple of hours after nightfall Atan came to tell me that we could start now. He was grave and solemn: it was clear that he regarded the impending transfer of a cave as a serious event. Personally I had a feeling that I was starting on a long and strange journey when I went into the tent to say good-bye to Yvonne and took the grinning death's head from a mail-bag under the bed. How this magic key was to be used I had no idea, and no one could tell me. Apart from the initiated owners of secret family caves I was the first person to hold such a stone in my hands. Yvonne sent along an S.A.S. air bag with presents to old Tahu-tahu, and then I crawled out into the night to tell Ed and the photographer that we could start.

We were to go by jeep past the lonely sheep farm at Vaitea on the high ground in the middle of the island, and from a point between there and the village we were to continue on foot towards the cave. By way of camouflage we filled the back of the jeep with bundles of washing, and the skipper drove us up to Vaitea. Here he delivered the washing to Analola, the native manageress at the sheep farm. With some girl friends she had undertaken to do all our washing since they had access to the only tap on the island: the water was piped from an overgrown crater lake in the volcano of Rano Aroi.

The photographer took the wheel and drove on with the three natives, Ed and myself. We had started in glittering starlight, but now came a shower. Atan, who was sitting solemnly on the tool-box between the photographer and me, looked uneasy and began to whisper to me about the need for some "good luck." I heard the village skipper mutter to Ed in a conspicuously gloomy voice that it looked as if the wind was changing. Strained as the natives were tonight I could not judge with certainty whether anything in particular worried them, or whether they were merely oppressed by the gravity of the occasion. I feared that something might happen to make them draw back at the eleventh hour. The sexton's brother was fresh in my memory.

In the back seat Ed and the two natives were no longer exchanging a single word. The photographer at the wheel was silent of necessity. He understood neither Spanish nor Polynesian and could converse with the natives only through pantomime and gesticulation. When he suddenly stopped the jeep and jumped out to look at all the wheels the two Atan brothers were terrified and asked what was wrong. I tried to calm them, saying that everything was all right. Obviously they were both in a state of nerves and looking for all sorts of omens and signs. I was almost in a panic myself lest the jeep should break down, because the photographer, ignorant of our conversation, began to gesticulate vividly, explaining with a worried look that he thought the engine was running on only three cylinders. But it bumped on in the deep crooked wheeltracks, and the stars again glittered above us between the scudding clouds. The two brothers still sat as if on pins and were visibly nervous. When we came to the place where we were to stop, Atan suddenly changed the programme. It would be better if we drove on right into Hangaroa and waited in his house till the whole village was asleep.

When we approached the village he changed his mind again: his *aku-aku* had said we were to drive to his brother's house instead of his own. We drove straight through the village with our lights on, swung down towards the coast in front of the church and went on for a short way northwards along a stone wall. Here we were told to turn the lights off and stop, and Enlique Teao was left to look after the jeep while the rest of us climbed over the wall and walked in a drizzle across a stony field. Small, light lava stones lay strewn so thickly over the

ground that walking was difficult and Atan offered the photographer, the oldest in the party, a shoulder to prevent him
from twisting his ankle or falling. He repeatedly whispered to
Ed that it was safe for his own friends to go over his land
because he had a good heart; his *aku-aku* therefore saw that
nothing happened to those who crossed his ground. He naïvely
added that he had always been kind to others: he gave food to
those who had none and listened to those who asked for help.
So his own *aku-aku* was satisfied with him.

In the middle of the stony field was a little white-washed hut.
The village skipper tapped cautiously at both the window and
the door before he succeeded in waking his wife. At last the
door was opened by a most lovely vahine, a grave woman in her
thirties, of almost savage beauty, with long raven-black hair
flowing down over a magnificent figure. The village skipper,
for all his family pride, had found among the short-ears a
worthy South Sea wife.

Two benches were drawn up to a small table in the middle of
the floor, and here the beauty, gliding round us like a silent
shadow, placed a small candle. The village skipper disappeared
into the other room and in a little while came back with a
coverless manuscript book which he carefully drew from an
old paper cement-bag and laid before us in the candle-light.

The book, whose leaves were yellow and faded, was once
made as a copy-book for children in the schools of Chile, but it
had been used for quite a different purpose. On every page
were pagan *rongo-rongo* signs: small neatly drawn figures of
bird-men, demons and other curious symbols which we knew
so well from the mysterious picture-writing of Easter Island.
When we turned the pages we saw some with nothing but
unreadable lines of hieroglyphs, while others were arranged
like a dictionary, giving the meaning of the different signs. The
rongo-rongo symbols were then nicely set out in a column down
the left-hand side of the page, and to the right of each sign its
meaning was given in Polynesian written in Easter Island
dialect by means of rather naïve Latin characters.

We sat round the candle and looked at the faded *rongo-
rongo* book, speechless with astonishment. It was obvious that
this was no mere bluff arranged for us by the village skipper;
and it was equally clear that if the person who had once

written these mysterious signs really possessed the secret of the *rongo-rongo* writing, then this simple coverless book was of enormous value, opening up undreamed-of possibilities for the interpretation of Easter Island's ancient picture-writing.

I noticed that 1936 was written on one of the pages, and asked the village skipper where he had obtained this fine book. He said that his father had given it to him a year before he died. His father could write neither *rongo-rongo* nor modern characters, but he had told his son that nevertheless it was he who had made the book: he had carefully copied an older book which had completely fallen to pieces and that one had been made by *his* father. The village skipper's grandfather was a learned man who could carve *rongo-rongo* on slabs of wood and also sing the text. At that time there were some men alive on the island who had learnt to write modern letters while they were in exile as slaves in Peru. One of them had helped the old *rongo-rongo* man to record the sacred meaning of the ancient signs to prevent their total loss since nearly all the experts had died during the slave raid.

Both Atan and the village skipper's own wife were as amazed at the book as we were, and the owner proudly confided to us that until now he had not let a single person see it. He had kept it in the cement-bag in his own cave, and only took it out now and then when he wanted to think of his father. He had decided to make a copy before this book too fell to pieces, but he had found that it was a fearful task to copy all the little figures on the forty-one pages of the book. I proposed that the cameraman should borrow the book and make an exact photographic copy for him, and after much hesitation he reluctantly consented.[1]

It was now growing late by local standards, and I asked if we should not be going soon. The village skipper replied that there was no need to go yet: he would know when it was eleven, for a particular cow always lowed then. I did not hear the cow but not long after we broke up and the black-haired vahine took us to the door with the candle. Again Atan carefully

[1] Thereby the irreplaceable contents of the book were saved for posterity, because one dark night after the expedition ship had left, the village skipper slipped off to sea in his little boat. Nobody knows his fate. Perhaps the book is still hidden in his cave, the entrance to which is lost. Perhaps it accompanied its owner into the distant ocean.

Ure vae inu   To ma nia kva

Two pages from the village

hehaga kite kupega.	korara ia hoa
kuaki a rurua.	tagata, mau ahi
kaka tava	ite muku, nuku, ahi,
kuahuki tegutu	~~maitae~~
kaki raua,	kua vero. koiaite mata.
noi a rurua.	maitae. oho mai
kovate	kaviri. e takae.
he motu. te ika	kituu
hehaga. kite mua ki	oho
hehaka. topa hia mai	kerima iruga ite puoko
kua oo te re re, oto vaka.	koira koiara kuahai kitoonu ma
e rua oona. maea kite puoko	leoho hekoti.
he koti koti.	kito iko.
hoko rua.	
karua, maori. ote kohou,	
hepoki. motu ite kohou.	
he maori. pte kohou.	
kaloru. maori. ote kohou.	
kaha, maori. ote kohou,	
garoki reo riva riva, mo kai ite kohou.	
ka mai taki, koe. erepae.	
ka mai taki tehuru. ote koro	

skipper's *rongo-rongo* book.

helped the photographer over the stony field, and we were soon back at the jeep, where our watchman Enlique lay deeply asleep over the wheel. We shook him awake and went on in the jeep following the cart-ruts northwards in the direction of the leper station. Soon we swung off inland along a veritable cattle track. It was so dark and the "road" so entirely hypothetical that Atan had to sit all the time like a traffic policeman with his hand outstretched pointing out our course over the rough ground. The only reminder of his blood-poisoning was a white rag on his first finger, highly suitable for showing the way at night.

After half an hour's driving we had left Puna Pau with the topknot quarry behind us on the right, and Atan made signs to us to stop and leave the jeep. We all six crawled out and stretched our legs after the bumpy ride. The village far behind us now lay dark and silent. The drizzle had stopped and the stars began a new conquest of the sky. The village skipper looked up and whispered that we had "good luck," for the rain had stopped. It struck both Ed and me that this was a most peculiar remark from an Easter Islander, since in the middle of the dry season a shower was always welcomed by the inhabitants, no matter where they were or what they were doing. Little Atan added eagerly that he was sure all would go well, for his aunt Tahu-tahu had great *mana* power. She had not only told him how he should behave, but she had personally prepared the earth oven at the cave.

Before we began our walk we had to climb over a high wall of loose stones. Here Atan took all the camera equipment from the photographer and nursed him across the barrier. I was terrified lest someone should tumble down and bring the top of the wall with him, for that would obviously be taken as a bad omen. On the other side of the wall we came on to a narrow path, and here I was asked to lead the way by carefully shining the torch downwards, but soon I had to stop because the cursed battery gave out. The two brothers were thoroughly scared and asked nervously what had happened. I tried to calm them, and when I had fiddled about until there was a faint glow, I began to walk on. But the brothers were visibly uneasy till the photographer stealthily passed me his torch so that I could go on with the same light as before.

The path wound through a field of maize, broken by open stretches of stony ground, leading into an area which Atan later told me was called Matamea. This was the name given by the Easter Islanders to the planet Mars. I was trying to keep my bearings all the time, but it was so dark outside the range of the light which the tips of my toes followed that I could see nothing but the silhouettes of three round hills against the starry sky, one of them straight ahead and the others to the right.

It was a strange walk through the night by six silent men, an absurd mixture of ancient and modern times. I myself marched at the head with the village skipper's precious *rongo-rongo* book in the S.A.S. air bag over my shoulder and Atan's grinning death's head in an official mail bag of the Royal Norwegian Foreign Department. Behind me in single file came the rest with camera equipment and empty cardboard boxes. We had now emerged upon a field of tall dry yellow grass. Atan whispered that we were to stop, and asked me to switch off my torch.

His brother, the village skipper, went fifty yards to the left out of the file and stood in the long grass with his back to us. Then we heard him slightly raise his voice as he began to talk Polynesian across the field, all in subdued tones. Out in the field the sudden sound of a voice was carried into the night with a strangely clear quality: he was talking so melodiously and with such control: even if he spoke loudly he was not using to the full the normal strength of his vocal chords. Neither indeed was there a living soul to talk to in the grass. We saw his back clear-cut as a lonely silhouette against the stars. Atan whispered excitedly that his brother was talking to the *aku-aku* in the neighbourhood to make sure that all would go well. When the village skipper rejoined us we were told only to whisper when we left the path. Nor must we smile; we must look serious. I was again asked to lead the way, this time through the high grass near the place where he had delivered his monologue.

The dry grass was scattered and scanty, and we stopped in a place where the village skipper squatted down and began to dig in the sand with his hands. At once a shiny green banana leaf appeared, and I realized that it was here that old Tahu-tahu had been early that morning to prepare the so-called *umu*, or

Polynesian earth oven. Layers of banana leaves were removed, each browner than the one before and more and more steamy and juicy, and at last the white flesh of a baked chicken and three sweet potatoes came to light, while a most powerful and unusual aroma rose up into our nostrils. It was a smell that made the mouth water and diffused into the night an indescribable fragrance.

Atan sat staring nervously while the earth oven was uncovered, and when the contents appeared in good order he seemed immensely relieved. Tahu-tahu's earth oven had been successful: we had "good luck."

While we all squatted reverently round the earth oven sniffing the curious smell, I was asked in a whisper to pinch off the little tail on the rump of the hen and eat it in the presence of the others, while saying aloud a magic Easter Island formula:

"Hekai te umu pare haonga takapu Hanau eepe kai noruego."

I later discovered that the natives themselves had difficulty in translating some old words in this phrase, the meaning of which was that we were to eat from this ceremonial earth oven of the Norwegian long-ears to get *mana* power to enter the cave.

The brothers were still visibly nervous, and I have never struggled so hard to repeat without stumbling a difficult sentence which I only partly understood, while at the same time my zoological knowledge of the anatomy of a trussed and contorted hen was strained to the uttermost before I fumbled my way to the right end of the bird, where its tail was. I noticed that head and claws were still intact although twisted out of position and the beak of the bird was clipped off at the roots. I recalled that the mayor had once told me how one could kill an enemy by doing something magic with a fowl's beak.

I wrenched off the little tail, put it into my mouth and chewed. It did not taste at all bad. I was next told to help myself to a small piece of the three sweet potatoes. It tasted excellent. But I was left with a round chicken-bone in my mouth and I did not know whether to swallow it or spit it out ; I must not blunder. I sat sucking the bone till Enlique signalled to me that I could spit it out, but Atan interfered and asked me to lay it on a banana leaf.

I was now told to break off a piece of chicken and a morsel of sweet potato for each of the others, and each time I who helped and those who ate were to repeat the same complicated formula. I was in a panic when the photographer, as the first man served, ventured on to thin ice by repeating the phrase without understanding a single word, but he mumbled something so indistinctly that at any rate no one heard that it was wrong, and Ed avoided the issue simply by swallowing the titbit as soon as I had said the difficult sentence for him.

When we had got through this needle's eye I really began to feel anxious, for my share of the fragrant-smelling chicken had been restricted to the short caudal lump. I was delighted when Atan whispered that now the *aku-akus* were pleased. They had seen us eating in their honour, so now we could help ourselves freely, and eat up the whole chicken for good luck. Never have I known a meal to smell better, and never have I come across chicken and sweet potatoes prepared in more masterly fashion than in those banana leaves in old Tahu-tahu's earth oven. In this one respect the old dancing spectre was a true sorceress who could, without cookery book or spices, outdo the most highly trained *chef de cuisine*. But then no restaurant could spread such a starry sky above its guests with a wall tapestry alive with waving silhouettes of grass, and scent of spices wafted in upon the food from open meadows and a burnt-out fire.

Yet we who sat there in a circle enjoying our chicken-bones were not the guests of honour. The ceremony was held for other guests, who had no stomachs and therefore lacked our splendid appetite; they just rejoiced to see how good the meal was tasting. I felt almost sorry for the *aku-akus* who sat around us in the grass, if at least they had the sense of smell. Atan whispered that now and then we must throw a gnawed bone over our shoulders and say: "Eat, family *aku-aku!*"

We spoke loudly to the *aku-akus*, but only whispered among ourselves. Apparently the stomachless guests of honour could not hear very well; sight must have been their keenest sense.

At the height of the meal a disgusting green blow-fly buzzed in and landed plumb in the middle of the food. I was just about to drive it away from the chicken, but hesitated for a second, and it was as well I did. For Atan stared hard at the fly and whispered eagerly:

"That's the *aku-aku* singing, it's good luck."

He grew more cheerful as the meal proceeded. When only part of a large sweet potato was left I was told to break it up and strew the pieces around us, on the banana leaves, and in the empty hearth.

When this was done Atan whispered that everything was ready. He rose and asked me to bring the "key": now we were to open the entrance to the cave. Never before had I felt so excited about something I was going to see. We walked only fifteen or twenty paces west: then Atan stopped. We both squatted down. I sat there with the grinning skull on my knee.

"Now ask your *aku-aku* where the entrance is," Atan suddenly whispered in an almost challenging tone.

I became nervous. We were in the middle of a plain as flat as the floor of a room: there was not a hill in sight except the three distant silhouettes against the stars. How could there be a cave here, without a rock even the size of a dog-kennel?

"No," I replied. "I cannot ask that. It is wrong to ask about the entrance to other people's private property."

Fortunately Atan agreed, and pointed straight to the ground at the tips of my shoes. I saw there a small flat stone half covered with sand and loose straw, exactly like ten million other stones in the neighbourhood. He asked me in a whisper to bend towards the stone with the death's head in front of me and say in a loud voice: "Open the door of the cave!"

I felt a fool, but did as he said. I bent down towards the earth with the grinning stone in my hands, and repeated the magic formula as Atan himself had said it: "*Mataki ite ana kahaata mai!*"

Then he took the stone head from me and told me to "go in." I brushed away the sand and straw till the whole of the stone appeared: it proved to be the size of a tea-tray. I felt it, and it was loose. When I turned it up a gaping black hole appeared in the earth. It was too narrow for anyone to force his way down. One by one I loosened four other slabs which appeared below, being extremely careful not to let sand or straw slip into the hole. At last the opening was just big enough for a man to drop through.

"Now go in!" Atan commanded.

I sat on the ground with my legs in the hole. It was impossible to see anything down in the black opening, and as I lowered my body I held on with my elbows and stretched down with my toes to feel if I could touch bottom. I could not, and on a signal from Atan I loosed my hold and let myself drop down into the unknown. As I let go I had a curious feeling of having done this before, and in a fraction of a second I remembered a night during the war when I sat like this with my legs down in a dark hole. That time it was a sergeant who bade me let go, but then I had a parachute on my back and knew that I should land among friends on a training ground in England. Now little Atan, looking at me with his strange big eyes, was the only person who knew where I was going to land, and he seemed vaguely uncertain about the friendliness of the *aku-akus* down below.

I let go and fell through the darkness, but not far, and my fall was remarkably soft and light. I could not see a thing, and had no idea what I was standing on. Only above me was there anything to see: a small round hole in the roof with a few brilliant stars. The black shadow of a head appeared, and of an arm which handed me my electric torch. I was able to reach it, and when I turned it on it revealed two shining white skulls at my feet. One of them had a patch of verdigris over its forehead, and a threatening black obsidian spear-point lay on top of each. I was standing on a mat of yellow *totora* reeds plaited together with twisted bark: it was so thick and soft that it was like standing on a mattress. The cave around me was small, with rock walls rising solid in front of me, to the right behind me, but under a sagging fold of lava it continued inwards to the left, and there I could see a confused mass of grotesque faces and figures staring at me as far as my feeble light could reach. The figures seemed to be standing along the walls on mats of the same kind as those under my feet.

I was only able to take a quick look round before Atan handed me the key-stone: then he turned about and wriggled his legs and backside into the hole. I noticed that above me the roof of the cave was artificially constructed of large slabs round the opening, but farther in it continued as a natural tunnel with round folds of solidified lava hanging down from the roof.

I crept aside so that little Atan could let himself drop. The first thing he did when he landed like a ball on the mat was to bow gravely to the two skulls, after which he bowed to a stone skull a little farther on in the tunnel, exactly like the one I now had in my hands. He whispered that I must lay the key-stone down beside this other "guardian," and then say in a low voice that I was a long-ear from Norway who had come there with my brother. Afterwards he showed me that his aunt had removed the magic bone-meal from the holes in the other stone skull too. He took a quick look round and whispered that there was no longer any danger. His aunt had arranged everything, he had meticulously carried out her orders, and the *aku-akus* were satisfied.

I turned my torch into the corners where diabolical faces and strange twisted figures of stone were drawn up for review.

"This is your house," Atan assured me. "Now you can walk about in it as you like."

He added that the name of the cave was Raakau, and explained that to the best of his knowledge *raakau* was a rather special name for the moon. Atan and I crept farther into the cave to make room for the photographer and Ed, who were now coming down through the hole. We went along a narrow passage between two wide ledges built of loose stones and covered with yellow reed mats. All the way the strangest sculptures lay closely packed on the mats on both sides. The tunnel was not very long, after a few yards it ended abruptly in an irregular wall; but Atan's "moon-cave" was indeed the most fabulous underground treasure-chamber. Here were curiosities which would make an art dealer tear his hair with excitement: the whole cave was full of unknown primitive works of art. No museum in the world had figures of this kind: every single object was an ethnographic novelty which gave us the strangest impression of the Easter Islanders' secret and bizarre world of the imagination.

Every single figure in this myriad of underground sculptures was quite different from what we had seen before. The only traditional Easter Island motif I recognized was a typical long-beaked bird-man standing erect with his hands behind him, but hitherto such figures had been seen only in wood; no one had yet heard of a *tangata manu* statuette in stone. There were also small stone models of the peculiar Easter Island paddles. Indeed, everything was represented, from human beings and mammals to birds, fishes, reptiles and invertebrates, nor were fantastic hybrids lacking. Here and there were groups of figures carved on the same stone, such as two bird-men holding between them a strange cat-like animal. There were also many distorted figures and monsters with an occasional head here and there, and some sculptures which none of us understood at all.

The central passage between the reed mats was thickly carpeted with dry hay. Atan said that his aunt Tahu-tahu had taken care of the cave for him when he was a little boy, and she still came down here and slept if she was depressed and was missing those who had gone. She had been there the same morning and attended to the stones. I noticed that two of them were wet.

As the time passed Atan felt more and more at ease, and in half an hour he suddenly said to me with his voice at normal pitch:

"It's all right now: we can talk and do what we like, in *your* home, my brother."

Atan obviously felt that he had carried out the last of his aunt's instructions; the cave with its pleasures, dangers and obligations was now legally transferred, now it was I who had all the responsibility. He himself was out of the danger zone. His own agitation had reached its climax when the earth oven was uncovered and Tahu-tahu's cooking had proved successful. Now his last anxiety had disappeared, he had escaped from the whole uncanny business. Whether his great relief was solely due to his freedom from responsibility, or whether he also thought the *aku-aku*s had resigned their office and moved to a more peaceful habitation, was not quite clear to me. But despite a certain formal respect for the stones Atan now gave the impression of a completely free man. He only asked us politely to leave the two human skulls where they were, as they were the heads of two of his own family. Otherwise we could take away as many cave stones as we could carry in the cardboard boxes we had brought.

We had entered the ground at midnight and we emerged again at two o'clock. We helped one another up out of the hole, and it was a relief after the stuffy cave to inhale deep draughts of fresh night air. The village skipper had picked a juicy water melon, which we consumed; then we covered the hole with stones but did not add the sand and straw, because members of the expedition were coming back next day for the rest of the stones. Silently groping our way back in the darkness, we suddenly aroused an invisible drove of horses, whose hoof-beats drummed away with a hollow sound across the field. We saw neither lights nor people, and Atan pushed ahead without troubling about the photographer, who now had to fend for himself. It seemed that *aku-akus* were no longer lying in ambush.

Ed asked Atan what he intended to do with his cave when the stones were no longer there.

"I've got to keep it," said Atan. "I shall need it in case of war."

There was not much sleep in the tent that night. The paraffin lamp glowed over the pages of the diary until the eastern sky began to redden, and I just got a little nap before the steward hammered on the frying-pan, the signal of another busy day. Lazarus was on the spot already, hanging about inquisitively while I was having my morning wash behind the tents.

The mayor had once told me that if several people entered a secret cave together, the *aku-akus* would move to another place. Without an *aku-aku* the secret entrance would lose its magic, and strangers would be able to find it at once. I began to see the practical value of this superstition, for the saying that what one person knows no one knows, but what two people know all know, is more applicable on Easter Island than any-where else. No sooner had Enlique been told that he was to enter Atan's cave than he had boasted of this impending event to Lazarus, and even in the village people were begin-ning to talk.

Some days earlier, before sunrise, Lazarus had come to my tent with some cave stones. He seemed nervous and upset and said nothing, but silently took from his sack a large bird exactly like a penguin. It was fully life-size and the likeness was so striking that I was utterly astonished, for I knew that, apart from the icy regions of the Antarctic, the penguin was found only in the Galapagos islands. Lazarus reached into the sack again, and this time extracted the head of a purely imaginary bird with its beak full of sharp pointed teeth. Finally he produced the head of a beast of prey whose muzzle had been badly scraped on the journey.

He sat silent for a long time, studying me belligerently. At last he told me that he had escaped death that night by a hair's breadth. To fetch the sculptures he had twice made a zig-zag descent of the precipice leading to his cave; on the second ascent a small projecting rock broke off in his hand. Below him was a sheer drop of a hundred feet, and he was left bent over with whirling arms, on the point of falling backwards into the abyss. By the merest chance he had grabbed hold of another projection with his left hand, had regained his balance and had cautiously climbed the remaining fifty feet to the rim of the plateau. When he had reached the top safe and sound he sat for a long time thinking: Why this piece of bad luck, was it wrong to take stones from the cave?

Lazarus had repeatedly asked himself this question on his way back to Anakena, and now he put it to me with a suspicious air.

"It's sheer madness to climb about on a precipice alone at night," I said. "Surely you must realize that *that* is highly dangerous!"

Lazarus looked at me sceptically, without visible reaction. It was clear that he was accustomed to such climbs, always alone, and always at night.

"Besides, it wasn't *bad* luck," I added, "on the contrary you really had incredibly *good* luck in grasping the other bit of rock!"

This gave Lazarus something to think about, and he began to look rather brighter. Indeed, he had not fallen; on the contrary, his was an extraordinary piece of good fortune to be sitting there without a scratch. But, he asked, why should he have suffered this frightening experience and be made to feel so miserable?

This was not so easy to answer. I sat silent and stared at his sculptures on the bed. Lazarus' stones were never washed or scrubbed, but today the head of the snarling beast had a nasty wound on its dark muzzle. I pointed to this, and Lazarus looked at the fresh scratch with concern.

"Do you think you treat your stones well?" I asked, trying to turn the conversation. "How would *you* like being shaken about in a sack with the mayor without any grass between you to take the knocks?"

Lazarus's conscience was uneasy, and it looked as if he had found sufficient reason for his sufferings in the night. Nevertheless we agreed that he should not continue to fetch more stones. As his cave was in such a dangerous position he must not risk these visits alone at night. So Lazarus crept out into the red glow of early morning, fully reassured that after all the night's adventure had been just another proof of "good luck."

On the night when our party was preparing to set off for Atan's cave, Lazarus was lurking about the tents. When he saw me alone for a moment he said that he knew what we were about, and that he too had decided to take me to his cave after I had been to Atan's. Now it was the morning after, and Lazarus could not restrain himself from sniffing around in the hope of getting a word with me while I was still behind the tents, head down in a wash-basin. He asked no inquisitive questions: he just sensed that no disaster had befallen any of us during the night. Then he disappeared.

At that time Lazarus and several of the long-ears were working for Arne in Rano Raraku, returning on horseback to eat and sleep at Hotu Matua's cave. All our native diggers had their daily rations, and those who lived in the Anakena valley also got the leavings from the kitchen tent in the camp. But today Lazarus did not seem satisfied with his daily allowance. He came loafing up in the twilight and asked me if he might have a chicken, a live chicken. The natives had often brought me live fowls as presents, and all those which did not cackle or crow at daybreak had been allowed to live and walk about freely among the tents, while the others gradually came to a mysterious end. The steward, who rose early, was said to have seen the photographer stealing about among the tents barefooted in his pyjamas with a little rifle in his hands. One thing was certain: he daily cursed the natives who filled the camp with crowing cocks and cackling hens.

I suspected that Lazarus was up to something, and I told the steward that he could certainly let him have a chicken. The steward crept upon the crowd of hens and flung himself on his stomach into the madly cackling, fluttering mob and managed to grasp a fleeing leg. Lazarus came back delighted, with a hen under his arm.

"This means good luck," he whispered happily. "The steward caught a *white* hen!"

Before Lazarus disappeared with his white hen, he made sure that we could take the motor launch along the coast next day: he was willing to take me to the cave. Late in the evening the skipper drove to the village to fetch Bill, for Lazarus had agreed that he and the photographer might come too.

The sea was unusually smooth in the bay next morning when we assembled on board the ship. Lazarus followed me down into the hold: he wanted something to put into the cave so as not to leave it empty when we took away the stones. He asked for two unopened rolls of dress material and, in addition, some small article, no matter what. He was very particular about the colour of the dress material, but the small object he accepted directly I offered it, in the shape of a pair of scissors. I guessed that the two rolls of material were for his two elder sisters, while the *aku-aku* would have to be satisfied with only the scissors.

When we climbed down the ladder into the launch, both the chief engineer and the motor-man came too: they were to put the four of us ashore at a place which Lazarus would indicate. We set our course westward along the cliffs on the north coast, congratulating ourselves that the sea was so calm that we should get safely ashore. But as we moved farther away from Anakena we felt to our surprise that the launch was beginning to roll heavily. Only Lazarus took this as a matter of course, saying that the *aku-akus* always whipped up the sea when someone was going to a cave. He sat goggle-eyed and held on tight. The coast was a mere chaos of lava blocks lying in wild confusion where the waves broke at the foot of a steep drop. In a little while Lazarus pointed to a stretch fifty yards long between two enormous piles of rock running down to the sea. There his grandmother had once climbed along, fishing, when she surprised another old woman who sat there washing and drying cave stones. His grandmother had passed by, pretending that she saw nothing. When she returned soon afterwards the other woman too was fishing and there was no sign of the stones. So Lazarus knew that there must be a secret cave in that place.

Shortly afterwards we passed the lonely windmill in the Hanga-o-Teo valley, once an important centre of habitation, but now abandoned and desolate. Soon afterwards, Lazarus pointed to another stretch of the wild coast about a hundred yards long. Within this area lay the secret cave where he had once told me his cousin, Alberto Ika, had been to fetch the *rongo-rongo* tablets, at the time when the *aku-akus* had forced him to bring them back to the cave.

Lazarus had scarcely shown us this spot when he became frightened: he could see people. The rest of us saw nothing, but Lazarus, who had the eyes of an eagle by day and those of an owl by night, saw four persons sitting on a rock. Why were they there, and what were they doing? He stared and stared till we rounded the next point. Now the seas were becoming steadily worse, and we all saw that it was useless to try to land in such conditions. Just under a steep cliff where Lazarus' own cave lay we circled several times close inshore, while Lazarus tried to point out to us a tiny ledge on the face of the precipice above our heads, behind which the entrance lay. This was an "open" cave, Lazarus explained. He went on pointing and explaining till we all thought we saw where it was, but when we checked up on one another, none of us agreed, and at last we gave it up altogether. And while the salt spray drenched our faces as the chief engineer put his helm over and set course for home, the launch rose on end and began a mad dance in the choppy sea. The waves grew worse and worse; the wind had not risen, it had merely shifted. It was no longer possible to keep a straight course: the steersman had continually to turn into the biggest seas, which came rolling in at us with foaming crests. Lazarus was silent, but sat holding tight. The rest of us merely followed with our eyes the steersman's skilful movements and every single tumbling sea, while the salt water dripped from our hair and faces and our clothes clung to our bodies like wet paper.

Just before we reached the Hanga-o-Teo windmill we all saw four small dots up on the edge of the plateau. Three of them climbed on to horses and rode in the same direction as ourselves, while the fourth turned about and galloped the other way towards the village.

"That's Alberto's brother," Lazarus exclaimed in surprise. "The others must be his sons."

We soon lost sight of the horsemen, and no one had time to wonder what they had been doing. Soon the expedition ship appeared beyond a bluff; she too was pitching heavily in the seas, and roaring breakers followed us right into Anakena Bay, where the surf was thundering on the beach.

Lazarus leapt ashore as if the devil himself was at his heels, and together we walked up to the camp in silence, as wet as drowned rats. Bill was as serious as Lazarus, and was trying to rub the salt water from his spectacles with a sodden handkerchief. He confided to me that he had felt so terribly seasick that he thought he would die, but he dared not show it for fear that Lazarus should interpret it as a bad omen for entering his cave.

After lunch we set off for the cave for a second time. But this time we saddled four horses and followed the remains of a prehistoric road which wound along the north coast between the screes of the plateau. After the creaking windmill at Hanga-o-Teo we came to a stretch of the road where the prehistoric paving was still intact, resembling the ancient Inca roads in Peru. Soon afterwards Lazarus dismounted and escorted us to a ledge where a huge winding snake with cup-shaped hollows along its raised back was cut into the solid rock. He had told us of this before, and Father Sebastian had mentioned it too. Bill was quite amazed: the fauna of these Pacific islands did not include snakes, so where had the old-time sculptors found their model?

Soon afterwards we passed a solitary statue which had once been abandoned en route to an *ahu* near the north cape. I thought of the transport problem with dismay: seven miles from Rano Raraku as the crow flies, and much more on such rough ground where riding was often difficult enough. Here we left the ancient trail and rode on over a wild stony plain just inside the steep drop to the ocean. The endless sea was still dotted with white caps. As we were riding steeply down into a little gully one of my stirrup-leathers broke, but I managed to hide it; Lazarus noticed nothing, and I rode on with one stirrup into very rough ground, which was getting worse and worse.

As we neared our destination, I observed for the first time that Lazarus was growing visibly nervous. He whipped up his horse with a little stick and begged me to quicken my pace, so that we might arrive before the others. We increased our lead across the stony plain by a couple of hundred yards, and when we came to the foot of two great lava blocks Lazarus leapt to the ground and tied up his horse, asking me to do the same. Then he pulled off his shirt and trousers at top speed and stood with nothing on but his pants. He rushed down the slope towards the edge of the precipice with a coil of rope in his hand, begging me as he ran to strip quickly and follow him with the hen. I had no idea where the hen was, and when I asked, I received an irritable and abstracted reply as he bounded down the slope. I caught sight of an old bag hanging from his saddle, seized it and hurried after him, completely stripped but for my pants. The other two came riding along about a hundred yards behind us, zig-zagging over the stony ground.

I overtook Lazarus on the very edge of the precipice, and without turning he hastily mumbled a scrappy and nervous order that I should eat the tail and give him a little bit when he came up again. Then he vanished down the cliff. When I asked in bewilderment if I was to eat the tail now or wait till he returned, I received no answer.

In the bag I found the hen plucked and baked and packed in banana leaves. I struggled to find head and rump of the twisted body inside the leaves, and had just wrenched off the little tail stump when Lazarus appeared over the edge again. I stuffed the tail into my mouth and chewed as I tore off a strip of the breast for him, which he gulped down like a wild beast, looking to left and right. It was a strange ceremony we performed in our pants on the very edge of the precipice. The others had now reached the rocks and were dismounting. Lazarus asked me to break a few pieces from the hen and lay them on the rocks, and when this was done he suddenly seemed relieved and said that we could now eat freely, and also give some chicken to the other two.

Lazarus was still in a great hurry. He slung the loop of his rope over a round stone which was only loosely attached to the rock by a dried lump of earth, and then flung the rest of the rope over the cliff. Then he disappeared over the edge yet again, without supporting himself by the rope or even testing it to see if it would hold. I looked down at him and asked cautiously if we could be sure that the rope was properly made fast. He gave me a queer look and said that he himself never used a rope, and what had I to be afraid of? He knew that nothing could happen to me.

It is not always pleasant to be regarded as supernatural. I felt that I had only too good a use for the rope, but dared not touch it, so badly was it secured. So I manoeuvred myself over the edge with only my pants on, as Lazarus had done, while holding the scissors, wrapped in paper, between my teeth: I had been expressly instructed to bring them with me down the cliff. I am no mountaineer, and loathed what I was setting out to do. I lowered myself down till the tips of my toes found a hold on a horribly narrow ledge, but it was almost impossible to find another hold for my fingers. There was a perpendicular drop of 150 feet below us, and down there foam and green water were whirling and roaring among sharp lava blocks. The ocean lay empty and blue beyond: but along the rocks beneath us a green sea monster seemed to be rolling and twisting as it foamed with rage and sent tongues of water licking in between the sharp lava jaws, greedily agape for anything which might break loose and fall from the cliff above. It was a horrifying maw to tumble into. We had to keep ourselves tight against the rock wall, for a single careless inch could tip us out of balance. Lazarus, straight-backed and light-footed, tripped sideways along the ledge like a rope-dancer, showing me the way. I suddenly lost all interest in his cave and cursed all *aku-akus*, not least my own, which had landed me in such a situation. My only wish was to clamber up again before it was too late. But I could not quite bring myself to do that either. So I followed slowly in Lazarus' wake, down the slanting ledge, with one cheek, my body and two outstretched arms pressed close to the rock face so as not to tilt outwards. Never again will I climb on a lava cliff in my underwear. The wide meshes caught on the jagged surface and I hung fast as though nailed to the wall by my own pants, jerking and pulling till I managed to tear myself loose.

If Lazarus had wished for a really vicious *aku-aku* to guard his cave, he could have hit upon nothing worse than an invisible one planted on this narrow ledge to catch ignorant intruders by their pants at the most inconvenient moment, just when they wanted to slip by like shadows. Certain it was that while I was staggering along the ledge, engaged in a constant struggle to release myself, Lazarus was tripping along gracefully on the tips of his toes without a single scratch.

We climbed down in zig-zags, coming upon the rope again at a steep place where it hung free down the cliff-side to the next ledge. I could not quite do without it here and pressed fingers and toes against the lava wall wherever I could, letting as little as possible of my weight on the rope, till I reached a little shelf on which Lazarus stood. He squeezed himself against the wall as stiff as a guardsman, and gave no sign of going farther. This was a most uncomfortable parking-place: the shelf was a foot wide and there was only just room for both of us side by side, with our backs to the rock.

There was no cave here. Lazarus stood motionless, pressed to the cliff, and merely stared at me with a strange, inscrutable expression. Suddenly he reached out and said quickly:

"Give me your hand!"

He could have asked nothing worse of me just at that moment, as I was standing with the scissors in my mouth, clinging fast to the rock with my pants in shreds. I pressed against the cliff so hard that I felt the rough lava cutting into my back like corals, and held out my right hand to him. He grasped it firmly.

"Promise me not to say a word to anyone on the island about what we're up to now," he begged. "You can talk to your own people, but they must keep their mouths shut so long as they are here."

He did not let go of my hand, but told me that if his name was mentioned in connection with this affair his sisters would be beside themselves with fury. When I had left the island I could talk freely, for if rumours got back to the village through the *Pinto* he would just say that he had made copies, and in a few months everything would be forgotten.

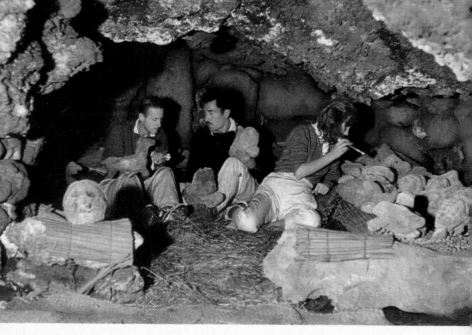

Above: A secret family cave. Atan Atan with inherited possessions in an underground cave, the secret entrance to which was closed with slabs of stone covered with earth and herbage.
Below: Enlique had his private treasure chamber deep down underground. Curious sculptures lay piled up along the walls.

The small secret sculptures of Easter Island lay hidden in great quantities in family caves underground. The skull seen above was a 'key-stone' which gave access to the secret opening of the cave. A powder made of human bones was placed in the hole in its forehead to kill intruders by pure magic.
Note also a three-masted reed boat, a slab with ideograms, a long-eared head and a foot.

The most curious figures, which no one but the inheritors had seen before, came up out of the family caves. Here are a beast with a human head; a bearded face; a whale with a reed hut and a typical Easter Island earth oven on its back and six balls under its belly; a woman with a fish roped to her shoulders, and the profile of a head.

Above: A magic guardian and a stone head. The figure on the right was Estevan's most powerful *aku-aku,* which guarded the hereditary possessions in the cave. It is a recumbent bust of a devil with a humped back, swellings on its head, and a beard.
Below: Modern wizardry in an underground family cave. The man with the flag believed himself to have supernatural qualities and had annexed the table flag from the camp, thinking it to have supernatural power. From the left: Juan the wizard, Tumu and Andres Haoa.

I promised to do what he had asked of me, and then he let go my hand and asked me to bend over the precipice and look down. I stretched out as far as I dared, and gazed in horror at the sharp lava blocks in the whirling foam. There was a small ledge, like that on which we stood, about a man's height below us, and under this again the cliff fell sheer to the bottom.

"Now, where is the entrance?" Lazarus asked with visible pride.

"Impossible to say," I admitted. My only desire was to get it all over.

"There, under your feet," he said, pointing to the small ledge beneath us. He held me while I cautiously leant out as far as I could. But still I saw nothing.

"You can't get to the opening unless you do exactly as I tell you," Lazarus said. And then, up on the ledge, he began a course of instructions the like of which I had not experienced since I stood before my first dancing-master. I was told to begin with the left foot and then follow a meticulous series of short steps and half turns which was to end in my sinking down on my knees and stretching out on my stomach on the shelf below. I was asked to wait where I was while Lazarus gave a demonstration of the difficult dance steps necessary to get safely down to the cave. I saw how he placed his hands and feet, how he twisted himself round on the ledge to be able to sink on to his knees and on to his stomach; after that I only saw his kicking legs, and then he was gone.

I stood alone and noticed more than before how the air was filled with the thundering of the surf against the cliff. A few hundred yards farther west, on a curve of the coast, I spotted the cameraman standing at the very edge of the plateau filming in the late afternoon sun. The ocean was still white-crested: it was out there we had been circling that morning, likewise without seeing this infernal cave.

Then a hand appeared on the shelf below holding a fiendish stone head: Lazarus' own head and body followed and he slowly repeated, in reverse order, the same carefully studied steps and turns until he was up on the ledge with me again.

"The key," Lazarus muttered, holding out the stone head.

Again I had to press myself hard against the wall, for now Lazarus asked me to give him the scissors. I had to take them

I

out of my mouth and hand them to him, while he gave me the
"key" in my other hand. This "key" had human features with
great bulging eyes, a bearded chin and a most hypnotic expression, but a long neck stretched horizontally from the back of
the head, as on an animal. Lazarus asked me to put the "key"
down on a tiny ledge by my head, and then it was my turn to
begin the horrible dance down to the cave.

There was so little room for manoeuvre that I soon realized
the necessity of following Lazarus' lessons in every detail. When
I had turned myself about so that I could crouch down on all
fours on the lowest ledge, I saw for the first time the opening
leading to the cave, hidden under a projection of the rock. The
hole was so small that I should never have dreamed of anyone
being able to crawl into it. The original discoverers of the cave
must have lived quite near, with time to explore every single
inch of this terrain. Lazarus had told me that the cave was
called *Motu Tavake*, which means "Cliff of the Tropical Bird":
the locality was called Omohi and lay at the foot of Vai-
mataa on the Hanga-o-Teo plain. The cave had belonged to
Hatui, who was the grandfather of Lazarus' mother.

I was crouching on all fours on a tiny ledge, and the narrow
hole in the rock opened on to a still smaller ledge, at the same
level, but a little way off. To get to it I had to stretch forward
and take hold of the edge of the other shelf. Lying flat, I got my
arms and head into the hole on one ledge, while my knees and
legs still lay on the other. My stomach was without support
above the abyss and the breakers. The hole through which I
was trying to worm my way in was so narrow that my pants
were pulled down several times. The rock scratched and cut
my back and thighs, for there was hardly any sand, only rough
hard lava.

At first I could discern nothing but a horribly narrow
passage and a very faint suggestion of light ahead. I lay for a
long time struggling with my legs out over the abyss, and when
at last I got my feet inside I felt that the passage was widening
a little, without any rise of the low roof. I began to discern
various contours around me; and then, beside my ear, I discovered a sculpture representing two mating turtles. On my
other side appeared a small statuette of the same type as the
giants from Rano Raraku. I crept farther in and found more

room: I could soon sit up and look into a cave which was dimly illuminated from a hole I could not yet see. Closely packed along the walls strange sculptures stood or lay piled up in several rows on the bare, dry rock. There were no mats here and no hay. A few yards in front of me and blocking the way stood a conspicuous figure, unmistakably of the male sex. He was in a straddled position with bent knees and his arms raised threateningly, and he was surrounded by a mass of other figures. There was a little step behind him leading to a lower level where two outstretched human skeletons were lying. A tiny hole in the wall to the right let a dim light fall on the crumbling bones and made it possible to see faintly the outlines of the ghostly treasure-chamber. I heard something breathing. I heard it as clearly as if it were in the corner beside me. But it was only Lazarus outside, squeezing himself in through the narrow opening. The acoustics were incredible: I could hear his bare skin rubbing against the sharp lava. Lazarus came in without ceremony and squatted down beside me. His big eyes and his teeth shone white. Lazarus was now quite himself again, just as I knew him on his nocturnal visits to my tent. He pointed out the big figure which straddled in a warning posture with its arms in the air, towering over the others; it suggested a traffic policeman directing the swarm of mysterious figures around him and along both sides of the cave down towards the opening.

"That's the most important stone," Lazarus explained. "He's the chief of the cave, an old king."

Otherwise Lazarus knew incredibly little: to all my questions about the other figures his only reply was a shrug of the shoulders and "don't know." The only other things he seemed to be sure about were two flat stone discs bearing symmetrical symbols: he declared that they represented the sun and the moon. We were not obliged to whisper, but the whole atmosphere and acoustics were such that it was natural to speak in a hushed voice.

Lazarus crawled round with me for a time, then he disappeared out of the passage again to fetch Bill down: it was too risky for the photographer to attempt the descent. A short time passed, and then I heard Bill's voice whispering an oath in the narrow hole. Bill had grown up in the heart of the Rockies,

and did not mind a precipice, but there were no such damned
rat-holes in the mountains of Wyoming. He managed to
wriggle in, and sat in silence for a while, looking round him
with unseeing eyes. Suddenly I heard an outburst: he had
discovered all the figures round him. Lazarus followed close
behind and brought an electric torch, and we could now see the
individual figures better. While a great number of the stones
in Atan's cave were scratched and rubbed by washing and
care, there was no sign of scratch or mark on any of the figures
in Lazarus' cave. In Atan's cave I felt as if I were entering a
magician's secret parlour with mats on the shelves and heaps of
hay on the floor: here it was like going into an old storehouse.

We asked Lazarus if he did not wash the stones. No, there
was no need to, because there was no growth here: this was a
perfectly dry cave because of the current of air.

Over by the little hole we noticed cold, dry air trickling in,
and there was not the smallest scrap of green on the iron-hard
walls, not even on the crumbling bones of the skeletons. In
Atan's cave there was a fine layer of mould and moss on the
wall beneath the entrance.

We lost all count of time inside the cave. We chose some of
the most interesting sculptures, and Lazarus and Bill crawled
out to receive them, while I was left behind to try to manoeuvre
the stones through the narrow entrance tunnel without scratching them. This was much easier said than done, for when crawling on the stomach it was impossible to transport a lava sculpture without injury unless one held the torch at the same time,
and an extra hand was really needed for dragging oneself along.
I realized now for the first time how skilful Lazarus had been,
who had crawled and climbed here alone at night without
scratching more than the muzzle of a single beast. When at last
I came to the cave mouth, and had moved several stones in
front of me inch by inch, I heard anxious cries from Bill, but
all words were lost in the noise of the breakers. My way was
blocked by my own sculptures, and I could not get farther till
Lazarus removed them from outside. When I peered past the
sculptures I thought I could distinguish his arm, and suddenly
I discovered what had happened; outside it was dark. Night
had come upon us.

Lazarus removed the stones one by one, and sent them up to

Bill. When the opening was clear, I crawled out and found a complete change of scene. It was barely possible to detect the outlines of the cliff in the faint light of a crescent moon. I had gooseflesh all over my body and was trembling at the knees when at last I reached the plateau safely: I tried to console myself with the thought that it was due simply to the night chill. For it had been cold in the cave and cold to climb nude in the night wind. While Bill and I were on our way up Lazarus went down yet again; this time he had with him the two rolls of dress material to leave them in the cave.

We flung our clothes on and regaled ourselves with hot coffee from a thermos, while the photographer admired the night's haul. I noticed that Lazarus had begun to cough a little, and Bill confided to me that he too did not feel well. We both knew that the *cocongo* from the *Pinto* had begun to spread during the last few days: it did not yet seem to be as bad as usual, but there were already signs that more serious cases were developing. I was really afraid that either Bill or Lazarus would now fall ill, for in that event, instead of gradually overcoming his inherited fear of *aku-aku* and taboo, Lazarus would become more superstitious than ever. Bill had a wind-jacket, so I gave mine to Lazarus and put the sack with the priceless haul on my back. Before we walked up to the horses Lazarus made sure than no scraps of paper or other traces were left on the ground, and then our little caravan set off homeward in the faint moonlight. The sack was heavy and the going was incredibly rough, so I had more than enough to do to keep myself on the horse's back with only one stirrup. But when we came up on to the ancient trail I rode forward alongside Lazarus and said he could see now that there was no *aku-aku* in the cave that wished us any harm.

"That was because I went down beforehand and said the words," Lazarus replied calmly.

What words Lazarus had said I never found out. Nor the object of undressing when one was to go down into the draughty cave. Perhaps the *aku-aku* in the rock was an old-fashioned survivor, accustomed to visitors wearing only a small loincloth. I dared not ask. For Lazarus believed that I knew all about *aku-akus* just as well as he did, if not a good deal better.

We rode on in silence, and our horse' hoofs clattered in the dark when we passed over the paved section of the road. Just afterwards we heard the low creaking of the lonely windmill at Hanga-o-Teo. Driving clouds sped across the crescent moon, which peered curiously down into my sack, and the night was full of mystery. The wind was chilly, and we urged the horses forward, without watering them at the mill.

For Lazarus was coughing.

CHAPTER IX

AMONG GODS AND DEVILS IN EASTER ISLAND'S UNDERWORLD

A DANGEROUS spectre was wandering about on Easter Island in company with the *aku-akus* during those very days when we were obtaining entrance to the secret caves. It had appeared some weeks before: it came and went among the houses in the village, and no one could shut it out. It became more and more daring, and soon it appeared also among our people in the tents at Anakena. Creeping in by the mouth and nose, it ran amok through the whole body. It had come to the island as a stowaway on the *Pinto* and sneaked ashore under the name *cocongo*.

The mayor had been in his cave for stones only twice when the *cocongo* knocked at his door. He kept on his feet for several days, though feeling wretched; then he took to his bed. When I went to see him he declared with a cheerful smile that the *cocongo* was usually much worse and that he would soon be quite well. A week later I went over to see him again. He was then in the village hospital. I called on the new village doctor who had come in the *Pinto* to relieve the other, and was shown into the little sick-room where the *cocongo* patients lay coughing. I could not find the mayor among them, and was becoming anxious when a skinny old man raised himself on his elbow over in a corner, and said in a hoarse voice:

"Here I am, Señor Kon-Tiki!"

I was quite horrified when I recognized him.

"Pneumonia," the doctor whispered. "He nearly died, but I think we shall save him."

The mayor lay there pale and hollow-cheeked with a peculiar forced smile on his thin lips. He summoned me to the bedside with a feeble gesture and whispered in my ear:

"It'll be all right. When I'm well again we'll do great things together. My granddaughter died of the *cocongo* yesterday. She'll guide me from heaven, she will. This is no punishment, I realize that. Just wait, señor, we'll do great things."

I left the hospital sick at heart. It had been terrible to see the jolly mayor again in such a condition. He had been so odd, I did not quite understand what he had meant. Perhaps it was the fever that had given him that queer look in his eyes and made him talk so strangely. That the superstitious man did not believe his illness to be a punishment by the *aku-aku* was of course excellent, but it was most peculiar.

The days passed. This wave of *cocongo* carried off no one except the mayor's granddaughter, and he was soon well enough to go home. When I went to see him, he smiled the same queer smile. He had no temperature now, but he repeated all that he had said in hospital. For the first few weeks he was too weak to return to us and to his friends in the cave at Anakena. He stayed at home with his wife, and we regularly sent him butter and other nourishing food to help him to put on a little flesh.

The mayor's youngest brother, little Atan, slipped through the needle's eye with ease. He did not have even a touch of *cocongo* that year, and had gradually rid himself of belief in punishment by the *aku-aku*. He was released from both the duties and menaces of the cave. Instead of punishment he had received a reward large enough to get his family through many a tight place in the future. By local standards he was now a well-to-do man, but both clothes and money were hidden in Nature's big safe under the ground. Though the mayor had hung between life and death, Atan did not consider his brother's illness to be a cave punishment; on the contrary, Atan had indeed no idea that his brother had brought stones from his cave, and was continually advising me to ask him about his cave as soon as he was well again, for it was sure to be the most important cave of all.

Lazarus was on the verge of illness. The morning after the ride from his cave he was outside my tent at an early hour to ask me, coughing and hoarse, how I was.

"Absolutely first-rate," I said, and saw Lazarus' face light up at once. I was glad he had not asked after Bill, for he was not at all well that day. Lazarus went about for two or three days, hawking, coughing and taking medicine, and then was as fit and well as ever without even going to bed. He too clambered down into the cave with rewards for himself and his sisters.

While the village doctor was fighting the *cocongo* at Hangaroa, the expedition's doctor had his hands full with all our own workers, now nearly a hundred strong. We were well supplied with antibiotics and other medicines, which were increasingly popular with our native diggers. They were also very fond of headache tablets and ate them as sweets if we did not keep an eye on them. Thus we rode out one wave of *cocongo* after another, and we soon began to feel more secure again. But problems seldom come alone, and something else happened just then which caused a considerable stir in the village.

On the last day before his illness, when the mayor was sitting with his room full of cave stones waiting for transport to the camp, he had suffered two serious shocks. The worst had been when the skipper, who fetched him, filled the jeep with white-clad nuns while the mayor was sitting there with a sack full of cave stones. But before the skipper arrived, Gonzalo, our Chilean representative, had come in at the door unexpectedly and caught sight of a stone lobster before the mayor could hide it away.

"This is *old*," Gonzalo said, eagerly picking up the sculpture from the floor.

"No, it's *new*," lied the mayor.

"I can see that it's old," said Gonzalo suspiciously.

"I made it myself," the mayor insisted.

Gonzalo was obliged at last to give way.

When the mayor came to the camp in the jeep he told me at once of the episode with Gonzalo, and repeated that on no account must I say a single word to anyone about his having taken stones from the family cave.

"Señor Gonzalo must have known something," the mayor said mistrustfully. "He was much too suspicious, and would hardly believe me when I said I had made the lobster myself."

Later Gonzalo came to me in the tent and gave an account of the same episode. He thought he had unveiled the whole mystery of the caves.

"The mayor's deceiving you," Gonzalo said. "I've seen an incredibly fine lobster which he admits he made himself: you must be on your guard if he comes and says it's from the cave."

I*

Gonzalo was astonished when he heard that the mayor had already brought me the lobster and, in addition, had told me all about Gonzalo's visit.

The mayor was now on the alert, and tried to cover himself by continually announcing that he personally made curious stone sculptures. When the *cocongo* began to be troublesome and he had just taken to his bed, he had a visit at home one evening from Gonzalo and Ed. They met the mayor's brother-in-law, Riroroko, inside the garden gate. They had hardly greeted him when he began, quite unasked, to testify in a boastful fashion to the mayor's skill at carving stone; he had special tools with which he made lobsters and animals and boats, afterwards washing them and whipping them with banana leaves to make them look old.

Neither Ed nor Gonzalo had asked for information about the mayor's stones. They were therefore all the more amazed at this frank confession, and they told me at once what they had heard. Meanwhile the mayor lay helpless in bed with a rising temperature, and able neither to make nor fetch more cave stones. But Gonzalo went about among the natives with ears wide open trying to find out more: he was staying in the village at the time, working with Bill at Vinapu.

At this time young Estevan's pretty wife, the strong-minded woman who had sent me the first cave stones, had recovered her health. Being cured of her serious abdominal trouble, she went to the cave with Estevan every night to fetch grotesque figures, which they stacked in a locked outhouse. I no longer asked to be taken into her family cave, the first of which I had been told. In return she had given me important information about some of the stones which came from it.

I had told Gonzalo that I was expecting a load of sculptures from her cave, and one evening when he was walking about and surveying the neighbourhood, he saw a heap of uncut lava blocks stacked up behind the house of Estevan's neighbour. Smouldering suspicion blazed up. Gonzalo thought they had been left there by Estevan for making sculptures and he decided to act.

That very day there had been an accident in the village. A woman had been sitting outside her hut melting pig's fat in a cauldron, while her little boy ran about playing. The child had tripped and fallen head-first into the hot fat. The mother had rushed the child to hospital and he was now completely enveloped in cotton-wool and bandages.

Next day Enlique came to me in the camp with a gloomy face. It was he who later went with us into Atan's cave. Some days before he too had brought me a little sack with cave sculptures. I knew that Enlique was uncle to the child who had just fallen into the cauldron and his gloomy countenance at once suggested that he wanted to blame me for the disaster, since I had persuaded him to go into the cave. Now things were beginning to get complicated. On this island nearly everybody was mutually related in some way or other, and any mishap in the village could be interpreted as a punishment of the one who had broken a taboo.

Enlique asked me to go with him behind the newly erected statue.

"Something awful has happened now," he began in a low voice. "There's trouble in the village. Estevan and his wife do nothing but lie in their house all day weeping. Señor Gonzalo has said that they have cheated Señor Kon-Tiki, that they made 'stones' themselves."

"Rubbish," I said. "There's nothing for them to cry about. Ride over and tell Estevan and his wife that all is well. I'm not angry."

"All is *not* well," Enlique said despairingly. "The whole village will soon be furious. If the stones are new, everyone will be angry with Estevan and his wife for trying to cheat Señor Kon-Tiki. And if the stones are old, everyone will be still angrier with them for removing things from a family cave. Everyone's bound to be angry with them now."

Enlique said nothing about the child who had fallen into the cauldron. Evidently he regarded this as his brother's misfortune, not his own. And his brother had *not* brought me any stones, though I later learned that he too had a cave.

That evening I was sitting sealing up fresh pollen samples and could not leave the tents, but the next night the skipper drove me into the village, where we went into Estevan's hut. He was sitting alone on a bench, whilst his wife was lying on the bed: the eyes of both were red with weeping. We gave them a friendly greeting, but before Estevan could speak he burst into tears again. He declared for two days and nights they had neither slept nor eaten, but had just wept. For Señor Gonzalo had said that Estevan had made false stones to deceive Señor Kon-Tiki. He had seen a heap of lava stones next door and thought that Estevan had collected materials for making sculptures. What he had not seen was that their neighbour was building an extension to the back of his house, and that the stones were being used to make the wall.

I tried to console them as well as I could. We had brought several presents with us, and when we left they both promised to have a meal, go to bed and try to forget the whole thing.

Lower down the street we went in and knocked at the mayor's door. We found him in bed in a completely shattered condition. He had had a visit from his powerful aunt Tahu-tahu. She had been in a towering rage and said that he was a good lad, and so was Señor Kon-Tiki, so he ought not to sell me fakes as was rumoured in the village. He had not been able to tell her that these stones he had given me were old, for he had not yet obtained her consent to take anything from Ororoina's family cave. So he had merely told her that he was a sick man: he would explain everything as soon as he was well again.

"Other people get angry for a short time," said the mayor. "But old people like her get so angry that they can't speak for three days."

He had given her a roll of cloth and a carton of cigarettes as a token of friendship from me, but she had just flung them on the floor and said she would have nothing he had obtained by fraud. Only when he had explained that the things were not his, but a direct gift from me to her, had the old lady picked them up again, and made for the door.

We tried to talk the sick mayor into a calmer frame of mind, but this was a waste of time. His old aunt was a generation ahead of him, with all the rights and all the wisdom this implied. Tahu-tahu was a dangerous woman. If she was angry, she could kill a man by burying a chicken's head.

The rumours about Estevan and the mayor caused a great stir in the village. Many of the natives came and assured us that there were no secret caves in the island: we must not believe anything of the kind. If there had been any, the entrances had been lost long ago. If anybody brought me sculptures, they had made them themselves: there was nothing like it on their island. Some of those who came and denied the existence of the caves were so sincere that they obviously believed what they said. But others made the opposite impression because of their nervous, almost panic-stricken efforts to induce us to believe otherwise. Some of the older people in particular quite lost their heads in their eagerness to remove from our minds any suspicion that there was anything on the island today except sheep and statues.

For several days one piece of information nullified another, while all who had contact with the natives cautiously attempted to get to the bottom of the problem.

Ed came down to see us one day from Orongo; he had again come round to the opinion that, after all, there must be secret family caves on the island: only we must be on our guard against imitations. He had managed to elicit from his native workers that it was usual for whatever was kept in caves to be taken out now and then to dry. Some of the objects were packed in *totora* reeds.

Bill, too, had been utterly confused by all the rumours with which the village had been buzzing. To get more reliable information he had left the governor's house and was lodging with a native family. He stopped me outside the church one Sunday and whispered:

"I am sorry I can't speak freely, but I can say one thing: there *are* secret caves on this island, and they *do* contain things of the kind you have."

The next to come to me was Gonzalo. He had felt profoundly unhappy for several days over the row he had caused in the village. He had been honestly convinced that he had discovered that the cave sculptures were fraudulent, but something had now happened to make him change his mind: a strange experience of his own. A native boy had confided in him. The boy had been used by an old woman to climb down into a secret cave at Hanga Hemu, from which the woman wished to fetch figures for Señor Kon-Tiki. The boy had found a sculpture of a hen which lay as a kind of key-stone in the first room of the cave, along with two skulls. But the tunnel into the next room had been blocked by fallen rock, so he did not get into the chamber where the old woman had said he should fetch some figures wrapped in plaited *totora* reeds.

Gonzalo was so excited when he heard this story that after a long struggle he eventually secured the boy's promise to show him the place. Gonzalo found the cave exactly as the boy had described it, with the two skulls and an artificial opening in the side-wall, where the tunnel leading farther in was blocked. But he found more. Someone had been there after the boy and had dug desperately both in the floor and the roof over the place where the rocks had fallen. Gonzalo managed to force his way ten feet into a crack above this spot, and at the end of the crack he found that someone had dug a hole straight down to the tunnel beneath. Through the hole he thrust his arm down until he could grab a handful of loose earth; in the earth lay pieces of rotten *totora* reed. Someone had been there before him and removed ancient reed packages.

I asked Gonzalo if he knew who the old woman was. Yes, he knew. It was Analola's mother.

For me this was a valuable clue. It was Analola's mother and sister who had defended the four great round stone heads with tooth and claw when a young couple had found them in the field outside the village fence and wanted to sell them to me. The old woman had then furiously abused the finders as thieves of her family property, and had been delighted when I merely let the four grotesque heads roll back into position face down. Did she now want to show her gratitude by bringing me cave stones instead?

I thanked Gonzalo for this important piece of information, and left the village in the jeep together with the skipper. I sat chuckling to myself. So Analola's mother had a cave. Fine, I had a special reason to make a note of this.

The evening sun had already sunk into the sea and it was dark. We were to stop on the high land at the Vaitea sheep farm on our way home, to fetch water for the camp. Analola was manageress at the farm, and she always came out for a friendly chat when we called for water. Analola was the most influential woman on the island. She was an intelligent beauty with flowing black hair and smiling brown eyes. Perhaps her nose was too wide and her lips too full to win a beauty contest in our own world, but out here in the Pacific she was the uncrowned queen of Easter Island. She was able and honest: everyone respected Analola.

When we drew up in front of the tap outside the wall at Vaitea, Analola and a couple of her girl friends came out with a light to help us draw the water. It was usually the skipper who came to fetch it, and for the past few days Analola had been going on at him about the mayor having cheated Señor Kon-Tiki.

"There are no such things as secret caves. There's no one on the island who has stone figures," Analola declared. "I was born here and have lived here all my life, *capitano*. Tell Señor Kon-Tiki that he mustn't believe it."

Analola was an honest soul who never cared for loose talk, and at last the skipper began to get upset.

"You see, when Analola says it—" the skipper mused with a worried look. "The mayor is a bit of a rascal, you know."

Analola was what the natives called "a child of our time." Of her ancestors' characteristics but little remained. She was civilized not only in dress and manners. Only once had I seen a spark of superstition in her brown eyes.

"Is it true that you have talked to a stone statue?" she once asked me after the mayor, Lazarus and I had found all the whales by the *ahu* at Anakena. "My mother says that a stone statue comes into your tent at night and tells you where to search."

"Nonsense," I said. "A stone statue can't come into my tent."

"Well, a little one could," said Analola.

Now she stood shivering in the chill of the evening and held a light for us as we worked the hose into the hole of the water-tank.

"How's your mother, Analola?" I asked cautiously.

"Funny that you should ask that. She's just come to Vaitea to see me, and she's lying in my bed now."

I took Analola gently by the arm and asked her in a whisper to come with me behind the jeep while the others filled the water-tank. I had suddenly had an idea. I knew the vivid Polynesian imagination, and their bent for obscure, allegorical references to sacred things, of which it was not good form to speak openly. I also knew from Gonzalo's report that Analola's mother had taken a stone chicken from her cave, and I guessed that there was probably a sculpture of a dog there too, as these were motifs recurring in the mayor's, Lazarus' and Atan's caves.

We went and stood under a dark eucalyptus tree.

"Analola," I whispered, and she looked up at me with a sweet expression. "Go in to your mother and give her this message from me: 'Chicken is good, but dog is better.'"

Analola looked completely bewildered. She stared at me with her lips apart for a long time; then she drifted up the steps and disappeared silently into the house. The water-tank was full now. We waved to the other vahines and started up the jeep for the drive down to Anakena.

The next evening the skipper went up for water as usual. He returned to camp with a detailed report. Analola had told him at once all that had happened the previous evening, and the skipper repeated it in her own words. She had told him that I had first spoken to her quietly in the night. Then her heart had told her: "Surely, Señor Kon-Tiki wants to make love." But afterwards, when I whispered to her that chicken was good but dog was better, she thought: "Surely, Señor Kon-Tiki must have taken much wine." Nevertheless she had gone in to her mother and given the message. And she had never seen her mother so queer. She had sat up in bed with a jerk and replied:

"That's why I'm here. To go into the cave with you and Daniel Ika."

Analola had been utterly perplexed. Nothing of the kind had ever happened to her before. Her mother was *mama-tia* to Daniel Ika, his aunt on his father's side. Analola had been so upset by what her mother had said that she had not slept all night. Next day her mother had come and asked her for two chickens, a piece of lamb and four candles. When Analola asked if she was going to give a party, her mother had not replied.

Next evening the skipper came with a fresh report: Daniel Ika had arrived at Vaitea the night before, and had slept in a room on the sheep farm. Analola had peeped through the key-hole and had seen that her mother was there as well. The two of them had been planning the visit to the cave, and Daniel had managed to persuade his aunt not to take Analola. She would bring "bad luck," he had said: for Analola was a child of our time and would give her secrets away to anyone who could win her favours.

The other two had decided to visit the cave two nights later, and had agreed where they should dig an *umu* to bake the hens. Analola had understood that this cave was at Vai-tara-kai-ua, which was just west of the Anakena valley.

"That's funny," the chief engineer said when the skipper repeated the story at lunch. "The Second and I have often been for an evening walk over to the place with that queer name. It's so pretty over there, with a little clump of green trees where wild chickens are often sitting about. Each time we've been there we've seen old Timoteo, the man who made the reed boat. He says he sleeps there at night because he's so fond of chicken."

The night watch on board told us that he had seen faint smoke from that direction the last few mornings.

Then came the night when Analola's mother and Daniel Ika were to steal to the cave. They came back next morning with long faces. Analola told us that they had baked their chickens somewhere up on the plateau, but they had not got down to the cave: they had found someone spending the night at Vai-tara-kai-ua. Exactly the same thing had happened the next night. This time they had seen that the mysterious person was old Timoteo and they guessed that he had another cave there himself and was watching the entrance so that Kon-Tiki's men should not find it. Analola's mother had decided to make a third attempt, and if they were again unlucky it was a sign that they ought not to enter the cave. In that case she and Daniel would give up and return to the village.

We learned from Analola when they were next to visit the cave at Vai-tara-kai-ua, and I decided to entice old Timoteo away from the place that night. When the appointed evening approached, the sea was calm and glassy. Some of our men had been out by moonlight the night before catching rock lobsters with native girl friends. This was one of the island's great delicacies: it is really a big lobster without claws. Our frogmen could often spear it in underwater caves, but the simplest way was to wade breast high along the shore at night with flaming torches. The native vahines were very skilful at this. They trod on the great creatures and held them fast with their toes till they could plunge down to pick them up and put them in a sack.

That evening the cook had twenty-one big red fellows in his pot, and we were going to have a lobster party in the mess tent. Lazarus had brought us a huge sack of newly gathered pineapples, the juiciest we had ever tasted.

I had kept old Timoteo at work all day. He had been on board the ship and repaired his own reed boat, which had been knocked about a good deal on deck before we hung it out of the way down in the hold. I now had no further need for the old man, but I wanted to keep him away from the valley to be visited by Analola's mother that night, so when evening came, and Timoteo wanted to go ashore and back to his post at Vai-tara-kai-ua, I brought him a large meal and asked him—purely as a ruse—to take the night-watch on board.

"We're going to have a *fiesta* in the camp," I explained. "All hands are going ashore tonight to eat lobsters. The sea's quite calm, so nothing can happen."

Timoteo did not look altogether happy. I had a feeling that the old man would be capable of taking a reed *pora* to swim ashore. I therefore took him up to the barometer and gave him a chair in front of it.

"If the barometer goes down to that mark," I said, pointing right down to the bottom figure to be on the safe side, "then you must blow the siren at once."

Timoteo took his instructions in deadly earnest. He sat down with his nose against the glass of the barometer and his eyes fixed rigidly on the needle while he swallowed his food. I knew that he would not move now. When the night-watch and the engineers came on board again, they would see about sleeping quarters for him.

Timoteo sat dutifully staring at the barometer, we of the expedition were gathered for our lobster party in the mess tent, and up in the hills somewhere above Vai-tara-kai-ua Daniel and Analola's mother were creeping down the valley towards the cave. As I was picking out the meat from the last leg, I realized that they had certainly dug the baked fowl out of the earth oven, and no doubt were now moving on, bringing the candles with them for use underground.

The night passed.

Early next morning Timoteo came ashore with the engineers. He said he must ride off at once to talk to his wife.

"Where is she?" I asked.

"In the village," he replied. He turned slowly and looked at me with a peculiar smile. Then he added: "But tonight she may have slept at Vai-tara-kai-ua. Who knows?"

This was a curious remark.

"What's your wife's name?" I asked.

"Her name is Victoria Atan. But she likes to call herself Tahu-tahu. And she is a bit *tahu-tahu*."[1]

Timoteo had climbed up on to his horse. He pulled the reins and off he rode.

The skipper drove up to Vaitea for water extra early that day. The report he brought back was that Daniel and Analola's mother had returned to the village. They had given up all hope of getting into the cave at Vai-tara-kai-ua unseen. When they made their final attempt the night before, Timoteo was not there, but his old wife was sitting there instead.

How Timoteo had managed to warn Tahu-tahu we never discovered. She relieved him only for that one night. But the old man continued to guard the little valley zealously so long as we were on the island. The veil of secrecy lies undisturbed over the two family caves at Vai-tara-kai-ua. It is for Timoteo, Tahu-tahu and Analola's old mother to decide whether they will try to hand the secret on to their own "children of our time." And they must decide soon. For if anything happens to these aged people, two caves with all their irreplaceable contents will disappear for ever into the depths of Easter Island.

Daniel had one twin- and one half-brother. The twin was Alberto: it was he who had shown two *rongo-rongo* tablets in the village and put them back in the cave because he was invaded by *aku-akus* at night. The half-brother was called Enlique Ika; he was of royal birth and had the right to the noble title *Ariki-paka*. Both Father Sebastian and the governor had pointed him out as a unique specimen, because he simply could not tell a lie. This was a rare virtue on Easter Island. Among us in the camp he was known as the "Royal Son," by reason of his proud nature, his stately appearance and his noble birth. He could not read,

[1] Tahu-tahu=sorcery.

but his unshakable honesty had made him the Navy's most respected shepherd, and he lived in a stone hut on the road to Rano Raraku.

One day he came riding in and offered us a deal. We had brought some enormous pine beams with which we supported the tall statues when we dug around their bases. He wanted to build himself a new house on the treeless island. If I was willing to do a deal, I should get a fat ox for every third beam.

"You shall have all the beams if you'll give us cave stones in exchange," I said.

This was quite a random shot, a sudden inspiration. I had no idea whether the "Royal Son" had a cave at all, or even knew what cave stones were. He was completely taken by surprise and wriggled for a moment in a desperate attempt to lead the conversation into other channels. But I stuck to my offer, and as he realized there was no escape, he said firmly:

"But I don't know where the entrance is. I wish I did know, Señor Kon-Tiki."

"Have you tried to bake a chicken in an *umu takapu*?" I asked curtly. "Have you tried to make a *tahu* in front of the cave?"

He was utterly flabbergasted. His expression changed completely.

"I'll talk to my brothers," he said at last. "I can't decide myself. I have only a share."

I learned that the entrance to one of his family caves had been lost. But he and his brother Daniel were sort of "sleeping partners" in another cave, the entrance to which only Alberto knew. The "Royal Son" knew that the stones there were in packages of *totora* reeds, and that the cave also contained *rongo-rongo* and some old paddles. But the finest objects were a stone sailing vessel, which he referred to as a *vaka oho*, and a statue of smoothly polished black stone, so large that it reached to a man's stomach.

The "Royal Son" had searched for the cave many a time, for Alberto refused to show the entrance to his brothers. He did not mind sitting in the village describing the position of the cave to them but he dared not point it out on the spot for fear the aku-aku might see him.

Several days passed before the "Royal Son" appeared again.

Then one day he came riding in with some large water-melons, and while he was unloading them he whispered across the back of the horse that he would be able to get me some old figures. His wife had been weeping and complaining for several days because she had an incompetent husband who could not find his own family cave. When nothing availed, and her husband always came home empty-handed, she had set to work on her own old uncle instead, and begged him for help, so that they could get beams for a new house. She had heard from her grandmother that the uncle knew the entrance to a cave in which she herself had a share, because her father was dead. The uncle, who was living with them in the stone hut at the time, grew weary of all this weeping. Eventually, therefore, the old man promised to show them the way to the cave.

The uncle was old Santiago Pakarati, who had helped his brother Timoteo to build the reed boats. The four old brothers were now working for me as fishermen. I had to provide full board for the working team which was digging at Rano Raraku, and I did what old traditions described as customary in the stone-cutters' time: I selected a special team, with no other duties than to work in shifts day and night catching fish and lobsters for all the men in the quarry. This helped us to eke out their daily rations of meat, rice and sugar, which were coming ashore from the ship in alarming quantities. We now had to keep all the flour for our own use. Only the four old Pakarati brothers came to the camp regularly and received old loaves: they dipped them in coffee and ate them as cake. We had become especially friendly with old Santiago, who was in the camp every day and collected his brothers' bread and tobacco rations.

We had once attempted to simplify the rationing system by making the distribution once a week instead of daily. But such an arrangement was not practicable on Easter Island. The whole native labour force sat up all night eating and smoking, and came to work next day with green faces, having consumed the whole week's ration. They had spent a splendid night, but then Santiago declared that they must have more cigarettes or they would have to go for a whole week with nothing to smoke. Everyone was pleased when we introduced daily rations again: saving is an incomprehensible idea; let the morrow take care of itself. *Haka-le* was the island's motto. It means something like "never mind." A native would say it if he lost his knife, smashed a bowl—or indeed, if his whole house was burnt down. Arne was lying on the bed one day in old Santiago's house, smoking. He dropped his cigarette and grubbed about feverishly in the straw to find the stump, from which a rather alarming cloud of smoke was ascending.

"*Haka-le*," said old Santiago, puffing cheerfully away at his own cigarette. "Just light another!"

In this atmosphere of smiles and easy-going *haka-le* the *aku-akus* were sadly out of place. The natives accordingly did all they could to avoid them, though nothing to get rid of them. They lurked on the cliffs, a blot on the general happiness. Old Santiago was a cheerful, carefree character. He was always satisfied with life and ready to joke and laugh. But his face fell into gloomy furrows and he grew almost angry when Arne wanted to camp alone by the crater lake in Rano Raraku. Santiago would not at any price have set foot inside the statue crater alone at night. For the *aku-akus* lurked behind the statues and whistled at him from the reeds in the lake. I was therefore particularly surprised that old "uncle Santiago" was the one who had now offered to accompany us to a cave.

It was late at night when the jeep stopped at the little stone hut on the road to Rano Raraku. I had chosen Arne among the archaeologists because he knew Santiago best. The skipper, the second officer and Sanchez from Chile came too, in the hope that they also might be allowed into the cave. The "Royal Son" came quickly out of his hut with his wife and a young man who, they explained, was Santiago's son.

"But where is Santiago?"

"He's ill. He can't come. But he has explained to his son where the cave is."

I knew that old story. It was a disappointing change in the programme which never led to any result. I went into the hut to see how ill Santiago was. There he sat squatting in the corner and looked at me with a sad expression. He gave a dry forced cough when he saw me come in. Santiago had no sign of fever. There was nothing to indicate that the old man was ill. But it was easy to see that he profoundly regretted what he had promised to do.

"Santiago, you're as fit as a tuna fish, you old rascal. Surely you aren't afraid of the *aku-aku* when I'm with you?"

Santiago eagerly grabbed a cigarette and whinnied so that all the smile-wrinkles moved up to his ears like the folds of an accordion.

"I've got a pain in my back, señor."

"Then you must give up smoking."

"It isn't all *that* bad."

I went on chaffing the old man for a long time until, half resisting, he came out and crawled up into the jeep with an uncertain grin. Now we were nine in the jeep. Santiago sat squeezed in by my side, silent and grave, and showed the way. From Rano Raraku we turned off along the south coast and followed some faint cart-ruts along the edge of the cliff. We had to hold on tight, for although it was almost impossible to see the track, it was very easy to *feel* it.

"This isn't a cave for hiding things, señor," said the old man suddenly, in the hope of my losing interest.

"Isn't there anything in it, then?"

"Oh yes, a little. I haven't been there since I was seventeen. An old woman showed me the place before she died."

The old man asked us to stop the jeep before we came to Vaihu, and we covered the rest of the way on foot. There was bright moonlight when we went down to the edge of the cliff. Again I saw silver-grey breakers in the night, hammering away at the lava barricade beneath us. Santiago was carrying a home-made rope ladder, composed of two thin ropes with a few scattered sticks as rungs. Right out on the edge of the cliff he was handed a bag by the "Royal Son's" wife and took out the familiar baked chicken wrapped in banana leaves. He asked me to eat the tail, "because it was to me he was showing the cave." There were the usual baked sweet potatoes in the bag too, but only the bony tail-stump was eaten, and I was the only one to taste anything. The rest of the delicious chicken was left behind on a rock.

Then the old man suddenly began to sing a monotonous song in a subdued voice over the cliff-side towards the sea. The tune stopped abruptly, as if broken off in the middle. Then he turned quietly to me and said I must promise to leave one thing behind in the cave. It did not matter what it was, but something must be left there. This was "the law," he explained. The cave was his. There were some distant relatives of his lying in it. That was why he had sung the name of the legal owner of the cave for the *aku-aku*.

Santiago slipped the top rung of the rope ladder over a lava block on the very edge of the plateau, and flung the rest of it over the precipice.

I lay prone with my head over the edge and turned the light of the torch downwards. We were on an overhang, for the rope ladder was dangling loose in the air just below. Santiago ordered only his son to undress, and to keep only his pants. He was to go down first. It was difficult to get a grip where the ropes were stretched tight at the edge, and the few rungs were a long way apart. The roaring breakers were only thirty feet below, but a drop of even six feet would have been enough for a man to kill himself on the jagged lava in the surf.

About twelve feet below us the descending man vanished. The rope ladder hung empty. We reached as far out as we could with the torch, but saw nobody. He had obviously abandoned the ladder and crept into an invisible hole. When the "Royal Son" followed suit a little later, he too disappeared from the ladder at the same place. When the next man was about to descend, we saw to our astonishment that the "Royal Son" was on the ladder again, climbing up as fast as fingers and toes could grip.

"Did you see anything?" I asked.

"Yes, a long tunnel going into a cave."

"And what was in the cave?"

"Oh, I didn't see. I didn't go in, for I'm not used to caves."

"Because he isn't used to caves, he's afraid of the devils," old Santiago explained.

And the "Royal Son" had to admit that this was so. His wife looked at him in alarm and was clearly glad to have him back.

When I was on my way down the rope ladder, I was quite as frightened as my native predecessor. But my fear was due to rather different causes. I thought of the lump of lava which held the ladder and my own weary fingers striving to get a hold where rope and sticks lay tightly pressed against the rock. Not till I had a knee bent up to my chin could I reach to the next rung with the tip of my toe. I was soon down to the point at which the ladder hung loose in the air, and immediately I caught sight of the narrow hole in the cliff-face into which the others had disappeared.

Holding tight with a hand on each rope I had to work myself through the dangling ladder, face upwards, till I got my legs into the little hole. I managed to push them in as far as the thighs, and with my whole body swaying in the air and my arms clinging to the ladder, I struggled to force myself farther in. I could get no purchase at all. The rope ladder only swung farther from the cliff if I pushed, and I had to drag myself into the crack with my heels until I had got my stomach in. I had hardly any back left when at last I got so far in that I could let go of the dangling rope with one hand while I fumbled for a hold on the rock wall with the other. The rope swung away as if it wanted to drag me out of the hole again until finally I let go with the other hand too. There I hung, face upwards, half inside the rock and half outside. This part of the trip had been child's play for the "Royal Son." Not till I was inside the rock up to my neck did I feel safe. I breathed a sigh of relief when I had shoved myself some yards into the crack to where it opened into a cave half the height of a man. It was not until this point that the "Royal Son" had begun to feel uncomfortable. This was where he became scared and had to give up.

Santiago's son had lit a candle inside. When I sat up I saw that we were surrounded by skeletons. Here Santiago's distant relatives lay. They had been packed in *totora* reed mats which were now brown and quite rotten; they fell to pieces at a touch. Some of the bones inside had a curious blue-green colour. I saw that small packages of the same decomposed reed lay alongside two skeletons which were stretched side by side just by my knees. I felt one package cautiously with my fingers. The reeds were brittle and crumbled at the slightest touch, but there was something hard inside.

At this moment we nearly had a fatal accident. Arne was now busy doing acrobatics at the entrance to the cave. While struggling desperately to get himself free of the rope ladder and into the narrow hole, he broke a rib. He broke it so emphatically that he afterwards insisted that he had heard it crack, and the pain was so intense that he was barely able to retain his grip.

We got Arne into the cave, and what he saw almost made him forget his pain. He crawled about patiently in the low, uncomfortable grotto. It was incomprehensible how in old days they had managed to get their dead down the cliff and into the narrow hole. Father Sebastian had told me of natives who had crawled into caves like this to die there of their own free will. After Christianity was introduced in the last century, with compulsory burial in the churchyard at Hangaroa, some of the old people had tried to get into their secret caves by stealth so that their skeletons might remain hidden there for ever. The last person who had succeeded in burying himself alive in this manner was old Teave, grandfather to some who were still living.

But the skeletons we had round us now had been packed up in reed mats. Here the relatives must have let their dead down the cliff with ropes, while others had lain in the crack and drawn the bodies in after them.

The skipper, the second officer and Sanchez had also come in. Only Santiago and the disheartened "Royal Son" remained with his wife on the plateau above us. We photographed and made sketches as well as we could under the low roof, and then we began to examine the cave's contents. Skeletons lay scattered about on the stone floor, and the only burial goods which accompanied them were the small parcels of reeds. A few of the parcels were already in complete dissolution, enabling us to see the contents.

The largest parcel contained a female figure carved in stone. From another a double face peered out, with four eyes and two noses which vanished in a curve round the stone and met as spear-heads on the other side. At the far end of the cave lay a solitary skeleton with a parcel beside it, and the plaited reeds had kept so well that large pieces held together when we took it with us. Inside the parcel was a sculpture of a lobster like the one which had started all the row about the mayor's cave stones. Perhaps it was an old fisherman who was lying there in the corner with his favourite magic stone, since a fisherman would have a special interest in increasing the power and fertility of lobsters.

There were only ten sculptures in this cave. All had been packed in reeds. Two of them were almost alike, a small statue of a standing man with a bird's beak. We left one of these behind in accordance with our promise to old Santiago.

To crawl out into the cool night again, we had to lie on our backs and kick ourselves along head first. Next, to reach the rope ladder, we had to edge ourselves out of the hole until the back was unsupported from the waist upwards, our arms stretched over our heads. Then we had to swing ourselves out backwards and up the dangling ladder. It was an unpleasant piece of acrobatics with the surf below us in the moonlight. Unpleasant was a mild word when Arne's turn came. But all went well, and the three who stood waiting anxiously up on the cliff thought that Arne was merely stiff from the climb.

We carefully packed the contents of the cave, and hauled them up with the aid of ropes. When the last load was up, and Santiago had made sure that we had left one article below, I caught sight of the chicken lying on the rock. The smell tempted me irresistibly. I was not going to let the *aku-aku* have this. And the *aku-aku* took no revenge when I helped myself freely to his portion and shared it with the rest in brotherly fashion. But the natives refused to touch a scrap, and kept away with worried looks until the last gnawed bone was hurled into the sea. Then the woman began to pluck up courage. She laughed contemptuously at her husband for having been afraid to crawl into the cave. The farther she got from the cliff the bolder she became, and when we sat squeezed together in the jeep, bumping home in the moonlight, I felt sorry for the proud man in the back seat. His wife screamed and laughed and teased him till he could not help smiling at himself. He shook his head and declared that he would never be so silly again. Now he knew better. Never again in his life would he let himself be frightened by ghosts and devils. He would go straight home and build the family a new house.

There was another person on the island who was more accustomed to converse with devils than the "Royal Son." As it happened, it was the mayor's youngest brother, little Atan, who unconsciously dragged me right into the hornets' nest. When he had disposed of his own cave and obtained more useful things in exchange, he was no longer in doubt that it brought "good luck" to get rid of the underground business

altogether. Atan had many friends in the village and no
enemies. Everyone liked Atan. And he tried with the greatest
caution to worm out of them information as to who had
caves.

One evening the photographer rode off across country,
followed by the skipper, the three engineers, the cook and the
mess boy. Ostensibly they were going along the north coast to
take film shots in the sunset. The mayor, little Atan and
Lazarus were standing with us by the tents and waved to the
others as the party rode away. We who remained were going to
a party at the governor's later in the evening, and Atan and
the mayor were then given a lift over to the village in the
jeep, while Lazarus now stood waving good-bye. No sooner
were we in the jeep and out of sight than Lazarus leapt upon a
horse and rode off at a gallop after the photographer and his
party. They had fixed a secret rendezvous where Lazarus was
to join them. The other natives were not supposed to know a
thing, for the horsemen had their rucksacks full of empty bags
and cartons. They were to fetch the rest of the sculptures from
Lazarus' cave, and bring them back to the camp unseen in the
course of the night.

I was to set out on a fresh adventure that night, conducted
by little Atan. He had long suspected that his brother-in-law,
Andres Haoa, had a cave. Now at last his suspicion had been
confirmed.

"Do you remember Andres Haoa, Señor Kon-Tiki? It was
he who showed you fragments of *ipu maengo*. He has those
pieces and the whole jars he showed to Father Sebastian
hidden in his cave."

That it was Andres Haoa was particularly unfortunate. He
was greatly offended with me because I had accused him of
trickery and had not given him the full reward on the occasion
when he had strewn tiny bits of his fragment in our excavation
at Ahu Tepeu. Little Atan realized this, but proposed that I
should send Andres Haoa a present, which he felt sure would
put things straight. I gave him a few dollars and two packets of
cigarettes, and it was agreed that I should come to Atan's
house when the governor's party was over late that night.
Meanwhile Atan would try to arrange a meeting.

Just before midnight I left the governor's bungalow. I

had informed him that I was taking part in secret expeditions into the island underworld, but that I was pledged to silence and could give no complete report till it was all over. The governor was grateful for the information and somewhat relieved. He had heard strange rumours in the village, but queer things were always being said in Hangaroa, and no one took the native gossip seriously.

At midnight I entered Atan's little hut. He opened the door himself, and the first thing I saw in the light of a flickering candle was my old "enemy" Andres Haoa, the pottery man, staring at me unshaven and bristly, with bloodshot eyes. He jumped up from the bench, embraced me and called me brother, assuring me that he would give me all the help he could. The tiny room was full of big words. Good-natured little Atan flung out his chest and boasted of his own *mana*: it was he who had saved the friendship between us two who now met again in his house. He had inherited his powerful *mana* from his mother. She had chosen him to take over all the strength of her soul: she had liked him best of all her children, although he was the youngest.

He told me that Andres Haoa had been quite beside himself when he saw my gifts of friendship. Andres himself admitted that he had wept for joy when he received the presents and heard the message of reconciliation. He had been in an awkward corner that time when, purely as a friendly act, he had brought me a fragment of real *maengo*, for I had at once demanded that he should show me the place where he had found it. Of course he could not show me his family cave, and that was where it had come from. He was therefore compelled to take us to another place to distract our attention.

Andres' story did not sound improbable. But now he had heard so much from Atan that he would like to give me the key, that I might see the pottery with my own eyes. Yet he had a younger brother who was as hard as flint, and he must first be won over to my side. This younger brother was the chief of the cave. He had been given the key by their father, although he was not the eldest. He "lived with" the *aku-aku* and had been much annoyed when Andres had called at his home that evening to propose that they should give the key to Señor Kon-Tiki.

"Let us go to this brother together," little Atan proposed. "We must be able to persuade him with our combined *mana*."

I was in white tropical dress after the party, but was able to change into a darker shirt and shorts I had with me; then we all three crept out into the night and sneaked out of the village in a northerly direction. We walked and walked in the moonlight, and the more we walked and whispered the more vehement became the talk of friendship and brotherhood. Atan had unlimited confidence in our own combined *mana*, and declared that he was a more genuine Norwegian long-ear than I. Both of them impressed upon me that if Andres' younger brother, Juan Haoa, tried to lead me into a trap by giving me the key to the cave, I was to say "no!" and cross my arms. If he then gave the key to his elder brother Andres, I was to accept it from Andres with thanks.

Outside the village we came to a desolate region, where at last we stopped before a high stone wall. Behind the wall great glistening banana leaves stretched up stiff and motionless against the moon, and half withdrawn among them lay a low white-washed stone hut. There were no windows and the place had a sinister, uninhabited look. Nothing indicated that anyone lived there. A rotten ladder, with some of its steps broken, led up to the stone wall, and another led down on the other side.

Little Atan braced himself: he was to go in first and announce our arrival. The ladder gave a nasty creak as he climbed over the wall; a moment later he was at the door, knocking slowly and cautiously. We saw a glimmer of light from the chink of the door as someone let him in.

Atan was gone for five minutes. He came out alone, and when he was with us again he looked forlorn and miserable. Andres' younger brother had been terribly hard and difficult. We must all three go in and get our combined *aku-akus* to work on him. We climbed over the wall and went up to the hut together. I entered first with the other two at my heels. In a room that was furnished with nothing but a white-painted table and three short benches, we were confronted by two tough gangster types who stood staring at us with hostile expressions. They looked as if they were ready for anything but a joke. One might have been about thirty, the other a little over forty.

I said good evening, and they returned my greeting without stirring, without moving even a muscle of their faces. The younger stood erect, head back, with a stoical expression like an Indian in a Wild West film. He had piercing black eyes, and round his mouth and chin he had a black stubbly beard just like his brother behind me. It was unusual to see a beard on the island, even if the mayor, Atan and some others had managed to grow moustaches. He stood straddle-legged with his arms inside the opening of his shirt, so that part of his chest was bare. He gave me a penetrating look with half-shut eyes and said, slowly and intensely, like a man in a trance:

"Watch my *aku-aku*. This is the *aku-aku*'s house."

Now I had to keep a cool head. I had put my foot into it and the expressions of those fellows showed unmistakably that I was in it up to my neck.

"I know," I said. "I can see."

He brushed my remark aside as if in irritation, and took a few slow steps towards me in a challenging manner, till he was looking right into my face. Then he almost hissed, with suppressed and quivering anger:

"Show me your *aku-aku*'s power!"

It was evident that Atan had been talking big about me and my *aku-aku*: the four men expected to see a miracle. All their faces were eager and tense, with an added mixture of contemptuous challenge in the bearded face which was now so close to my own. He gave the impression of being drunk, but he was not. He was in a state of self-hypnosis, almost in a trance. He was his own *aku-aku*.

I went two inches nearer, till our chests almost touched, and then took a deep breath to be equal to the situation.

"If your *aku-aku* is as powerful as mine," I said, putting the same note of suppressed contempt into my voice, "you can send him out through the door. Send him up to the top of Orongo. Down into the crater of Rano Kao. Across the plain at Vinapu. To the statues in Rano Raraku. To Anakena, Hangaroa, all round the island. Ask him if the island is changed. Ask him if everything has not become better. Ask him if old walls and buildings have not reappeared, and unknown statues risen up out of the ground. When you get your *aku-aku*'s answer, I'll ask you: Do you need any more proof of my *aku-aku*'s power?"

The man did not hesitate for a moment. He promptly agreed. He asked me to sit beside him on one of the benches.

Little Atan felt quite on top again. He and Andres at once began to ask the brother to give me the key, and soon the other tough fellow joined them and politely suggested that I should have it. But the chief actor, sitting beside me, did not move a muscle and did not condescend to listen to what they said. He sat with folded arms as on an invisible golden throne, bolt upright with mouth shut tight and lips protruding exactly like those of the great statues. Through pure self-suggestion, he inflated himself in his own and his friends' eyes, like a self-worshipping medicine-man or priest-king brought out of the mists of antiquity and thrust into shirt and trousers.

The other three stood before him, begging him for the key, but he ignored them completely. They continued their entreaties with hands and arms outstretched in humble prayer: one of them, indeed, went down on his knees in supplication.

The man beside me sat for a long time enjoying the others' humiliation, as if basking in artificial sunlight, slowly turning his head from one side to the other. Now and again he turned to me stiffly and emphasized his own immense spiritual power, his *mana*. His supernatural strength came from many sources, for he had in his veins the blood of two of the most important tribes. And this was the *aku-aku*'s house; *aku-akus* protected him on all sides. Behind him he had the mightiest *aku-aku* in the island: he lived in front of old Tahu-tahu's hut, and she was his wife's aunt. They had no other living neighbours. A little to the right was a deserted hut; it belonged to a woman who had died, and only an *aku-aku* lived there now. He had an *aku-aku* behind him, one on each side, and one in the house.

An uncanny glow came into the bearded fellow's eyes: the more he inflated himself the more dangerous and fanatical he became, so I hastened to interrupt him. Now I started to brag: it was just as if I had borrowed his pump and was using it to inflate my own reputation, while the air gradually went out of my neighbour as he listened.

I told him that I had inherited a powerful *mana* from Teri-ieroo, my mighty father by adoption, the last great chief of

A hula evening in Tahiti. Both before and after its work on Rapaiti the expedition had to call at Tahiti for provisions and equipment. No one on board regretted it. Yvonne is seen in red skirt in the background singing with the hula girls.

Above: The song of the South Seas has entranced people of many nations. The last verse is being sung, but that verse will never end as long as the palms wave and the evening air is filled with the sweet scent of the *tiare* blossom.
Below: Heaven or hell? A grunting pig-dance in the Taipi valley on Nuku-hiva.

Above: Rapaiti's green hills were covered with overgrown terraces and myste-rious pyramids which could not have been the work of nature.
Below: All the men of the village going up the hill to take part in the first real excavation ever done on this amazingly unexplored island. Of the twelve artificial hill-tops we chose Morongo Uta.

Above: Women leaving home to replace the men. The men had never done any paid work before, and as soon as they had started they laid down their spades, because they had heard that everyone who worked went on strike.
Below: Cheering vahines marching uphill to take over the men's work, led by Lea, the Joan of Arc of the South Seas. Lea, half Tahitian and half Corsican, had come to the island to teach the natives to read and write.

Tahiti. Before he died, he gave me the royal name Terai Mateata, or "Blue Sky." And when our raft landed on Raroia ten years later I got still more *mana*, for a feast was held in memory of Tikaroa, the first island king, and I was adopted as *Varoa Tikaroa*, the "Spirit of Tikaroa."

No more was needed. As I spoke my opponent was visibly losing ground, and at last he gave way. He rose slowly, and the rest of us did the same. Then he pointed to his big solemn friend and said:

"Tumu! bear witness."

I had read of the word *tumu* before. It was not a name, but a title. Earlier explorers had mentioned it as a mystic word dating from the original social system of Easter Island, a word which even the natives no longer quite understood and could not explain. Now a *tumu* stood before me in the flesh. His functions were not buried with the past: here he was in full activity. Atan told me afterwards that Juan Nahoe was *tumu* for the Haoa family. He was arbitrator and judge in the brothers' internal affairs.

The bearded fanatic drew himself up close in front of me, and Tumu stepped silently up beside him.

"Hereby I transfer to you the key to one of my two caves," he said in a sepulchral voice, as if pronouncing a sentence of death.

The others stood silent as the grave and even the flame of the candle did not flicker. Now I felt that I was in a dilemma. Was *this* the moment when I was supposed to fold my arms and say *no*? Verbally he now offered me the key indeed, but he did not hand it to me nor did I see it. I hesitated for a moment, and then replied drily "thank you," without moving a finger. He stood motionless for a long time, peering at me with his jet-black eyes. Then he quickly turned and marched out of the door with such bombastic pride in his bearing that he almost leaned backwards.

The other three seemed unspeakably relieved. Little Atan wiped away the sweat from his brow, though the only source of warmth was the little candle now flickering in the wake of the departed man. Eagerly gesticulating and relaxed, the three left in the room were in marked contrast to the one who had just stalked out.

K

A few minutes passed, and then the unpleasant fellow came back with a light flat parcel under his arm, and a heavy basket in his hand. Both were made of plaited *totora* reed. He gave the flat parcel to his brother, who laid it on the table, and then he again stood motionless before me, holding the basket. He fixed me intently with his eyes, but did not hand me the basket. I also remained motionless, with no expression but defiant contempt and utter indifference.

He turned abruptly to his elder brother Andres and gave him the basket. Andres handed it to me and I accepted it, thanking the younger brother for having first given the key to his elder brother and not directly to me. The aggressive fellow did not seem to be at all mollified. He stood for another moment or two without speaking: then he pointed to the parcel on the table and demanded:

"What is inside this parcel? Show your *aku-aku*'s power!'"

Once more all four were standing round me staring, tense and expectant. I racked my brains. It was like a nightmare examination; anything might happen if I did not pass the test. The parcel was as large as a brief-case and much too flat to contain any stone or wooden object. It was made of nicely plaited reeds and had seemed as light and as flexible as a large envelope when Andres laid it on the table. I realized that what I had in my hand must be the key to the cave, and I took it for granted that the parcel on the table also came from the cave. The plaiting of both parcel and basket were exactly the same.

I thought of the pretty feather work the natives had often brought us. They were copies of old feather hats and long strings of feathers used in dancing. Early visitors to Easter Island had seen prominent men with waving crowns of feathers on their heads, wearing feather cloaks, just like kings in ancient Mexico and South America. Was it possible that there was something of this kind, but more recent, in Andres' cave? Feather work was certainly not a bad guess. But if it was right was it a headdress or what? The others waited, tense with excitement. I must stand the test.

"My *aku-aku* says *con pluma*, 'with feather,' " I said cautiously, trying not to be too specific.

"*No!*" the fanatic snarled, leaping up like a tiger. "*No! !*" he repeated in a frenzy. "Ask your *aku-aku* again!"

He stood in triumph, crouching forward like a cat about to spring, enjoying the situation with an angry grin on his face. Little Atan wiped away the beads of sweat and looked quite desperate. He gazed at me entreatingly, as if to tell me that now I must do everything I could to make my *aku-aku* see reason. Tumu and Andres seemed menacingly suspicious, and they too had slowly come nearer. I did not like the situation. These people were fanatical, and I had, uninvited, poked my nose into the most inflammable recesses of their private lives. If anything happened, not a soul knew where I was. From this remote hut not a sound would reach the village. My friends would think that I had fallen over a cliff or been trapped in a secret cave. Nowhere in the world were there so many hiding-places in which a man could disappear for ever without leaving a trace.

I had no idea what the parcel could contain. It could only be pure guesswork. Could it be *tapa* or bark-cloth?

"Something to wear," I hazarded.

"No! Ask your *aku-aku* once more and ask well!"

They all drew closer to me in a threatening manner, and half my brain worked on the chance of fighting my way out, while the other half went on speculating what there could be in the parcel.

"A material," I tried as a last hope, using the technique of "animal, vegetable or mineral" on the radio programmes.

A queer grunt was the reply, and I was asked to open the parcel while they all stood round me, black as thunder. I untied a string of reed fibre and drew out an unbound book full of *rongo-rongo* signs. It was something like the priceless book I had been shown by the "village skipper." The hieroglyphic ideograms were drawn in ink, ink that had faded with age.

Suddenly it flashed into my mind that in Spanish the word for "pen" was the same as for "feather." I slammed the book down on the table so hard that I almost put out the light, and drew myself up indignantly.

"My *aku-aku* was right!" I said. "He said *con pluma*, and this indeed is written *con pluma*!"

All their faces changed immediately. They drew themselves up and looked at each other foolishly. It was they who had been wrong. The savage fellow with the stubbly beard and the

flashing eyes had changed completely. He had not thought of
it in that way. Little Atan broke the ice. He was utterly astonished and could only stammer:

"Oh, what a powerful *aku-aku* you have!"

This kindled a spark of jealousy in my bearded opponent.

"Look at the *aku-aku* in the book," he said. "Look at it!"

He turned over the large pages like those of a fantastic
picture-book, till he came to a page at which he let it lie open.
The left-hand page was covered with mysterious picture-writing
without explanation. On the right twenty picture signs were
repeated and translated into the natives' own tongue in clumsy
Latin characters. At the bottom of the page a separate line was
written in faded brown ink.

"There's the *aku-aku*," he grunted, pointing to the single
line.

I read: *Kokava aro, kokava tua, te igoa o te akuaku, erua.*

" 'When worn out at the front and worn out at the back,
make a new one,' that's the name of the *aku-aku* in the book,"
the owner said proudly, and gave me thereby an approximate
translation of the old sentence.

It struck me that this was very clever. The original maker of
the book had added a piece of practical advice, so that his
heirs would never dare to let the book fall to pieces and the
text be lost before a careful copy had been drawn. He had
turned his advice into an *aku-aku*, that no one would fail to
respect it.

"There's the *aku-aku*," the man repeated proudly, placing his
finger on the sentence, that we might all admire it.

"It's a *powerful* book," I said, and realized that I had chosen
the right adjective instead of saying *interesting, pretty* or *well-
made.* It appeared that the man could not read the contents,
but regarded the book as pure magic.

Henceforward we were all the best of friends: I was called
brother and received admiring looks from all sides. But still I
did not feel wholly secure.

"Now we are brothers," the man said, placing both his
hands on my shoulders. "Now we will drink each other's
blood!"

Little Atan looked at him with mingled fear and admiration. I hardened myself in soul and body and tried not to show

any feeling. After the mental suffering I had endured, no one was going to frighten me that night with a scratch from a knife. But the thought of drinking that horrid fellow's blood was unendurable. I remembered the mayor and Atan once telling Ed and me that they sometimes mixed their ancestors' bone-meal with water and drank it to get "power." Presumably it was something of the kind that we were going to do now.

The grim man marched as stiff as a post into a little back room, and I expected him to return with a knife. Instead he came back just as gloomily with a bottle and five glasses. He opened the bottle and poured something into each glass; the others only got a red splash at the bottom, but I had a full glass. Then each of us had to repeat the magic word *takapu* again and again. Atan had told me before that this was a word which gave *mana*, so that the *aku-aku* could see. Earlier investigators have translated this Easter Island word as "ceremonial earth oven," but this is wrong. The word has nothing to do with an earth oven unless *umu* precedes it, and then it is *umu* that means "earth oven."

When we had repeated the magic word often enough, I sniffed at the dirty glass unnoticed. It was red wine he had procured on board the *Pinto*. Before we drank, the leader said in a gruesome voice:

"Now we will drink our mingled blood."

The idea that wine was blood he must have acquired from the church. We emptied our glasses and he filled them again, an inch for himself and the others and a full glass for me.

"You are our leading brother, drink well," said the bearded fellow good-humouredly, and I was glad that he was not the one to drink freely. But now everything was pure friendship. There was big talk of *aku-akus* and brotherhood. I was their chief, and I had the key. The key to their cave and to "good luck" for all five of us. As far as I could understand, Tumu was now responsible for the second cave, but even that was mine if I came back and settled down among them for good.

The bottle was soon empty. I had had the benefit of most of it.

"Look at my beard," said the black-stubbled bandit, who had now become my younger brother. "That's where my strength lies," he said triumphantly.

I was sorry they did not see me as I looked when I had been on a raft for 101 days. But they had now accepted my strength even though I was clean-shaven. I had never enjoyed a drink so much, or needed it so badly. I felt in excellent form and looked at my watch. It was three in the morning. It was a long way to the camp, and I must see about getting home. I thanked them heartily and took my leave. As I was eagerly picking up the valuable *rongo-rongo* book and the basket containing the key to the cave, my brothers said that they would come and see me at the camp next day, and then we must have a meal of my food together. I bade them all welcome, and walked out into the fresh cool night with Tumu, Andres and Atan.

Next day my new brothers called for me and took me to the top of a hill. Here the fanatic clambered up on to a mound and began a speech in a hushed voice to an invisible audience out over the sea to right and left of him. He held the *rongo-rongo* book in a reed case under his left arm while he gesticulated heavenwards with his right. He talked in Polynesian in a low, almost inaudible voice, but looked like a mob orator mounted on a soap-box in the corner of Hyde Park. He pointed towards the sky and towards us, as excited as if he was trying to hold the attention of a great invisible crowd out over the sea and the plain below us. He stood there with open shirt and unbuttoned jacket fluttering in the wind, with one foot far away in antiquity and one foot with us—typifying a people in transition.

When the speech was over, he clambered down in an emotional state into the trench where we stood, and presented me with a fine wood-carving of a sail-fish. Then he took out the *rongo-rongo* book and turned the pages vigorously till he came to the page where the *aku-aku* was. He delivered another speech in a hushed voice to all the invisible people round him, keeping his finger on the line, and then he asked me to take the book from him and read the *aku-aku* aloud.

With the three men standing reverently beside me, and a view over a great part of the strange island below us, I read again:

Kokava aro, kokava tua, te igoa o te akuaku, erua.

They listened reverently and impressed, and the ceremony was at an end. Their forefathers had been taken to witness that the book was now legally made over to me. We climbed down from the hill, down to the green tents, where the steward had laid a cold meal for us.

The meal which followed recalled the lunch before we went to little Atan's cave. But the ceremony was even more grotesque and the hoarse voices even more brutal as they whispered compliments about the "power" and "strength" of the dishes. And that day each of us had his own vahine with him. Yvonne was terrified when I myself began to speak in the same unpleasant hoarse voice and behaved as queerly as the rest. She told me afterwards that she had been quite sure I had gone out of my mind.

Towards the end of the meal my sinister brother rose and pointed to the little Norwegian table flag, standing and stroking his black stubble-chin.

"That is your strength, my brother," he suddenly said to me, and seized the flag. "That is your strength, I must have it."

I gave him the flag and also a little model of the *Kon-Tiki* raft in a cellophane case, which he wanted to take at all costs. And carrying these two presents triumphantly under his arm, he left the mess tent at the head of the party and disappeared with the others on horseback in the direction of the village.

I managed to get a few hours' sleep before midnight. It was the turn of another new cave. Enlique Teao, who had been with us in Atan's cave, had blabbed. This time Yvonne, Carl, the photographer and Thor junior were coming, besides Atan. The cave was most skilfully concealed, but easily accessible through a rock-fall at the foot of a bluff on the west coast. Again I had to eat the tail-stump of a hen and crawl down a narrow shaft into the underworld. In an underground ante-room we were received by two skulls lying on a newly raked floor. Inside was a kind of bay decorated rather like a Christmas crib, with hay on the floor and yellow reed mats ranged in the form of a horseshoe round the walls, and covered with fantastic stone figures. It was really cosy in this inner cave. Enlique was friendly and naïve, like a child proud of a doll's house, and I felt pleasantly relaxed, with the memory of last night's visit to the fanatical brothers. The moon shone on us round and smooth when we came up to the surface again: the wind was light and mild and allowed the moon to play with its own silvery reflection on the gentle swell of the dark sea.

Next day we had arranged a huge barbecue and dancing for
the village population on the plain at Anakena. Our doctor
and the village doctor were sitting in the mess tent squeezing
drops of blood from the ear-lobes of those of our guests whom
Father Sebastian had pointed out as pure bred. When the
turn of the mayor and his family came, they gave their blood
as proudly as if the doctor was picking diamonds from their
ears. There was no doubt in their minds that a drop of blood
from a genuine long-ear's ear-lobe could be sold for dizzy
prices to museum owners. When they saw how carefully the
little red drops were mixed with chemicals and conveyed to the
ship's refrigerator in special containers, their looks showed that
they had no doubt about it: we were swindling them hopelessly,
but what would they not do for us for friendship's sake?

While the place was a scene of life and gaiety, the mayor
himself went round in a straw hat collecting the chosen in
order. We were surrounded by songs and laughter, twanging
guitars and neighing horses. I had just been to the fire pit and
helped myself to a juicy piece of meat when a scraggy old man
in a discarded army overcoat halted his horse in front of me.
He was ragged and toothless and his sunken cheeks were
covered with grey stubble. He gave me a friendly greeting, and
I asked him to dismount and help himself from the open earth-
oven. But he only leaned down towards me and muttered in a
low voice:

"This is why I'm here: to say you will have double luck.
El brujo, the wizard, has told me that you will have luck at
midnight on Sunday if you come to the house. After that, good
luck will follow you."

The old man would not reply to my questions: he merely
gave a jerk to his reins and rode off into the crowd, and I did
not see him again. I had never heard of *el brujo* before: as far
as I knew only old Tahu-tahu was concerned with *tahu* and
witchcraft. But I quickly guessed that it must be my strange
new brother, if there was anyone on the island who deserved
such a designation. He had behaved exactly as if he considered
himself a medicine-man. He lived in the *aku-aku*'s house, in
front of old Tahu-tahu's lonely hut, and thought himself surrounded by devils. I was in no doubt, the "wizard" must be
my newly acquired younger brother, Juan Haoa.

When Sunday came, we went over to the little church as usual. The birds flew in and out under the roof and twittered as freely as ever. Father Sebastian, as always, came down from the chancel in his gaily-coloured chasuble, and the atmosphere of opera was unchanged. But we were no longer surrounded by a mass of native heads which just blended into an unfamiliar whole. We now knew most of the faces. Friends sat on every bench. There sat the "policemen" Nicolas and Kasimiro. There sat old Pakomio with Lazarus and young Estevan; the "village skipper" and the "Royal Son" and the four old Pakarati brothers. And Atan and Enlique, Alberto and Daniel. And together with all the rest the trio Tumu, Andres and Juan the Wizard came in and sat down side by side in the middle of the congregation. At midnight today, Sunday, I was to see them again, according to the old horseman. Time and again I caught myself staring at the trio. There they sat sincere and reverent, drinking in every word that Father Sebastian spoke, and they sang the Polynesian hymns with the same fervour as the rest. The devilish look in their eyes had gone; they had a positively good-natured appearance, and the black stubble no longer made them look like bandits but rather like saints doing penance. If I had approached them and asked why they were in Father Sebastian's church when they had dealings with *aku-aku* and underground devilry, they would certainly have been surprised and probably replied, like little Atan:

"We are good Christians. All that is *otra cosa aparte*, 'another thing apart.' "

Today there was a christening in the church. I was god-father and sat on the first bench on the women's side. Behind me sat Analola with her old mother and the whole colourful crowd of vahines. Beside me sat the mayor beaming, all dressed up, with his wife, his red-haired son and his old black-clad aunt Tahu-tahu. This was the mayor's great day. He had become a grandfather. His daughter-in-law had presented him with a strapping grandson as compensation for the little girl who had died of the *cocongo*. The mayor was overflowing with happiness and wanted to call his grandchild after me. When Father Sebastian asked beforehand what the child was to be named, the mayor replied:

"Thor Heyerdahl Kon-Tiki El Salvador de Niños Atan."

K*

Father Sebastian tugged at his beard in desperation and begged for a shorter name. When the child was held over the font, the grandfather nudged me delightedly in the ribs.

"Look at his hair," he said.

The little boy's skull was covered with stiff, flaming red hair.

And the child was christened Salvador Atan. He was the last scion of the long-ears' race. He was the thirteenth generation after Ororoina, who escaped alive from the battle at Iko's ditch.

When night came and the whole village was dark and still, a candle was blown out in the mayor's house and two shapes crept out of the door unseen. Both the jeep and the horses of the expedition's Sunday party had returned to Anakena long before. In the village and in the camp people had been asleep for some hours, for it was nearly midnight.

But the jeep had returned to the village and was standing waiting without lights at the mayor's garden gate. The red-haired father of the just-baptized child, and its little uncle Atan sat waiting in the jeep and made room for the two shadows which came out of the house. Quietly, and without lights, the jeep rolled along the village street to the church, thence down to the sea and up along the coast towards the leper station.

I was beginning to feel uneasy as to what might happen. Ed was to wait in the jeep with the red-haired boy, whilst Atan and I were to walk on in the dark up to the *aku-aku*'s house. Quite secretly, Ed and I had stayed with the mayor for the early part of the night.

A few hundred yards from the house Atan and I left the jeep.

When we came up to the wall with the half-rotten ladder and saw the ghostly house between the great shining banana leaves, Atan stopped.

"You must go in alone first," he whispered to me. "You are our leading brother. You must knock at the door and say: Wizard Juan, stand up for good luck!"

I climbed over the creaking ladders and went up to the house. It was as silent as the grave. I raised my fist and with my knuckles tapped cautiously three times on the old door.

"Wizard Juan, stand up for good luck!" I said in a measured tone.

No answer. Not a movement within. Only the wind blowing round the ghostly house caused a faint rustling of the great glistening banana leaves that reached like spreading fingers towards the full moon. In the distance I heard the faint washing of the sea.

"Try once more," little Atan whispered on the other side of the wall.

I knocked again and mechanically repeated the phrase. Only the wind replied.

Now I was beginning to feel insecure. Perhaps this was another trap. Perhaps they were, this very moment, putting me to a new test. Atan saw that I was hesitating. He whispered that I must try once more: they must have gone to sleep inside for good luck. I realized that it was impossible for all three to be sound asleep now, just when they were to receive us, and I was beginning to be afraid of losing the battle. Were they standing behind the door and waiting for my *aku-aku* to see them? Incidentally, it was remarkable how much rustling there was over there to the left, where the great waving leaves caught all the moonlight so that the ground beneath was invisible in the dark. Had they hidden there behind the bushes to see if I got any help from my *aku-aku*? I thought once or twice, too, that I heard a faint sound from within, but no one opened. When I had tried six times, I gave up and turned to go. Then I distinctly heard a quiet movement behind the door. I turned and knocked for the last time.

"Wizard Juan, stand up for good luck!"

The door opened slowly. A young woman came out and turned on me the light of a home-made tallow lamp. I looked over her shoulder, but no one else was there, only the empty wooden benches round the little table at which I had received the *rongo-rongo* book and the key to the cave.

The three men had gone, she told me. She thought they had gone to the cave.

That was it. Presumably they would now wait for my *aku-aku* to follow their track so that we could meet at the cave.

Fortunately Atan at once decided to go into the village to look for Andres. He quickly set off across the field southwards.

The woman put out her lamp in the brilliant moonlight, and sat down on a wooden bench along the wall. She asked me to sit beside her. I remembered the face. She was Juan Haoa's wife and the mayor's youngest sister. I could not help noticing her lovely profile in the moonlight. There was nothing in the least Polynesian about her. She reminded me strikingly of an Arab or Semitic beauty. It was a classic profile with a narrow, slightly curved nose and thin lips. It was incomprehensible that she was a pure-bred Easter Islander. This was a genuine long-ear who sat beside me. We had a sample of her blood on board the ship.

She was an intelligent woman, and I had no difficulty in starting a conversation with her. We were left alone for a long time, for one o'clock came, and two, and Atan had not returned. I had a good deal of information from her as we sat on the bench, chatting in the moonlight. The three men had decided that I ought to have a sort of *aku-aku* of feathers, she told me, because we had talked about feathers the night before. But to give it power they had been up at old Tahu-tahu's, and she had killed a chicken and made a feather crown for me to wear on my head. They had kept it between them on the table a few hours ago, when she herself went to bed, but now it was gone. She thought, therefore, that they were waiting for me in the cave with the feather crown. The whereabouts of the cave she did not know, all she could say was that her husband went northwards when he visited the cave at night. She knew a good deal about caves and cave customs, but had never seen a cave herself.

This inside information about the feather crown could be very useful in the event of the three putting me to another test. I could now surprise them with my own knowledge.

Another hour passed, and when it was three o'clock little Atan came trotting across country from the village. He had at last found both Andres and Juan in their own sister's house, and Tumu was with them. Tumu had demanded that they should talk to their sister too about giving me the cave, as she had a share along with the brothers. But now she was furious because the brothers had not asked her before instead of after giving me the key. They tried to mollify her by holding handsome presents from me in prospect, but she was still in a rage and threatened to make trouble if they gave the cave away. She would not even listen to Atan. The three men had been in complete despair, not least Tumu, who was with them to find a solution which would satisfy all three. They had begged me to excuse the delay, but I must just wait.

We waited till four, when I went off to reassure the two who were still waiting in the jeep. We decided to give it up, and the jeep had already started for the village when we heard the hoofs of a galloping horse behind us. It was Juan the Wizard, riding after us in the moonlight at breakneck speed. He came from the north and not from the village, and said that we must turn and follow him. He seemed excited and overwrought. We turned the jeep. Juan rode ahead, and we followed him without lights along the coast in the moonlight, nearer and nearer to the leper station. I thought they would soon be sure to hear us up there. Our guide signalled to us to stop and get out beside some big lava-blocks on a rolling plain covered with stones.

As I crawled out of the jeep, sleepy, cold and stiff, two figures rushed out from a hiding-place behind the rocks and were upon me in a single bound. Before I could do anything they stretched their arms aloft over me and placed a crown of waving feathers on my head. Juan the Wizard leapt from his horse, tethered it to a stone, and swiftly hung a long string of feathers bandolier-wise over his chest. He explained that this was to show that I was the chief brother, while he came next in rank. He asked me to follow him, and we set off across the stony plain as fast as we could go, with Ed, Tumu, Andres and Atan at our heels. The red-haired boy remained to watch the jeep.

Tahu-tahu's waving feather crown was a faithful copy of a *ha'u teke-teke*, a well-known headdress among the original population of Easter Island: specimens of it exist in several museums. I felt rather an idiot striding across the scree with the waving crown on my head: it was as though I had returned to childhood and was running about the stony plains of Easter Island playing Indians in the moonlight. Things seemed no less crazy when soon after I was squatting down eating the tail-stumps of two hens.

Soon afterwards we raised a few stones amid the remains of

an old crumbling lava flow, and I crept down through the shaft ahead of the others, with the feather crown on my head. Down below we entered a roomy cave, but it was low under the billowing roof. Again the floor was covered with old hay. To the right of the entrance was a little altar covered with a reed mat, and on it was a large and majestic stone head, flanked by two human skulls. One of the skulls was real, the other was of stone and had a curious sucker-shaped mouth which was twisted forward and up, ending in a small bowl or oil lamp on which it gazed down with great hollow eyes. Facing this gruesome trio lay another white skull and a slender stone pestle with a head at the upper end.

In the middle of the floor was a low stone platform, covered with hay and a reed mat on top. Juan the Wizard asked me to sit there and look in a given direction, as his grandfather had always done. Round the walls was another platform covered with the most extraordinary figures, some from reality and some from a world of dreams. In addition there was a yellow reed parcel on each side of the platform on which I sat enthroned.

The first thing Juan the Wizard did was to produce the little model raft and the Norwegian table flag.

"This is your blood," he whispered to me in a hoarse voice, gripping the flag tightly. "And there you have new power yourself, there you have *ipu maengo*!"

I was so excited that I held my breath as I took the wrappings from the parcels and stared at the contents. In each of them lay a brown unglazed earthenware jar. These must be two of the three mysterious jars Andres had defiantly shown Father Sebastian at the time when he was angry with me.

"He's got many of different kinds in the other cave," Tumu put in. "It's full of *maengo*, and it'll be yours when you come back to us."

One of the two brown jars had a simple band of incised ornamentation. Juan declared that "grandfather" had made it, and that the incisions represented men who had gone to the wars. The jars had been placed here so that the dead might drink when they wished to.

When we unpacked the two jars later in the camp, only Gonzalo recognized the type. He had seen jars like them in

Chile, where the Indians had made them for generations and where they are probably made in remote regions at the present day. A new problem arose. These hand-moulded jars were not turned out by modern man, using the potter's wheel. They were made of coils of clay pressed together in the true American Indian manner. How did this type of jar find its way to Easter Island, whether in ancient or modern times? And what was there about these jars that made them worthy of a place among the figures in the family cave? Why did he not put water for the spirits into a glass, a can or a coffee-pot? Earthenware was unknown in the native huts, and yet Juan must possess more. For we found that neither of these two jars answered the description of the three Andres had shown to Father Sebastian.

Only on one other occasion did I hear of a cave on Easter Island with old jars in it. This belonged to a cousin of Enlique's, but he had left for Chile in the *Pinto*.

Day was breaking and the cocks crowing when I tried to slip quietly through the mayor's garden gate. Not a soul was to be seen, and my bed was as I had left it. Invisible hands had put out fruit and a roast chicken, but best of all was to relax between the fresh white sheets which I had once presented to the master of the house when he was planning a voyage in the *Pinto*.

"Don Pedro mayor," I said when my smiling friend tip-toed in with a bowl of water next morning. "Thank you for a splendid night's hospitality. But when will you show me your cave?"

"Take it easy, señor, surely you weren't out last night without good luck?"

"I had good luck. But I shall soon be leaving the island. When can I see Ororoina's cave?"

"Take it easy, señor, you've had the key from me. Isn't it lying under your bed?"

It was. And I could not help smiling inwardly when I thought of it, for what I had under the bed was a "long-eared" head of a rather different type from what I had expected.

But there had been so much that was unexpected about the mayor of late. Ever since he came out of hospital he had been a little queer, and I did not recognize him as quite the man I had known. He had grown thin and wan, as was to be expected,

but above the sunken cheeks a new gleam had entered the
cunning eyes. He seemed exalted and over-optimistic and was
full of fantastic plans. He was no longer afraid of his grandmother. Now we would empty the cave and both of us would
become multi-millionaires. He was going to buy a small steamer
and start regular tourist traffic from the mainland. His brother,
the "village skipper," could steer by the stars, and his red-
haired son, who had learnt to drive a jeep, could look after the
engines. Everyone on the island would become incredibly rich,
for the tourists he brought would buy more bird-men and
moai kava-kavas than the whole population could produce.

I tried to damp the mayor's colossal optimism, but it was
quite useless. For "good luck" I must not talk like that. But in
spite of all his boasting and big promises the mayor did not
bring me a single stone after he left hospital. Nor did he come
and work for me. Suddenly he had no time for anything at all.
After all, he was mayor and therefore a fearfully busy man.

But then one day, quite unexpectedly, he came rushing to
meet me outside his garden gate. "Good luck!" he said.

This was a day of real good luck, he whispered excitedly.
And then he told me, quite openly and in the skipper's presence,
that Tahu-tahu had agreed to his giving me the key of Ororoina's cave, on one condition: that I should take Tahu-tahu's
eldest son, as well as the mayor and his son, with me when I
left the island. I promised to talk to the governor about it, and
the mayor positively jumped for joy. He eagerly invited the
skipper and me to come into the house at once. At the round
table where I had so often sat we found a rather brutal-looking
fellow with a flat, broad nose and curly hair. He did not look
particularly amiable, even though he tried to smile. Two empty
glasses and an opened bottle of Chilean peppermint stood on
the table. The man who sat there with bloodshot eyes looked as
if he had made certain of the lion's share of the contents. But
he was not drunk, and he rose and genially stretched out a
large hand in greeting.

The mayor assured us unctuously that this was a good fellow,
inasmuch as he was his own cousin, his mother being Tahu-
tahu. But his father's family came from the Tuamotu islands.

"He has helped us," the mayor assured me. "He has persuaded Tahu-tahu."

He dragged up a bag, held it out in front of him, and whispered mysteriously that the key-stone was a head with three small holes in it: these had been filled with a deadly meal made from his ancestors' bones. The man with the bloodshot eyes nodded gloomily. Now they had carefully removed all the bone-meal and the head was no longer dangerous.

This detail was common to the mayor's and little Atan's caves. But when the mayor took the key-stone out of the bag, it was no grinning death's head that appeared. On the contrary, it was a really jovial pig's head of stone, an amiable snout with round cheeks and long hanging ears, exactly like the most cheerful of "the three little pigs" in the fairy tale, the one who danced before the wolf and built his house of straw. But unlike the nice little pig in the story this cave pig had curved teeth, worse than a wolf's, and three holes for human bone-meal on the top of his head.

The mayor and his cousin turned a gloomy gaze up to us. I tried to look as grave as they were, but the mayor must have detected a suppressed gleam in my eye, for he suddenly smiled and gave the pig's head an affectionate kiss on the snout. Both the skipper and I were on the verge of collapse. I hastened to thank the mayor gravely for the pig's head, the skipper took a cardboard box full of other sculptures, and we made for the door. The mayor asked me to wait in patience for a few days with the pig's head under my bed: for several nights running he must bake chickens in *umu* so that all might go well when we entered the cave.

Days had now become weeks. The mayor seemed never to have finished baking his chickens. And the pig's head was by no means safe from Anette under the bed. She was always crawling under it to play with Daddy's piggy-wig. The figures from all the other caves had been taken on board the ship: we did not like to have them lying in the tents, for scorpions often crept out of the holes in the stones.

"Yes, indeed, I had good luck last night," I repeated, getting out of bed to take the washbowl from the mayor's hands. "And the key-stone's in my tent. But I must take it on board now. We're going."

When the mayor heard this, he had apparently baked

enough chickens, for he at last fixed a night to enter the cave.
Bill was permitted to come, and the photographer, but he
would have no more.

On the afternoon of the day the mayor had fixed we had a
number of native visitors to the camp. The first party to
arrive brought their traditional wood carvings for sale, and
there were lively barter dealings outside the tents. Among the
horsemen was a taciturn half-wit who came over to my tent
with six weather-worn stone figures tied up in a cloth. Moss
was growing on one of them.

"Who made these?" I asked.

"I," the boy replied apathetically.

"You can't have. There's moss growing on one of them."

The boy did not answer, but his mouth fell and it looked as
if he was going to weep. Then he told me that his father would
give him a thrashing if he knew about it. For the boy knew the
entrance to his grandfather's cave.

I gave him a lot of presents for himself and his father, and
the lad rode home overflowing with happiness. He probably
knew of a cave which no one tended and we never heard another
word about the matter.

The wood-carvers remained in the camp till dark, then they
all rode home in a crowd. They had scarcely left when a
solitary horseman came down from the hills. He tethered his
horse and came to my tent. It was Juan the Wizard. He looked
grave and troubled, embraced me and called me brother; then
gave me an urgent warning. If anyone came to me with more
stones, I must not accept them: it would bring me "bad luck."
What I had now was all right, but it must go no further: I
must not accept a single stone from now on. His *aku-aku* knew
everything that happened in the village. If I accepted one
more stone he would get to know of it, and for our brotherhood's sake I must promise to do as he begged me. If I did not,
I should regret it and I should never see his other cave with *ipu
maengo* in it.

He gave me a wonderful sculpture of a reed boat with a
figure-head and two sails. He had taken it from the second
cave, so that I might not forget. He was so sincere in his
warning, almost imploring, that I realized that he had discovered something which he could not disclose.

As soon as Juan the Wizard had discharged his peculiar mission, he crept out in the dark again to his horse and vanished into the night.

Not very long afterwards a young couple came riding along the jeep-tracks from the village. They were two of the most humble and decent natives in the island. The man's name was Moices Secundo Tuki, and he was one of my best workers. His wife, Rosa Paoa, was as quiet and simple as her husband. I had never talked about caves to them, and I was surprised when they silently unloaded a heavy sack from one of the horses and asked if they might show me the contents privately. When they had emptied the bag, seventeen fantastic stone sculptures lay in a row on my bed, among them some of the most curious I had seen till then. A figure of a woman with a large fish in a rope on her back strikingly recalled a typical motif in ceramics from old desert graves in Peru.

Rosa answered all questions openly and frankly. Her father, a short-ear of the Ngaruti clan named Simon, had given her the sculptures to barter with me. He had inherited them from his great-grandfather, whose name she did not know. But the stones came from a closed cave in the cliff near Orongo, and the cave was called *Mata te Paina* or the "Eye of the Straw Image." Another family had hidden their sculptures in the same cave, but no one had washed them after Marta Haoa had died.

I was eager to obtain these unique sculptures. But respect for Juan the Wizard and his urgent warning were fresh in my mind and kept me on my guard. Who could know if he was hiding in the darkness and spying on me? There was some mysterious reason for the hurried visit he had paid me. But I did not want to lose the stones. I told the couple that my *aku-aku* warned me against accepting stones just now. But he might change his mind. Therefore they must hide the sack well and come to me again the day our ship was to leave the island.

The couple looked most distressed and puzzled. They remained seated, their faces like two question marks. But when I gave them some presents as a mark of friendship, they stuffed them gratefully into the sack with the stones and crept out silently to their waiting horses.

I scratched my head in an endeavour to understand what was going on. Then I blew out the lamp and tried to get some sleep before we went in to meet the mayor at midnight. I had little more than a nap before the cameraman came and told me that the jeep was ready. We were to pick Bill up at a rendezvous in the village, and we were giving a lift to the mate. He was going on another secret mission. An old native had confided to me that he knew of a red-haired human head in a cave. He himself dared not touch the hair, but he was willing to point the place out to anyone who was not afraid of a swim in the sea at night. And the mate Sanne was not afraid of anything. The mayor too had once spoken of such a head which was supposed to be in his cave. Could there be mummified heads in any of these caves? We bumped off into the night, heavy with sleep, while white flocks of sheep silently scattered from our headlights like clouds of dust. We should soon find the answers.

It was long past midnight when our little party of six came stealing up to Tahu-tahu's house. In addition to the mayor, his red-haired son and his cousin, there were Bill, the photographer and myself. In the scree just below her little hut I smelt the well-known odour of chicken in an earth oven, and we were soon squatting in a circle, devouring the delicacy, I first with the chicken's tail. The ceremony at an *umu takapu* was beginning to be familiar to me, but never one so cheerful as that night. The natives were not nervous, and the mayor seemed almost theatrically self-confident as he sat at his ease, tossing chicken-bones to the *aku-akus* as nonchalantly as if they were dogs standing round us begging for morsels. When he had had enough, he went a little way to one side and lit a cigarette: then he came up and proposed in a friendly way that we should go to the cave.

This time the entrance was not just a few steps away: it was surprising how far the cave itself was from the scene of the ceremony. We clambered over walls, stumbled forward over rough stony fields and followed winding tracks. We must have walked for ten minutes, and the place where we had eaten was far behind us, when the mayor stopped at last by a natural pile of stones. Once we stood and examined it, it was easy to detect that the stone in the middle had recently been moved.

The mayor asked me to produce the key-stone which I had in the bag. I must try to find the entrance with its help, he said. When I found it, I must shout three times into the pile that I was a long-ear from Norway, open the door.

I walked straight up to the stones, with the pig's head in front of me like a mine-detector, and tilted its snout down towards the suspicious stone, repeating the mayor's magic words. A moment afterwards I had removed a number of stones and was on my way backwards down a narrow shaft into the underworld of Easter Island.

At the bottom I slowly came out of the shaft backwards and was just about to straighten up cautiously like a blind man inside the dark cave, when I felt a sharp bump against my neck. It was not the roof I had hit: I had run into some moving object. There must be someone in the cave. Before I had time to think I had flung myself aside and round, switching on my torch as I did so. It was as I thought: I caught a glimpse of something moving. But what on earth was this? The light fell on a large bird of prey with outspread wings and a hooked bill, carrying a human skull on its back. It was of stone, and hung from the roof by a string. It was still swinging slowly from the bump I had given it. The bird looked strangely bright and new to have hung there for eleven generations since Ororoina's time, and the piece of fibre string by which it hung was new.

I swung my torch around. The cave was not at all large. Three reed mats with parallel rows of round flat stones lay on the earth floor: on each stone was carved one magnified figure of the types which made up the *rongo-rongo* writing. A small head with a goatee beard lay on each mat as guardian. I saw at once that this cave could not have been the source of the varied choice of sculpture the mayor had brought me. The only outstanding objects here were a vessel with sails and a large stone bowl over in a corner. Both were well done, but looked as conspicuously fresh as the bird hanging from the roof.

I looked into the bowl. In it lay eleven small locks of human hair of every range of colour from red to black. Most of the locks were red, and were bound together separately with thin strips of bark with elaborate knots. But the locks of hair were not at all dry and faded as on old mummies: they must have been cut recently from living persons, for they were still fresh and glossy.

The suspicion that had lurked in my mind since seeing the bird that swung from the roof was now definitely confirmed. The sculptures in this cave were not old. They had been made quite recently, and the whole cave was sheer contrivance. We had walked straight into a trap. My first thought was to get out. This was what Juan the Wizard had meant to warn me against.

Bill's legs were already feeling their way through the shaft opening in the wall of the cave, and it was too late to stop him. Behind him came the photographer. It was no use making a row now, for if the three natives up there realized that we had seen through the plot, they would probably be terrified. And if, for this reason, they had the idea of filling in the shaft above us with stones, then we should be in a nice spot here under the solid rock.

"We've been cheated," I said to Bill directly his head was clear of the shaft. "Let's get out of this as quickly as we can. It isn't a family cave. These are not old stones."

Bill looked astonished and quite uncomprehending. He crept across to the *rongo-rongo* stones to take a closer look.

"There's nothing necessarily old here," he whispered back to me.

"Look at the bird and the boat and the bowl with the hair in it," I replied.

Bill swung the light round him and agreed. Now I saw the bloodshot eyes of the mayor's cousin behind me. He was studying me intently, but did not understand what we were whispering to each other in English. Then I saw the mayor's face in the torchlight too. He was dripping with sweat from sheer nervousness. His son looked round him with large eyes. The ascent of the shaft must now be clear.

"The air is bad down here," I said to the mayor, rubbing my forehead.

He cordially agreed and wiped away the perspiration.

"We'll go up and have a bit of a talk," I said and made for the shaft.

"Agreed," said the mayor and headed for the same hole.

I felt a thrill of relief when I stood under the open sky and saw the others climb out of the shaft one by one.

"We'll go now," I said curtly, picking up the damned pig's head which lay on the stone pile looking at me with a crooked smile.

"Agreed," said the mayor and jumped up as if to confirm that this was no place to remain.

And so the little procession went back the way it had come, in silence: not a single word was exchanged. I led the way, sleepy and tired and cursing inwardly, with the mayor close at my heels. Behind him came Bill and the rest. The mayor's cousin lost little time in making off in the dark, and soon after the son had gone too.

When we came to the first houses in the village, the photographer and I said good-night to Bill. It was two o'clock, and he had to get home to the native house where he was living. On parting he whispered that if I could persuade the mayor to take us to his real cave the very same night, he would not have time to prepare another hoax. In the village I asked the photographer to wait with the jeep and marched straight up the garden path to the mayor's house with the mayor himself close at my heels like a dog.

I went in and sat down at the round table without a word. The mayor immediately sat down beside me and let his eyes wander innocently round the walls with a vacant expression. I drummed with my fingers. He shifted slightly in his chair. I tried to make him look me in the eyes. He returned my gaze for a moment or two with large innocent eyes. Then he stared round at the walls again. We could have sat like this for the rest of the night. He was unwilling to accept defeat. He clung to the hope that the game was not yet lost. I had not said a word.

"That was bad luck, Pedro Atan," I began, and noticed that my own voice shook. "Bad luck for you, for me, and for your trip."

The mayor's chest began to heave. He held his breath. Then he burst into tears and let his head fall upon his arms. He lay for a while sobbing violently; then he jumped up and rushed out through the door. I heard him dash along the front of the house and into the little side room, where he threw himself on

the bed and lay there moaning. Then he grew quiet and came
back into the room where I sat.

"It was all the fault of my cousin, that bad, bad cousin of
mine. I thought as you did that we were going to a cave with
old figures."

"But it was you who showed the way—your cave," I replied.

He stood for a moment or two collecting his thoughts. Then
he burst into tears again.

"It was *his* idea. I should never have listened to him," he
howled. He rushed out of the door and once more into his bed,
where he lay for a long time. Then he came rushing back again.

"Señor, you can ask me for anything. Anything. But not for
the gate of the cave. Not the gate of the cave. I'd be willing to
bring out all the stones to you!"

"You don't *have* to show us the cave, but then no one will
believe in you. For you're much too clever at making figures."

I nodded angrily towards the accursed pig's head which lay
in a bag on the table. It was admirably done, and tired and
depressed as I was, I could not help smiling inwardly at the
thought of the cunning mayor, who had made me dance round
like an idiot holding the pig's snout over the stone pile.

"If you don't take us straight to the real cave tonight, you'll
be making a lot of new stones for another hoax," I said.

I rose to go.

"I can take you to *another* secret cave now, tonight," said the
mayor, in genuine despair.

"Is it Ororoina's?" I asked.

"No, but it's full of old things."

I took the bag containing the pig's head, the only souvenir
of the night's adventure, and walked uninterestedly to the
door.

"If you change your mind tonight, you can go and fetch
Bill from Rapu's hut. I'm returning to Anakena."

The mayor was standing at his door, wellnigh desperate and
cursing his cousin, as I walked down weary and depressed to
join the patient photographer in the jeep.

We had scarcely disappeared along the road when the
unhappy mayor went straight off to Rapu's hut. He woke Bill
and offered to take him to a genuine cave there and then. Bill
was very sleepy and utterly sick of the mayor, and when he

heard that the photographer and I had returned to Anakena, he would not go to the cave either.

The mayor had to go home alone empty-handed just before dawn.

About the same time the mate Sanne swam ashore not very far from the leper station. The old man had refused to let him use a boat, and he had to swim in the starlight out to a bare lava island. Here, following the description the native had given him, he had found his way to a couple of burial caves. In one of them he had actually come upon a human head with completely red hair. A thick tuft of uncommonly fine reddish-brown hair had come off on one side, and he had put this in a bag and taken it with him when he swam back to the rocks on the coast. The hair had no sheen and was bone-dry and brittle.

This was how the hair in the mayor's bowl ought to have looked if he had not gone round after leaving hospital cutting locks from the heads of his red- and black-haired relatives. That confounded *cocongo*! It had evidently given the mayor a bad shock and restored his faith in his dead grandmother and the *aku-akus*, while I myself had been degraded to the rank of a quite ordinary person who had tried to cheat him. The result was that he had decided to cheat me in return, to stop me from pestering him about his own cave. But in order not to irritate unknown *aku-akus* unnecessarily, he had made his sham *umu* far away from all caves and close under the wall of Tahu-tahu's house, where he counted on sympathy and protection.

The following afternoon the mayor's red-haired son Juan rode into the camp alone, looking very grave. Juan was an exceptionally handsome and well-built lad. As with the rest of the long-ear Atan family, there was nothing in the least Polynesian in his appearance. He could quite well have been an Irishman; certainly no one would have thought that he came from a South Sea island.

Juan told me gloomily that he thought his father was going to die. He refused to see his wife, he refused to eat or drink. He just lay in bed and moaned and wept and talked of "bad luck." Juan had seen by my face the night before that there was something wrong with the cave. He had never been in a cave of this kind before, so he had thought everything was all right.

When I told him what had happened, not a muscle of his face moved, but the tears gushed out and ran down his cheeks. He said that his father had gone straight to Señor Bill afterwards to show him another cave, but Señor Bill would not go without a message from Señor Kon-Tiki. But if I would write a message to Señor Bill, the boy would try to find out from his father where the other cave was, and so he himself and Señor Bill would bring "good luck" back to the island.

I wrote a note to Bill, and the boy galloped back to the village.

After Bill had received my note he was shadowed for the rest of the day by two men as soon as he left Rapu's hut. The natives had begun to shadow Lazarus too, so that I never got into his second cave, which was at Vinapu. But at midnight Bill had contrived to get away from his shadowers, and had met Juan at an agreed place. With him the boy had a crude map drawn by his father on a piece of paper.

It appeared from the map that they must first go to Ahu Tepeu, which lay far away in the stony region on the coast north of the leper station. Juan had obtained two saddled horses and a long coil of rope, and they set off in the dark. When late at night they reached the great *ahu*, the map had to come out again. They were to go on over a high sheep fence, where they had to leave the horses. The next clue was some big lava outcrops to the right. Directly below them, on the edge of the coastal cliff, was a firm round stone to which to fasten the rope. They were to climb down almost to the end of the long rope, and there they would find the cave.

They found the fence, lava outcrops and a round stone on the edge of the plateau, and when the rope was made fast Juan climbed down in the dark. They did not eat chicken first and made no *umu takapu*, no kind of ceremony. Juan was down for a long time and came up again tired out: there was no cave. They found another stone and tried that, with the same negative result. They moved the rope from stone to stone along the coast, till at last the boy came up completely exhausted: he could only just pull himself up over the edge with Bill's help. But this time he had found the place.

Bill set off down the rope in the dark. First he went down a sheer drop to a ledge with decent foothold: but from there the

rope hung free in the air. He went on down, and heard breakers
far below him in the dark, but could see nothing. Then suddenly as he hung there he saw a horizontal crack in the rock
just in front of his nose. He thought he could discern something inside but too far in for him to reach it, and the crack
was so narrow that he would not try to get his head in. With
the help of a torch he and Juan had at last been able to see
that the narrow cave was packed with figures buried under a
thick layer of dust. Juan had managed to squeeze his legs in up
to his stomach and had drawn out with his foot a hook-
nosed head with a flowing beard, the style of which recalled a
mediaeval ecclesiastical sculpture. They were both so weary
that they had only just been able to climb the sixty feet up to
the top of the rope with the piece they had been able to secure.

They did not risk another descent.

Next morning Bill sent me a letter. His impression was that
this cave hit the bull's eye. So far as he could see, there was
every reason to think that this time it was the real thing.

We examined the remarkable head they had brought with
them. It was something entirely different from the fresh sculptures we had been shown the previous night. This was old stuff.

I picked two of our best climbers: the cook and the second
engineer. In pouring rain, with Juan and Bill leading the way,
we rode off in broad daylight to the cave at Ahu Tepeu. In the
middle of the dry season the rain was "good luck," and Juan,
shivering with cold on his horse, was smiling broadly. At last
we were at the sheep fence, where we dismounted from our wet
horses. When we reached our destination the rain stopped. We
stripped naked to wring out our clothes, and I ran to and fro
on the edge of the cliff to keep myself warm.

Suddenly the breeze filled my nostrils with a familiar smell.
I would have recognized it among a thousand scents. It was
umu takapu, with chicken and sweet potatoes. I called Bill's
attention to it, but being a heavy smoker he noticed nothing. I
could see neither smoke nor people, but someone had been
here doing something mysterious. It was not natural for the
village people to come out here with chickens and cook an
ordinary dinner for themselves on the cliffs.

Juan made the rope fast and flung it down the cliff-side. I
was quite horrified when I saw where Bill had been climbing

in the night, and Bill himself was rather pale and silent when he saw the place again in daylight. There was a drop of some 300 feet down into the sea, and the cave was a good 60 feet below the edge of the plateau.

Bill had no desire to make the descent again, and I was glad that we had two skilled climbers with us. I had experienced enough of such trips for the present, and I gladly left the pleasure to others now that I no longer had my *aku-aku*'s reputation to defend. The climbers had with them a sack and a stick with a net on the end to fish the figures out of the rock. And soon the sack began to come up full and go down empty.

Out of the sack came the most incredible sculptures of men, animals and demons. Suddenly I heard a violent outburst from Bill. He held in his hand a large stone jar: a tall and gracefully curved water-jar with a handle. An almost obliterated demon's face and two flying birds in the Easter Island style could just be seen in relief when we blew away the fine dust.

"This is exactly what I had expected to find," Bill exclaimed. "Not real pottery, but something like this in stone, with pottery as its prototype, showing some memory of that art."

Bill was a quiet man, never prodigal of superlatives. But now he was afire with excitement. This cave would have been a quite logical place to hide possible sculptures from Ahu Tepeu when civil war and devastation reached that imposing structure and the great statues on the *ahu* were overthrown.

Now the sack came up again. There was another stone jar with a handle, but this one was much smaller. There were also a phallic figure with three incised human heads, and a warrior in a long feather cloak sitting on the back of a turtle. But the most remarkable figure was a whale with grinning jaws full of teeth; its tail terminated in a death's head and on its back was a model of the boat-shaped Easter Island reed house, with a square door in the side and a five-sided kitchen-*umu* behind. Six round balls as large as oranges projected under its belly, and along its side ran parallel lines which suggested a kind of fabulous boat lashed together with bundles of reeds. A short flight of steps or road ran from the house and down along the side of the whale to what might be regarded as the waterline of a ship.

Juan could give no explanation of any of the strange things that came up the cliff; all he knew was that his father had once been shown the cave by an old aunt.

Finally the cook and second engineer came up with the last sackful. They had taken the sculptures out of a little room inside the crack. The larger figures stood behind and the smaller ones in front. All the things were covered with a thick layer of fine dust and over some of them were spiders' webs. There were neither mats nor burials in this cave; it contained twenty-six sculptures.

On the way home from the cave in the cliff-side the red-haired boy rode up alongside me with a question in his eyes.

"This was excellent," I said. "And it will be well rewarded. But tell your father from me that it was not Ororoina's cave."

We unloaded all the stones at Rapu's house where Bill was living, and as we passed the village church I slipped in to see Father Sebastian. He clasped his hands together and marched up and down the floor, quite carried away when he heard that the mayor had now shown us a genuine cave. He had been truly distressed by the episode of the night before. Father Sebastian had been kept in bed for some time with a serious attack of *cocongo*, but even on his sick-bed he had closely followed all the strange things that were going on. When I stole in to see him at the most peculiar hours of the night he sat up in bed in his nightshirt and listened wide-eyed to what I had to tell him, and he always had interesting supplementary information to give me. That day he told me he had heard from old people that there were several caves with "something" in them in those very cliffs on the coast north of Ahu Tepeu.

The events of recent days quickly became known in the village and the strangest things began to happen. The people all went for the unfortunate mayor and shouted "*reoreo*"—liar— as soon as he set foot outside his door. Everyone tried to exploit the situation to his own benefit.

Some of the worst in abusing the mayor went home to carve stone figures in secrecy. Now that the secret cave stone motifs had been revealed by others, they saw no reason to sit and toil at the everlastingly repeated wooden figures. When they now tried their hands at stone-work, they no longer produced models of the great statues, or naïve boulders with nose and eyes. A distinctive and quite mature style suddenly burst into full flower under the hands of several natives at the same time. It was clear that a new industry had been opened up, based on an old form of art which had been taboo to the unprivileged.

Till now no one had tried to sell a cave stone. All deals had taken the form of an exchange of presents. But the new stones ranked with the wooden figures which were offered for sale. Some rubbed the stones thoroughly with earth, others whipped them with rotten banana leaves to give them the appearance of having once been wrapped in parcels of decayed leaves. Several men came sneaking into the camp with these products to try their luck. Perhaps, after all, Señor Kon-Tiki's *aku-aku* was not all-knowing, for if it had been, would he have let himself be enticed into the mayor's sham cave?

On Easter Island anything may be expected. While some men brought new sculptures and said they were old, some tried the opposite line in the last days before the boat sailed. They did as the half-wit had done: they offered old figures and said they had made them themselves. They hit upon the strangest explanations if we pointed to moss and old broken surfaces, or found weathered details which they themselves had not seen. They declared that their styles and motifs were taken from photographs in old books on Easter Island, despite the fact that no sculpture of the cave-stone type had been seen till now by any explorer or writer. And when I asked if they had seen them in Lavachery's book they fell into the trap and said yes, that was the very book.

I could not understand what was going on, but it soon became clear. Respect for taboos had begun to crumble. Some of the village people had become much less afraid of *aku-akus* after all that had happened. Señor Kon-Tiki had no all-knowing *aku-aku*, but neither had the caves. Superstition had been matched against superstition, and in many a village hut it had been extinguished, as a forest blaze would be by a counter-fire. But although the respect for *aku-akus* was dwindling there was still something which troubled the native mind, the dread of a neighbour's criticism if it became known that a man had broken a taboo and taken stones from his family cave.

Only the mayor was silent and stayed at home in his house. As we were striking camp I had another visit from his son. He

said his father was tired of being branded as a liar. He had not
lied to me from the time of our landing till we went to that
unlucky cave. Now he would show my friends and me that
everything he had told us about Ororoina's cave was true.
Father Sebastian and the governor could come too and see
that he had not lied. He would take us all to the cave. For Don
Pedro Atan was not a poor creature who went in for *reoreo* and
loose talk.

The night on which we were to visit Ororoina's cave was
fixed. I drove into the village late in the evening with Bill and
Ed and Carl and Arne to pick up the governor and Father
Sebastian. But the mayor had changed his mind at the last
moment and had hurriedly got hold of forty sculptures, which
he had exhibited on the floor of his own hut. He had warned
Father Sebastian that he could not take us into Ororoina's
cave after all, because there was such an enormous quantity
of figures in the cave. There were too many for him to be able
to hand them all over to me, and if he took us to the cave
entrance, the secret would no longer exist and he would have
no place in which to keep the great collection.

Father Sebastian and the governor accompanied us to the
mayor's house. He received us at the door with open arms,
loud-voiced and smiling, and took us into the sitting-room.
The round table was drawn back and the floor was covered
with sculptures. A fair number looked really old, but most of
them were obviously quite fresh. I at once noticed some
figures of recent make which had already been offered to us
by some other person. There were also a few clear attempts to
copy sculptures from his own crack in the steep rock-face.
What on earth was the mayor up to now? This was a second
and absolutely futile attempt to deceive us.

"What are you playing at?" I asked him. "Why haven't
you kept your promise to take us to Ororoina's cave, if it is
true that you have it?"

"It *is* true, señor. But when I was in Ororoina's cave last
night, I saw that there was such a colossal quantity of figures in
the cave that I could not hand so much over to you."

"You must have known that before. Didn't you tell me that
you washed all the stones regularly?"

"Yes, but all those I found tonight lay farther inside the

cave. I hadn't seen them before. They were completely covered
with dust."

"But you told me once, didn't you, that you had a kind of
account book in which you had put down every single sculpture
you owned?"

"Not every single *sculpture*, señor. Every single *cave*."

"You mean that you put down in the book only the number
of caves you owned?"

"Yes, certainly, señor. It's quite a tiny, tiny book," the
mayor said amiably, holding up finger and thumb to show its
size—that of a small postage stamp.

I gave up.

I was extremely sad as I walked down the steps from the
little house with all the others behind me. The mayor, quite
forlorn, stood abandoned in the doorway with all the stones on
the floor behind him. That was the last I saw of the mayor
Don Pedro Atan, the strangest personality on Easter Island,
the last standard-bearer of the long-ears—the man whose head
was so full of secrets that he himself hardly knew where fantasy
began and truth ended. If the island was once upon a time
inhabited by a few thousand like him, it was not surprising
that giant statues on the verge of the unreal crawled out of the
quarry and walked about to set themselves up as desired. Nor
was it strange that *aku-akus* and invisible treasure-chambers
had been invented as bank vaults for a surplus of imagination
in the form of queer sculptures small enough for sinful humans
to carry off.

When orders from the bridge brought the anchor chain
rattling up from the depths and the engine-room telegraph set
wheels and pistons humming and beating down in the ship's
bowels, there were few cheerful hearts either on board or
ashore. We had grown on to the little community and become
part of it. The green tents were completely at home on the
king's site at Anakena. Now the newly erected giant stood once
more alone and betrayed, staring out over the solitude of a sun-
filled valley where no one lived any longer. He looked so lonely
when we struck the last tent that we felt he was asking to be
thrown down again, as he had lain for the last few centuries,
with his nose deeply buried in the sand.

Above: The women worked better than men. They wanted to get clothes and food for themselves and the children from the ship.
Below: The strike was called off, for the men wanted to serve too. Men and women were given separate hill-tops and competed with one another at the most fantastic working tempo the archaeologists had ever seen.

Above: The work of ancient man. Ruins of walls, terraces and tower appeared as bushes and herbage vanished. Every single stone had been carried up from the valley deep down below.
Below: Popoi was Rapaiti's daily bread. *Taro* grew on irrigated terraces in the valleys: it was boiled, kneaded, hung up in leaves and eaten as a fermented dough.

But the giant at Anakena was of stone, while at Hangaroa village we left a giant of flesh and blood. Father Sebastian, bare-headed in his white gown, towered above the swarm of native friends down on the quay. We felt that he belonged to the expedition as much as any of us. But he had both feet firmly planted on the soil of Easter Island. He did not stand alone like the giant at Anakena: he stood as the central figure of the living population of the island, a unifying force and an inspiration. King Hotu Matua had once so stood among their ancestors when first he brought them ashore on this remote island.

We had to go round and say good-bye to every single native. And last of all the members of the expedition had, one by one, to take leave of Father Sebastian. He had taken on a special significance for every one of us. After Yvonne and little Anette it was my turn. I stood shaking Father Sebastian's hand. We did not say much in the way of good-byes. It is easier to find words at a railway station than bid farewell for ever to a friend on the shore of the world's loneliest island.

Father Sebastian turned away abruptly and the natives made room for him as, in his large black boots, he tramped off alone to the top of the hill. His new red jeep was waiting for him there. Now, as long as its tyres held out, the old priest would be able to spare his shoe-leather on his errands of mercy to the sick and suffering as far as the leper station among the stony plateaux to the north.

The governor and his family had jumped into the launch to escort us out. I was turning to jump in after the others, when old Pakomio took me gently by the arm and led me aside. It was he who had first gone out with me to the bird island to show me a secret cave which we never found. After that he had become Arne's right-hand man and foreman of the diggers in Rano Raraku. When Arne dug up a tiny statuette at the base of one of the giants, Pakomio had offered in a whisper to show him a cave full of similar figures. But when all the row about the caves started, Pakomio was frightened and withdrew his promise. Then he was the first to come running after me feverishly assuring me that there was nothing of the kind nowadays. In their fathers' time such caves had existed, but now all the entrances were forgotten, and if anyone had stone

L

sculptures today they were only copies of those that had been lost.

With the others silent in the background, Pakomio stood before me bare-headed, awkwardly twisting his home-made straw hat.

"Will you come back to our island, señor?" he asked timidly, looking up at me with large brown eyes.

"That depends on the stones I have with me. If it's all lies and humbug, as you say, the stones will bring me bad luck. Then I shall have nothing to return for."

Pakomio looked down. He stood fingering a wreath of white feathers round his hat. Then he looked up calmly and said in a low voice:

"Not all the stones you have are lies. They will bring you good luck, señor."

The old man looked at me with large, timid, friendly eyes: we shook hands for the last time, and then I jumped down into the launch.

The natives streamed along the coast, on foot and on horseback, to wave to the ship till the last moment. I fancied there was a hollow drumming under the horses' hoofs on shore, for Easter Island is a world in two storeys. But all I could really hear now was the surf breaking against the steep cliffs.

CHAPTER X

MORONGO UTA: A RUINED CITY
IN THE CLOUDS

O N a hill-top east of the Sun and west of the Moon, beyond seven billowing ridges, lies the golden castle of a Norse fairy tale. But who believes in fairy tales nowadays? *We* did, when we breasted the last ridge and looked at Morongo Uta.

Round us on all sides lay the sea—the endless sea, which we had crossed in our little ship from the other side of the globe. Below us lay deep green valleys encircling a bay as smooth as glass: we looked right down into the funnel of the small vessel which had brought us here from Easter Island. On the next summit, straight ahead of us, lay the fairy-tale castle, lulled in the slumber of centuries, like the Sleeping Beauty. As in a spell, its towers and walls overgrown with brushwood and herbage, it lay there just as the king and all his men had left it in the days when the world still believed in fairy tales.

I was tense with excitement as we climbed along the last ridge and approached the foot of the castle. It bulked vast and majestic before us, against an eerie background of drifting clouds and purple peaks and spires. Although it stood free and heaven-soaring beneath the blue sky, there was something earth-bound—almost subterranean—about this ancient edifice, which seemed to rise from underground in a vain attempt to push its way through turf and vegetation.

A big blue bird swooped down the cliff with a shrill cry. As we drew nearer, three white goats rose out of the herbage on one of the walls, leapt down into a moat and disappeared. Considering that Easter Island is the world's loneliest island, it is perhaps not so remarkable that this is one of its nearest neighbours, even though the distance between the two is the same as from Spain to the eastern point of Canada. Here among the green hills we felt farther away from the madding crowd than ever. This must be the most secluded corner of the Pacific. Who ever heard of Rapaiti? The little island had almost been

gnawed in two by the vast ocean round it. Too steep for a foothold, the ridge we stood on sloped down on both sides to two
sheltered bays, which reflected the dream castle in turn as the
wind changed. And if we looked about us, we saw no less than
twelve castle-like formations, all equally curious, on the other
green hill-tops around—but no sign of life. Down by the shore
of the bay where the ship lay mirrored, we saw smoke rising from
a little village of reed-thatched bamboo huts and a handful of
whitewashed houses. Here lived the entire population of the
island, 278 native Polynesians all told.

But who had built this lofty dream castle, and its counter-
parts on all the other hill-tops? And what purpose had these
buildings really served? No living soul on the island could tell
us. When Captain Vancouver discovered this remote speck of
land in 1791, he thought he saw people running about on top
of one of them; he thought he saw, too, a blockhouse, and
palisades further down the slope, and presumed that it was a
man-made fort. But he never went ashore to examine it. When
the famous South Seas missionary Ellis came to the island
some years later, he declared that Vancouver had been
mistaken: the strange contours up in the hills which looked
like forts were simply natural formations. After Ellis came
the well-known explorer Moerenhout. He praised Rapaiti's
strange mountain scenery, with its peaks that resembled
towers, castles and fortified Indian villages. But he too
failed to go up and have a closer look at these extraordinary
formations.

Twenty-five years ago Caillot wrote a little book about this
lonely island.[1] Both he and others climbed up into the hills and
saw here and there sections of masonry protruding through the
greenery. These were thought to be the walls of some strange
and long-forgotten forts, though others believed them to be the
remains of old agricultural terraces. Only one ethnologist ever
went ashore to study the natives: his name was Stokes, and his
unpublished manuscript has been preserved in the Bishop
Museum.

No archaeologist had yet set foot on the island. When we
stood looking out over hill and valley, we knew we were in
virgin country. We could begin just where we liked. No

[1] Eugene Caillot: *Histoire de l'Ile Oparo ou Rapa*, Paris, 1932.

archaeologist had dug there before us. No one knew what we might find.

There was an old legend once current among the natives of Rapaiti recorded nearly a hundred years ago, and describing the original settlement of the island. According to this legend Rapaiti was first settled by women who arrived from Easter Island, after sailing their primitive craft across the sea. Many of them were pregnant, and from them sprang the population of Rapaiti.

From the fairy-tale castle up in the mountains we could see for many miles across the sea. Far away to the south the sky was black and gloomy. Down there cold ocean currents, moving *east*, skirted the drift ice of the Antarctic. That was a dangerous region full of storms and dense fog-banks, and empty of islands and human life. But to the north the sky stretched bright and blue, flecked with little feathery trade-wind clouds drifting *west*, in company with the mild and all-embracing Humboldt Current that laps the countless islands on its way, including this lonely outpost of Rapaiti. It would have been quite natural for primitive craft to have drifted this way from Easter Island. That was why we had now followed the very same route to Rapaiti.

Day after day we had ploughed the rolling ocean in a westward race with the current and drifting clouds. Day after day we had stood on the bridge, or on deck, or at the rail, gazing into the boundless blue. It was remarkable to note how many of us would often wander aft and stand staring where the seething wake ran like a green highway through the blue expanse, marking the way back to vanished Easter Island. It looked as if many would like to be back there. Some, perhaps, were dreaming of vahines, others of unsolved mysteries and untrodden paths now left behind. Certain it is that very few indeed stood in the bows longing for the romantic palm-fringed islands ahead.

In our midst, but farthest aft of all stood Rapu, Bill's native friend and foreman of his team of excavators at Vinapu. Bill had trained this bright fellow and asked if he might bring him along to help him with the surveying. Rapu had embarked on his journey into the outside world with the smile of a film hero. But his heart was tied to the World's Navel, and when it sank into the sea astern his heart sank with it. And when his world vanished and there was nothing left but sky and sea, no one would have recognized the dashing Rapu.

He had a flair for the technical, and we first gave him a trial as a handyman down in the engine-room. But the ship's noisy underworld was not the place for Rapu. He assured the engineers that below deck the ship was full of "diabolos," and the good-natured chief let him spend his watches sitting on a chair at the top of the engine-room ladder. But the sea breeze sent Rapu to sleep as soon as he sat down, and the engineers suggested that he was better suited to keeping watch on the bridge. He quickly learnt to steer the ship by compass, and the mate went into the chart-room to attend to his own work. Then the wake astern began to assume a peculiar shape, and hopeful souls on deck thought the skipper and I had come to our senses and decided to return to Easter Island. But Rapu was quite innocent. He had curled up on the bench and gone to sleep while the ship sailed her own course. What was the point of steering, when the eternal horizon was just as empty whichever way you looked?

Rapu was not particularly superstitious. He was "a child of our time," as the natives on Easter Island put it. But to be on the safe side he pulled his blanket right up over his head when he slept, as was the custom among all the natives on his island. Arne had asked them the reason, and the answer was that they wanted to avoid seeing all the nasty things that were about at night. Not many of Rapu's friends would have put up a better show than he did, if they had set out into the great blue immensity of space in a ship whose cargo was a thousand cave stones, key-stones, skulls and bones. The Flying Dutchman was nothing to us. We were faring across the ocean in a ship laden with *aku-akus*.

Pitcairn had risen out of the sea, dead ahead. We had reached the island of the *Bounty* mutineers. The sky behind it was aflame with a low red sun, as though the desperate fugitives were still burning their ship behind them. Rapu woke up here. Now he stood in the bows. He counted the coconut palms—one, two—no, he had never seen so many in all Easter Island. Wild goats on the hills; bananas, oranges, and all sorts of Southern fruit he had never seen. This must be the

Garden of Eden. Rapu would come here with his wife as soon as he got home to Easter Island and could build himself a boat.

Now we saw red roofs amid all the tropical luxuriance up on the forbidding cliffs. A huge boat with six pairs of oars, gleaming in the light as they swung in time, emerged from a little cove set behind a point. The descendants of the *Bounty* mutineers hailed us. The islanders climbed on board—robust, bare-legged, picturesque characters, some of them types usually only encountered in historical films from Hollywood. A grey-haired giant clambered aboard and jumped down on to the deck ahead of the others: Parkins Christian, great-great-grandson of Fletcher Christian, who led the historic mutiny and set Captain Bligh adrift in a ship's boat that sailed west nearly as far as Asia, while Christian himself tacked against the wind and ran the *Bounty* ashore off this desolate island. Not a soul lived here when the mutineers burnt their ship in the bay and established themselves with their pretty vahines from Tahiti. Yet they found old abandoned temple platforms with skulls and a few small statues which faintly recalled the giants on Easter Island. Who had been there before them? Nobody knows. And till now no archaeologist had been ashore on Pitcairn Island for more than a few hours.

Parkins Christian invited me and my family to stay in his own house, while the others were distributed among all the other homes. We had a splendid reception from a truly hospitable little British community, which talked English very much as their ancestors had done when they landed there in 1790, with an admixture of Tahitian phrases and a local accent.

We enjoyed a carefree existence on the mutineers' island for several days. While the archaeologists wandered round and dug and poked about, the sailors visited Christian's cave and Adams' grave, and the frogman went down and had a look at the scanty remains of the *Bounty*: the inhabitants helped us to locate the ballast from the old sailing ship, which lay in a crack on the sea-floor on the bottom of Bounty Bay, a rusty heap of iron bars.

The inhabitants were constantly finding stone adzes in the soil. And there were rock carvings at the foot of a fearsome precipice on the north coast. But generally speaking, Pitcairn was poor in archaeological remains. The mutineers' descendants, as good Christians, had levelled the temple platforms to the ground, smashed the small statues, and thrown them into the sea to rid their island of strange gods. On a sheer cliff-face Arne and Gonzalo, with the aid of the inhabitants, found a cave quarry where, judging by appearances, the red statues had been hewn out of the rock. Worn-out stone adzes from the quarry still lay where they had been flung among the rock chippings on the floor of the cave.

Strangers rarely set foot on this island. The surf pounds the cliffs at the narrow hazardous landing place. But the shipping route from New Zealand to Panama passes close by, and whenever a passenger liner is expected the natives row out to sea and sell wood-carvings of flying fish and turtles, or little models of their ancestors' proud ship. This trade has proved so brisk that Pitcairn has run out of *miru* trees, which they need for their vitally important wood-carvings.

In return for hospitality we took the whole male population of the island, and a good many of their womenfolk, on board our ship and made for uninhabited Henderson Island. On its shores our sixty Pitcairn passengers felled 25 tons of *miru* wood in a single day. The palm-fringed beach looked like the scene of a pirate battle as the gaily-coloured throng of Pitcairn people of all ages dashed into the surf with crooked logs and branches, and manoeuvred them out to the boats rearing and plunging on the reef. These were rowed off to the ship laden to the gunwales, to return empty for another load. To anyone not accustomed to the breakers and backwash, which alternately covered and exposed the coral reef off the tropical island, disasters repeatedly seemed imminent. But men and women on the reef clung to the boat each time the breakers foamed over them and lifted them off their feet, and a bellowing giant at the tiller, shouting orders to twelve toiling oarsmen, kept the craft afloat and braced against the onslaughts of the sea.

Next day, as we unloaded the ship off the cliffs of Pitcairn, a smiling Parkins Christian assured us that his people had now enough *miru* wood to carve *Bounty* models and flying fish for another four years to come.

From Pitcairn we set a course for Mangareva. We anchored in crystal clear water above a wild and colourful coral garden set with pearl shells and peopled with myriads of queer fish, in a pretty lagoon girdled by rugged mountains. The only statue we saw in this palm-clad South Seas paradise was on a painting in the church, where it lay broken in two under the foot of a triumphant missionary. The French administrator was away, but his capable wife drummed the natives together for a big welcome party, which included a dance in honour of the legendary King Tupa. With a grotesque mask fashioned from a hollow palm stem drawn over his head, "King Tupa" danced in at the head of his warriors. According to legend he had come to the island from the east with a whole flotilla of large sailing rafts. After a stay of some months he had returned to his mighty kingdom in the East, never to reappear in Mangareva. In time and place this legend tallies astonishingly well with the Incas' legend of their own great ruler Tupac. He caused an immense flotilla of balsa sailing rafts to be built and set out to visit distant inhabited islands he had heard of from his own sea-faring merchants. According to Inca historians, Tupac spent almost a year on his cruise in the open Pacific, and returned to Peru with prisoners and booty after visiting two inhabited islands. I knew now, thanks to experiments we had carried out subsequent to the Kon-Tiki expedition, that such a raft cruise was entirely feasible, as we had finally rediscovered the lost Inca art of navigating a balsa raft by their *guara* or centre-board method. This enabled a raft to work to windward just as readily as any sailing boat. And Inca Tupac may well have been the Tupa remembered at Mangareva.

The next land we had sighted was Rapaiti. It lay among the cloud-banks to the south-west like a dream-land sailing on the sea. From far off we could see through our binoculars that there was something curious about the highest summits. They looked like overgrown pyramids from Mexico, or like stepped Inca fortifications in the wild mountains of Peru. This was surely something worth investigating.

With our hearts in our mouths we stood on the bridge as the skipper, with incredible skill, felt his way through a maze of rents and gaps in the live and growing coral reef which barred the entrance to a wide bay in the heart of the island. He manoeuvred the ship right into a smooth lagoon formed by a sunken crater lake, encircled by jagged peaks and lofty ridges. Anette stood looking reverently at the skipper as, at short intervals, he swung the handle of the engine-room telegraph

L*

back and forth between "stop," slow ahead" and "astern," the ship gliding imperceptibly forward between the corals. Suddenly she rose on tiptoe, took a resolute grip of the handle and pulled it down to "full speed ahead." "Full speed ahead," the engine room replied, and we should have run smack into the reef like an ice-breaker, had not the skipper hastily swung the telegraph in the opposite direction.

We breathed a sigh of relief when we rode securely at anchor in the unruffled water off the picturesque little village whose inhabitants came paddling out in tiny canoes to stare at us.

And now at last we had ascended to the topmost crest of the mountain chain after a climb among steep ravines and ridges.

"Morongo Uta," muttered a native who had shown us the way.

"Who built it?"

He shrugged his shoulders: "Perhaps a king, who knows?"

We walked across and began to peer about among the dense vegetation. Here and there elaborately built walls projected. I heard a shout from Ed, who was investigating a steep terrace, where a section of a platform had subsided, leaving an open earth bank full of shells and fish-bones. In the midst of the debris the slender and graceful outlines of a bell-shaped mortar appeared; it was made from flint-hard basalt, and had been turned and polished in masterly fashion. I had not seen a finer piece of stone-work in all Polynesia.

Bill, too, emerged on the crest.

"This is something big," he said, and stared in amazement at the gigantic structure before us. "We must dig here!"

We held a council of war on board the ship. We were beginning to run short of certain supplies. The large native staff of workers and our cave friends on Easter Island had stripped the ship of all our trade goods and the bulk of our provisions— indeed, most of our requirements for the months ahead. The only thing we could do was to weigh anchor, proceed to Tahiti and provision ship: then we could come straight back here and attack the castle on the hill.

We battled our way through rough weather till the familiar contours of Tahiti rose out of the sea. My old adoptive father, chief Teriieroo, was no more. His house stood empty among the tall palm trunks. But Tahiti was full of old friends, and no one

had time to be bored, day or night, till we laid our course
straight back to the waiting island down near the fringe of the
fog belt—east of the Sun and west of the Moon.

As we once more crept cautiously through the dangerous
reef of Rapaiti, Arne and Gonzalo were no longer on board.
We had passed Raivaevae on our way back from Tahiti, and
they had been landed to explore the overgrown ruins of some
taboo temples in which we had discovered a number of little
stone statues. But there was no extra space on board, as we had
taken on passengers from Tahiti. One was my old friend Henri
Jacquier, curator of the museum at Papeete and president of
the Société des Études Océaniennes. He was joining the expedition at my invitation. There was also a native family with us;
the authorities at Tahiti had asked me if I would take them
back to Rapaiti, which was their original home. Jacquier came
on board with one suitcase, but we had to swing out the derrick
for our native passengers. They brought innumerable crates,
boxes, parcels, sacks, chairs, tables, chests-of-drawers, cup-
boards, two double beds, a quantity of planks and beams, bales
of corrugated iron, live animals and huge clusters of bananas,
till we could hardly move on board. It was a full-scale operation
getting all this stuff ashore when we reached smooth water at
Rapaiti a week later. As transport had been free of charge, the
owner thought it so cheap that he never even bothered to say
thank you, but paddled cheerfully ashore with his family in a
canoe while the rest of us had to look after the unloading. Nor
was this the last we heard of the man.

However, we had met a remarkable couple ashore. The
woman, called Lea, was a high-spirited, humorous vahine, half
Tahitian and half Corsican. She had been sent to the island as
a schoolmistress, to teach both grown-ups and children to read.
The man, called Money, was one huge grin from ear to ear,
Tahitian by birth with a dash of Chinese in the corners of his
eyes. He had been a bus driver in Tahiti; now he had simply
accompanied his wife to roadless Rapaiti, where he lounged
about doing nothing.

As Lea could both speak French and write, she was the old
chief's right hand. If any problem arose, Lea's advice was sought
and she settled the case with great vigour. She was the life and
soul of the little community. Firmly planted on her feet, arms

akimbo and with bristling plaits, she reported for duty when I
came ashore. Money stood modestly behind her, well fed and
happy, wreathed in smiles.

I asked Lea if she could get me twenty strong men to dig in
the hills.

"When do you want them?" she asked.

"At seven tomorrow morning," I said, expecting that at
best a dozen fellows would come wandering in during the next
week.

When I came out on deck next morning to stretch myself and
watch the sunrise I caught sight of Lea standing on the shore
with twenty men drawn up beside her. I swallowed a glass of
fruit juice, crammed a slice of bread into my mouth and hurried
ashore in the launch. We agreed on Tahiti wages and working
hours, and by the time the sun was at the zenith we were high
up in the hills with Money and twenty strong fellows cutting
ledges and steps in the steep hill-side, so that we could reach
Morongo Uta without daily peril to life and limb.

Money led the way, giggling and laughing, and infecting the
whole team with his high spirits. They sang and shouted and
worked with a will, for this was something new: they were not
accustomed to work on this island. Who else should they work
for? Certainly not for their own families. It was the women who
cultivated the *taro* in the fields, it was the women who brought
the *taro* home and kneaded it to a fermented dough which they
ate for a whole week. And once a week, when they grew tired
of this *popoi* porridge, they went out fishing in the lagoon, and
with raw fish and *popoi* on the bill of fare they could retire into
the shade and sleep and make love for another week. Once a year
a native trading schooner from Tahiti called. Then some of the
men spent a few days in the woods gathering wild coffee berries
which had already fallen to the ground, and which they bartered
for various simple commodities on board the schooner.

In our cheerful working team there was only one man, always
last in the line, who shirked as much as he could and encouraged
the others to go slow. When Money protested, the shirker
enquired in surprise what he was worrying about, as Money
was not paying for the work. The man at the back was the
returned traveller whom we ourselves had brought free of
charge from Tahiti, complete with family and luggage.

Up on the sharp ridge which formed the watershed there was a saddle-shaped depression; the brushwood had crept up into it from the other side and obtained a foothold. Here we cleared a camping-ground on a ledge just wide enough for a two-man tent, where the occupants could sit and spit orange-pips down the slopes into the valleys on either side of the island. Bill was to have his base here. He had been given the task of directing the excavation of Morongo Uta.

When we were ready to go up into the hills next day, not a single one of our merry workers had shown up. Money was standing gloomily on the shore struggling with the corners of his mouth, which otherwise would have curled up in their customary smile, and Lea came rushing like a thunder-cloud out of a large bamboo hut in the village.

"If only I'd had a machine-gun!" Lea cried in a rage, swinging round and aiming at the bamboo hut with outstretched arm and one finger crooked under her eye.

"What's happened?" I asked in alarm, thanking heaven that the enraged woman was unarmed.

"They're holding a council of war in there," Lea explained. "That fellow you brought from Tahiti says it's unfair to the others simply to pick out twenty men to work. They now want to decide themselves how many are to work. Anyone who wants to should be allowed to: they say they won't stand for any dictatorship. And if you don't let them decide who is to work, they'll stop you going up into the hills again. They'll drive you away from the island. There are *fifty* of them who want to work."

Lea was really furious. The natives, she added, had solemnly invited us to a meeting in the big hut after sunset. For the time being we must return to the ship.

By six o'clock the sun had set, and we were engulfed in pitch darkness intensified by the stupendous cliffs which rose just behind the village and walled in the old crater lake, where our ship lay at anchor, imprisoned by the reef. The skipper put Jacquier and myself ashore alone, and we walked up to the dark village by the light of our flashlights. Three natives stepped out of the night without a word of greeting and followed us noiselessly on their bare feet.

Not a soul was to be seen in the village. The only sign of life

was an occasional heap of embers glimpsed through the doorway of an oval, thatched bamboo hut. But the glare of a
paraffin lamp led us towards the assembly hut, where we
stooped under the straw roof and walked in on to soft mats of
plaited pandanus leaves. On the floor round three of the walls
squatted thirty native men as grim as warriors before a battle.
In the middle of the floor, in solitary state, sat a large fat
woman with a map spread out between her bare legs.

We greeted the gathering with a cheerful *ia-o-rana* as we
straightened up inside the door, and received a murmured reply
from all those sitting there. Lea and the native pastor were
standing by the fourth wall. Lea stood with folded arms, dark
and menacing as a thunder-cloud, but flashed a smile of
welcome as we entered. Money was not there. Lea pointed to
four empty chairs which had been placed for her, the pastor,
Jacquier and myself.

She asked Jacquier to speak first, as officially representing
the French Colonial Ministry. He rose and read a speech in
French, very slowly and very quietly. One or two of the natives
seemed to understand, for they nodded and looked contented.
All the others looked eager and alert, with their eyes fixed
keenly on us, but they obviously did not understand a
word.

Jacquier told them that he was head of the Société des Études
Océaniennes, at which the large matron in the middle of the
floor nodded, visibly impressed, and pointed to the map. He
went on to say that he had been sent by the Governor of French
Oceania for the sole purpose of helping us. He had left family,
museum and chemist's shop in Tahiti for that very reason. And
I—pointing to me—was no tourist. I was the man who had
travelled to Raroia with my friends on a *pae-pae*. And now I had
come here with some learned men just to study their ancient
buildings. People from many countries had come to work
peaceably with the inhabitants of Rapaiti—from Norway,
America, Chile, Easter Island and France. We had come to
learn about their forefathers. We had just visited Rapanui—
Easter Island. Might we receive as good treatment on Rapaiti—
Little Rapa—as we had in Rapanui—Great Rapa.

Lea translated the speech into the Tahiti dialect, adding a
good deal that came from her own heart. She spoke softly,

almost daintily, but with emphasis and a note of admonition. Her hearers squatted motionless, swallowing every word, and every one of them seemed to be making an honest attempt to weigh her arguments. I studied with interest the alert types on the pandanus mats round the low bamboo walls. The whole occasion gave me an intense feeling of re-living events that were commonplace in the South Seas during the days of Captain Cook and the early explorers. Here on Rapaiti generations had gone by like months or years. The gleaming eyes of the men round the walls reflected so vividly the keen alertness of the uninhibited child of nature, that for a moment one forgot that they were wearing ragged shirts and trousers: they might have sat there in the loin-cloths of their ancestors. We saw only rows of attentive eyes, intelligent eyes, without a trace of the degeneration of the half-civilized, but with a primitive gleam I had seen till now only in isolated jungle tribes.

When Lea had finished the old chief rose. He talked to his men almost in a whisper, but we could see from his expression that he took a favourable view. After him another old native jumped up. He spoke for a long time in the Rapaiti dialect, eloquently and emphatically—he seemed to be the local public orator.

Finally I too rose, with Lea as interpreter, and said that their ancestors might have had good reason to offer resistance and defend their hill-top forts when strange vessels approached. But times had changed. *We* had come to climb the hills in their company, and remove the turf and scrub, so that the forts would be as fine as in the days of their forefathers. I was ready to yield to their demand and give work to all who wanted it, but only on condition that I could send down again any man who did not work well enough to deserve his daily wage.

They all sprang up and rushed towards us, and we had to shake hands with each one in turn. Next day Lea appeared with fifty-six men, while Money stood on one side smiling contentedly. This was the entire adult male population of the island, except for two old men who could not climb the hills. Money and I led the army up into the mountains, and Bill nearly fell over backwards into the other valley, as he sat in front of his tent up on the saddle and saw the seemingly endless

procession that came climbing into sight round a corner of the
rock-face just below him, yelling and shouting and swinging
axes and long machete knives.

When the great battle began up on the walls of Morongo
Uta the work went like child's play. Hibiscus and pandanus
and giant tree-ferns were powerless to withstand the assault:
heavy tree-trunks crashed down from the walls and went
thundering into the depths, followed by leaves and ferns and
herbage.

When evening approached, the besieging army retired without a single casualty. They cheered and danced like boys as
they scrambled down the hill. They had hardly taken a breather
apart from their midday rest, when they had opened the bundles
of large green leaves they had brought with them. Inside lay
the greyish-white dough called *popoi*, which they ate with two
fingers. Money descended the slope and came up twice as fat as
usual, having stuffed his shirt full of big wild oranges, which he
distributed to all who wanted them.

While the rest of us went down to the village or the ship, the
second officer stayed up in the tent with Bill. We were to keep
contact every evening by walkie-talkie. But long before contact
time we saw light signals flash out from the mountain fort in
the dark night. The second mate was sending an SOS: the
camp was being attacked by a million rats.

"The second mate always exaggerates," the skipper reassured
us. "If he says there are a million, you can bet your boots there
are not more than a thousand."

Next morning our army paraded afresh, and picks, spades,
netting screens and all kinds of excavating gear were carried up
the hill. The two rats which had visited the camp had over-
eaten themselves on *popoi* and had returned to their own orange
trees.

For a few days the work went splendidly. But then one
morning, all of a sudden, not one of our fifty-six natives turned
up. Through the field-glasses we could see the figures of Bill and
Larsen silhouetted on the hill-top, while Lea stood on the shore
waving to us. More trouble. I went ashore in the motor
launch.

"They're on strike," said Lea, as I landed.

"Why?" I asked in astonishment.

On Rapaiti the women worked and the men slept. Two vahines packing *taro* roots up in bundles of grass to take them to the village. The men went out fishing every Saturday when they were tired of eating *popoi*.

Morongo Uta lay like a fairy castle in the wild hills of Rapaiti. Sites of houses and tools appeared in masses when we began to dig. It was found that the original population had once lived in twelve fortified hill villages on the highest peaks, and had only gone down into the valley to till the *taro* fields and catch fish. Another excavated hill village, green-clad, is seen in the background to the left.

Work is over. The first fortified mountain village in Polynesia has been exposed. Bill, who directed the excavation of Morongo Uta, Yvonne and the
author plant the expedition's flag on the ruins of the largest building ever discovered in the whole of Polynesia.

"That man you brought back from Tahiti has told them that everyone who works must strike."

Flabbergasted at the news, I went to the village, where some of the toughest fellows were standing with their hands in their trousers pockets, looking truculent and surly. The rest had withdrawn into the huts. All I could see were a few eyes peeping through chinks in the doors.

"Why are you on strike?" I asked, addressing one of the men directly.

"I'm not the one that knows," the man replied, looking round for support. But he got none. For when I went from man to man none of them could answer my question: they just stood there, looking discontented and grumpy.

"There's another man who knows," a fat woman called from one of the doors. "But he's not here."

I told them to go and fetch him, and several of the men rushed off. They came back, escorting between them a half-reluctant fellow, a brutal type in an old green army overcoat with no buttons, bare-footed like the others, and with one of our own cigarettes drooping from his lips. It was our friend the free passenger.

"Why are you on strike?" I asked again, as he stood before me with an arrogant air. Everyone came out of their huts, men and women, and crowded gloomily round us.

"We want more wages for food," he answered, with the cigarette sticking up at the corner of his mouth and his hands in his coat pockets.

"But aren't you getting the wages you asked for yourselves, the same daily wage that is paid in Tahiti?"

"We want more, because we provide our own food and lodging."

I saw behind him the green leaf-bags of *popoi* hanging in the trees among the bamboo huts. I knew something about daily wages in French Oceania, and that what he was asking was absurd. If I gave way now, there would be a fresh strike and fresh demands the day after tomorrow.

So I said plainly that I meant to stick to the agreement made on the evening I accepted their previous demand. Their reply was that they were all downing tools.

An excited vahine of imposing dimensions was standing

beside me, with muscles that might have frightened any man. There were others of the same build nearby, and I had a sudden inspiration. I turned to the vahines:

"Are you women going to let the men lie and sleep in the huts, when for once there's paid work to be had on Rapaiti? When a ship full of food and clothes and other goods is lying out in the lagoon?"

It was a bull's-eye. The stout matron beside me spotted her own husband in the crowd, and at the mere sight of her pointing finger, the man slunk off backwards into the crowd, and was gone. A deafening clamour arose among the vahines. Suddenly Lea stepped out in front of the throng of gaping men, like a regular Joan of Arc, and with her hands planted resolutely on her hips, she called out to me:

"Why do you want men to work for you? Why can't you use us?"

This caused a proper landslide. I looked at all the robust girls gazing at me expectantly, and closed with the offer. After all, it was they who were accustomed to doing the work on this island.

Before I knew what was going on, Lea was rushing from hut to hut. She pointed to Morongo Uta and shouted her orders. The women came pouring out. Vahines with infants in arms handed them over to daughters and grandmothers. Others washing in the brook flung down their soapy clothes and the *taro* fields were left to themselves till the men should grow hungry. And then Lea, erect as a soldier, marched off uphill at the head of her regiment of vahines. Napoleon would have been proud of his Corsican blood if he had seen her striding in front singing the Marseillaise, which in the rearward files became more and more blurred, gradually blending with local tunes, till those who came last were singing regular hula melodies, waggling their hips seductively as they danced along. Money and I were the only representatives of the strong sex in the procession, and if Money had been smiling before, he was splitting with laughter now.

Bill and the second mate, up on the ridge, came crawling out of the tent when they heard the noise, and again I thought they would tumble down into the valley on the other side when they saw what was coming.

"Here are the diggers," I shouted. "Bring out the spades."

When Bill had pulled himself together, he seized a pick and handed it to one of the prettiest girls. She was so delighted that she flung herself on his neck and gave him a smacking kiss. Bill managed to save his spectacles and his hat and sank down slowly on to a packing-case, wiping his cheek and looking up at me with a bewildered expression.

"In all my career as an archaeologist," he said, "I've missed all this. I never knew archaeology could produce so many surprises. What'll you come marching up with next?"

Lea and her women's corps did credit to their sex. Neither in the United States nor in Norway had we seen such a working tempo. Masses of turf and soil were heaved down the cliff-side, so fast that Bill was run off his feet ensuring that everything was done properly according to his orders. The vahines were intelligent and quick learners, and with Lea at their head they formed a first-class clearing team. They were as meticulous in working on detail features with the trowel as they were energetic when their task merely involved getting rid of roots and surplus earth with pick and shovel. Gradually the towers and walls of Morongo Uta began to gleam rust-red and steel-grey in the sunlight. When the vahines had finished for the day and Bill was able to withdraw to his tent, he was completely exhausted. Nor was there the slightest falling-off in tempo in the days that followed.

The men were left sitting in the village eating *popoi*. When pay-day came, and the vahines kept both money and goods for themselves and all their children, the men began to throw down their *popoi* bags and approached the 'wise guy' from Tahiti with scowling faces: this was a result of their action that no one had reckoned with.

All this time the chief and the native pastor had stood by us, loyally but helplessly, together with the smiling Money. Now they came with all the men to sue for peace. They were all willing to resume work for the original Tahiti wages. We set men and vahines to work on two separate wings of the huge structure. This proved a challenge for the sexes, creating competition, and speed and efficiency now became a matter of prestige. Never was a ruin excavated by a more energetic team of diggers. From the ship down in the bay it looked as if a swarm of locusts had descended on the peak and was eating its way downhill: the vegetation covering Morongo Uta gradually receded and disappeared, and every day the expanse of reddish-brown rock increased. Terraces and walls stood out, and soon the stepped summit was stripped and shone like a chocolate temple against the blue sky.

On the other peaks surrounding us the pyramids still lay like the moss-grown palaces of mountain trolls. But Morongo Uta was not a palace. It was not a castle. Anyone who came up into the hills now could see that it was not a single building. It was the deserted ruins of a whole village. It was wrong to call it a fort. It was wrong to call it agricultural terraces. For up there on the topmost heights the whole population of the island had once upon a time had its permanent dwelling-place.

There was plenty of level ground on the floor of the valleys for those who had first found their way to this island. But instead of settling there they had climbed up the most inaccessible precipices and established themselves round the topmost peaks. There they had clung fast and built their airy eagles' nests. They had attacked the very rock with stone tools and turned the hill-top into an impregnable tower. Round and below it the whole cliff had been carved out in great terraces, on which the village houses had stood in rows. The ancient fireplaces were still there, full of charcoal and ashes. They were curious built-up stone ovens of a type hitherto known only from Easter Island and not found anywhere else in Polynesia. Bill carefully collected the precious scraps of charcoal in his bags. From them, with the help of radio-carbon analysis, it would be possible to determine the date of this strange hill village.

Stone adzes of different kinds, whole and broken, were lying about in great quantities. And equally common was the indispensable stone pounder used by the women of the past for beating *taro* into *popoi*. Some of these *popoi* pounders were so perfectly formed and balanced, with their slender lines, graceful curves and high polish that our engineers refused to believe that such work was possible without a modern lathe. Even the charred remains of an old fishing-net were carefully dug up out of the earth by Bill's trowel.

Once this must have been a well-fortified village. A huge

moat with a rampart on the raised village side barred the way to anyone coming along the southern ridge. Hundreds of thousands of hard basalt stones had been painfully carried up from the bottom of the valley to support the terraces on which the huts rested, so that they should not plunge down into the abyss under Rapaiti's violent rain-storms. The uncut blocks were fitted together in masterly fashion without mortar: here and there a drainage channel ran out through the wall, or long stones projected and formed a kind of stair from one terrace to the next. There were more than eighty terraces in Morongo Uta village, and the whole complex was 160 feet high with a span of 1,300 feet. It was thus the largest continuous structure ever discovered in the whole of Polynesia. According to Bill's calculations Morongo Uta alone must have had more inhabitants than the population of the entire island today.

Square stone ovens, wells and store-pits for *taro* were all that was left of the houses, apart from debris and tools. The local type of dwelling had been oval huts made of pliant boughs stuck into the ground, bent and bound together on top and covered with reeds and dried grass like a haycock. This too was suspiciously reminiscent of Easter Island. These hill-top dwellers had found no room in their mountain village for the huge temples which dominate the ancient architecture of all the other islands. The population of Morongo Uta had solved this problem in a manner so far unknown in the whole Pacific: they had cut small dome-shaped niches in the rock behind the terraces, and there they had built themselves miniature temples, on whose flat floor rows and squares of small stone prisms stood on edge like chessmen. Such ceremonies as could not be performed in front of these pocket-size temples could be carried out on the topmost platform of the pyramid, under the open vault of heaven, in company with sun and moon.

While Bill and his assistants were supervising the excavation of Morongo Uta, Ed and Carl went about with the ship's crew exploring the rest of the island. All the other peculiar hill-tops were ruins of fortified villages of the same type as Morongo Uta. The natives called them *pare*. Old house sites lay as close together as space allowed along the narrow edge of the lofty watershed which ran from peak to peak. Deep down in the mountain-girt valleys were the walls of old agricultural terraces. They often continued far up the sides of the valleys like flights of steps, and everywhere could be found the relics of artificial irrigation, with conduits which branched off from streams and conveyed water to hill-side terraces which otherwise would have remained dry.

Although the strange community of ancient Rapaiti had dwelt upon the highest peaks, the villagers had gone down daily along paths cut into the precipitous slopes to cultivate *taro* in the valleys and to catch fish and other sea-food in the bays. Few eaglets can have nestled in a more exposed eyrie than the children of these Pacific hillmen up on their lofty ledges. What had frightened these people and made them take to the heights? Had those who settled on one summit taken to the hills for fear of those who lived on the others? Hardly. The villages were all connected by house sites strung out along the ridges, forming a continuous defence system that faced the endless sea. Had they fled to the heights for fear that their island was sinking into the sea? Hardly. From the hill-tops we could see that the coast-line way below us was the same as in their time, for where the sea was shallow for some way out, the stones had been cleared away for landing-places, fish-traps and fish-ponds which could all still be used today.

The answer was plain enough. The people of Rapaiti were afraid of a powerful outside enemy, an enemy who was known to them, and whose war canoes might appear above the horizon without warning.

Perhaps they had themselves been driven to this out-of-the-way spot from another island which this enemy had already taken. Could this island be Easter Island? Could the legend of Rapaiti have sprung from a grain of truth, like the story of the battle at Iko's ditch? The cannibal battles in the third epoch of Easter Island would be enough to frighten anyone out to sea, even expectant mothers with their infants. As recently as in the last century a wooden raft with a crew of seven natives landed safely on Rapaiti after drifting from Mangareva, which we ourselves had visited on our way here from Easter Island.

There were no statues in Rapaiti, but there was no room for them on the hill-tops. And If Easter Island women and children had been the founders of the island's culture, they would have thought of house, food and security rather than flaunting monuments and aggressive campaigns: they would have built themselves curved reed houses and rectilinear stone ovens, as on Easter Island, instead of rectilinear houses and round earth ovens as on all the islands in the neighbourhood. They would put secure defences for their own homes before warlike expeditions to those of others. And if they came from Easter Island, it is less surprising that they had the enterprise to reshape entire mountain peaks with their small stone tools. Curiously enough it is the women of Rapaiti who keep the community going, even at the present day, while the men are coddled and cared for almost like overgrown boys.

It had hitherto been maintained that on Rapaiti there were neither dressed stone blocks nor human figures carved in stone. Up in the hills we found both. The natives took us to a bluff high above the valley east of Morongo Uta. Here they showed us a remarkable rock chamber where, according to legend, the bodies of kings in ancient times had lain before their mortal remains were taken off on their last journey. It was an outstanding example of the stone-mason's art. A repository shaped like a large sarcophagus had been cut in profile into the actual cliff face, and the open side carefully sealed up by four square blocks of stone fitted together so neatly that it looked as if the stones were living organisms that had in the course of time grown naturally together. In the cliff beside it a human figure, as large as a child, had been cut in high relief. It stood with raised arms, ominous and menacing, reminding me of the "king" in Lazarus' burial cave on Easter Island.

According to tradition, when they died, the kings of Rapaiti were carried up to this burial chamber in broad daylight, with pomp and splendour. Here the king lay, with his head pointing east, until one dark night he was taken away by two of his henchmen, who carried him stealthily over the ridge to the Anarua valley on the other side. There, from generation to generation, all the past rulers of Rapaiti were carefully hidden in a secret cave.

We found burial caves on Rapaiti. The largest was in the Anapori valley, behind a waterfall which fell straight down from the rock thirty feet above. A little stream trickled into the cave, and we had to wade knee-deep in a clayey mass inside the rock till we came to dry ground with burial cairns on the shore of a subterranean lake. The shore beyond could only be reached by swimming seventy-five yards through ice-cold water, yet here too, in pitch darkness, lay remains of human skeletons.

In the cliff below Morongo Uta we also found a burial cave from more recent times. It was hewn into the friable rock and the entrance was sealed with a stone slab. Three bodies had been laid in the cave, but we quickly replaced the slab when a native climbed up to tell us in a friendly manner that the contents were his closest kin. There were several sealed chambers of the same sort close by, apparently in recent use, and as we did not touch them the man confided that his own grandfather too reposed in a secret cave in the cliff close to where we stood, behind a similar slab. Beside him in the man-made cave lay a great many other people who had been placed there one after another during a period of generations. To this very day the inhabitants of Rapaiti adhere as best they can to their old custom: although they now bury their dead in consecrated ground near the village, they immure them in lateral chambers dug in the earth wall at the bottom of the grave.

The man-wrought peaks of Rapaiti rise in solitude out of the sea like some elaborate marine monument to the nameless navigators of a forgotten age—navigators who had many hundreds of miles behind them when they landed on this lonely spot. But many hundreds of miles were not enough to remove their fear that other seafarers might follow in their wake. The ocean is vast, but even the tiniest craft that will stay afloat can get across, given time. Even the smallest stone adze will make the rock yield if persevering hands hammer away long enough. And time was a commodity of which this ancient people had inexhaustible supplies. If time is money, they had a larger fortune on their sunny mountain shelves than any modern magnate. If time is money, their riches were as plentiful as the stones in the walls of Morongo Uta. And in this philosophic mood, looking at the ruins of the village shimmering in space between sea and sky, one could well imagine that this was the golden castle of the fairy tale, east of the Sun and west of the Moon.

But the Cave of the Kings in the Anarua valley was something that no one on the island could show us. For the king's henchmen, who had known the way, were themselves now hidden in the rock. And the people of Rapaiti did not know the trick of finding secret caves.

No one here had an *aku-aku*. No one knew how to eat chicken tail.

CHAPTER XI

MY AKU-AKU SAYS . . .

THERE was a smell of wild pig at the head of the Taipi valley. But not a sign of life was to be seen, of either man or beast. It was impossible to hear a thing. With a hissing noise a gushing waterfall lost its hold on the sheer rock above me, and hung wavering in thin air for sixty feet before it crashed down into the pool where I was swimming. On three sides I was hemmed in by cliff walls which rose as high as the fall, and were cushioned thickly with juicy green moss, cool and wet from the eternal spray. In the green moss were glistening little ferns and evergreen leaves, dripping and waving as they caught and shed their drops of crystal rain. The pearls sprang rainbow-tinged from leaf to leaf and down into the deep pool, where they danced round in the nectar for a while before they vanished over the rim and into the jaws of the green forest god down in the valley below.

Today it was boiling hot in the valley. I revelled in the sheer joy of living, lying in the refreshing pool high up in the hills and cooling off. I ducked and drank and at last lay half floating, completely relaxed, with my arms round a stone. There was a magnificent view over the roof of the jungle. Down there I had crawled and waded and jumped from stone to stone, making my way up the middle of the stream through a tangle of live and dead trees which lay across it at all angles, thick with moss, ferns and creepers.

In this virgin forest no axe could have been at work since the time when iron was first introduced into the Marquesas group. The population today lived only under the coconut palms down by the shore in the largest valleys. This was true not only here in Nukuhiva, but also in all the other islands of the Marquesas group. It is estimated that 100,000 native Polynesians lived here when the Europeans first arrived. Now the number was down to two or three thousand. In former times people lived everywhere, and I had seen many overgrown walls peeping through the vegetation as I made my way up the stream. But

where I now lay I had the whole of Melville's famous Taipi
valley to myself, for the little village near the bay where our
own ship lay at anchor was hidden behind a distant curve of
the valley.

Down there, just round the bend and well up the slope of
the valley, eleven sturdy red shapes stood motionless in a
clearing we ourselves had made in the jungle. Eight of them

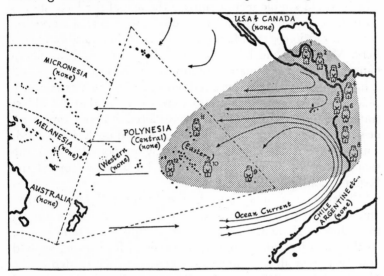

Area containing large stone statues in human form. All of
unknown origin. 1: Mexico. 2: Guatemala. 3: Panama.
4: Colombia. 5: Ecuador. 6: North Peru. 7: Central Peru.
8: Peru–Bolivia. 9: Easter Island. 10: Pitcairn. 11: The Marquesas. 12: Raivaevae.

were standing in the undergrowth when we came. But when we
raised the other three, they looked Christian men in the face
for the first time. They had lain on their bellies with their faces
stuck in the mud ever since the days when people came up
to the temple to pray and sacrifice to these ancestor-gods.
When one giant was raised with ropes and tackles under its
armpits, we saw to our surprise that it was a monster with two
heads: the only statue of its kind in the Pacific.

While Ed mapped the ruins, Bill started excavating in the
hope of being able to date the old stone figures. Incredible as it

was this was the first time an archaeological excavation had
been started anywhere in the whole Marquesas group
with its wealth of ancient culture. Only one archaeologist had
carried out a field study in the islands, and he had done no
digging.

Bill was lucky. Underneath the massive stone platform on
which the statue stood he found plenty of datable charcoal,
which would enable us to compare the age of the local statues
with those on Easter Island. In addition we received a greeting
from an old long-ear. Maybe he had been honourably buried
here. Maybe he had been sacrificed and eaten by Marquesan
cannibals. All that remained of him were his large ear-pegs and
a handful of withered bones hidden in a shaft in this masonry
platform. Radio-carbon datings were to reveal that the oldest
statues in the Marquesas group were raised in about 1300 A.D.,
or some 900 years after man had first settled on Easter Island.
This rules out the theory occasionally propounded that the
small Marquesas stone figures might be the ancestors of the
Easter Island giants.

While we were at work up in the jungle of Nukuhiva, Arne
and Gonzalo were left behind with a team of diggers among
the palms on Hivaoa, an island farther south in the same group.
As they had just completed their survey of Raivaevae, we had
now examined all the stone statue centres which existed in the
islands of the open Pacific. On Raivaevae they had excavated
a couple of old temples and found a number of small statues
which no one had seen till then. Now they had landed on
Hivaoa to obtain a date by digging, and to make a cast of the
largest statue in the Marquesas group. This measured only
some eight feet from head to foot, and was a dwarf by Easter
Island standards. They had taken with them the expedition's
last bags of dental plaster for we had used up most of our three
tons on Easter Island, making a cast of a thirty-foot giant to be
set up in the Kon-Tiki museum in Oslo, over a grotto filled
with cavestones.

As I lay there in the cool basin, re-living the journey in my
mind, I suddenly realized to the full to what extent the lonely
outpost of Easter Island stood out among the rest of the Polynesian islands as a culture centre of supreme importance. The
eleven grotesque little figures in the valley below me, and the

handful of others examined by Arne in the Puamao valley on
Hivaoa—all the Marquesas group had to offer—seemed almost
incidental and insignificant in contrast to the multitude of
proud giants erected during the two earliest epochs of Easter
Island. In fact they seemed by contrast like crumbs blown from
the rich man's table. It was the same with the few figures on
Pitcairn and Raivaevae. Easter Island, with its deep-rooted
culture, towered above the rest, a corner-stone in the pre-history
of the East Pacific. No other island could possibly have usurped
the proud title: "Navel of the World."

A modern scholar gives the credit for all that happened on
Easter Island to its climate. He considers that the comparatively cool weather did not encourage love life and indolence
as in the other islands, and that the lack of trees for wood-
carving led local settlers to attack the rock instead. As to the
love life of Easter Island, we heard a rather different verdict
from some of the sailors on board our ship. And if low tempera-
tures and lack of trees suffice to make man raise stone monuments, one would expect to see really enormous statues left by
the Vikings who settled Iceland. But no monoliths in human
form were ever raised by any of the ancient civilizations of
Europe or North America. Not even among the Eskimos. On
the other hand, they are found in a continuous belt running
from Mexico to Peru through the tropical jungles of Central
America.

It does not come so natural for just anybody to make for the
nearest mountain side with a stone in his hand, and set about
quarrying the solid rock. No one has even seen a Polynesian do
anything of the kind, even in the coldest parts of New Zealand.
Generations of experience in stone-carving are normally required for such projects. And experience alone is not enough.
People are needed with a fanatical urge to work and create,
people of the type of the mayor of Easter Island. He was certainly not a Polynesian type, that confounded mayor. I could
still see him in my mind's eye, standing at the door with the
whole floor behind him covered with queer figures. Beside him,
to the left, and on a level with his knee, stood his little invisible
aku-aku.

I shivered, and crawled out of the cold pool to stretch
myself on a sun-warmed slab of stone. The misty spray drifting

from the fall settled on me like dew as I lay there dozing, and made existence beneath the tropical sun cool and utterly delightful. In my thoughts I was on Easter Island. My thoughts were my *aku-aku*: I could send them anywhere I liked, just as swiftly as the mayor's *aku-aku* could travel to Chile or other distant lands.

I tried to get a clear picture of the mayor's *aku-aku*. It was doubtful whether he himself had any real idea of its invisible outer appearance. But behind it all, it must have been his own thoughts, conscience, intuition, all that could be put together to convey the idea of an invisible spirit: something free and unconstrained, without bones, which could lead the body to do the strangest things while it lived, and still remain behind alone to guard a man's cave when he himself and his crumbling bones had vanished.

When the mayor asked his *aku-aku* for advice, he stood as still and as silent as when he was talking with his dead grandmother. She disappeared, with his own train of thought, the moment I allowed myself to speak. He stood deep in meditation, searching his own conscience and listening to his own intuition. He was talking to his *aku-aku*. Call it what you will, everything in a human body that cannot be measured in feet or pounds. The mayor called it his *aku-aku*. And when he had nowhere else to put it, he let it stand by his left knee. Why not? It was always roaming about in the strangest places anyhow.

I felt sorry for my own *aku-aku*. It had followed me for a year on a lead, without the freedom to wing its way into the unbounded universe. I thought I could hear its complaining voice.

"You're getting stale, and too prosaic," it said. "You're no longer interested in anything but dry facts. Think a little more of all the romantic aspects of life in these islands in former times. All the human destinies. All the things you can't scrape out of the earth with a trowel."

"This is a scientific expedition," I said. "I've lived most of my life among scientists and have learnt their first commandment: the task of science is pure research. No speculation, no attempt to prove one thing or another."

"Break that commandment," said my *aku-aku*. "Tread on their toes."

"No!" I replied firmly. "I did that when we came to these islands on a raft. This time it's an archaeological expedition."

"Pooh!" said my *aku-aku*. "Archaeologists are human too. Believe me, I've seen 'em!"

I told my *aku-aku* to shut up, and splashed a little water at a mosquito which had ventured up here into the mist from the fall. But my *aku-aku* was there again. It could not restrain itself.

"Where do you think the red-haired strain on Easter Island came from?" it asked.

"Be quiet," I said. "I only know they were living there when the first Europeans came. And the mayor is descended from such stock. Besides, all the old statues depict men with red top-knots. If we say any more, we shall no longer be on firm ground."

"Nor were the red-haired men when they discovered Easter Island. If they had been, they would never have got there," said my *aku-aku*.

"I don't want to speculate," I replied, turning over on to my stomach. "I don't want to say more than I know."

"Fine. If you can tell me what you know, I'll add what you don't know," said my *aku-aku*. And so we were on talking terms.

"Do you think the red hair, too, was caused by the climate on the island?" it continued. "Or what is your explanation?"

"Nonsense," I said. "Of course, people with red hair must have landed on the island in the past. At any rate, the aboriginal settlers must have included *some* red-heads."

"Were there red-heads anywhere in the neighbourhood?"

"On several of the islands. In the Marquesas group, for example."

"And on the mainland?"

"In Peru. When the Spaniards discovered the Inca Empire, Pedro Pizarro wrote that, while the mass of Andes Indians were small and dark, the members of the Inca family ruling among them were tall and had whiter skins than the Spaniards themselves. He mentions in particular certain individuals in Peru who were white and had red hair. We find the same thing occurring among the mummies. On the Pacific coast, in the desert sand of Paracas, there are large and roomy man-made burial caves in which numerous mummies have been perfectly preserved. When the colourful, still unfaded wrappings are removed, some of the mummies are found to have the thick, stiff, black hair of the present-day Indians, while others, which have been kept in the same conditions, have red, often chestnut-coloured hair, silky and wavy, as found among Europeans. They have long skulls and remarkably tall bodies, and are very different from the Peruvian Indians of today. Hair experts have shown by microscopic analysis that the red hair has all the characteristics that ordinarily distinguish a Nordic hair type from that of Mongols or American Indians."

"What do the legends say? One can't see everything through a microscope."

"Legends?" I said. "They don't prove anything."

"But what do they say?"

"Pizarro asked who the white-skinned red-heads were. The Inca Indians replied that they were the last descendants of the *viracochas*. The *viracochas*, they said, were a divine race of white men with beards. They were so like the Europeans that the Europeans were called *viracochas* the moment they came to the Inca Empire. It is a historical fact that this was the reason why Francisco Pizarro, with a handful of Spaniards, was able to march straight into the heart of the Inca domains and capture the sun-king and all his enormous empire, without the vast and valiant Inca armies daring to touch a hair of their heads. The Incas thought they were the *viracochas* who had come sailing back across the Pacific. According to their principal legend, before the reign of the first Inca, the sun-god Con-Ticci Viracocha had taken leave of his kingdom in Peru and sailed off into the Pacific with all his subjects.

"When the Spaniards came to Lake Titicaca, up in the Andes, they found the mightiest ruins in South America— Tiahuanaco. They saw a hill reshaped by man into a stepped pyramid, classical masonry of enormous blocks beautifully dressed and fitted together, and numerous large stone statues in human form. They asked the Indians to tell them who had left these enormous ruins. The well-known chronicler Cieza de Leon was told in reply that these things had been made long before the Incas came to power. They were made by white and bearded men like the Spaniards themselves. The white men had finally abandoned their statues and gone with their leader,

Con-Ticci Viracocha, first up to Cuzco, and then down to the Pacific. They were given the Inca name of *viracocha*, or 'sea foam,' because they were white-skinned and vanished like foam over the sea."

"Aha," said my *aku-aku*. "Now that was interesting."

"But it proves nothing," said I.

"Nothing," said my *aku-aku*.

I had to plunge into the pool and cool down once more, but when I came back my *aku-aku* was there again.

"The mayor came from such a red-haired family too," it said. "And he and his ancestors who had made the great statues on Easter Island called themselves long-ears. Is it not strange that they should bother to lengthen their ears so that they hung down to their shoulders?"

"It's not so strange," I said. "The same custom existed in the Marquesas Islands too. And in Borneo. And among certain tribes in Africa."

"And in Peru?"

"And in Peru. The Spaniards recorded that the ruling Inca families called themselves *orejones*, or long-ears, because they were allowed to have artificially lengthened ear-lobes, in contrast to their subjects. The piercing of the ears to lengthen them was a solemn ceremony. Pedro Pizarro pointed out that it was especially the long-ears who were white-skinned."

"And what does legend say?"

"On Easter Island it says that the custom was imported. Their first king had long-ears with him when he reached the island in a sea-going vessel, after having steered for sixty days towards the setting sun on a journey from the east."

"The east? To the east lay the Inca Empire. What does legend say there?"

"It says that Con-Ticci Viracocha had long-ears with him when he sailed off westward across the sea. The last thing he did before he left Peru was to stop at Cuzco in the north on his way from Lake Titicaca down to the Pacific coast. In Cuzco he appointed a chief named Alcaviza and ordered that all his successors should lengthen their ears after he himself had left them. When the Spaniards reached the shores of Lake Titicaca, they heard from the Indians there too that Con-Ticci Viracocha had been chief of a long-eared people who sailed on Lake

M

Titicaca in reed boats. They pierced their ears, put thick
sheaves of totora reed in them and called themselves *ringrim*,
which meant 'ear.' The Indians added that it was these long-
ears who helped Con-Ticci Viracocha transport and raise the
colossal stone blocks weighing over a hundred tons which lay
abandoned at Tiahuanaco."[1]

"How did they manoeuvre these enormous stones?"

"No one knows," I admitted. "The long-ears of Tiahuanaco
did not leave a mayor behind who preserved the secret; no one
who could show posterity how the trick was done. But they had
paved roads as on Easter Island. And some of the largest blocks
must have been carried for thirty miles across Lake Titicaca
itself in huge reed boats, as they were hewn from a particular
kind of stone found only in the extinct volcano of Kapia on the
other side of the lake. Local Indians have shown me the
assembly point near the shore where gigantic dressed blocks
still lie abandoned at the foot of the volcano, ready to be
shipped across the great inland sea. The ruins of a wharf was
still there, and the local Indians call it *Taki Tiahuanaco Kama*,
'The Road to Tiahuanaco.' Incidentally, the neighbouring
mountain they refer to as the 'Navel of the World.' "

"Now I'm beginning to like you," said my *aku-aku*. "Now
I'm beginning to feel happy."

"But all this has really nothing to do with Easter Island," I
said.

"Wasn't the reed they used for building these boats the
Scirpus totora? Wasn't it the unaccountable fresh-water reed
which the Easter Islanders brought and planted down in the
marshy recesses of their extinct volcanoes?"

"Yes."

"And the most important plant on Easter Island when
Roggeveen and Captain Cook came there was the sweet
potato, which the Easter Islanders called *kumara*?"

"Yes."

"And botanists have proved that this plant too is South
American, that it can only have come to Easter Island if carefully transported by man, and that the same name *kumara* was

[1] The various Inca legends of their white and bearded predecessors in
Peru are recounted on pp. 224–268 of the author's book *American Indians
in the Pacific*.

also used by the Indians in large parts of Peru for exactly the same plant?"

"Yes."

"Then I've only one more question, and I'll tell you the answer. Can we assume that the Incas' predecessors in Peru were seafarers, just as we know the Incas themselves were when the Spaniards arrived?"

"Yes. We know that they repeatedly called at the Galapagos islands. And we know too that large numbers of raft centre-boards with carved hand-grips are preserved in the pre-Inca graves of Paracas, just where the tall red-haired mummies are found. A centre-board can't be used without sails, and a sail can't be used without a vessel. A single centre-board in a pre-Inca grave can tell us more about the highly developed sailing technique in Old Peru than any dissertation or Inca legend."

"Then I'll tell you something."

"I won't listen to you. You draw conclusions. You don't stick to dry facts. This is a scientific expedition, not a detective agency."

"Granted," said my *aku-aku*. "But how far would Scotland Yard get if they only collected finger-prints without trying to catch the thief?"

That was a question to which I found no ready answer, and my importunate *aku-aku* was off again:

"All right, forget it. But on Easter Island long-eared men with red hair have made long-eared statues with red hair. Either they did it because they were cold, or they did it because they came from a country where they were accustomed to messing about with big stones and erecting statues. But after them the short-ears came. And they were Polynesians, who were not cold and who found enough wood on Easter Island to carve all they liked. They carved bird-men and models of mysterious spooks with beards and long-ears and huge curved Inca noses. Where did these short-ears come from?"

"From the other islands in Polynesia."

"And where did the Polynesians come from?"

"Their language shows that they are distantly related to the small, flat-nosed people in the Malay archipelago, between Asia and Australia."

"How did they get to Polynesia from there?"

"No one knows. No one has found as much as a single trace
either there or on any of the alien island territories that lie
in between. Personally I believe they followed the current
along the coast of Asia up to north-west America. In that area
the most striking traces are found on the islands off the coast,
and the enormous decked double canoes there could easily
carry men and women on with the same current and wind
down to Hawaii and all the other islands. One thing is certain:
they must have reached Easter Island last, perhaps only a
hundred years or so before the Europeans came," I concluded.

"Then if the long-ears came from the east and the short-
ears came from the west, it must be possible to sail both ways
in this ocean?"

"Of course it's possible. Only it's a thousand times easier
one way than the other. Look at our own early explorers.
Until America was found no one possessed the necessary key
to the discovery of the Pacific Islands. The Europeans had
maintained a foothold in Indonesia and along the coasts of
Asia for a long time without a single ship trying to beat her
way oceanwards against the prevailing wind and current into
the open Pacific. It was not till Columbus had brought them
to America that Portuguese and Spaniards pushed on from
there, with the wind and current at their back, to discover the
whole vast Pacific. Indeed, both Polynesia and Melanesia were
first discovered by Spaniards who followed the current from
Peru on the advice of Inca mariners. Even Micronesia, with
the Palaus and other islands just off the coast of Asia, was first
discovered from South America. Expedition upon expedition
poured into the open Pacific, all from America, none from
Asia. The ships of the time were not even able to return the
way they had come across the Pacific. For two centuries all the
caravels left Mexico and Peru to cross the tropical belt of the
Pacific westwards to the coast of Asia, but to get back to
America they all had to go north with the Japan current,
following the desolate North Pacific route, well above the islands
of Hawaii. We should not expect more of Malay canoes or
Inca balsa rafts and reed boats than of European caravels. Do
you remember the Frenchman de Bisschop who was ready to
start on his bamboo raft when we called at Tahiti? He once

tried to sail from Asia to Polynesia in a primitive craft. It
didn't work. Then he tried the opposite way, from Polynesia
to Asia. Success, and at a spanking pace. Now he's going to try
sailing a raft from Polynesia to America. He'll have to go a
long way down into the cold eastbound Antarctic current. As
a European he may endure the icy gales down there. But if he
should ever get safely within a few hundred miles of the South
American coast, he'll have the worst part to face, as the eastbound current suddenly turns north. If he can't overcome the
current he'll start drifting straight back to Polynesia, the
same way as the *Kon-Tiki* raft and a solitary American rafts-
man who followed in our wake.[1] It's one thing to go by steamer.
It's one thing to travel with pencil on a chart. It's quite another
to travel in primitive craft on the restless ocean."

I listened for my *aku-aku*. It had fallen sound asleep.

"Oh, where did we leave off?" it said, when I shook it awake.
"Oh yes, we were talking about the short-ears. They were distant relatives of the Malays?"

"Right. But very, very distant, for they themselves were certainly no Malays. On their Pacific wanderings they must have
stopped off in some inhabited area where they greatly changed
their language and entirely changed their race. Physically, the
Polynesians and Malays are contrasts in every respect, from
shape of skull and nose form to body height and blood type,
according to the *race* experts. Only the *language* experts can
point to any relationship at all. That is what is so peculiar."

"Then which of them is a poor fellow to believe?"

"Both of them, as long as they simply put their facts down on
the table. But neither of them, if they fail to consult each other
and start to piece the whole puzzle together on their own.
That's the strength of pure research," I said.

"And that's its greatest weakness," said my *aku-aku*. "In
order to penetrate ever further into their subjects, the host of
specialists narrow their field and dig down deeper and deeper
till they can't see each other from hole to hole. But the treasures
their toil brings to light they place on the ground above. A

---

[1] We subsequently learnt that de Bisschop's raft sent out distress signals
and her crew were picked up by a warship, while the bamboo raft itself
broke up in the fierce Humboldt Current before reaching the Robinson
Crusoe island of Juan Fernandez.

different kind of specialist should be sitting there, the only one still missing. He would not go down any hole, but would stay on top and piece all the different facts together."

"A job for an *aku-aku*," I said.

"No, a job for a scientist," retorted my *aku-aku*. "But we can give him a useful hint or two."

"We were talking about a possible link between Malays and short-ears," I said. "What would your view be, as an *aku-aku*, if language said yes and race said no?"

"If language suggested that Harlem negroes and Utah Indians came from England, I'd back the race experts."

"Let us stick to the Pacific. You're a fool if you ignore the conclusions of the language experts. Language just doesn't blow by itself with the wind."

"Language spreads by devious ways," said my *aku-aku*. "It certainly can't blow by itself *against* the wind, and when the physical traits just don't tally, something strange must have happened en route, whether migration went directly west-east or east-west by the southern route, or more indirectly by the extreme northern route."

Far down in the valley a solitary horseman was riding. It was the expedition's doctor returning across the hills from Taiohae village with a bag-full of test-tubes filled with blood. He had collected samples on all the islands where we had been. Chiefs, elders and local authorities had helped him select those who could still be reckoned as pure-blooded. We had sent the samples by air in ice-filled thermoses from Tahiti to the Commonwealth Serum Laboratories in Melbourne. Our next consignment would be dispatched by air from Panama. The *Pinto* had taken the first. Never before had living blood from natives of these islands reached a laboratory in such a condition that all the hereditary genes could be studied and determined. Till now only the A-B-O blood group had been studied. It showed that the native tribes of Polynesia lacked the important B factor, which was also absent among all American Indians, while B was dominant in all the peoples from India and China right through the Malay archipelago, Melanesia, and Micronesia.

"I wonder what the blood will tell us?" I said to my *aku-aku*.

I did not know then that Dr. Simmons and his colleagues would carry out the most thorough blood analysis that had ever been applied to any people up to now. Nor did I know that they would find all the hereditary factors directly indicating descent from the original population of America, and at the same time clearly separating the Polynesians from all Malays, Melanesians, Micronesians and other Asiatic peoples. And not even my *aku-aku* could have told me this in my—or his—wildest dreams.

I began to feel chilly and put on my clothes. I glanced for the last time up at the cliff where the fall roared and the drops of water trickled through the moss. A few yellow hibiscus flowers came whirling along with the current and danced over the edge, down towards the jungle beneath us. Now I too was going to follow the current. That would be far easier going; for moving water was the early traveller's guide, to the ocean— and beyond.

A few hours later we were all standing on the bridge and on the afterdeck. Even the engineers had come up to gaze reverently at the scene, as our little ship slipped off down the precipitous coast, and the imposing red mountain wall slowly closed on the lovely Marquesan valley like a giant sliding gate. We could still see the untamed jungle rolling, green and heavy, down the steep slopes of the valley towards the sea. Elegant coconut palms, as though escaping from the green army behind, lined the beach on their slim legs, waving a friendly welcome to new arrivals and a wistful farewell to those departing. But for them the island showed no culture: but for them all was just savage beauty. We drank in the view and the scents. Soon it would all blend and blur into a vague shadow on the blue rim of heaven, before sinking with the sun into the sea behind us.

We stood there in the tropical sun, with cool, scented wreaths of flowers round our necks. Following the local custom, we were now supposed to throw them into the sea and wish ourselves back to these enchanted islands. But we hesitated to do so, every one of us. When they went overboard they would lie drifting astern marking a full stop to our adventure. Twice before I cast my wreath on bidding farewell to this enticing island-world of the South Seas, and had come back for a third time.

There came the first wreaths floating through the air to land on the sea. From the skipper and the mate up on the bridge. From Thor junior and the mess boy at the top of the highest mast. From archaeologists and sailors, from photographer and doctor, from Yvonne and myself. Up on the boat deck little Anette was standing on a chair peeping over the high rail. She struggled for a while to get the wreath off her neck, raised herself on tip-toe, and flung it with all her might over the rail and straight down.

I lifted her down from the chair and looked overboard. There lay twenty-three red and white wreaths rocking gaily in our wake. Anette's was not among them. Her little wreath had been caught up on the rail of the deck below. I stood watching it for a few moments. Then I went quickly down and flipped it overboard. I did not know why. I looked around me contentedly, and went up again to the others. No one had seen me. But I distinctly felt I heard someone laughing.

"You're as bad as the mayor," said my *aku-aku*.

THE END

Readers who wish to know more of Thor Heyerdahl's theories concerning the origins of the Polynesians will find them in his book American Indians in the Pacific.

INDEX

Incas, 12–13, 180, 185, 329, 351, 352, 353, 355, 356; buildings, 98, 103, 104, 108, 109, 127, 217, 218, 253
India, 358
Indians, American, 134, 180–1, 303, 351, 352, 353, 354, 355, 358
Indonesia, 97, 356
Influenza, see Cocongo

Jacquier, Henri, 331, 333, 334
Josef, sexton, 113, 117, 126
Josef's brother, 226, 227, 228–9
Juan Fernandez Island, 33, 357n.

Kansas University, 26
Kapia, 354
Kasimiro, 60–1, 72, 99, 100, 101, 227, 297
Katiki, 75
Kioe, 156
Kon-Tiki Museum, 348
Kon-Tiki raft, 12, 13, 14, 15, 47, 105, 231, 295, 302, 329, 357
Kon-Tiki, Señor, 44
Kon-Tiki, sun-god, 352, 353, 354
Kumara, 354–5

La Pérouse, 31, 32, 33, 91
La Pérouse Bay, 169
Larsen, see Second Officer
Lavachery, 37, 318
Lazarus, 150–1, 161, 163–5, 167–70, 171, 172–6, 193, 194, 195, 196, 198, 201, 204–5, 206, 207, 208, 211, 213, 220, 226, 228, 229, 230, 231, 264, 274, 284, 297, 314, 343; takes author to his cave, 248–62
Lea, 331–2, 333, 334–5, 336, 338, 339
Leon, Cieza de, 352
Leonardo, shepherd, 93, 175
Leper station, 63, 321
Lobster, catching, 273–4; sculpture, 205–6, 265, 282
Long-ears, 28, 38, 73–4, 85, 122–4, 139–40; descendants of, 131–2, 133, 135, 136, 139, 140–2, 143, 149, 150, 160–1, 163, 173, 179, 207, 228, 229, 233, 296, 298, 300, 313, 320, 353; ditch, 121–7, 342; in Marquesas, 348; as coming from Norway, 233, 242; origin of, 353–5

Maengo, 97, 231, 284, 285, 302
Mahute, bushes, 182
Make-make, 62, 130
Malay Archipelago, 355, 358
Malays, 357, 358, 359
Mamama niuhi, 174

Mana, 168 169, 171, 240, 242, 285, 286, 288, 289, 293
Mangareva, 328–9, 342
Mariana, 65, 66–73, 93–4, 97, 144, 166, 175
Marquesas Islands, 12, 96–7, 346–9, 351, 353, 359
Mars, planet, 241
Marseillaise, 338
Matamea, 241
Mata te Paina, 307
Melanesia, 356, 358, 359
Melbourne, 358
Melville, 347
Métraux, 37, 124, 137
Mexico, 108, 290, 329, 349, 356
Micronesia, 356, 358, 359
Miro manga erua, 149
Miru tree, 328
Missionaries, 35, 62, 324
Moai, see Statues
Moai kava-kava, 159, 160, 215
Moerenhout, 324
Moko, 196, 205
Moko Pingei, 122
Money, 331, 332, 333, 334, 335, 336, 338, 339
Morongo Uta, 323, 324, 330, 332, 333, 336, 338, 339, 340—1, 343, 344
Mostny, Dr., 39
Motuha, 140
Motunui, Bird-men's Island, 61, 99–102, 321
Motu Tavake, 258
Mu, 190
Mulloy, Dr. William, 26, 59, 73, 102–3, 104–6, 138, 142, 161, 172, 189, 201, 218, 251, 253, 259–60, 261, 264, 266, 269, 306, 308, 310–17, 319, 325, 330, 333, 335, 336, 338–41, 347, 348
Mummies, 206, 282, 308, 313, 351–2, 355
Mustad, 19

Nahoe, Juan, Tumu, 289
Naval sheep farm, see Sheep farm
Navel of the World, the, 27, 53, 107, 216–17, 325, 349, 354
Neru maidens, 74–5
New Mexico, 127, 134
New Mexico Museum, 26
New Zealand, 328, 349
Ngaruti, Simon, 307
Nicholas, 60–1, 227, 297
Norway, 13, 127, 233, 334, 339
Norwegian Foreign Office, 20, 21, 23
Nukuhiva, 346, 348
Nuns, 113, 114, 115, 148, 204, 205, 265

GEORGE ALLEN & UNWIN LTD
London: 40 Museum Street, W.C.1

Auckland: 24 Wyndham Street
Bombay: 15 Graham Road, Ballard Estate, Bombay 1
Calcutta: 17 Chittaranjan Avenue, Calcutta 13
Cape Town: 109 Long Street
Karachi: 254 Ingle Road
New Delhi: 13-14 Ajmeri Gate Extension, New Delhi 1
São Paulo: Avenida 9 de Julho 1138-Ap. 51
Sydney, N.S.W.: Bradbury House, 55 York Street
Toronto: 91 Wellington Street West